بسم الله الرحمن الرحيم

www.shaykhabdalqadir.com

First edition: Madinah Press 2010
This edition: Madinah Press 2013

Madinah Press
Postnet Suite 402
Constantia 7848
Cape Town
Republic of South Africa

madinahpress@gmail.com

ISBN: 978-0-620-46930-2
Printed by Lightning Source

DISCOURSES

ON

TAWHID HUBB

'AMAL SAFAR

SHAYKH DR. 'ABDALQADIR AS-SUFI

DISCOURSES

CONTENTS

CONTENTS

- CONT'D -

Text of Qur'an: taken from
the Algerian State Edition of Imam Warsh.

English meanings: from the Emirates-approved
text of the Hajjis Abdalhaqq and Aisha Bewley.

THE BOOK

OF

TAWHID

Nine Discourses
given between March 27th
and May 29th 2004
at Al-Jami'a Mosque,
Claremont, Cape Town

PREFACE

Due to the interregnum, soon, inshallah, to be brought to an end, which marks the period from which Islamic governance was interrupted, that is to say in the Mughal and Osmanli Dawlets, we, the Muslim World Community, experience Islam without its utterly necessary dimension of political command. One oddly regrettable result of this has been that we have started to take our Imams as leaders, making them into a priesthood, and allowing them to rule us like a slave population, which, having no power over either war or wealth, allow themselves to be commanded in the private matters of births, marriages and deaths. In this sense our Muslim population have taken on the form of a totally different religion, Shi'ism. The proof of this is that we have allowed the kuffar to define us as belonging to "Sunni Islam", as if accepting their definition that the Islamic religion has historically been split into two sects. There can only be one Deen al-Haqq, and it has Divine authorisation to be called Islam. Allah the Exalted says in Surat al-Ma'ida (5:3):

ٱلْيَوْمَ يَئِسَ ٱلَّذِينَ كَفَرُوا۟ مِن دِينِكُمْ فَلَا
تَخْشَوْهُمْ وَٱخْشَوْنِ ٱلْيَوْمَ أَكْمَلْتُ لَكُمْ دِينَكُمْ وَأَتْمَمْتُ عَلَيْكُمْ
نِعْمَتِى وَرَضِيتُ لَكُمُ ٱلْإِسْلَٰمَ دِينًا

Today the kuffar have despaired of overcoming your deen.
So do not be afraid of them but be afraid of Me.
Today I have perfected your deen for you
and completed My blessing upon you
and I am pleased with Islam as a deen for you.

Another result of this is, that in treating the Imam as an Authority, rather than that utterly replaceable figure whose noble task is to lead the Salat, the members of the Jama'at have lost that dynamic relationship with the text of the Qur'an on which a vibrant Islamic community has to be founded. In our books of Seerat and Hadith we find that the Sahaba used to gather after Fajr, and those among them who knew some Qur'an would recite it, after which they would reflect in order to see how they could apply its guidance to the day's affairs.

It was in that spirit that we decided to hold a series of gatherings in order to give a start to this dynamic relationship between the Jama'at and the Book of Allah. In reviving this Madinan 'Amal, it was only fitting that we should begin the matter by extracting from the Qur'an itself the clear explications of Allah, glory be to Him, about Himself, that is, the knowledge of Tawhid.

So it was that in these nine gatherings, each one of the Fuqara, men and women, sat with the Qur'an in front of them, and at every reference to the Qur'an in the text which follows, the Jama'at would themselves look up the Ayats, and they would also be recited by our Hafidh. As a result, by the end of the study series the group felt at home with handling the Qur'an, looking it up, and finding the Surat and the Ayat. One could say that the Jama'at, in this small event, had recovered for themselves the Clear Book which had, after all, been sent down from Allah, glory be to Him, for them, and not just some priestly class who used it to assure them a living, to take it out in the rituals of birth, marriage and death, and even, astaghfirullah, hold it over the householder's head when he left the house on a journey!

One could add a further result to this matter. It is precisely this Jama'at that has most fully grasped that the paid Imams (a Makruh situation in the Shari'at) have neither taught, nor called for, nor activated the need for a community to be governed by an Amir, and that the Amir, in turn, must impose with his Zakat Collectors that collected Zakat without which there simply is no Islam at all.

Shaykh Dr. Abdalqadir as-Sufi

I

March 27th 2004

We will Look at Surat al-Ahzab (33:34-35).

وَاذْكُرْنَ مَا يُتْلَىٰ فِي بُيُوتِكُنَّ
مِنْ ءَايَٰتِ ٱللَّهِ وَٱلْحِكْمَةِ ۚ إِنَّ ٱللَّهَ كَانَ لَطِيفًا خَبِيرًا ﴿٣٤﴾
إِنَّ ٱلْمُسْلِمِينَ وَٱلْمُسْلِمَٰتِ وَٱلْمُؤْمِنِينَ وَٱلْمُؤْمِنَٰتِ وَٱلْقَٰنِتِينَ
وَٱلْقَٰنِتَٰتِ وَٱلصَّٰدِقِينَ وَٱلصَّٰدِقَٰتِ وَٱلصَّٰبِرِينَ
وَٱلصَّٰبِرَٰتِ وَٱلْخَٰشِعِينَ وَٱلْخَٰشِعَٰتِ وَٱلْمُتَصَدِّقِينَ
وَٱلْمُتَصَدِّقَٰتِ وَٱلصَّٰٓئِمِينَ وَٱلصَّٰٓئِمَٰتِ وَٱلْحَٰفِظِينَ
فُرُوجَهُمْ وَٱلْحَٰفِظَٰتِ وَٱلذَّٰكِرِينَ ٱللَّهَ كَثِيرًا
وَٱلذَّٰكِرَٰتِ أَعَدَّ ٱللَّهُ لَهُم مَّغْفِرَةً وَأَجْرًا عَظِيمًا ﴿٣٥﴾

And remember the Signs of Allah
and the wise words
which are recited in your rooms.
Allah is All-Pervading, All-Aware.

Men and women who are Muslims,
men and women who are muminun,
men and women who are obedient,
men and women who are truthful,
men and women who are steadfast,
men and women who are humble,
men and women who give sadaqa,
men and women who fast,
men and women who guard their private parts,
men and women who remember Allah much:
Allah has prepared forgiveness for them
and an immense reward.

Regarding "Men and women who remember Allah much," the Arabic term used there is "Dhikr." It is "Men and women who do dhikr of Allah," men and women who do the act of remembering.

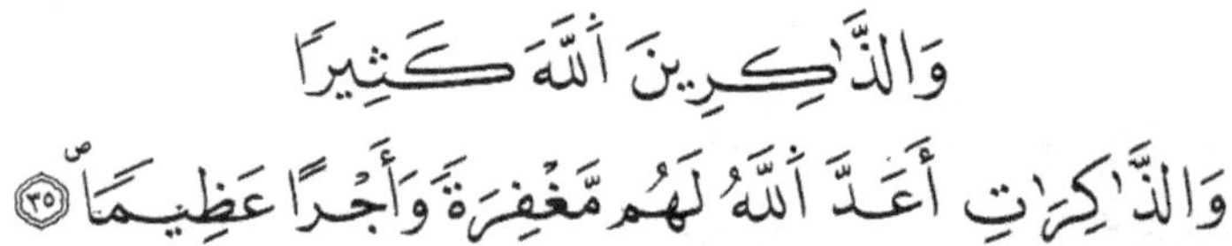

Men and women who remember Allah much:
Allah has prepared forgiveness for them
and an immense reward.

I

Here we have the statement that is the defining ayat of the fuqara and the faqirat, this ayat defines them.

وَاذْكُرْنَ مَا يُتْلَىٰ فِي بُيُوتِكُنَّ
مِنْ ءَايَٰتِ ٱللَّهِ وَٱلْحِكْمَةِ ۚ إِنَّ ٱللَّهَ كَانَ لَطِيفًا خَبِيرًا ﴿٣٤﴾

And remember the Signs of Allah
and the wise words
which are recited in your rooms.
Allah is All-Pervading, All-Aware.

So Allah, subhanahu wa ta'ala, mentions the worship that you do – not in the mosque – but the worship that you do privately, and He begins in this ayat from that. This already distinguishes these muminun and muminat who have a special place with Allah, subhanahu wa ta'ala.

وَاذْكُرْنَ مَا يُتْلَىٰ فِي بُيُوتِكُنَّ
مِنْ ءَايَٰتِ ٱللَّهِ وَٱلْحِكْمَةِ ۚ إِنَّ ٱللَّهَ كَانَ لَطِيفًا خَبِيرًا ﴿٣٤﴾

And remember the Signs of Allah
and the wise words
which are recited in your rooms.
Allah is All-Pervading, All-Aware.

"Buyut" here has been translated as "rooms", and that is interesting because if you go to Surat an-Nur (24:36):

فِي بُيُوتٍ أَذِنَ ٱللَّهُ أَن تُرۡفَعَ
وَيُذۡكَرَ فِيهَا ٱسۡمُهُۥ يُسَبِّحُ لَهُۥ فِيهَا بِٱلۡغُدُوِّ وَٱلۡأٓصَالِ ٣٦

The translation is: "In houses which Allah has permitted to be built," but it is not so much 'houses' – you could almost say zawiyyas. It is the place where people have set themselves apart to do dhikr of Allah, subhanahu wa ta'ala.

Now Allah specifies the spiritual, ruhani qualities of these special people in the next ayat:

إِنَّ ٱلۡمُسۡلِمِينَ وَٱلۡمُسۡلِمَٰتِ وَٱلۡمُومِنِينَ وَٱلۡمُومِنَٰتِ وَٱلۡقَٰنِتِينَ
وَٱلۡقَٰنِتَٰتِ وَٱلصَّٰدِقِينَ وَٱلصَّٰدِقَٰتِ وَٱلصَّٰبِرِينَ
وَٱلصَّٰبِرَٰتِ وَٱلۡخَٰشِعِينَ وَٱلۡخَٰشِعَٰتِ وَٱلۡمُتَصَدِّقِينَ
وَٱلۡمُتَصَدِّقَٰتِ وَٱلصَّٰٓئِمِينَ وَٱلصَّٰٓئِمَٰتِ وَٱلۡحَٰفِظِينَ
فُرُوجَهُمۡ وَٱلۡحَٰفِظَٰتِ وَٱلذَّٰكِرِينَ ٱللَّهَ كَثِيرٗا
وَٱلذَّٰكِرَٰتِ أَعَدَّ ٱللَّهُ لَهُم مَّغۡفِرَةٗ وَأَجۡرًا عَظِيمٗا ٣٥

Men and women who are Muslims,
men and women who are muminun,
men and women who are obedient,
men and women who are truthful,
men and women who are steadfast,
men and women who are humble,
men and women who give sadaqa,

men and women who fast,
men and women who guard their private parts,
men and women who remember Allah much:
Allah has prepared forgiveness for them
and an immense reward.

So Allah, subhanahu wa ta'ala, has meant that for these people, there is something prepared for them. They have a reward. This group of people have the reward with Allah, subhanahu wa ta'ala. They have forgiveness and a vast reward. What would be the vast reward after forgiveness? For the common people it would be like the bill being paid. But there is more than that, there is a vast reward. With Allah, subhanahu wa ta'ala, there is only one thing that would be fitting for the people He has defined and that would be Ma'rifa. The reward of Allah, subhanahu wa ta'ala, is Ma'rifa.

The Arabic word for reward is 'ajra'. This word comes again and again in the Qur'an, and it is to do with this contract Allah has made with the special muminun, the ones who are picked out, the ones who are elevated, and this is the vast reward.

Now we look at Surat al-'Ankabut (29:45):

ٱتْلُ مَآ أُوحِىَ إِلَيْكَ مِنَ ٱلْكِتَٰبِ
وَأَقِمِ ٱلصَّلَوٰةَ ۖ إِنَّ ٱلصَّلَوٰةَ تَنْهَىٰ عَنِ ٱلْفَحْشَآءِ وَٱلْمُنكَرِ ۗ
وَلَذِكْرُ ٱللَّهِ أَكْبَرُ ۗ وَٱللَّهُ يَعْلَمُ مَا تَصْنَعُونَ ﴿٤٥﴾

Recite what has been revealed to you of the Book
and establish Salat.
Salat precludes indecency and wrongdoing.
And remembrance of Allah is greater still.
Allah knows what you do.

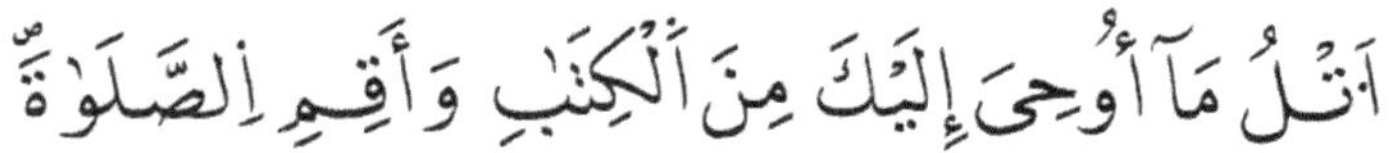

Recite what has been revealed to you of the Book
and establish Salat.

So the first order is the recitation of Qur'an. Allah, subhanahu wa ta'ala, puts the two together because the Salat implies the recitation of Qur'an, thus it is really one thing. This, again, is the command to Salat which has built into it the recitation of the Book. There are three stages, and this is the first stage. The next stage is:

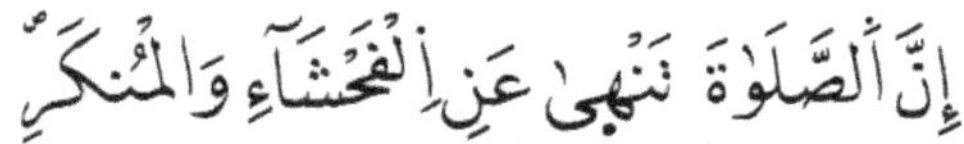

Salat precludes indecency and wrongdoing.

Having established that, Allah then puts another level on to constructing the complete human being. The next level is, "Salat precludes indecency and wrongdoing," so the moral behaviour cannot be imposed on him if you have not already established the recitation of Qur'an, and the Salat. Then you can impose on man the correct moral behaviour. It is as if the kuffar, who are nowadays attacking Islam, were saying that we are harsh with people, and in fact you could say that people in Arabia are harsh with their own people because they have not established the recitation of Qur'an which leads to the understanding of its meaning, and the Salat – so then they can ask of their people to have a moral behaviour and if they do not, with that situation the Shari'ah is there to put the limits on human behaviour. Human behaviour has to be limited, otherwise man will go to the extremes of destruction.

And remembrance of Allah is greater still.

So the highest aspect of this is that you are now another type of human being. You are people who make Salat, who worship Allah with the knowledge of the words of Qur'an, and therefore you have taken on this correct behaviour – but greater is the dhikr of Allah. So that which gives you access to Ma'rifatullah is the highest aspect of the human being. Then we come to the inescapable reality of the Muslim situation:

وَٱللَّهُ يَعْلَمُ مَا تَصْنَعُونَ ٤٥

Allah knows what you do.

The dynamic of this superior being, the Muslim – that is superior to the kuffar – is that he knows that Allah knows what he does. This is another kind of being. The Wird as-Sahl, of the great Sufi of the East, Sahl at-Tustari was from Qur'an:

الله معي الله ناظر إلي الله شاهد علي

Allah is with me, Allah sees me,
Allah is the Witness of my acts.

This is what made him have direct experience, 'Ilm al-laduni, of Allah, subhanahu wa ta'ala.

Now we go to Surat al-Baqara (2:152):

Remember Me – I will remember you.
Give thanks to Me and do not be ungrateful.

This ayat is an ayat 'adhim because this is a very high thing that Allah is telling the muminun. Look at the construction:

فَاذْكُرُونِيٓ

Remember Me,

أَذْكُرْكُمْ

I will remember you.

It has exactly the same construct but is like a mirror image of it. It is like saying "If we remember Him, He remembers us" – and the Sufis say, "Who is the rememberer?" Allah, subhanahu wa ta'ala, says, "Remember Me and I remember you." So the lover becomes the beloved. Who is the lover and who is the beloved? This is the secret, this is the very heart of what can be spoken, because beyond that you cannot say. But Allah, subhanahu wa ta'ala, has openly said in the Qur'an that the lover is the beloved and the beloved is the lover. "Remember Me – I will remember You." Love Me and I will love you.

Let us look now at Surat al-Muzzammil (73:8-9):

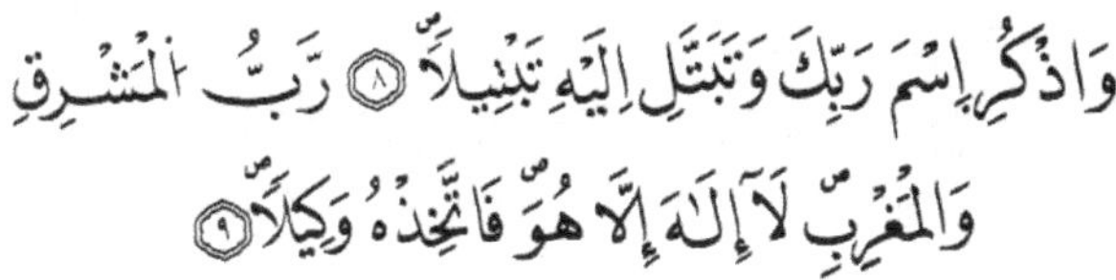

Remember the Name of your Lord,
and devote yourself to Him completely.
Lord of the East and West –
there is no god but Him –
so take Him as your Guardian.

This is the command. This is what runs through the Qur'an. Remember that the Qur'an is full of very ferocious things, terrible things – it is full of these warnings to the kuffar about the Fire, about the destruction of cities, about the punishment of Allah, about how He will not allow these deviations of the human beings and how in every age He has smashed them. But then underneath this running all the time is this message to the muminun: "Allah has prepared forgiveness for them and an immense reward." This is what you have to do. This is your business. "Remember the Name of your Lord." Dhikr is the order on these ones who are the elite, and the elite of the elite is to be people who live in dhikr. They are created for dhikr because Allah, subhanahu wa ta'ala, says in Surat adh-Dhariyat (51:56):

وَمَا خَلَقْتُ الْجِنَّ وَالْإِنسَ إِلَّا لِيَعْبُدُونِ ۝

I only created jinn and man to worship Me.

This is the order from Allah. This is what you are created
for, and is what only these special people have understood.

وَاذْكُرِ اسْمَ رَبِّكَ وَتَبَتَّلْ إِلَيْهِ تَبْتِيلًا ۝

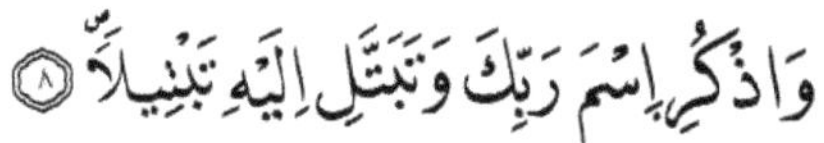

Remember the Name of your Lord,
and devote yourself to Him completely.

Allah, subhanahu wa ta'ala, says: "Devote yourself to
Him completely," which means you do nothing else! The
people who did not have the Sirat al-Mustaqim would
think therefore that they had to go up into a mountain
and stand on one leg, and that they had to shut themselves
off from the world in order to do this thing. But Allah,
subhanahu wa ta'ala, explains in Surat al-'Imran (3:191):

الَّذِينَ يَذْكُرُونَ اللَّهَ قِيَامًا وَقُعُودًا وَعَلَىٰ جُنُوبِهِمْ

...those who remember Allah, standing,
sitting and lying on their sides.

This means that in every situation you remember Allah.
Also Allah, subhanahu wa ta'ala, says in Surat an-Nur
(24:37):

رِجَالٌ لَّا تُلْهِيهِمْ تِجَارَةٌ وَلَا بَيْعٌ عَن ذِكْرِ اللَّهِ

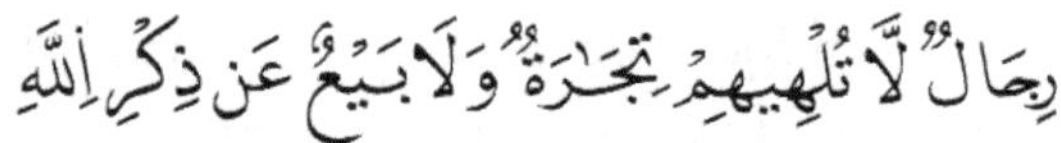

Men who are not distracted by trade or commerce
from the remembrance of Allah.

So trading, doing business, does not distract you from the remembrance of Allah. So this order: "Devote yourself to Him completely," means that you live in the Presence of Allah, the Hadrat ar-Rabbani in every situation.

If you look at the Diwan of Shaykh Muhammad ibn al-Habib, radiyallahu 'anhu, he says that the thing which stands in your way is your nafs. If you remember yourself, you are forgetting Allah. Surat al-'Asr (103):

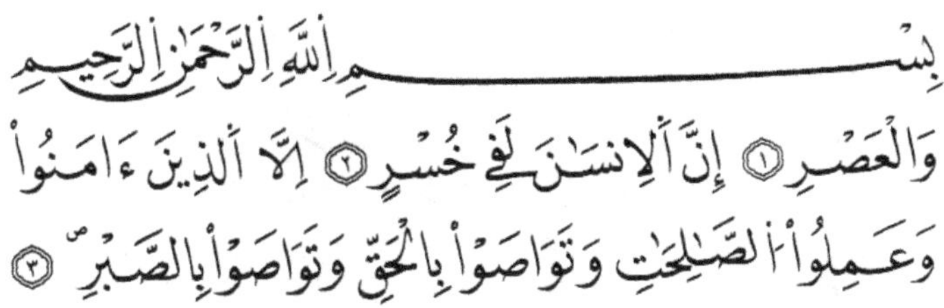

In the name of Allah, All-Merciful, Most Merciful
By the Late Afternoon, truly man is in loss –
except for those who have Iman and do right actions
and urge each other to the truth
and urge each other to steadfastness.

So man is in forgetfulness and what he is forgetful of is the reality of his own existence. He owes his existence to Allah. His existence is evidence of Allah, and he forgets! And Allah says: "When you forget, remember."

Now we look at part of Ayat 165 in Surat al-Baqara:

وَالَّذِينَ ءَامَنُوٓا۟ أَشَدُّ حُبًّا لِّلَّهِ

But those who have Iman have greater love for Allah.

So Allah, subhanahu wa ta'ala, is placing a certain group of the humans higher because they have greater love of Allah, subhanahu wa ta'ala. This is a qualitative difference. All men are not equal. With Allah they are not the same. There is no equality, because there is a portion of the human race who are the muminun, who are pleasing to Allah, and who have a greater love for Allah, and this places them higher.

Look now at Surat al-'Imran (3:31):

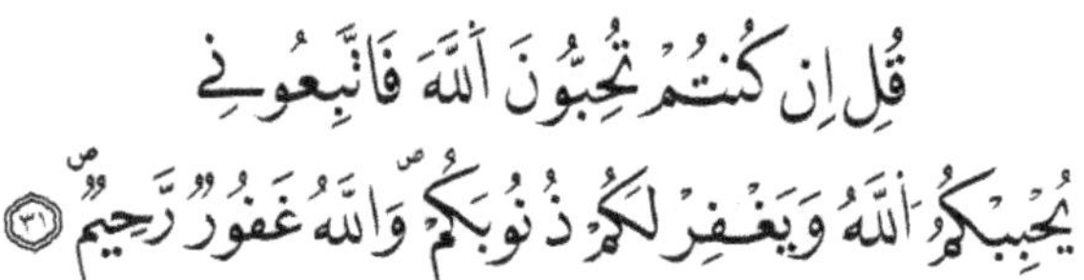

Say, "If you love Allah, then follow me
and Allah will love you and forgive you
for your wrong actions.
Allah is Ever-Forgiving, Most Merciful."

Now is revealed the whole process by which this happens, because it begins with this vital word in Qur'an which is 'Qul'. This means that it is a command from Allah from the angel to Rasul.

Now we get the whole story: "Say, 'If you love Allah, then follow me.'" So Rasul is ordering the people, "If you love Allah, then follow me." You cannot love Allah and not follow Rasul. This means we have no dialogue with other religions. There is nothing to say to other religions. If you love Allah then you have to follow Rasul – finished! That is the end of our dialogue – go back, go away! If you really love Allah then you will follow Rasul, sallallahu 'alayhi wa sallam.

This is an order from Allah where He says: "Say!" Sallallahu 'alayhi wa sallam is not saying it from himself, he is saying it under the Divine imperative.

قُلْ إِن كُنتُمْ تُحِبُّونَ ٱللَّهَ فَٱتَّبِعُونِى
يُحْبِبْكُمُ ٱللَّهُ وَيَغْفِرْ لَكُمْ ذُنُوبَكُمْ ۗ وَٱللَّهُ غَفُورٌ رَّحِيمٌ ﴿٣١﴾

Say, 'If you love Allah, then follow me
and Allah will love you and forgive you
for your wrong actions.
Allah is Ever-Forgiving, Most Merciful.'

The Prophet's order is to tell the people that if they love Allah, they have to follow the Rasul. Then Allah will love them, which means, again, in this contract which we have taken, that if Allah loves the mumin then the lover becomes the beloved. Then the door is open to Ma'rifatullah. Once the sentence is read, that is Ma'rifa. There is no other way that you can go. You have now reached the point where you have available to you Ma'rifatullah.

"Allah will love you" means that you love Allah so that you follow Rasul, sallallahu 'alayhi wa sallam, and you have Ma'rifa of Allah, subhanahu wa ta'ala. And you are forgiven for your wrong actions. In other words, the life-term is wiped out, the whole thing is gone. Then you are told:

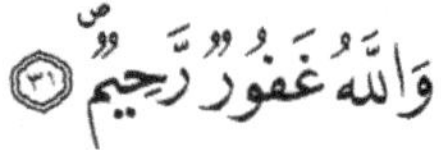

Allah is Ever-Forgiving, Most Merciful.

About this matter which we have been looking at: first of all, it is like the Qur'an has one aspect for everybody because the Book is revealed for the whole world. So there are a few places in the Book where Allah, subhanahu wa ta'ala, says, "Ya ayyuhann-Nas." He speaks to mankind because there is always the possibility among these millions and millions of people that there would be one who hears the message.

Then Allah, subhanahu wa ta'ala, warns with tremendous warnings which are terrifying. He says, "Ya ayyuhal-Kafirun" – to the kafirun this is going to happen, make no mistake about it. There is the inevitability that the darkness of that inner life will in the next world have a punishment which will be a torment greater than the torment they had in this world.

Then He says, "Ya ayyuhalladhina amanu," and he speaks to the muminun and gives them guidance. Then he tells them that He has set up the people on different levels, and He has mentioned, as we saw in the Surat al-Waqi'a, the Muqarrabun, the people who come near. He has now revealed this whole structure for the access to Ma'rifa.

You might think that this is not in the Qur'an, but these

ayats are embedded like jewels among the other decorations and beauties of the Qur'an. That is that Allah, subhanahu wa ta'ala, talks about Ma'rifa. He talks about love in a very high and exalted way which is connected to direct knowledge. There is a knowledge that is not information, there is a knowledge that is illumination – 'Ilm al-laduni, direct from Allah, subhanahu wa ta'ala.

One of the shuyukh of the East made a very similar description to Imam al-Ghazali's, radiyallahu 'anhu. He said that this love has ten stages. The first is Muwafaqa – Compatibility. The way of having this compatibility with Allah, subhanahu wa ta'ala, is to regard the enemies of the Beloved as our enemies, and His friends as our friends. So right at the beginning he makes this division that is in the Qur'an: Do not take the kafirun as your friends. You separate yourself from them and regard the enemies of the Beloved as our enemies and the friends of the Beloved, of Allah, subhanahu wa ta'ala, as our friends.

The next is Mayyal – Inclination. The heart is an instrument and the heart begins to move. The word for heart in Arabic is 'qalb' from the root QLB which means to turn over. So the heart is always turning over, it is always in motion. It is like that part of the steering of a ship or submarine which is like a fulcrum that is always turning. So the heart will always go to something, and if it does not go to the halal it will go to the haram, and if it wants the haram it will get the haram because it is like a magnet – if it wants the bad it will get the bad, if it wants the good it will get the good. If it wants food, then the food is coming to it, and the secret of understanding the destiny is that the food is coming to you before you get hungry. It is actually on its way! It was a sheep in a field which has been slaughtered, and then it has been hung, and then sent to the butcher's, it has been bought, it has been taken to the kitchen – you think, "I'm hungry," and there it is on the plate in front of you. The Awliya say that this meal has been coming to you from before the creation of the world, because Allah is the Provider. The rizq is from the Razzaq.

This is the first movement of the heart. First you are compatible, you are in tune with the Beloved because you have learned not to like the enemies of Allah. That makes you compatible, it makes you acceptable. Then comes inclination, and this is to busy yourself on your quest for the Beloved. In other words, your heart begins to ask, "Why is it so difficult? What do I do? What should I do? How am I to move about? How am I to have knowledge? How is it that I sit through the dhikr and am not having something happen inside me?" and the heart begins to incline.

Then the next stage is Muanasa – Fellowship. The heart begins to want to be with the people who love Allah because one of the signs of the lovers is that they love to hear the name of the Beloved. It is like the story of Layla and Majnun. It is enough for Majnun to hear the name of Layla that he is happy. So he wants to go where her name is said. The beginning of Muanasa is to attach yourself to Allah sincerely and to detach yourself from everything else. The way you detach yourself from everything else is by beginning to get into the habit of sitting with the people who love Allah, subhanahu wa ta'ala.

Then this closeness begins to take on a dynamic. The next stage is Hawa – Passion. But this passion is the opposite of the passion of the world, it is to keep the heart in zuhd. In other words, not to let it have anything except the passion for the dhikr, for the Presence of Allah, for the knowledge of Allah. So with this, the heart begins to become certain, it begins to become pliable, it begins to become accessible to things it was not accessible to before. That is the explanation of the famous sentence of Imam al-Ghazali, radiyallahu 'anhu: "The person who has put one foot on the path is like a star. The one who is advanced on the path is like a moon. The one who has achieved knowledge of Allah is like the sun. But the one who has not put one foot on the path is like a stone."

The fifth stage is Muwadda – Friendship. What makes the friendship with Allah is that before anything else the dominant experience of the heart is yearning. So you are reaching beyond the business of living. You have a yearning that reaches out past everything to do with 'thing'. Shaykh Muhammad ibn al-Habib, rahimahullah, says in the Diwan,

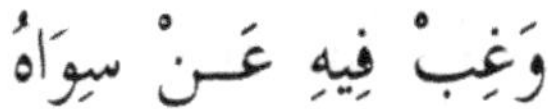

Withdraw yourself in Him
from all that is other-than Him.

The sixth stage is Khulla – Exclusive Friendship. You book in not just your intellect and your heart, but you book in all the limbs of the body to be in this condition. This is what Salat is for, this is what fasting is for, and this is what the imara is for – that the limbs of the body become worshipful.

The seventh stage is Mahabba – Affection. Mahabba is that the intensity of this longing and love and desire begins to burn up in the faqir the things which are no good, the things which are not right. They just galvanise and in their place comes the possibility of doing good actions. You move from being concerned with yourself, which brings about bad actions, to not being concerned about yourself but having compassion for others, because this love spills out into a love for the fuqara. It spills out, it overflows so that your body overflows to take in all the people and you do not know which is you and which is them. This is because you then have taken on good actions. Living in good actions, in what is called birr – birr is active, it is not just goodness, but that you are actively doing good.

Then you come to the eighth stage which is Shaghaf – Violent Affection. So the intensity increases and the Shaghaf becomes so that you are so intoxicated that you are liable, as he says, "To risk tearing the veil of your secret," because to disclose the secret is like kufr. In other words, in the dhikr you become so intoxicated that you might reveal this knowledge which is coming into your heart of Allah, subhanahu wa ta'ala, yet no-one must know. Shaykh Muhammad ibn al-Habib says in his Diwan:

وَاذْكُرْ بِجِدٍّ وَصِدْقٍ   بَيْنَ يَدَيْ عُبَيْدِ اللهِ

Do dhikr with gravity and sincerity
in front of the slaves of Allah.

The Ninth stage is Taym – Enslavement. You become a captive slave of love, and that is to put on tajrid which is to strip away. There are two tajrids: there is the tajrid of the outward which is to do without, like zuhd. Zuhd is not, "I won't have it," it is "I don't need it." Imam al-Ghazali tells of Sayyiduna 'Isa, 'alayhi salam, having a comb and a mirror. He saw a child running its hands through its hair and he threw away the comb. Then he saw the animal go to the water, and realised that if you look into the water you can see yourself, so he threw away the mirror.

This is outward tajrid, but the inner tajrid is to strip away the body itself. In the khalwa there is a tajrid of the batin which is that you lose the hearing, the sight, the touch – you lose all the senses one by one, so that what is left is a consciousness which in its turn vanishes which is, in the language of Tasawwuf, 'Fana fillah'. One of the Sufis said about Taym, about this enslavement: "You wish to buy Him – first sell yourself." This is the counsel of the 'Arif to the one who wants this knowledge.

The tenth stage is Walah – Bewilderment. Muhiyuddin Ibn al-'Arabi has written many things about Walah. This shaykh says it is, "To place the mirror of the heart before the Beloved to be intoxicated in the wine of beauty." There is another of these shaykhs – Yahya al-Muniri, who said, "Love (hubb) sends a message from the Beloved, and the message to the heart is: 'Be always in motion, restless.'

To life: 'Let go of joys.' To the head: 'Do not settle.' To the face: 'Lose your complexion.' To the body: 'Say goodbye to vanishing strength.' To the eyes: 'Shed tears,' and to the lover himself: 'Hide your condition. Shut your mouth. Pull back from friends. Get rid of both the worlds.'"

II

April 3rd 2004

Last week we were looking in the Qur'an at the use and presentation by Allah, subhanahu wa ta'ala, of one word, 'Hubb' – the love of Allah, subhanahu wa ta'ala, and the meanings of this love for the muminun.

Tonight we look at the meanings of one other word which is 'ibada. We will look at what defines 'ibada, which is that the way in which the mumin aligns himself with worship of Allah, subhanahu wa ta'ala, this 'ibada is from 'abd. So the worship of Allah, subhanahu wa ta'ala, is itself slavehood. It is putting oneself under the acknowledgement of the power of Allah, subhanahu wa ta'ala, and it is from the knowledge in which the 'ibada is performed that it takes its meaning.

There is a very famous hadith in the Sahih collection which recurs in various versions, where Rasul, sallallahu 'alayhi wa sallam, in defining the importance of Salat refers to a Salat with understanding. This is not the same as someone just going through the motions of Salat, but it is someone who knows what this standing, bowing and prostrating means. Who is being worshipped is what gives it meaning. This is what we will look at in the following ayats.

Look at Surat Al 'Imran (3:175), the second part of the ayat:

فَلَا تَخَافُوهُمْ وَخَافُونِ إِن كُنتُم مُّؤْمِنِينَ ﴿١٧٥﴾

But do not fear them – fear Me if you are muminun.

The word khawf is fear, actual fear. It is not a psychological condition, but physical. Khawf is what goes through the body, like the man seeing the wild tiger. Allah, subhanahu wa ta'ala, says, "Do not fear them – fear Me if you are muminun," so Allah is taking the mumin and changing his whole identity so that 'them' in this general sense refers to the enemy, and it therefore also refers to everything in the creation that the mumin is afraid of. Do not be afraid of what opposes you and what confronts you, but "fear Me," fear Allah, subhanahu wa ta'ala.

Here He is using a structure by which He says, "Me," and when Allah, subhanahu wa ta'ala, says that, it is as though He is speaking from His Essence because He is speaking about Himself in the first person. Sometimes He speaks in the Qur'an to the people about Himself as 'He', but here He is saying 'Me,' so this is an absolute command from the very core of our understanding of Allah, subhanahu wa ta'ala.

"Fear Me if you are muminun." In other words, the condition of being mumin, of being one who trusts in Allah, is that he has fear of Allah. Fear of Allah means that you cannot have fear of anything else. It is a change in the condition of the human creature who has become mumin, and at this point the fear that he would have of the other, and of the enemy, and of what opposes him, this khawf becomes something very deep that is fear of Allah, subhanahu wa ta'ala. That in itself would be so great that it would paralyse the mumin if it were the only condition under which he could live, and great Awliya have had such a great fear of Allah, subhanahu wa ta'ala, at a certain stage of their journey to Allah that they have become transfixed by it and Allah, by His power, has taken them out of that and this is because in the language of Tasawwuf, khawf is balanced against raja', hope.

There is a famous story of the man who came to Shaykh Muhammad ibn al-Habib, rahimahullah, from the Sahara to give him the Idhn of being in the Darqawi Tariqa. Shaykh Muhammad ibn al-Habib, rahimahullah, was then teaching Arabic in the Qarawiyyin mosque in Fes, and this man had been sent with an instruction from his shaykh: "Go to the Qarawiyyin and when you get there, there will be a circle of 'ulama sitting. Go up to them and say, 'I am the guest of Allah'," which is a way of asking for hospitality, "and whoever accepts, you go with that man."

So this man, who was one of the salihun, went there and said, "I am the guest of Allah," and they all bowed their heads, they did not want the bother of this guest from the Sahara. "I am the guest of Allah." The third time he asked, Shaykh Muhammad ibn al-Habib, rahimahullah, said, "Marhaban," and took him.

He took him to a tiny little room he had in the wall of Fes. The room is built inside the wall and so the steps up are very steep. As he climbed the steps, this man who had been sent to Shaykh Muhammad ibn al-Habib put one foot up on the step and said, "Khawf," then his next foot up and said, "Raja'." "Khawf! Raja'!" Shaykh Muhammad ibn al-Habib, who at that point was one of the great 'ulama of Fes, who had no experience of Tasawwuf directly, suddenly was confronted with another kind of man and it had an effect on him. This man stayed with him and Shaykh Muhammad ibn al-Habib never asked where he had come from or why he was there, he accepted him as his guest and asked him no questions, and the man stayed with him for almost two years.

In this time Shaykh Muhammad ibn al-Habib had seen that this man was someone who never said anything against anybody and if people spoke badly, liking to gossip and attack people, he would leave the room. Also, all the time he was doing Wird and making Ismul-'Adham. Then one day he said, "I have a letter for you."

Shaykh Muhammad ibn al-Habib said, "I am not expecting any letters!" The man said, "It is for you!" He said, "Well then, it is from you. You read it." So he read out from his shaykh in Tinjdad giving Idhn to Shaykh Muhammad ibn al-Habib to take the Tariqa.

In all this the resonance which made him enter the Sufic path was the impact of this man climbing a stair where on every step he was poised between fear and hope. So this khawf is a reality for the mumin – that he has fear of Allah. "Do not fear them – fear Me if you are muminun." This is the beginning of the correct relation of 'ibada.

Now we look at Surat az-Zumar (39:36-37):

أَلَيْسَ ٱللَّهُ بِكَافٍ عَبْدَهُۥ ۖ
وَيُخَوِّفُونَكَ بِٱلَّذِينَ مِن دُونِهِۦ ۚ وَمَن يُضْلِلِ
ٱللَّهُ فَمَا لَهُۥ مِنْ هَادٍ ﴿٣٦﴾ وَمَن يَهْدِ ٱللَّهُ فَمَا لَهُۥ مِن مُّضِلٍّ ۗ
أَلَيْسَ ٱللَّهُ بِعَزِيزٍ ذِى ٱنتِقَامٍ ﴿٣٧﴾

Is Allah not enough for His slave?
Yet they try to scare you with others apart from Him.
If Allah misguides someone, he has no guide
and if Allah guides someone, he cannot be misguided.
Is Allah not Almighty, Exactor of Revenge?

We are now understanding the 'Who' of Allah, how we can speak of Allah, Who is dealing with us because we cannot say that we are dealing with Him.

Allah is asking, “Is Allah not enough?” You must remember that we have all been educated with a materialist education. We have all received an education which believed that we had to master things and by mastering things it extended that we had to master people. The Deen of Islam does not accord with this, which is why in the present day you have such a chaos because people are trying to behave with that education and viewpoint as Muslims. This is why you have this horrible situation in Palestine and the horrible situation of all the Arab peoples for whom this is their language they use over breakfast.

They do not know, because they have taken on this world-view of the kuffar, and yet here the Revelation is saying: “Is Allah not enough for His slave?” This is a tremendous statement. Are you then looking for some other power to take you through the whole process of your life? Do you really think that there is some process that you can do that is going to support you when the Islamic position is that all you are called upon is not to do nothing, but to obey Allah? And if you obey Allah, He is enough for you. You do not need anything else. The things in turn will obey you.

“Is Allah not enough for you? Yet they try to scare you with others apart from Him” – that is coming out of the television set every day. That is what the news is – to make you feel that power lies elsewhere than with Allah, subhanahu wa ta’ala.

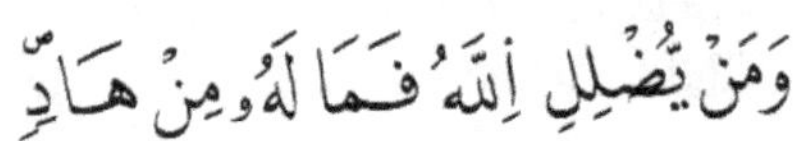

If Allah misguides someone he has no guide.

The word for guide is Hadi. One of the Names of Allah is Al-Hadi so if you are not guided by the One who Guides then you are not going to be guided. There is not some other guidance that you will get that will take you through the process of life with success. "If Allah misguides someone, he has no guide and if Allah guides someone, he cannot be misguided." In other words the people who follow in this path of Allah, subhanahu wa ta'ala, they are safe, they are secure.

Then Allah says: "Is Allah not Almighty, Exactor of Revenge?" He is All-Powerful but he also takes revenge. So it is reminding you that this One you are being guided by is not going to let off those people who oppose you. They are not going to escape. This One who is All-Powerful, who is guiding the muminun, is also the One who will take a terrible revenge on those who do not obey Him. This also means that what you might call the 'foreign policy' of the Muslims has to be based on this. The transaction of the Muslims has to be based on this. This is part of the power of Allah, subhanahu wa ta'ala – that He does not let the enemy of Allah escape.

We come now to a very important thing which you have to remember because it is something that the Sufis lean very heavily on for the knowledge to give them strength and insight. It runs right through the Futuhat al-Makkiyya of Shaykh Ibn al-'Arabi where he talks about Allah, subhanahu wa ta'ala, as the Creator. Allah says in Surat az-Zumar (39:38):

وَلَئِن سَأَلْتَهُم مَّنْ
خَلَقَ ٱلسَّمَٰوَٰتِ وَٱلْأَرْضَ لَيَقُولُنَّ ٱللَّهُ

If you ask them,
'Who created the heavens and the earth?'
they will say, 'Allah'.

What Allah is telling us by this is that the kuffar are not necessarily atheists but that they have in fact limited Allah. The kuffar think they live in an already-created reality and then on this created reality they run wild and do what they like. This is not the truth of the matter.

In the rest of the ayat Allah, subhanahu wa ta'ala, shows them that that is not how it is. There is nothing in creation that is not in the process of action. Allah is One in His Names and His Attributes and His Essence, and He has created the things in a dynamic state. Therefore not only the human beings, the animals, the living organisms, but even the chemical foundation of the world, the mountains, what Ibn al-'Arabi called the 'gypsum foundation' of creation – all of these things are in motion. Anyone who has any doubt should look at what has been happening in Turkey and look at what has been happening in Iran. The mountains and valleys have been erupting, splitting, everything is in motion – there are gases coming out of the earth at every minute, the whole thing is alive.

The evolutionary lie is that there were these simple organisms which got more and more complex and then, poff! you have man, and that is the creational process. Then this man does what he wants, he makes up his rules, he makes up his ideas – the whole of the eighteenth century was men making up ideas about how they should live and what existence was – they invented the whole thing!

Allah is telling us that the kuffar will say that Allah created the heavens and the earth but that is not understanding because you cannot separate a man from his actions. Therefore the creation of man enclothes the fulfilment of the destiny of the man. That is part of His creation, it is part of the creativity, just as the creation of the birds, the animal kingdom involves the whole cycle of mating and reproduction. For instance, the whole cycle of hibernation of the bears – there is no such thing as a bear without hibernation, it is not possible. So creation goes through the seasons, it goes through life.

When the kuffar give this insufficient answer, Allah, subhanahu wa ta'ala, tells us to respond with this:

قُلْ أَفَرَءَيْتُم مَّا تَدْعُونَ مِن
دُونِ ٱللَّهِ إِنْ أَرَادَنِىَ ٱللَّهُ بِضُرٍّ هَلْ هُنَّ
كَٰشِفَٰتُ ضُرِّهِۦٓ أَوْ أَرَادَنِى بِرَحْمَةٍ هَلْ هُنَّ مُمْسِكَٰتُ رَحْمَتِهِۦ

Say: 'So what do you think?
If Allah desires harm for me,
can those you call upon besides Allah remove His harm?
Or if He desires mercy for me
can they withhold His mercy?'

In other words, all this dynamic process of life which the kuffar call history and which the sociologists call social relations and so on, is actually under the command of Allah, subhanahu wa ta'ala. When good comes it is from Allah, when trouble comes it is from Allah and they cannot control how Allah works with His creation, making it happen.

The position of wisdom is then given:

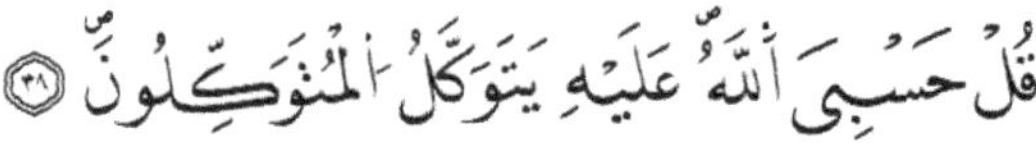

Say: 'Allah is enough for me.
All those who truly trust put their trust in Him.'

Allah, subhanahu wa ta'ala, has set out that there is in the human race a body of people who have another orientation which by its nature, because it contains the wisdom about how existence works, has to triumph. But they can only triumph if they are in that circle of the muminun who are defined by 'ibada, and their visa, their passport is 'ibada.

Look at Surat al-Hadid (57:22):

مَآ أَصَابَ مِن مُّصِيبَةٍ فِي الْأَرْضِ وَلَا فِيٓ أَنفُسِكُمْ إِلَّا فِي
كِتَٰبٍ مِّن قَبْلِ أَن نَّبْرَأَهَآ إِنَّ ذَٰلِكَ عَلَى اللَّهِ يَسِيرٌ ﴿٢٢﴾

Nothing occurs, either in the earth or in yourselves,
without its being in a Book before We make it happen.
That is something easy for Allah.

This is the depths of the wisdom of Qur'an which is only to be found in Qur'an. Allah, subhanahu wa ta'ala, opens up all His treasures of His secrets to the muminun. "It is in a Book," means that it has already been stated, it has already been sent down. The history is told.

Sayyiduna 'Umar ibn al-Khattab, radiyallahu 'anhu, was with Rasul, sallallahu 'alayhi wa sallam, and he asked, "O Rasul! Are we on a matter that is just beginning or are we on a matter that is just finished?" Rasul, sallallahu 'alayhi wa sallam, said, "The Book is written and the ink is dry." 'Umar ibn al-Khattab then said, "If that is the case, what then is the use of my making an effort to do things if it is already determined what is going to happen?" Rasul, sallallahu 'alayhi wa sallam, said, "Every creature is on a pattern from Allah and he will do that which is the destined thing for him, and he cannot escape it." 'Umar ibn al-Khattab said, "Now I can go back to work." Look at the quality of those people. That did not stop him, he said that he was one of those people who would do the utmost to serve Allah and, "I will go back to work."

It was not an imprisoning thing or a crushing thing but a liberating thing. That is why the muminun make the du'a, "O Allah, give me an Iman that is lasting." You want the seal of the destiny to be secure so that you die in Islam, so that your path all the way through is dynamic. This is something easy for Allah. Then in the next ayat of Surat al-Hadid Allah says:

لِّكَيْلَا تَأْسَوْا عَلَىٰ مَا فَاتَكُمْ وَلَا تَفْرَحُوا بِمَا آتَىٰكُمْ

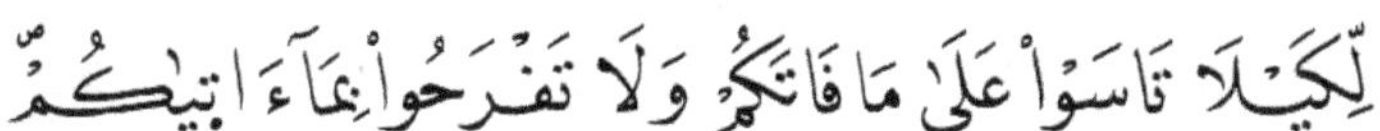

That is so that you will not be grieved
about the things that pass you by
or exult about the things that come to you.

This is very significant because Allah defines for the mumin, like the question of 'Umar ibn al-Khattab, the condition in which he is left. These two opposites do not anymore impinge on your heart. Once you understand how things are, you will not be grieved about the things that have passed you by. There is no such thing as having missed something. That is it! That is the who-ness of you. And you do not exult about the things that come to you because they have come by the destiny and by the same power of the One who has held other things back from you. So you become unified in your understanding of Tawhid.

Surat az-Zumar (39:62-64):

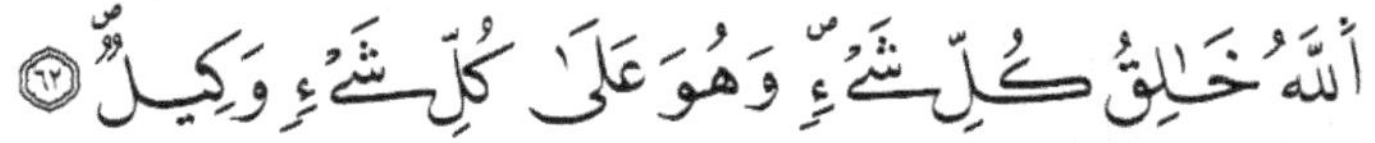

Allah is the Creator of everything
and He is Guardian over everything.

Look at the uncompromising viewpoint that is offered the Muslim, it is like standing on granite, it puts you on firm foundations. You cannot be shaken because once you grasp the Tawhid of Allah you are men of knowledge, you know how existence works. You must realise that the kafirun do not know what is going on. They do not understand the process. The Muslims who have taken knowledge from the Book of Allah and from the Sunna of Rasul, sallallahu 'alayhi wa sallam, they know that Allah is the Creator of everything and He is the Guardian over everything. If He is the Guardian over everything, then He is the Guardian over you and you will move in a confidence that what you will do is that which will best secure your safety. This includes everything, including war. It is an understanding of security and safety that is inside the person.

This next thing is very important. Allah, subhanahu wa ta'ala, says:

لَّهُۥ مَقَالِيدُ ٱلسَّمَٰوَٰتِ وَٱلْأَرْضِ ۗ وَٱلَّذِينَ
كَفَرُوا۟ بِـَٔايَٰتِ ٱللَّهِ أُو۟لَٰٓئِكَ هُمُ ٱلْخَٰسِرُونَ ﴿٦٣﴾

The keys of the heaven and earth belong to Him.
It is those who reject Allah's Signs who are the losers.

He does not say that just the heavens and earth belong to Him, we have already established that, He also says the keys of the heavens and earth. That is the patterns, and the patterns of the heavens are all those things that bring to life all the living forms from the Unseen into the Seen. So the disappearance of the species is under Allah's law as well as the appearance of the strong mumin at the time the Muslims need it. All these things are because Allah has the keys and He, subhanahu wa ta'ala, unlocks events.

We may not like the events which are unlocked, but the ones who have this strong Tawhid can read events and know what to do. For example, Rasul, sallallahu 'alayhi wa sallam, said that there will come a time when the best property will be sheep and to hide and retire in the mountains. Alhamdulillah, we have not reached that point, but there is a point when that will be the thing the mumin knows to do. The keys to the heavens are with Allah and also the keys of the earth belong to Him. This means that He unlocks events just as He unlocks living forms. He unlocks the earth and makes this earth sterile and makes this earth fertile. He makes this earth shake and He brings down a city. All of this is in His power that the patterns of existence are in His hands.

Allah says: "Those who reject Allah's signs are the losers." Allah's signs are those manifestations in existence of His power. Everything which is happening in the world is to teach the mumin, even the things we do not like, even the situation today with our Ummah – there are signs and Allah is giving us indications. What He disapproves of and what He approves of have not changed, so we have to interpret them and there are those things which awaken in the Muslims this vibration which we call khawf, that you fear Allah. At the same time, when things become intolerable, Allah also has a guidance that He never puts on the mumin more than he can bear.

Finally Allah says:

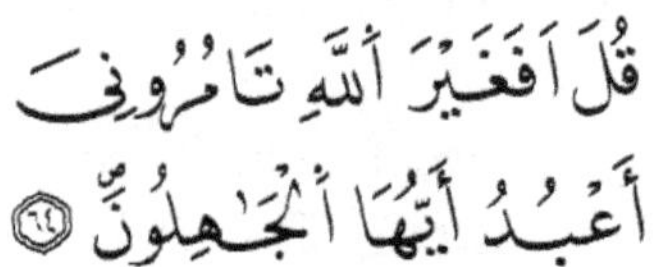

Say: 'Do you order me
to worship something other than Allah,
you ignorant people?'

The ignorant people are all those we are dealing with in the world today, the atheists and the people who have corrupted former religions who are completely lost. They are ignorant. Our strength lies in our knowledge Allah has given us through the Qur'an and through the pattern of what is pleasing behaviour to Allah, subhanahu wa ta'ala, which is that of the Rasul, sallallahu 'alayhi wa sallam.

Now we look at Surat al-Ahzab (33:41-43):

يَٰٓأَيُّهَا ٱلَّذِينَ ءَامَنُوا۟ ٱذْكُرُوا۟ ٱللَّهَ ذِكْرًا كَثِيرًا ﴿٤١﴾ وَسَبِّحُوهُ
بُكْرَةً وَأَصِيلًا ﴿٤٢﴾ هُوَ ٱلَّذِى يُصَلِّى عَلَيْكُمْ وَمَلَٰٓئِكَتُهُۥ لِيُخْرِجَكُم
مِّنَ ٱلظُّلُمَٰتِ إِلَى ٱلنُّورِ ۚ وَكَانَ بِٱلْمُؤْمِنِينَ رَحِيمًا ﴿٤٣﴾

You who have Iman! Remember Allah much,
and glorify Him in the morning and the evening.
It is He who calls down blessing on you,
as do His angels,
to bring you out of the darkness into the light.
He is Most Merciful to the muminun.

Allah gives a direct order how to keep in you this inner fulcrum, this inner compass that is going to put you into a knowledgeable state about the events which come in your life. You will know how to deal with the different things of existence because everything in existence is alive – you are not wandering in a desert but living through a situation where everything is alive and full of possibilities which Allah is offering you and giving you at every moment. You will know how to discriminate – one of the names of the Book is the Furqan – and you will know from this wisdom how to react in every situation.

Allah, subhanahu wa ta'ala, says: "You who have Iman!" and then He says that the way the whole thing is kept alive is: "Remember Allah much." This is the famous phrase which repeats in the Qur'an, 'dhikr kathiran' – lots of dhikr. Allah is saying that this reality you are living in is so tremendous that while you have been given the pattern which is enough for you there is much more. You can go on and on by degrees because Allah explains in Qur'an that the muminun are raised up by degrees of Divine knowledge which they receive from Allah.

One of the Bedouin came to Rasul, sallallahu 'alayhi wa sallam, and said, "Is it true that I have to confirm that Allah is One and Muhammad, sallallahu 'alayhi wa sallam, is His Messenger?" He said, "Yes." Then he asked, "Is it true I have to make Salat five times a day?" He said, "Yes." "Is it true I have to fast every year?" He said, "Yes." "Is it true I have to pay the Zakat?" He said, "Yes." "Is it true I have to take the Hajj?" He said, "Yes." "Well that is all I know, I am not doing anything else!" Rasul, sallallahu 'alayhi wa sallam, said, "Then you will have success."

Another time, a Bedouin said to him, "I do the five prayers, I am not doing anything else. That's it!" Rasul, sallallahu 'alayhi wa sallam, smiled and said, "Allah will give you the Garden. He will reward you." In other words, because of the mercy of Allah the minimum is enough. Yet among the muminun there is an elite body of people who are not content with this, they want more. They have read in the Qur'an that Allah raises people up by degrees and the highest degree is the people called the Muqarrabun, the people who draw near to Allah. Because He has not got place, Allah has explained: "Allah is nearer to you than your jugular vein," so it is a nearness which has no spatiality in it at all. This nearness is the condition of the 'Arifin and the salihun. This is the Qur'anic language for the Sufi. The Muqarrabun are the Sufis.

"Glorify Him in the morning and the evening" – that is in the Fajr and after the Isha. "It is He who calls down blessing on you, as do His angels, to bring you out of the darkness into the light." The interesting thing is that in another part of the Qur'an (Surat al-Ahzab, 33:56), Allah specifically says about the Rasul, sallallahu 'alayhi wa sallam:

إِنَّ ٱللَّهَ وَمَلَٰٓئِكَتَهُۥ يُصَلُّونَ عَلَى ٱلنَّبِيِّۚ
يَٰٓأَيُّهَا ٱلَّذِينَ ءَامَنُواْ صَلُّواْ عَلَيۡهِ وَسَلِّمُواْ تَسۡلِيمًا ٥٦

Allah and His angels
call down blessings on the Prophet.
You who have Iman! call down blessings on him
and ask for complete peace and safety for him.

But here it is more. One cannot make a mistake about this so we went to the great tafsir of Shaykh Ibn 'Ajiba who says that Allah says: "My Salat is a mercy on you, sallallahu 'alayhi wa sallam, and on your Ummah." Now, with overflowing love of Allah, subhanahu wa ta'ala, He makes the salat on Rasul, sallallahu 'alayhi wa sallam, and the angels on the whole Ummah of the Muslims. So we are a community overwhelmed by the protection and love and the blessing of Allah, subhanahu wa ta'ala. It is because of him we all get this direct, Divine covering and protection and blessing of Allah, subhanahu wa ta'ala.

Then Allah, subhanahu wa ta'ala, says: "He is the Most Merciful to the muminun." We are in a position of absolute security, absolute safety and we cannot go wrong as long as we remember that He is the Lord of the Universe, and the Lord of our destinies. I think we will stop there, but there is more!

HADRA

We ask Allah, subhanahu wa ta'ala, to cover us in His Rahma. We ask from Allah a great forgiveness beyond anything we could merit. We ask Allah, subhanahu wa ta'ala, to cover our wrong action. We ask Allah, subhanahu wa ta'ala, to strengthen us in our good action. We ask Allah, subhanahu wa ta'ala, to make us people of good actions. We ask Allah, subhanahu wa ta'ala, to raise us up to degree after degree of knowledge. We ask Allah, subhanahu wa ta'ala, in all the destiny to give us an Iman that lasts to the grave. We ask Allah, subhanahu wa ta'ala, to let us die among the salihun and in the best of company.

II

We ask Allah, subhanahu wa ta'ala, to give victory to the Muslims. We ask Allah, subhanahu wa ta'ala, to pardon the Arabs for their having abandoned the Deen of Islam. We ask Allah, subhanahu wa ta'ala, in His Mercy to bring them back to the Deen by the secrets of His Qur'an. We ask Allah, subhanahu wa ta'ala, to revive the Muslims in every land. We ask Allah, subhanahu wa ta'ala, to remove the false 'ulama from their places. We ask Allah, subhanahu wa ta'ala, to remove the thrones from their places. We ask Allah, subhanahu wa ta'ala, to place thrones of honour and thrones of 'ibada to rule the Muslims. We ask Allah, subhanahu wa ta'ala, to give us leaders to restore us to our full splendour. We ask Allah, subhanahu wa ta'ala, to let it happen during the lives of the people here assembled. We ask Allah, subhanahu wa ta'ala, to protect the children of the people here assembled and to give them a world in which the Deen is stronger than it has ever been.

We ask Allah, subhanahu wa ta'ala, to make the people of this Tariqa travel wherever they want in the world and to establish the Deen wherever they go. We ask Allah, subhanahu wa ta'ala, for benefits beyond anything we deserve. We ask Allah, subhanahu wa ta'ala, to be generous to us by His promise of generosity and to give us generosity on our fellow Muslims in order to merit such generosity from Allah. We ask Allah, subhanahu wa ta'ala, whose generosity cannot be compared to ours, to be merciful to us, to strengthen us and to give us the Sirat al-Mustaqim into a future with hope dominating our fear.

III

April 10th 2004

We started with the subject of the adab of the mumin in relation to his 'ibada and I am just going to continue. It is something that has an ongoing path and this is one bit of it. Also, inshallah, we are going to stop at a very, not confusing, but contradictory part, so that I will also have to introduce the subject for next week, because otherwise you will think that this is the whole story! We are now moving into a very serious, deep matter so I ask you to please try and sit still and concentrate. Fold your hands, or look at the Qur'an.

We are now going to look at the subject of Allah as the Creator and then His creation, His creatures. We are looking at Allah in His power as Creator. So we look at Surat al-Hadid (57:1-3 and 6):

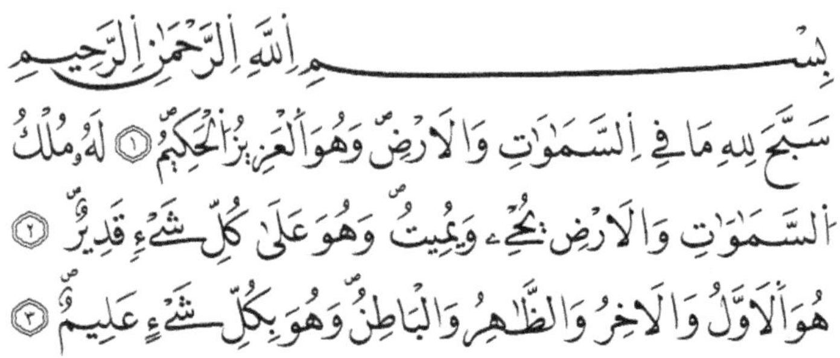

In the name of Allah, All-Merciful, Most Merciful
Everything in the heavens and the earth glorifies Allah.
He is the Almighty, the All-Wise.
The kingdom of the heavens and the earth belong to Him.
He gives life and causes to die.
He has power over all things.
He is the First and the Last,
the Outward and the Inward.
He has knowledge of all things.

Then the last ayat is:

يُولِجُ ٱلَّيْلَ فِى ٱلنَّهَارِ وَيُولِجُ ٱلنَّهَارَ فِى ٱلَّيْلِ
وَهُوَ عَلِيمٌۢ بِذَاتِ ٱلصُّدُورِ ٦

He makes night merge into day
and day merge into night.
He knows what the heart contains.

III

We are beginning to get an understanding in these ayats about Allah as the Creator. “Everything in the heavens and the earth glorifies Allah. He is the Almighty, the All-Wise.” The first thing is that everything in the heavens and the earth glorifies Allah. This is an indication of something that the Sufis and the salihun have understood for hundreds of years, and which the scientists have belatedly discovered in the last hundred years – the things of the heavens and the earth are not static and dead. Everything is alive. Everything is in action. The atom is not a static thing but a whirling, speeding thing. Everything is in motion and this motion is the glorification of Allah, subhanahu wa ta’ala.

مَا فِي ٱلسَّمَـٰوَٰتِ وَٱلْأَرْضِ

Everything in the heavens and the earth.

‘Heavens’ is samawati, which also means those things which are in the Unseen, which are going to come into the existent realm to glorify Allah. In other words, the forms that have not emerged into the created world are also glorifying Allah, subhanahu wa ta’ala.

لَهُۥ مُلْكُ ٱلسَّمَـٰوَٰتِ وَٱلْأَرْضِ

The kingdom of the heavens and the earth,

– the kingdom of the unseen world and the visible world – belongs to Him.

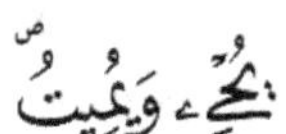

He gives life and He causes to die.

Part of this nature of the created event is the giving of life and the making to die. What happens in the span of time, between birth and death, coming into existence and going out of existence – this is all under the power of Allah, subhanahu wa ta'ala. It is His Action that brings to life and also terminates it. This means also that the creation of the living forms is under the power of Allah in its totality.

You must remember that part of the essence of kufr is the idea that the creation is a static thing into which comes man with an intellect which is then free to behave in a certain way. The understanding of the Muslims is that Allah is the Creator of the creatures, and also this means that the human being's actions are part of his existence. You cannot separate a man from his actions. What a man does in that span of time is all under the command of Allah, subhanahu wa ta'ala.

He has power over all things.

This means that He is the activator of them. Power is not some magical thing that intervenes with 'free radicals' doing what they want and suddenly some divine force pounces on them. Power over them is, by His power, to let them do that which they are going to do. This is very important for the Muslims to understand.

III

هُوَ ٱلْأَوَّلُ وَٱلْءَاخِرُ وَٱلظَّٰهِرُ وَٱلْبَاطِنُ ۖ وَهُوَ بِكُلِّ شَىْءٍ عَلِيمٌ ③

He is the First and the Last,
the Outward and the Inward.
He has knowledge of all things.

This is a very important ayat for the Sufis. It is an ayat which has openings, Fatiha, in it for the 'Arif. Moulay al-'Arabi ad-Darqawi, radiyallahu 'anhu, explains how he achieved his Tawhid with Allah: when he was in khalwa, he heard a voice declaring this ayat. He heard this and said, "I understand that He is the First and the Last, and I understand that He is the Inward, but I do not understand how He is the Outward." He was saying that in his correct upbringing as an 'alim, of course, that Allah is exalted above everything that could be associated with Him. The voice then said, "If He had meant anything else He would have said it." This confirmation that He was not only the Inward but that He was the Outward was what gave him his Tawhid and he passed out of the consciousness of this world.

At the minute we are looking at this aspect of exalting Allah over everything with which He can be associated and yet, at the heart of it, we have to come back to this element about the nature of what we can say about Allah, confirmed by what He tells us, that He is the First and the Last, the Outward and the Inward.

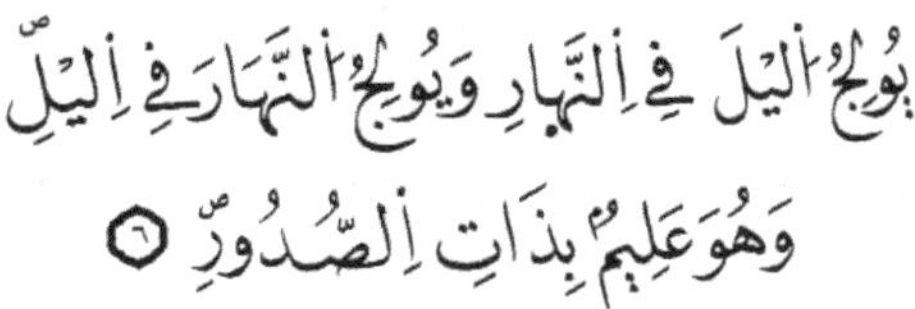

He makes the night merge into day
and day merge into night.
He knows what the heart contains.

While we are getting an understanding of Allah being exalted above the creation and having power over the creation, we also discover that the One who is the Master of the cosmic events of night and day – which means the whole nature of the creation of the stars and the sun and the moon –

He knows what the breasts contain.

Sudur in Arabic means 'breasts' but it is more correct to say 'hearts' because it is saying that Allah knows what is inside the human creature. Inside the human creature is the impulse to action, the force to move and make things happen, to do things. It is not an emotional thing about being angry or not, "He knows what is in the heart," and the heart moves by impulse. The word qalb, which means heart, is from the root 'qalaba' which means to turn over, to transform, to change. So the very central organ of man is itself in motion with this Divine commotion that has been set up in it.

So you will find that Allah being exalted above everything and the Creator of everything is put alongside His power to know what is in the breasts of man.

Now we will go to Surat Ya Sin (36:82). We have come

to the point where we have to look at the created things because we have to understand the nature of how Allah is with His creation, which is not a simple matter and yet it is not a complicated matter. It is simply that you must see it with the eye of understanding. One of the great Sufis of India said: "This matter will never be settled by logic." It is like when you tell someone something and they get it: "I've got it!" It is not a mental process but a 'seeing the whole point of something.' This is how you will understand the nature of Tawhid.

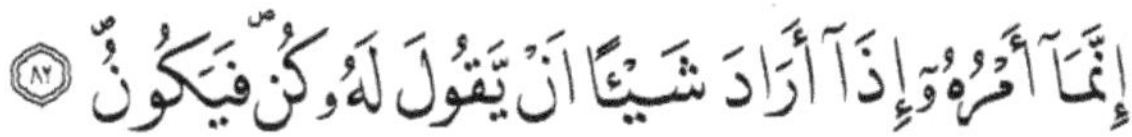

His command when He desires a thing
is just to say to it, 'Be!' and it is.

Here Allah plunges us right into the secret of His secrets. He unveils it for the muminun openly. There are no mysteries in Islam, what is unveiled is unveiled. What the heart is able to grasp is another matter.

Allah's command when He desires a thing is just to say to it, 'Be!' and it is. Kun fa yakun – it is almost like the grammar breaks down because the 'fa' is very fine usage. It is not 'and' or 'it follows that', rather it is like you could put 'Be' then a stroke, then 'it is' – Be/it is. You have to concentrate on this because it is very strange. When Allah wants a thing, He just says to it "Kun fa yakun," "Be!" and it is. If you look at it one way it does not make sense. I am not being discourteous to Allah, I am unlocking this so you see it. Astaghfirullah, if Allah said this to it and it was there, it would not make sense because if it is already there, how does He say to it to be there? If it is not there, how can He say to it, "Kun fa yakun?" We have to understand this because neither of the ordinary outside situations click with common sense.

When Allah's Command, the Amr, comes on His desire, His Irada – when He wills it, it means that the thing is already in His knowledge, so He orders it and it is in being. In this sense we can understand, by metaphor, that the creator of forms has an idea of a form and then he makes it happen. At the moment we will stick with this very crude metaphor because we are going to find out something even more devastating and overwhelming about how Allah deals with His creation, to do with something that is not 'exalted above' but intimately close.

Before the thing comes into the creation – and we cannot say 'it is in the mind of Allah' because we have no authority to say that – but it is in the knowledge of Allah, subhanahu wa ta'ala. The thing is in His knowledge and when He is ready and when He wills it, it comes into being. So we have taken one step into an understanding of Tawhid.

Now we go to Surat Maryam (19:9). Now Allah, subhanahu wa ta'ala, opens the doors, reveals the secrets. He explains His way of dealing with existence openly. Remember that we are not dealing with ayats of hukm, we are dealing with ayats that explain about existence. We would have to take a different adab to the ayats that say what is forbidden and permitted. At the moment we are dealing with Allah being the Creator.

قَالَ كَذَٰلِكَ قَالَ رَبُّكَ هُوَ عَلَيَّ هَيِّنٌ
وَقَدْ خَلَقْتُكَ مِن قَبْلُ وَلَمْ تَكُ شَيْـًٔا ﴿٩﴾

He said, 'It will be so!
Your Lord says, "That is easy for me to do.
I created you before, when you were not anything."'

This is about the gift of a child. There are just two things in this ayat and first of all – although we will not go into the details of it – the slave is being told of a generous gift of life to a child from Allah on the parent. The first part of it is that the slave, because he is of the salihun and of the exalted knowers, when he is told how it will be, although it does not seem to be possible, he accepts it. It is that acceptance of Allah's dealing with his slave that allows Allah, subhanahu wa ta'ala, to inform the slave of a knowledge that he did not have until he heard this.

قَالَ رَبُّكَ هُوَ عَلَيَّ هَيِّنٌ

Your Lord says, 'That is easy for Me to do.'

'Lord' means the Rabb, Allah, in His capacity to create all the living forms and all the inter-connectedness of all the forms. This is Rububiyyat, which is from Rabb, and Rububiyyat involves not only the creation of the forms but also their connectedness, like all the levels of the forest from the tops of the trees down to the insects at the root of the tree. All these are interconnected just as the nations of men and the movements of men, and the vast migrations of men all come under Rububiyyat.

So this is the Lord saying that He will give this child, and then He says:

I created you before, when you were not anything.

So He explains to the father the commentary on Kun fa yakun: "I created you before, when you were not anything." First of all you were not anything, the command came, "Kun!" and you were. Allah created you so that there was a 'you' to create. We find when we look elsewhere in Qur'an that in fact all the human creatures were called before Allah, subhanahu wa ta'ala, before the creation of the world and He said to them (7:172):

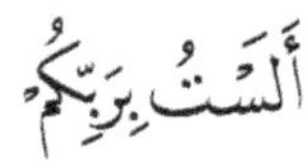

Am I not your Lord?

This is how Allah, subhanahu wa ta'ala, deals with the creation. It is a dynamic, ongoing event in the in-time. All the in-time is under His power, which is beyond time and is not associated with anything.

We go to Surat al-Mulk (67:13-14):

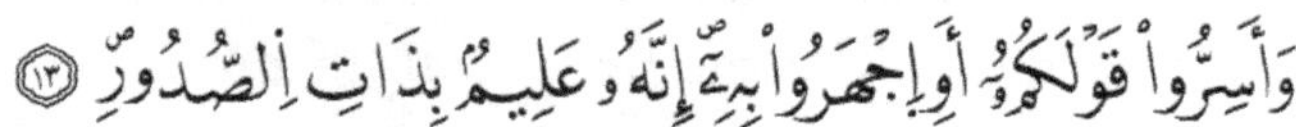

Whether you keep your words secret or say them out loud,
He knows what the heart contains.

Again we get this reminder that He knows what the breasts contain. This impulse of the human heart to go this way or that way, to be secretive or open – all this, He knows what the heart contains. This is about the absolute command that Allah, subhanahu wa ta'ala, has over the slave.

Does He who created not then know?
He is the All-Pervading, the All-Aware.

He is the Creator so Allah, subhanahu wa ta'ala, says, 'How am I not to know since you are my creation?' This is the dynamic relationship into which Allah, subhanahu wa ta'ala, is putting his slaves. He is not only putting the muminun into this position, He is putting the kuffar in this position. He is keeping those who behave in one way in this position, and those who behave in another way in this position, which means that this Divine knowledge is present in every situation.

"Does He who created not then know?" You must not think that Allah made the universe and the stars and the constellations, and then life came into things – this is the position of the kuffar. The position of the Muslim is that alongside this enormous cosmic majesty of Allah's creation, subhanahu wa ta'ala, there is also the fact of His intimate connection to His slave. The Names He gives are Al-Latif and Al-Khabir, which Hajj 'Abdalhaqq Bewley has heroically called the All-Pervading and the All-Aware. He has also said that Latif has the meaning of graciousness and kindness and also of penetrating right through everything, pervasive but with infinite kindness and closeness. Khabir is total awareness that takes in everything all the time. This is how we must understand Allah, subhanahu wa ta'ala, all the time.

We go back to Surat Ya Sin (36:79) for a vital phrase:

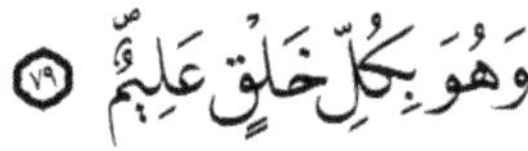

He has total knowledge of each created thing.

The One you worship when you say, "Allahu akbar," – the 'akbar' of your takbir is that He has total knowledge of each created thing. Total knowledge not only means the biological creature but everything that is in it, its history from the moment of it coming into the world until the moment of its death. Allah, subhanahu wa ta'ala, knew you at birth and was aware of you when you died. This is the knowledge Allah has when He says that He has total knowledge of each created thing.

To realise the majesty of Allah and also this reality of Divine Presence is to realise that it is also a knowledge that involves all the creatures from the beginning of time until the in-time comes to an end. It is one process, and this process is the knowledge of Allah, subhanahu wa ta'ala.

We are going to look at how the mutakallimun see this.

What we are faced with is that the creature is known to Allah in the Unseen and the 'Kun' brings the creature into the seen world, into the existent world. The mutakallimun call the forms in the knowledge of Allah before they are created, the 'known'. They are known by Allah, but the Sufis have a special term for them because they think it is very important to get this thing right, so the Sufis have invented a vocabulary based on the Qur'anic ayats. They call this 'al-'Ayan ath-thabita' which means 'source-forms', although it is difficult to translate. 'Al-'Ayan ath-thabita' is when Allah has the – I do not like to use the word – 'idea' because this is not correct, but He has the form in His knowledge before the 'kun' brings it into existence. The Sufis call it a source-form, a form from the Source.

At this stage of our understanding of Tawhid we have to make a complete division, otherwise we will go outside Tawhid. We make a division between the known – that is the 'ayn ath-thabita before it comes into creation, before the 'kun' – and the Knower, Allah, subhanahu wa ta'ala. The known has a form, limited, determined, individualised, specific. The Knower is free of limitation, free of determination and is not a form. The known subsists only in the knowledge of the Knower, it has no independent existence until the 'kun'. The Knower exists in Himself, totally independent, He is not dependent on anything. Surat al-Ikhlas:

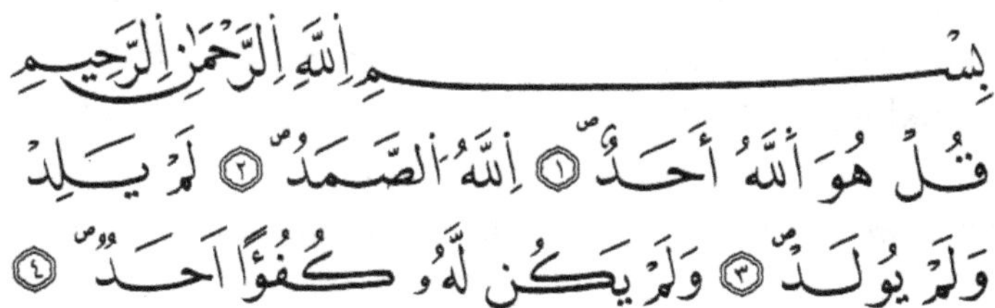

In the name of Allah, All-Merciful, Most Merciful
"Say: 'He is Allah, Absolute Oneness,
Allah, the Everlasting Sustainer of all.
He has not given birth and was not born.
And no one is comparable to Him.'"

The known has no attribute but it has a capacity in its form to receive attributes. The Knower is the possessor of these Source Attributes. Allah, subhanahu wa ta'ala, has these Attributes: life, knowledge, will, power, hearing, sight and speech. So when He makes the order: "Kun! fa yakun," He gives a bit of life, a bit of knowledge, a bit of will, a bit of power, a bit of hearing, a bit of sight, a bit of speech – we call them the borrowed attributes because they are in-time, and Allah is outside time but He lets the form, when it comes into being, have a limited 'rental'. The human being has a rental on these capacities or attributes because he is designed in order to be able to receive them.

The known forms, before they come into existence, are passive, have no existence, no attributes and no activity. When the 'kun' comes they can then have these things from Allah, subhanahu wa ta'ala, because the Knower has activity, the Knower is active, He is the Actor. All the actions of the creatures come from the Actor. There is no action of the creatures but from the gift of Allah, subhanahu wa ta'ala, in the order of the 'Kun! fa yakun.' Power belongs absolutely to Allah and He gives these, like sprinkling water, onto the forms to bring them to life.

Thus we are able to say that the relation of the known to

the Knower, of the forms to the Creator of the forms is otherness. The forms are other-than-Allah, they are ghayr, they are masiwallah. Everything that is existent, in the world, in the cosmos is other-than-Allah: we have two. This may sound very strange but to arrive at Tawhid we must posit a very powerful 'two' because otherwise we are not going to get it right. We would end up like the mushriks or the kuffar.

Let us look at Surat Al 'Imran (3:28 & 30). It is one phrase which comes twice:

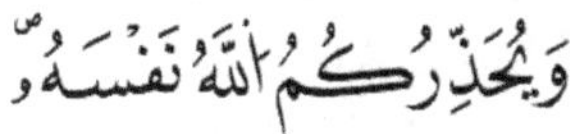

Allah advises you to be afraid of Him.

Hajj 'Abdalhaqq has very wisely given a different aspect of the word 'yuhadhirukum' in each of these two ayats. In one ayat: "Allah advises you to be afraid of Him," and in the other: "Allah advises you to beware of Him." What this is, is that Allah says not to try to understand the Essence. The Act of Allah you must understand, the Attributes of Allah you must understand, but when we come to the Essence from which these complex things emerge – do not try. Be afraid. Beware, because you cannot penetrate it.

Also, Rasul, sallallahu 'alayhi wa sallam, in a famous hadith, because of these revelations, warned the muminun not to contemplate, in the language of the mutakallimun, the 'Dhat', the Essence of Allah, subhanahu wa ta'ala. Imam al-Ghazali goes to great lengths very beautifully trying to understand it by looking at all the processes of the Act. Dependent on the Act are the Attributes: without the capacity to move and so on, you cannot realise something, but when you go from the Act to the Attributes that make it happen you ask, "Where do the Attributes come from?" and you reach the Essence. Imam al-Ghazali tries very beautifully to see if he can get any further but he stops and says that you cannot go any further. That is as far as you can go.

So let us say, in the language of the mutakallimun and the 'ulama, that Allah is Khaliq, the Creator, and the creatures are makhluq. Allah is Rabb, and the creatures are marbub. Allah is Ilah, He is worshipped, and the creatures are maluh, worshippers. Allah is Maalik with a long 'a', He is Master, Controller of all the destinies, and the slaves are mamluk. The Sufis say very beautifully:

"The Haqq is Existence, the 'abd is non-existence. Transformation of Reality is not possible, so the Haqq is Haqq and the 'abd is 'abd." The Lord is the Lord and the slave is the slave.

This means that all these shayateen of the orientalists who say that the Sufis are pantheists and say that God is the creation, have not understood anything at all of what is being taught. People talk about 'Wahdat al-wujud' yet the term does not appear once in all the four hundred books of Ibn al-'Arabi. When they talk about that they imply that God IS the universe. But the slave is the slave and the Lord is the Lord. Shaykh Ibn al-'Arabi says, "There is no limit to slavehood. There is no line by which he can pass over from created to Creator. There is no way that the Creator in His vastness will allow that He should be slave. He has, by His wisdom, determined it this way, this is how He set up creation."

We now go to the famous and well-known ayat in Surat Fatir (35:15):

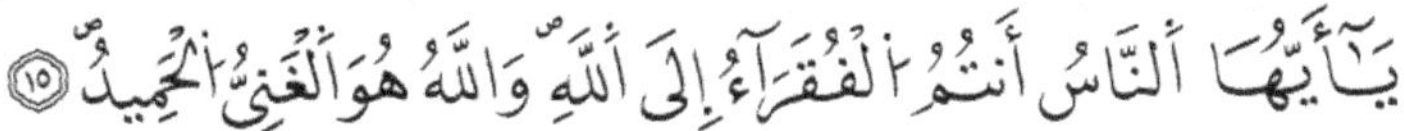

O Mankind, you are the poor, in need of Allah,
whereas Allah is the Rich-beyond-need,
the Praise-Worthy.

This is a statement of what I have just said. The creature is totally dependent and Allah is totally Independent. The position of the slave in need of Allah is that he is in need of Allah for his living, his knowing, his seeing, his hearing, his willing – for all these attributes he needs this gift of Allah which has been given because He has made a form that can receive these capacities during the in-time span that is destined for him. But he is totally dependent, and Allah is totally independent of that creature and of that creature's functioning with these attributes that He has allowed him in the in-time to touch upon.

At this point we have to say that the essence of Tawhid is based on this fundamental duality, that Allah is highly exalted above anything that can be associated with Him. This does not change, but we are going to enter into another zone of knowledge which Allah has opened to us in the Qur'an which involves the nearness of Allah, subhanahu wa ta'ala. The slave is not just looking up in terror and awe at the majesty of a distant Creator, he is also conscious that the One who is the Creator of the universe, of the stars, of the planets, of the sun and moon and the other creatures and the land that they are on, is this One Who is close to you.

I think we had better look at one more ayat, otherwise I would leave you with a position which is not actually the whole, proper position of the Muslims. We have to look at the 'ananiyya', the 'I'-ness of the creature in this position of 'abd, before this Almighty Creator – otherwise we would all go home depressed! We will put just one foot in the door of this subject.

Look at Surat al-Hadid (57:4). By the way, this refers to the creation in six days. We know from other ayats in the Qur'an that the six days are not literally six days. You have to remember something which many people forget – there were not 'days' until Allah placed the earth in orbit around the sun. Days only happen once the whole thing is already done. When, in another place, Allah says that a day with Allah is like fifty thousand years in the way you count – it is like a phase in the creation over a time-span that is beyond our knowledge. The people who want to attack the Qur'an with ignorance say, "Six days? We know better than that, we are scientists," but they do not know anything.

هُوَ ٱلَّذِي خَلَقَ ٱلسَّمَٰوَٰتِ وَٱلْأَرْضَ فِي سِتَّةِ أَيَّامٍ
ثُمَّ ٱسْتَوَىٰ عَلَى ٱلْعَرْشِ

It is He who created the heavens and the earth in six days,
then established Himself firmly on the Throne.

By 'throne' He means the cosmic Throne of the might of the creation.

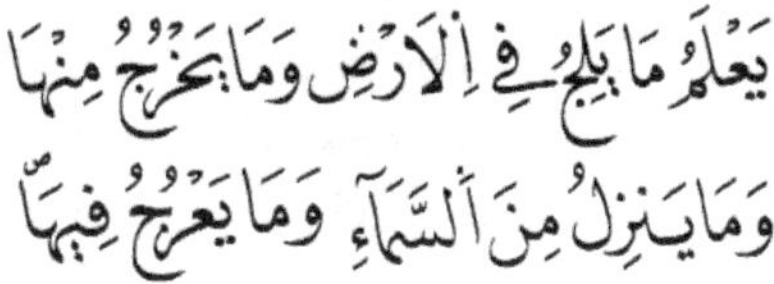

He knows what goes into the earth
and what comes out of it,
what comes down from heaven
and what goes up into it.

He knows the whole creational process. Then, having made this declaration about the majesty of Allah, He says:

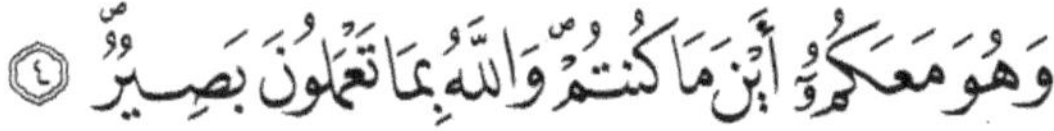

He is with you wherever you are –
Allah sees what you do.

Allah has what you might call an 'intimate' connection, but it is not a connection because one cannot use the word connection. He has an intimate presence with the slave. He is with you wherever you are and Allah sees what you do.

The one who has understood this has a different experience of existence. Allah, subhanahu wa ta'ala, says in Surat al-Kahf (18:24):

وَاذْكُر رَّبَّكَ إِذَا نَسِيتَ

Remember your Lord when you forget.

So it is not someone forgetting the 'Asr prayer, or just being distracted by something in life, by things in the dunya, it is this. When you forget that He is with you wherever you are, and Allah sees what you do – when you forget that, that is what you have to remember. How He is with His creation – this is what you have to remember.

Surat al-Asr (103:2):

إِنَّ ٱلْإِنسَـٰنَ لَفِى خُسْرٍ ۝

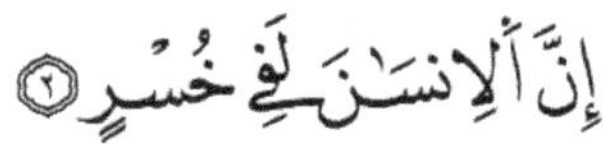

Truly man is in loss.

What is the loss of man? It is this. What does he forget? He forgets that Allah is with you wherever you are and Allah sees what you do. To finish, we remember the great Sufi of the East, Sahl at-Tustari, radiyallahu 'anhu, when he took as his wird, the Wird as-Sahl:

الله معي الله ناظر إلي الله شاهد علي

Allah is with me, Allah sees me,
Allah is the Witness of my acts.

That was the path to high Tawhid and to quick access to fana fillah and being obliterated in the Presence of Allah.

IV

April 17th 2004

What we have been doing is taking steps, and each gathering we have had is another step. This is just an instalment and there is, as it were, another chapter where we will join things that we have separated.

Hajj 'Abdalhaqq said something earlier which I was very pleased with in his understanding of what I had been saying last week. He said, "The wahhabis start with 'One', with a Tawhid which they declare, and they end up with two. What you are saying is that you start with two and you end up with One." So we are going towards a complete understanding of Tawhid but we have to go in stages because we are talking about the Tawhid of the people of the Tariqa, the people who are on the path to 'Ilm al-laduni, to direct knowledge of Allah, subhanahu wa ta'ala. You cannot afford to get it wrong.

All the foundations become the instruments and technical apparatus by which the Sufis reach their goal. They do not walk naked on their path. It is like the tawaf – before Rasul, sallallahu 'alayhi wa sallam, the people used to go naked around the Ka'aba. When Rasul came, sallallahu 'alayhi wa sallam, he did not abolish the tawaf but he had people clothed and gave them honour by being dressed, and he allowed the institution of tawaf to continue. Islam is not culture, Islam purifies culture. In the same way, for this knowledge that we want, you have to be clothed in this taqwa and this birr, this path of right action in order to arrive at the robe of honour which is Ma'rifatullah.

If we can continue the story as it were, we finished on the next stage of this matter which was in Surat al-Hadid (57:4). "It is He Who created the heavens and the earth in six days, then established Himself firmly on the Throne." We will look at it again because it gives us continuity: "It is He Who created the heavens and the earth in six days," and remember of course that the six days are not a literal thing but are part of this vision of the creation of the world where another ayat in the Qur'an refers to a day being an enormous length of time. "It is He Who created the heavens and the earth in six days, then established Himself firmly on the Throne" – then the whole cosmic reality came into being.

IV

هُوَ ٱلَّذِى خَلَقَ ٱلسَّمَٰوَٰتِ وَٱلْأَرْضَ فِى سِتَّةِ أَيَّامٍ ثُمَّ ٱسْتَوَىٰ عَلَى
ٱلْعَرْشِ يَعْلَمُ مَا يَلِجُ فِى ٱلْأَرْضِ وَمَا يَخْرُجُ مِنْهَا وَمَا يَنزِلُ مِنَ ٱلسَّمَآءِ
وَمَا يَعْرُجُ فِيهَا وَهُوَ مَعَكُمْ أَيْنَ مَا كُنتُمْ وَٱللَّهُ بِمَا تَعْمَلُونَ بَصِيرٌ ﴿٤﴾

It is He Who created the heavens
and the earth in six days,
then established Himself firmly on the Throne.
He knows what goes into the earth
and what comes out of it,
what comes down from heaven and what goes up into it.
He is with you wherever you are –
Allah sees what you do."

I shall just remind you that the significance of us looking at this ayat is that two knowledges which Allah reveals about Himself are put together. This is this next step that we are taking.

At the beginning of the ayat Allah, subhanahu wa ta'ala, declares Himself the One Who created the whole cosmic reality but the next stage is: "He knows what goes into the earth and what comes out of it, what comes down from heaven and what goes up into it." Therefore He also has an on-going knowledge. In the continual nature of existence Allah, subhanahu wa ta'ala, knows everything that is happening. It is not the primitive idea of a divinity that makes everything happen and then He has done His job, astaghfirullah. Allah is explaining that His knowledge also contains all the process of life for which, in another context, from the Qur'an, we take the term 'Rububiyya' from the word 'Rabb.'

Rububiyya is the Divine control over all the inter-related aspects of existence – how the chemicals come together to produce other chemicals, how the elements interact with each other, how in the whole life of the forest from the tops of the trees to the creatures at the foot of the trees, each creature has a capacity to eat another creature so that it can live – all these things are interconnected and inter-related by this Rububiyya.

Now we come to the last part which is what is important to us.

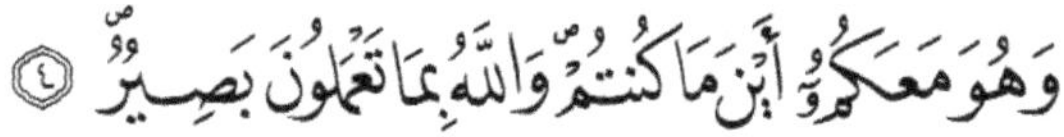

He is with you wherever you are –
Allah sees what you do.

This is a new knowledge that Allah is giving us. It has two things: it has 'ayna ma' which indicates place. So Allah knows the place where it is happening, and 'kuntum', 'you are', which indicates time, Allah sees the time and the place of any given human situation.

Allah sees what you do. As the mufassirin observe, Allah, subhanahu wa ta'ala, does not use the word 'know' which He could say if the meaning were about this earlier stage, but 'He is with you wherever you go' is Presence, and Allah sees what you do. 'Sees' from Basir, is the verb of eye-witnessing, and to witness you must be present.

وَٱللَّهُ بِمَا تَعْمَلُونَ بَصِيرٌ ﴿٤﴾

Allah sees what you do.

Basir is eye-witnessing. Therefore from this we have a knowledge that Allah witnesses us, this is a seeing.

Now we go to Surat an-Nisa' (4:108):

يَسْتَخْفُونَ مِنَ ٱلنَّاسِ وَلَا يَسْتَخْفُونَ مِنَ ٱللَّهِ وَهُوَ
مَعَهُمْ إِذْ يُبَيِّتُونَ مَا لَا يَرْضَىٰ مِنَ ٱلْقَوْلِ
وَكَانَ ٱللَّهُ بِمَا يَعْمَلُونَ مُحِيطًا ﴿١٠٨﴾

They try to conceal themselves from people,
but they cannot conceal themselves from Allah.
He is with them when they spend the night
saying things which are not pleasing to Him.
Allah encompasses everything they do.

People talk about the Qur'an as Revelation and you have to understand that it IS a revelation! The Revelation is not the descent of the Qur'an, it is that Allah reveals secrets of Himself that have not been known until then. He is telling us openly – it is a Qur'an al-Mubin, it is a clear message. The Revelation is that Allah shows all His secrets that He wants the human creatures to have, and He gives it to them in this Book.

Here He says that people try to conceal themselves from people, in other words these people are already in a process of hiding themselves. But the Revelation says: “They cannot conceal themselves from Allah.” In other words you can hide yourself from people but you cannot hide from Allah. This is a statement of how it is. This knowledge changes the one who has it. The one who knows this is not the same as the one who does not know. The ones who do not know try to conceal themselves from people. This is what kufr is – they cover over what is going on but they cannot be kafir with Allah, they are trying, but they cannot do it because Allah knows what is happening.

Then Allah says:

وَهُوَ مَعَهُمْ إِذْ يُبَيِّتُونَ مَا لَا يَرْضَىٰ مِنَ ٱلْقَوْلِ

He is with them when they spend the night saying things which are not pleasing to Him.

Do you not see the reality of this? People are actually involved in the business of scheming against Allah, subhanahu wa ta‘ala, against what is pleasing to Allah. So they are doing it as if they were in clandestine plotting against Allah. Allah says: “He is with them,” and ‘with them’ is Presence.

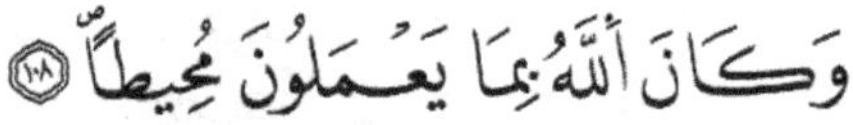

Allah encompasses everything they do.

It is not something psychic or magical, but a Presence which encompasses the whole event of what they are doing. Apply this to how we get the news today. You get the news about Iraq and the news about Afghanistan and it is all presented to us by kuffar who are trying to conceal themselves from people, who are spending the night saying things that are not pleasing to Allah, but He says: "Allah encompasses everything they do." We have to see it in the light of Allah's complete command of the situation, He knows exactly what is happening. What He tells us is that He is with them, and that is Presence.

You have to understand that over this last century there has been a whole false teaching of Islam, a Tawhid that does not take into account these ayats that we are looking at, as if they did not exist. They have made a Tawhid by what Ibn al-'Arabi says, "They have had Tanzih but they have not had Tashbih." They have had exaltation of Allah above what is associated with Him without also understanding this extraordinary reality that Allah has openly declared in His Book about His Presence.

Rasul, sallallahu 'alayhi wa sallam, said in a well-known hadith, the meaning of which is: "None of you while making Salat should spit in front of himself as Allah, the Majestic, is before him." From this, the great collector of Sira, Asqalani, said, "This hadith refutes the claim of one who confines Allah to the 'Arsh alone. This establishes omnipresence in every place." This is very important because we are now getting a comprehension of Tawhid which allows us to say that, as we have already established, nothing can be associated with Him, He is not dependent on anything, He is not contained in any form, and at the same time here we have this amazing revelation of His Presence in events.

Let us look at Surat al-Waqi'a (56:83-87). What we are finding is that each one of these ayats is giving another dimension of this Presence of Allah, this witnessing of Allah, this seeing of Allah of the human actions. Now this nature of the Presence of Allah, subhanahu wa ta'ala, gets more intimate, more intense.

فَلَوْلَآ إِذَا بَلَغَتِ ٱلْحُلْقُومَ ﴿٨٣﴾ وَأَنتُمْ حِينَئِذٍ
تَنظُرُونَ ﴿٨٤﴾ وَنَحْنُ أَقْرَبُ إِلَيْهِ مِنكُمْ وَلَٰكِن لَّا تُبْصِرُونَ ﴿٨٥﴾
فَلَوْلَآ إِن كُنتُمْ غَيْرَ مَدِينِينَ ﴿٨٦﴾ تَرْجِعُونَهَآ إِن كُنتُمْ صَٰدِقِينَ ﴿٨٧﴾

Why then, when death reaches his throat
and you are at that moment looking on –
and We are nearer him than you, but you cannot see –
why then, if you are not subject to Our command,
do you not send it back if you are telling the truth?

Allah is nearer the dying man than the man that is at his deathbed, but you cannot see. This is the most intense moment – a human being at the death of another human being, and at that moment the one who is watching the dying man does not understand that the nearness of Allah, subhanahu wa ta'ala, is nearer than his presence next to the dying man, and he cannot see. You are always on the edge of a Divine Presence, like that moment, for that moment is true at every moment.

"Why then, if you are not subject to Our judgment," to how We have decreed it to be – 'if you are telling the truth' – how the kafir sees it – 'why do you not send back this command of death, this destiny of death?' Allah has destined him to die. It is as if Allah were saying: 'If you,' the kafir, 'have this position that you claim then why do you not send back the order: 'Do not die!'' In other words you are denying the reality of the event of death thus denying the Presence of Allah, subhanahu wa ta'ala, in the act of death. This is the point that you have to understand. This knowledge of the Presence of Allah changes the experience of the one who knows it.

We go to Surat Qaf (50:16). Again, we will find two things coming together in this ayat.

وَلَقَدْ خَلَقْنَا ٱلْإِنسَٰنَ وَنَعْلَمُ مَا تُوَسْوِسُ بِهِۦ نَفْسُهُۥ
وَنَحْنُ أَقْرَبُ إِلَيْهِ مِنْ حَبْلِ ٱلْوَرِيدِ ﴿١٦﴾

We created man and We know
what his own self whispers to him.
We are nearer to him than his jugular vein.

Look how Allah is unveiling His secrets to the people. Allah says, "We created man," and we have already understood that Allah has connected together this enormous physical creation and organisation of existence. Even the kuffar, as Allah says in Surat az-Zumar (39:38):

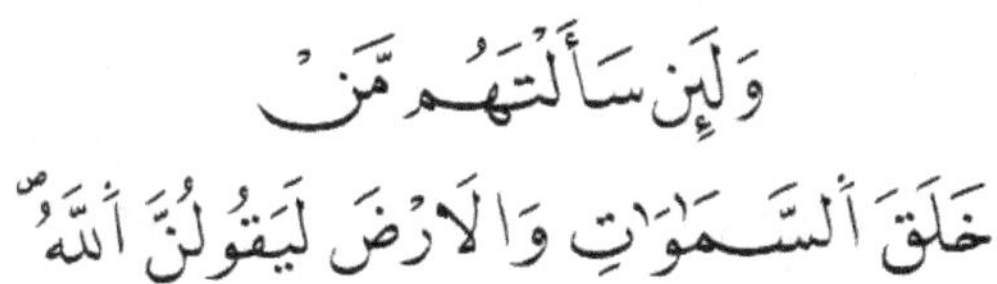

وَلَئِن سَأَلْتَهُم مَّنْ
خَلَقَ ٱلسَّمَٰوَٰتِ وَٱلْأَرْضَ لَيَقُولُنَّ ٱللَّهُ

If you ask them,
'Who created the heavens and the earth?'
they will say, 'Allah'.

What they do not see is (Surat Qaf, 50:16):

وَ

"Wa."

Every word in the Qur'an has meaning, every word is important.

لَقَدْ خَلَقْنَا الْإِنسَانَ

We created man

– it is not even 'created' but 'constructed', 'We constructed man, We put all the bits together that make up man,' and then comes, 'And'. You must think of creation in terms of the child in the womb. It structurally comes bit, by bit, by bit. The first organ to appear is the heart, then the other organs begin to form and come together bit by bit. This is what the 'khalaqna' is, it is almost 'constructed' in modern understanding.

So: "We constructed man," and the next bit is: "And we know what his own self whispers to him." The self's whisper is like a silent voice because it is inside the creature. Allah is saying that the One Who created this enormous cosmic event also knows what the self is saying to itself, what you are saying to yourself. So Allah is with you. You are accompanied by a Presence of Lordship – all the time. This is Tawhid! Now you are beginning to see what the true nature of Tawhid is.

Allah, subhanahu wa ta'ala, goes one step further to make the mind stop. He says:

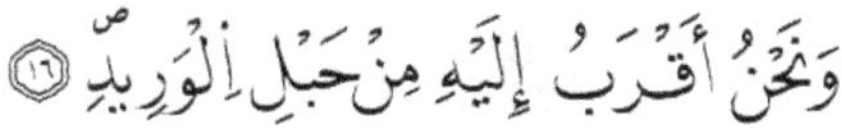

We are nearer to him than his jugular vein.

He uses the word 'aqrab' for 'nearer' and Al-Qarib is a name of Allah, subhanahu wa ta'ala. Allah has Nearness. "We are nearer to him than his jugular vein." The jugular vein is what gives you life. If you cut the jugular vein you cut the life off. "We are nearer," and the Sufis find that the 'We' is often used with direct reference to the Essence, and what we are dealing with here is the Essence because there cannot be Attributes without Essence.

If Allah sees, if Allah hears, it means also that His Essence is there because He is not also divisible, He cannot be divided. Therefore again, this is a complete contradiction of the false teaching of Tawhid that has been spread among the Muslims over the last century which is why we are in the terrible situation that we are in now, and it is only this knowledge which you have, which you will take and teach, which will establish the true Qur'anic teaching, which is the might and power of Allah, subhanahu wa ta'ala, which means He is completely present in all our actions. In that sense, as slaves of Allah, we also know what He wants. This is how we will be able to change things because we have a knowledge that can only come through the people who have Iman, who have trust in Allah, subhanahu wa ta'ala.

Now we go to Surat al-Baqara which is filled with things of this nature. Surat al-Baqara (2:186):

وَإِذَا سَأَلَكَ عِبَادِى عَنِّى فَإِنِّى قَرِيبٌ

If My slaves ask you about Me, I am near.

Again there is this name of Allah – 'I am Near.' Mu'awiya ibn Ja'ad said, "Once a bedouin asked Rasul, sallallahu 'alayhi wa sallam, whether Allah was near to him so that he could talk intimately to Allah, or whether Allah was far so that he should shout." Rasul, sallallahu 'alayhi wa sallam, remained silent for a while then this ayat was revealed. This was the answer to the question of the bedouin.

أُجِيبُ دَعْوَةَ ٱلدَّاعِ إِذَا دَعَانِ

I answer the call of the caller when he calls on me.

Now we have been given another bit of the secret. This nearness of Allah is not a passive thing, it is dynamic and active. "I answer the call of the caller when he calls on Me." It is beautiful. The one who calls on Him, Allah calls on him. This is the true relationship of the slave with his Lord, a merciful Lord. It is an indication of the mercy of Allah, subhanahu wa ta'ala.

IV

أُجِيبُ دَعْوَةَ ٱلدَّاعِ إِذَا دَعَانِ

I answer the call of the caller when he calls on Me,

– meaning that the one who calls on Him, He calls on them – so Allah calls, not His slave.

Then from this there is a conclusion:

فَلْيَسْتَجِيبُوا۟ لِى وَلْيُؤْمِنُوا۟ بِى لَعَلَّهُمْ يَرْشُدُونَ ﴿١٨٦﴾

They should therefore respond to Me and believe in Me so that hopefully they will be rightly guided.

In other words, once this knowledge clicks into place – and it is more than knowledge, it is an awareness of how things are – it follows that the person should respond to Allah. "They should therefore respond to Me and believe in Me," so you believe in Him, and you trust in Him because He is the Answerer. I cannot say it is a relationship because there is no relationship with Allah, but this possible reality comes into place through the knowledge that this is how things are. The calling makes the Iman.

Surat al-A'raf (7:7). This is another step in our understanding of this situation.

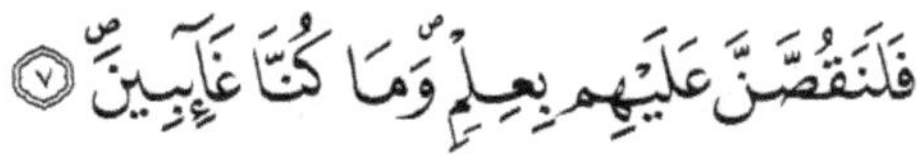

We will tell them about it with knowledge.
We are never absent.

This is not a state that comes and goes, but it is constant. This is a knowledge which underlies all understanding of visible reality, which must be understood: Allah sees you, Allah hears you and He is never absent.

Abu Musa al-Ash'ari said that once, travelling with Rasul, sallallahu 'alayhi wa sallam, a companion started to shout takbir, and Rasul, sallallahu 'alayhi wa sallam, said, "O people, do not strain yourselves. You are not calling on One Who is blind or deaf. You are calling on the One Who is listening to you, seeing you and is with you. The One you are calling on is nearer to you than the neck of your camel." This is Rasul, sallallahu 'alayhi wa sallam, teaching Tawhid to the Sahaba – and denied for a hundred years by these shaytans from Arabistan. We have seen from these ayats that Allah sees what is happening and He hears the one who calls. You are calling on the One Who is listening to you, seeing you and is with you. The One you are calling on is nearer to you than the neck of your camels.

We now connect "We are never absent" to Surat an-Nisa' (4:126):

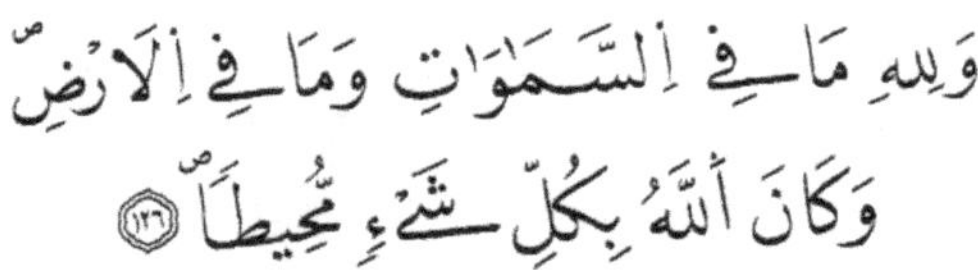

What is in the heavens
and in the earth belongs to Allah.
Allah encompasses all things.

– which is the completion of what we saw in that last ayat. Allah possesses the whole situation and Allah encompasses all things. Not only is He never absent, but He encompasses everything. Surat al-An'am (6:103):

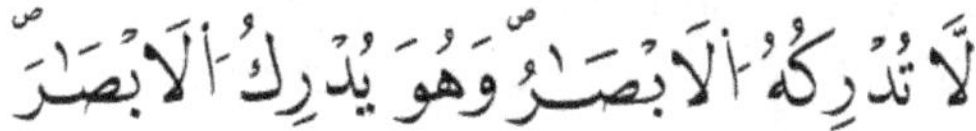

Eyesight cannot perceive Him
but He perceives eyesight.

Allah, subhanahu wa ta'ala, is constantly challenging the kuffar with the question: "On what grounds do you deny the Unseen, and given that you deny the Unseen how are you able to deny that you will be brought from your graves and held to account for your actions?" Allah, subhanahu wa ta'ala, says in Surat Fussilat (41:54):

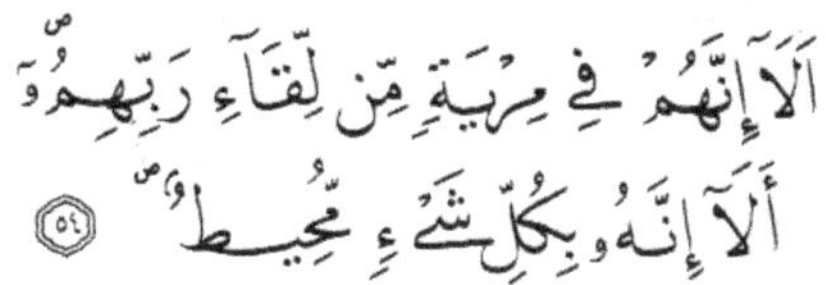

What! Are they in doubt
about the meeting with their Lord?
What! Does He not encompass all things?

It is like Allah has set up a contract with the human being and Allah, subhanahu wa ta'ala, is saying, "Do not deny it. How are you able to deny it?"

Allah says: "What! Are they in doubt about the meeting with their Lord?" He uses the word 'Rabb' which means 'Lord' in His aspect as the Ruler over all the created creatures. "What! Are they in doubt about the meeting with their Lord?" Qur'an is insisting that this cannot be avoided, it cannot be doubted and if it is doubted then you are in ignorance because this meeting with the Lord, the encounter which happens after death is an inevitable and inescapable part of understanding the nature of the One Who has created the whole universe, Who is speaking through Rasul, sallallahu 'alayhi wa sallam, in the Revelation of Qur'an.

Surat at-Talaq (65:12):

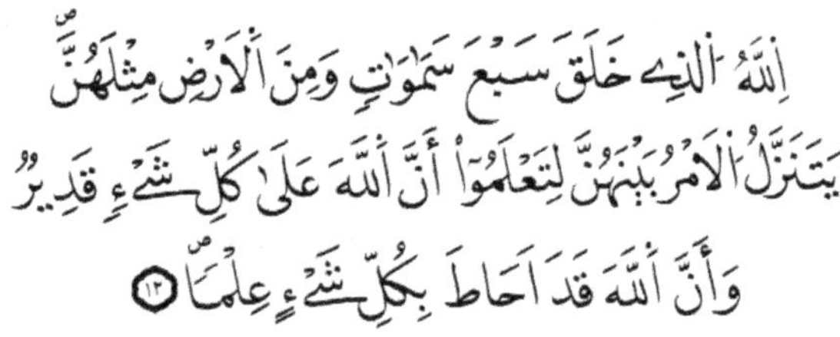

It is Allah Who created the seven heavens
and of the earth the same number,
the Command descending down through all of them
so that you might know
that Allah has power over all things,
and that Allah encompasses all things in His knowledge.

Allah, subhanahu wa ta'ala, is talking about His power as Creator not just of this earth but of the whole universe, the seven heavens and the seven realms of earth. Then He uses the word 'Amr' which is from the 'Kun!' – the Command of the creation of the cosmos descends through all the heavens and all the earth. This Amr goes to the furthest stars, to the furthest galaxies and constellations, "So that you might know that Allah has power over all things."

The Command has come through all the creation – in other words, part of the Command is that you are there on the earth to receive the message of Allah, subhanahu wa ta'ala, and know that He is the Creator of it, and that Allah encompasses all things in His knowledge.

Allah encompasses all things in His knowledge. He has made the whole cosmic event in His knowledge, but in the continuum He has created the time of the cosmos and knows it at every instant from its beginning, in its present, until its fulfilment. Remember the famous question of Sayyiduna 'Umar ibn al-Khattab, radiyallahu 'anhu, to Rasul, sallallahu 'alayhi wa sallam: "Are we on a matter that is finished or are we on a matter that is just beginning?" Rasul, sallallahu 'alayhi wa sallam, said, "The page is written and the ink is dry." "Allah encompasses all things in His knowledge" could not be true if He did not have a knowledge of everything to the Yawm al-Qiyama.

Remember also that time as we understand it stops with the creation. Again we come to the limits of thinking because it is in the nature of the Creator to create time. Rasul, sallallahu 'alayhi wa sallam, said, "Do not curse time because Allah is Time." There are two words for 'time', there is 'zaman' and 'dahr'. This means that Allah is the Creator of the instantaneousness of events, not just the measured distance of time. The measured distance of time will come to an end with the destruction of the world, but the moment in which the Command takes place is from Allah.

We now go back to Surat al-Baqara (2:115), and we are going deeper into this unveiling of Tawhid by Allah, subhanahu wa ta'ala.

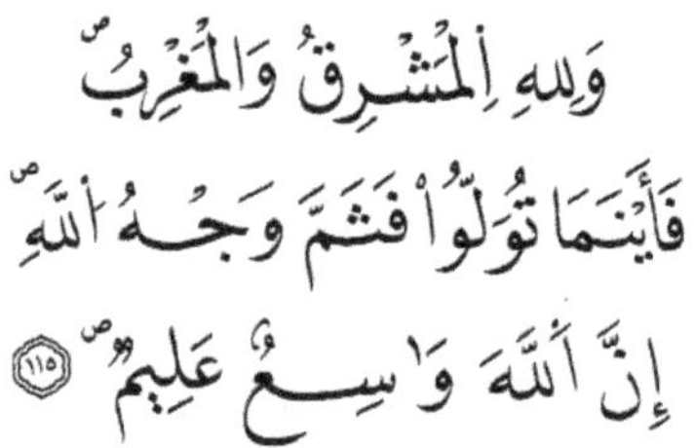

Both East and West belong to Allah,
so wherever you turn, the Face of Allah is there.
Allah is All-Encompassing, All-Knowing.

Let us look again at the Arabic:

وَلِلَّهِ ٱلْمَشْرِقُ وَٱلْمَغْرِبُ

Both East and West belong to Allah,

– so the directions belong to Allah.

فَأَيْنَمَا تُوَلُّوا۟ فَثَمَّ

"Fa thamma" – meaning, "right there –" and what comes immediately after that?

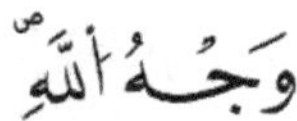

"Wajhullah". Face of Allah. Do you see that there is no grammar, it is the Revelation of Allah, subhanahu wa ta'ala? There is no gap, there is no space in it, there is nothing added. "Wherever you turn – Face of Allah."

Knowledge is in making a distinction about this. This truth is so deep and so profound. There was once a famous majdhoub and they went into the mosque and he was prostrating here, there and everywhere and they said, "What do you think you are doing?" He said,

فَأَيْنَمَا تُوَلُّوا فَثَمَّ وَجْهُ اللَّهِ

"Wherever you turn, the Face of Allah is there." He was mad in love with Allah, going around in circles because, "There is the Wajh of Allah."

Look at the two aspects of this. If you go back into the Qur'an, Allah, subhanahu wa ta'ala, speaks with this intimacy and love and concern for Rasul, sallallahu 'alayhi wa sallam, and says to him in Surat al-Baqara (2:144):

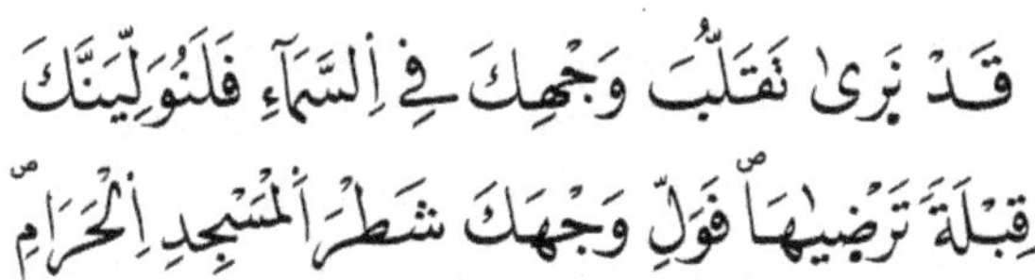

We have seen you looking up into heaven,
turning this way and that,
so We will turn you towards a direction
which will please you.
Turn your face, therefore, towards the Masjid al-Haram.

Take the qibla of Makkah. So the Muslim takes a qibla and he takes it because that is Shari'ah. Shari'ah is that you take a direction. We cannot ask 'Why?' of Allah but I am trying to explain how the meaning of the taking the qibla of Makkah is the event of setting Islam above and abrogating all other religions. Otherwise he would have been permitted to make qibla of Jerusalem. It means the end of Jerusalem. It is the Deen of the qibla and Allah, subhanahu wa ta'ala, has given the muminun the qibla of Makkah. That is why Ibn Taymiyya quite rightly says, "There is no rite of 'ibada connected to Al-Aqsa." None. It is not in the Deen. It has a place for us of love and respect because of the Mi'raj, but the Deen involves the rites of Makkah.

You are then holding in your understanding two truths. One can only be understood in someone drunk and intoxicated with love of Allah, who is then outside the Shari'ah. If a man is mad and commits a crime he is not punished, he is locked up as insane. But the people have to obey the Law and the Law is that they take a qibla, which is ignorance unless you know that you take the qibla in slavehood, in your 'ubudiyya to Allah, subhanahu wa ta'ala, because Rasul, sallallahu 'alayhi wa sallam, has been given the Revelation that that is how Allah wants us to make worship of Him. We do it, but we also know the Face of Allah is wherever you turn.

The Wajh of Allah, according both to the mutakallimun and the Sufis, is a way of saying the Essence of Allah. The Face of Allah is the Essence of Allah. The face of the person embodies, as it were, the person. Wherever you turn, it means that the Essence of Allah is present. This is also a denial of those who have set Allah on the Throne and say that He has no presence on earth. It also gives a lie to the ones who say, because of certain ayats in the Qur'an, that Allah has limbs and is a person. Ibn Batutta's famous observation was that he heard Ibn Taymiyya say, astaghfirullah, "Allah descends from His Throne as I descend from this mimbar," which is of course a horrific statement as far as we are concerned.

We now go to Surat al-Qasas (28:88) which we connect to the previous ayat.

Do not call on any other god along with Allah.
There is no god but Him.
All things are passing except His Face.
Judgment belongs to Him. You will be returned to Him.

Here you have it. This is the dividing point. When people say to you, "Dialogue with other faiths," there is NO other faith, because they do not know this. This is not to be debated or discussed, this is to be obeyed. This is a knowledge only the Muslims have and if people want knowledge they must come into the qasr, the fortress of the Deen.

"Do not call on any other god along with Allah. There is no god but Him. All things are passing except His

Face. Judgment belongs to Him. You will be returned to Him." Here is the complete contract.

All things are passing except His Face.

Everything that is in-time is passing, time is passing, all things are passing. This Divine Reality is before, during and after the 'all things' which are passing.

The Face of Allah is present, the Command – the 'Kun' is given, the things come into existence and by their coming into existence things move into an in-time sphere. From their beginning they are disintegrating and they pass. Everything passes except His Face, and when it is all gone – Wajh of Allah. The whole in-time movement of things comes to an end – Face of Allah. So Allah dominates and is the Reality in place and in time. Place is under His Command and under His Presence, and time is under His Command and under His Presence. This connects to another knowledge which is that judgment belongs to Him. He decides what is what. He is the Discriminator.

Then comes the intimate, existential message, as you would say. You will be returned to Him. In other words, you will enter the time-process and He will be present, you will go through the time-process and He will be present, and at your deathbed He will be nearer than the one near you. Then you will go into the grave and after that you will be returned to Him. That is the journey. That is the process.

IV

Surat ar-Rahman (55:26-27):

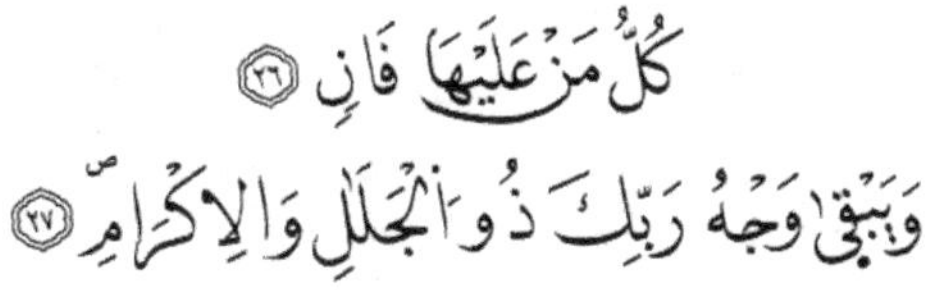

Everyone on it will pass away;
but the Face of your Lord will remain,
Master of Majesty and Generosity.

كُلُّ مَنْ عَلَيْهَا فَانٍ ﴿٢٦﴾

"Everyone on it will pass away"
is the reality of your life.

وَيَبْقَىٰ وَجْهُ رَبِّكَ

"There will remain the Face of your Lord." Then it tells us who our Lord is:

ذُو الْجَلَالِ وَالْإِكْرَامِ ﴿٢٧﴾

The Master of Majesty and Generosity. The One Who is the Master of this whole situation is One of Majesty because of the creation, and Generosity because of the creatures.

Surat Yunus (10:61):

وَمَا تَكُونُ فِي شَأْنٍ وَمَا تَتْلُوا مِنْهُ مِن
قُرْآنٍ وَلَا تَعْمَلُونَ مِنْ عَمَلٍ إِلَّا كُنَّا عَلَيْكُمْ شُهُودًا إِذْ
تُفِيضُونَ فِيهِ وَمَا يَعْزُبُ عَن رَّبِّكَ مِن مِّثْقَالِ ذَرَّةٍ فِي الْأَرْضِ
وَلَا فِي السَّمَاءِ وَلَا أَصْغَرَ مِن ذَٰلِكَ وَلَا أَكْبَرَ إِلَّا فِي كِتَابٍ مُّبِينٍ ﴿٦١﴾

You do not engage in any matter
or recite any of the Qur'an or do any action
without Our witnessing you
while you are occupied with it.
Not even the smallest speck eludes your Lord,
either on earth or in heaven.
Nor is there anything smaller than that, or larger,
which is not in a Clear Book.

You do not engage in any matter or recite any of the Qur'an or do any action without Him witnessing you while you are occupied with it. This is what is happening all the time. Allah says that He is witnessing us, while we are busy doing these things. Existence is our 'busy doing that'. Reality is Allah watching you while you are doing it. That was the famous Wird of Sahl at-Tustari, the great Sufi of the East:

الله معي الله ناظر إلي الله شاهد علي

Allah is with me, Allah sees me,
Allah is the Witness of my acts.

In case there is any doubt that Allah is generous, He

says: "Not even the smallest speck eludes your Lord either on earth or in heaven," there is no atom on the earth or in the sky but that it is known to Allah. "Nor is there anything smaller than that, or larger, which is not in a Clear Book." In other words, the mithal which Allah uses of the whole creation is this Book about which Rasul, sallallahu 'alayhi wa sallam, says, "The page is written and the ink is dry."

This is why Muslims cannot commit suicide thinking that they are somehow making things happen. They are in gross defiance of the Presence of Allah, subhanahu wa ta'ala. They have no permission to do such a thing, they have been ordered to worship, not to kill themselves, it is forbidden. They already have orders which are to fear Allah, not the enemy. It is of no use even to say that they do not fear death, because that is not what is happening at death as Allah, subhanahu wa ta'ala, has already explained: when you die, He is closer to you than the one watching you die. This is Whom you must fear, you must fear Allah.

Allah, subhanahu wa ta'ala, says: "There is not anything in it which is not in a Clear Book," which means from the mumin's point of view he says, "Alhamdulillah, we are safe. The foundations of our existence are secure. We are safe with Allah." Then you live your life knowing you are safe. This is the Yaqin which the Qur'an speaks about in varying degrees.

Now we will look at Surat Fussilat (41:53-54). Again Allah, subhanahu wa ta'ala, is challenging those ignorant people who do not get the point! If you do not have this knowledge of Tawhid, you do not know what life is about. You can only cause trouble and havoc. Allah says:

سَنُرِيهِمْ ءَايَٰتِنَا
فِي ٱلْءَافَاقِ وَفِيٓ أَنفُسِهِمْ حَتَّىٰ يَتَبَيَّنَ لَهُمْ أَنَّهُ
ٱلْحَقُّ أَوَلَمْ يَكْفِ بِرَبِّكَ أَنَّهُۥ عَلَىٰ كُلِّ شَيْءٍ شَهِيدٌ ﴿٥٣﴾ أَلَآ إِنَّهُمْ
فِي مِرْيَةٍ مِّن لِّقَآءِ رَبِّهِمْ أَلَآ إِنَّهُۥ بِكُلِّ شَيْءٍ مُّحِيطٌۢ ﴿٥٤﴾

We will show them Our Signs on the horizon
and within themselves
until it is clear to them that it is the truth.
Is it not enough for your Lord
that He is a witness of everything?
What! Are they in doubt about
the meeting with their Lord?
What! Does He not encompass all things?

This is reiterating the ayat we saw earlier. "We will show them Our signs on the horizon," meaning in the world, "and inside themselves." In other words, Allah will indicate this matter that we have been looking at over the last couple of hours, in your lifetime, in what is going on out there and in what is going on in here. There will be signs, and what are the signs? The signs are evidences of the power of Allah, subhanahu wa ta'ala. What are the evidences of the power of Allah, subhanahu wa ta'ala? They are your recognising that you are dependent and He is Independent. You are the needy and He is the One

Who Provides. Therefore you do not need anything because He will provide for you. "We will show them Our signs on the horizon and inside themselves until it is clear to them that it is the truth."

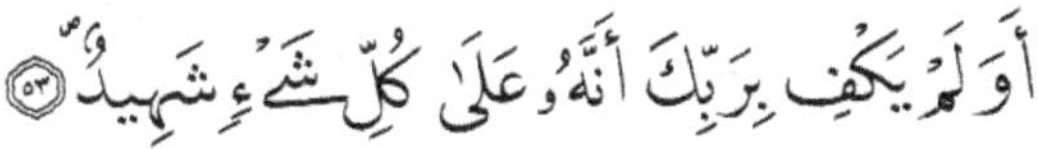

Is it not enough for your Lord that
He is a witness of everything?

This is the knowledge that matters. It is an experiential knowledge that He is the Witness of everything. This is the foundational reality of Tawhid. Allah, subhanahu wa ta'ala, then connects that to:

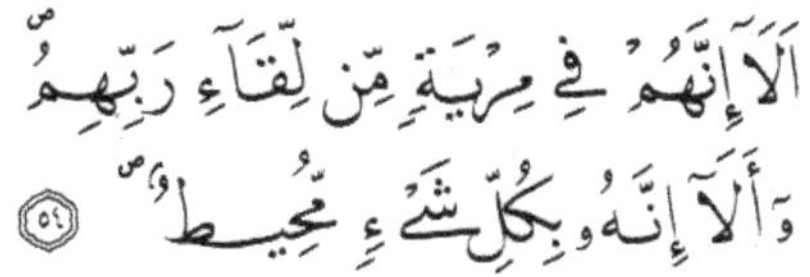

What! Are they in doubt
about the meeting with their Lord?
What! Does He not encompass all things?

This is the dividing line between the kuffar and the muminun. The muminun are those who are not in doubt about the meeting with their Lord, and that is the evidence and proof because He has given signs throughout their lifetime on the horizon and in themselves that confirm it. That is what Hajj is for. It is a sign on the horizon because when you see the muminun, you do not have a prayer at the Ka'aba or at Mina that is not also a prayer for the dead.

Hajj is a sign on the horizon and there are signs in yourself because there are things Allah puts in the heart on Hajj that you cannot tell anybody. There are these millions of hajjis and they all have a secret from Allah in the Hajj. Everyone has something that happened with them that is not the thing they tell. This is the sign on the horizon and the sign in themselves. So they are not in doubt about the meeting with their Lord. That changes the person. The one who is not in doubt about the meeting with his Lord knows: "Does He not encompass all things?" That is what the Sufis call Hadrat ar-Rabbani, the Presence of Lordship. The heart begins to move in singing the Diwan, and from being solid, it is like you become opaque and these lights begin to come through and manifest and that is this Presence of Allah that is with us all the time, until the heart fills up with it and the eyes begin to fill with tears and all that is outside on the horizon becomes mixed up with all that is inside in the heart.

This is the beginning of the Tajalliyat, the illuminations from the Essence of Allah, subhanahu wa ta'ala, on the people of dhikr. This is why we meet, this is the purpose of what we are meeting for. This apparatus of knowledge becomes with us direct states of the heart and this is what Tasawwuf is, this is what the Tariqa is. It is because of our knowledge of Allah, subhanahu wa ta'ala, and our understanding of Qur'an, that we are able to experience these lights in the heart. Without this knowledge you could not experience these lights in the dhikr. Moulay al-'Arabi ad-Darqawi said, "My ecstasy, my drunkenness is in the discourse, not in the hadra."

V

April 24th 2004

We now come a step further from what we were doing at our last reunion. To recap, we will go to a couple of ayats which will confirm what we have already seen in the Qur'an. What we are coming to is an examination of an important term which is 'Tajalli.'

The proper understanding of Tawhid is the engagement of the slave with his Lord. You cannot have a Tawhid that does not have one who understands it. The fullness of the meaning of this unity of Allah, subhanahu wa ta'ala, involves the human creature entering into this stage of knowledge.

We will first look at Surat ar-Ra'd (13:33):

What then of Him Who is standing over every self seeing everything it does?

We have to recognise, whether or not it is pleasing to these modernists and scholars who think they can decide what the doctrines of thinking in Islam are, that the Qur'an is Clear, it is Mubin. "What then of Him Who is standing over every self seeing everything it does?" Therefore Allah, subhanahu wa ta'ala, Who is on the Throne, Who governs the universe is, 'standing over every self.' This is an extraordinary metaphor which means He is dominating every self and seeing everything it does. This is the intellectual orientation of Iman and the one who recognises this is established in Iman.

The question challenges the ignorant people who do not understand the nature of existence, they are missing the point of existence so their actions lead them and everyone else astray. The human creature is bonded to an obligation to his Lord to an understanding that He is a witness of his acts.

Now we go to Surat al-Hadid (57:3):

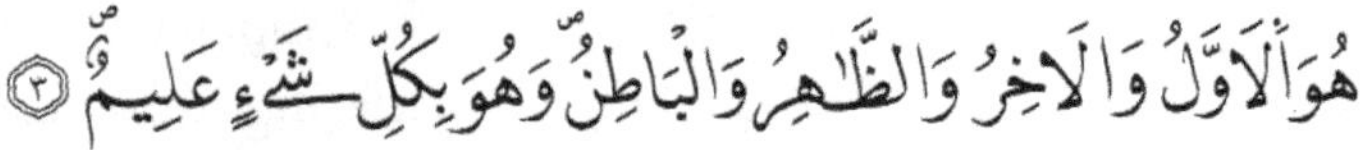

He is the First and the Last,

the Outward and the Inward.
He has knowledge of all things.

This is the famous ayat we all know and which encompasses everything of creation – firstness and lastness, outwardness and inwardness, that is time and space. Huwal-Awwalu wal-Akhiru – all the measure of time, the in-time from its beginning to the in-time at its end. Huwadh-Dhahiru wal-Batin – all the outsideness of things and all the insideness of things.

Look at how Allah, subhanahu wa ta'ala, specifically relates particular Attributes of His in explaining His reality to the human creatures. "He has knowledge of all things" – this is an Attribute of Allah, subhanahu wa ta'ala. So all the in-time things are in His present knowledge, His continuous knowledge, His absolute knowledge and there is nothing hidden from Him. Also, He has knowledge of all the outward of things and all the inward of things, and as we saw earlier He knows what is in the breast.

This is an absolute confirmation of the reality of Allah, subhanahu wa ta'ala, and there is nothing excluded, there is nothing outside of that. All of the creational realities therefore are declaring the Presence of Allah, subhanahu wa ta'ala. One of the shuyukh of the East, Al-Iraqi said, "How can love deny there is nothing in existence except Him?" This is where the kuffar, who do not want to face up to this, say that we equate Allah with the universe, that Allah is the universe. But what we are saying is that the existent things have no reality in themselves, therefore they are masiwallah, other-than-Allah, therefore they are non-existent.

"How can love deny there is nothing in existence except Him?" So the reality of existence is Allah, but again we are stuck at a point which seems to have no exit. We have established that existence belongs to Allah alone. Attributes and Actions must be His also because Allah is One in His Essence, His Attributes – seeing, knowing, hearing, doing – and Actions must be His also because the attributes of these faculties cannot themselves manifest without an action. You cannot have seeing and knowing and hearing and doing and speech without action, and action belongs to Allah, subhanahu wa ta'ala.

He has firstness and lastness, outsideness and insideness, and these relations are established with the essences of things. In other words, we have sight, we have knowledge, we have hearing, we have seeing – the essences of the things, of the creatures have these faculties but we do not have anything, we are not existent, only Allah is the existent. These essences of the things are subsistent in Allah's knowledge. Our reality comes by being existent in the knowledge of Allah. The created things are the result of the Divine 'kun!' emerging from the inward to the outward and they are other-than-Allah. All the created things are masiwallah.

Allah's Dhat, the Essence of Allah is not like anything, free from the determinations of the essences of things. Allah is not like the created creatures. We have essence, we have attributes, we have action but He is not connected to us.

V

Now we look at Surat an-Nahl (16:3). We still have to get out of this dilemma about our non-existence and yet our having these attributes that Allah, subhanahu wa ta'ala, has.

خَلَقَ ٱلسَّمَٰوَٰتِ وَٱلْأَرْضَ بِٱلْحَقِّ
تَعَٰلَىٰ عَمَّا يُشْرِكُونَ ﴿٣﴾

He created the heavens and the earth with truth.
He is exalted above anything they associate with Him.

You must concentrate very hard now, and you will understand it very clearly. "He created the heavens and the earth with truth," 'bil-Haqq'. Here Allah opens the door on the very core of this understanding of Tawhid.

We have established this dilemma that we have the attributes that Allah claims to be uniquely His and yet we somehow have an in-time experience of them – we see, we hear, we know, we judge, we act – but Allah has revealed here that He has created the heavens and the earth bil-Haqq, with the Truth. So there is not a connection, but it is how things are that all these created forms which have no existence in themselves, which are utterly dependent on Allah, subhanahu wa ta'ala, are nevertheless created bil-Haqq.

Allah will open out to us now what the nature of this bil-Haqq is, and again, without this you cannot have Tawhid.

He is raised above anything they associate with Him.

Allah is locking us into this stage of knowledge because we have to admit that He created the heavens and the earth bil-Haqq and at the same time He is exalted above the things. So it is still this impossible, apparent contradiction because He is exalted above everything they associate with Allah and what can you associate with Allah except the things, except the created existence?

Let us continue with discovering the Qur'anic ayats. We have to go to Surat Ta Ha (20:114):

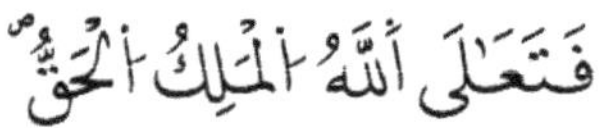

High exalted be Allah, the King, the Real!

Allah says He is exalted, He is raised above all the created forms and He says He is the King, which means He rules over all the created forms. Also He is Al-Haqq, the Real. The mutakallimun have always recognised that this name Al-Haqq is used very specially by Allah in the Qu'ran and it relates to the Essence, the Dhat of Allah. So the very Essence of Allah, the unknowable, the unthinkable, that on which you cannot meditate or try to grasp – the very core of the Divine Reality – is the Ruler Who is exalted above everything.

Now we go back to Surat ad-Dukhan (44:39):

We did not create them except with Haqq.

– so the created forms have been created from the very Essence of Him Who is exalted above all the things. Then He says,

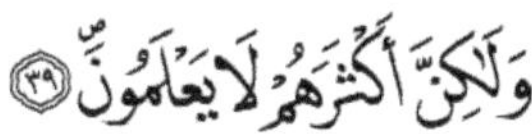

But most of them do not know it.

– most of the human creatures do not know this. This is also true of those Muslims who have abandoned the proper teaching of Islam which has remained constant from the beginning and has been in the hands of very respected and noble 'ulama. It is only in the last one hundred and fifty years that this whole understanding collapsed. The interesting thing is that the understanding of this highest aspect of the Deen went along with that thing which sustained the whole of the Deen throughout the whole of society, which is the Amr of Shari'ah. When the Amr was removed by which the Shari'ah was imposed, then the understanding of Tawhid went. These things are not disconnected.

Allah says:

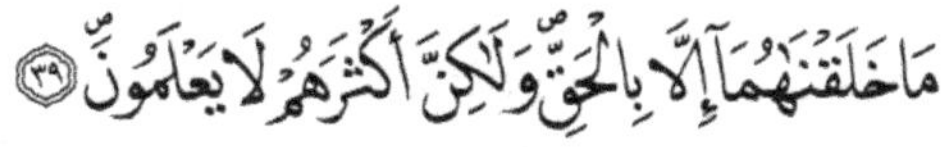

We did not create them except with truth,
but most of them do not know it.

The loss of the Amr was the abandoning of the Tawhid.

They could not have abandoned the Shari'ah if they had not lost the doctrine, the understanding of Tawhid. Therefore the responsibility for the disappearance of the leaders of the Muslims comes back on the common people who had been given this knowledge and who let it slip out of their fingers.

Now we go to Surat Yunus (10:5 and 6):

خَلَقَ ٱللَّهُ ذَٰلِكَ إِلَّا بِٱلْحَقِّ نُفَصِّلُ ٱلْآيَٰتِ لِقَوْمٍ يَعْلَمُونَ ۝٥
إِنَّ فِي ٱخْتِلَٰفِ ٱلَّيْلِ وَٱلنَّهَارِ وَمَا خَلَقَ ٱللَّهُ فِي ٱلسَّمَٰوَٰتِ
وَٱلْأَرْضِ لَآيَٰتٍ لِّقَوْمٍ يَتَّقُونَ ۝٦

Allah did not create these things except with truth.
We make the Signs clear for people who know.
In the alternation of night and day
and what Allah has created in the heavens and the earth
there are Signs for people who have taqwa.

Allah, subhanahu wa ta'ala, gives another chance, another possibility to grasp this tremendous thing that we are moving towards understanding.

"Allah did not create these things except with truth." We have established this, we have understood this. After that Allah says: "We make the Signs clear for people who know." 'Sign' is a very important word in the Qur'an which appears throughout the Qur'an in delineating the people of knowledge from the ignorant, that is the muminun from the kafirun. "We make the Signs clear for people who know." Remember that elsewhere Allah says: "There are signs in your self and on the horizon." Therefore a sign is an indicator and these signs have been created to give us an understanding of how existence is.

"We make the Signs clear for people who know," and the people who know are the people who glorify Allah, subhanahu wa ta'ala, because they have not been created except to glorify Him, subhanahu wa ta'ala. If they have knowledge it is because they worship Him, if they do not worship Him then they do not have knowledge of Him. The matter is not one of ratiocination, it is not one of reason, but one of seeing clearly.

Knowing is by confirmation – "We make the Signs clear for people who know." Then Allah indicates the sign:

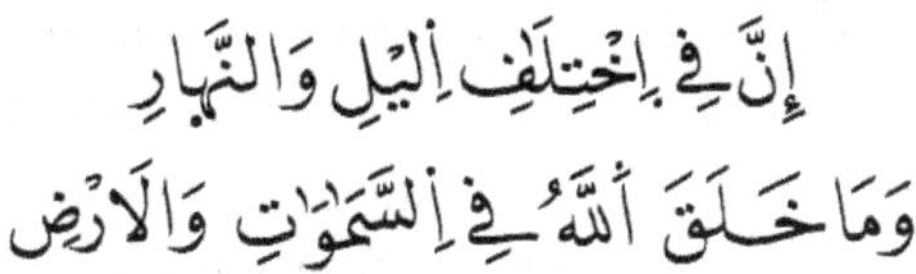

In the alternation of night and day
and what Allah has created
in the heavens and the earth.

The alternation of night and day means that this planet is moving in its orbit with a sun and a moon, and this regulates our existence on the earth. It is measured, it has order, everything is in its place. Our reality is based on the continuous flow of the time-process which only exists because the sun is there illuminating the earth, 'setting' – going out of our sight, and coming back into our sight with the day. These are signs which indicate the purposefulness, the meaningfulness of existence in the alternation of the night and day.

وَمَا خَلَقَ ٱللَّهُ فِي ٱلسَّمَٰوَٰتِ وَٱلْأَرْضِ

And what Allah has created in the heavens and earth.

– which therefore means that if you look out further beyond our immediate reality on earth with the sun and the moon, out to the stars, in all of this Allah then indicates the key of this knowing – the knowing clicks into something else. It is not knowing by the intellect, by measuring, it is knowing these are: "Signs for people who have taqwa." If you realise the power of Allah, subhanahu wa ta'ala, you change. This taqwa is something natural and connects to fitra. If you go to people who have not had the word of Islam, by their fitra they are in some way acknowledging their recognition of the movement of the stars. The people who have examined the ancient stone edifices of ancient peoples see that they have connected their understanding to the knowledge of the movement of the stars. It is an awareness of the harmony of the universe and this is from taqwa. Taqwa is therefore the foundation of knowledge. The person with taqwa is another kind of person, and this is the mumin. We are now moving closer.

We go to Surat al-'Ankabut (29:44):

V

خَلَقَ ٱللَّهُ ٱلسَّمَٰوَٰتِ وَٱلْأَرْضَ بِٱلْحَقِّ
إِنَّ فِي ذَٰلِكَ لَءَايَةً لِّلْمُؤْمِنِينَ ﴿٤٤﴾

Allah created the heavens and the earth with truth.
There is certainly a Sign in that for the muminun.

Now it is clear. Grasping this is an important indication that Allah has deemed necessary to mention who it is for. It is for the muminun. The ones who know are the ones who have taqwa and the ones who have taqwa are the muminun, the people who have Iman in Allah, subhanahu wa ta'ala. The Dhat, the Essence of Allah, is present in both the origination of the world and in its continuance. We have established that Allah is the Outward, because, "He has created the heavens and the earth bil-Haqq," and this is a sign for the muminun.

Now we go to Surat an-Nur (24:25):

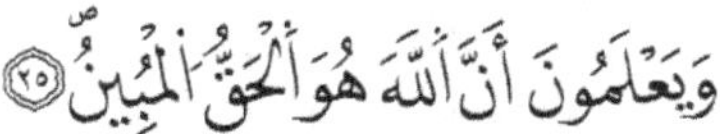

And they will know that Allah is the Clear Truth.

Now it is all being laid out. They will know that Allah is the Haqq al-Mubin, the Clear Truth, the Manifest Truth. They will know, and this is the knowledge that He says will come to the human creature, that Allah is manifest, clear Haqq – Essence, unknowable, exalted above everything they associate with Him. So the Dhat of Allah is present in the creation of the world and in the continuance of the world.

We stay with Surat an-Nur, ayat 35.

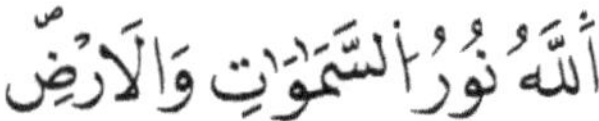

Allah is the Light of the heavens and the earth.

We are being taken further into the secret of existence. Further we find:

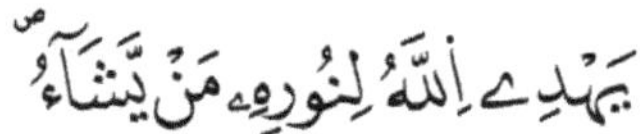

Allah guides to His Light whomever He wills.

So Allah is the Light of the heavens and the earth and He will guide to His Light whomever He wants. We have established that Allah is One in His Acts, His Attributes and His Essence, unalterable, and He manifests Himself through His Attribute of light in the forms of the created objects, which in reality are only reflected entities because they have no existence in themselves. They are made bil-Haqq, so they are a reflection of what is true, manifesting outwardly the essences which are in the knowledge of Allah. So the Divine Qualities emerge in the world of created phenomena. In other words, the human creature has knowledge, will, seeing, hearing, power and action reflected on him by this light from the Essence of Allah, subhanahu wa ta'ala, on His Throne.

Remember that things are not and cannot be created out of nothing. "Nothing can come of nothing," as Shakespeare said. Equally non-being cannot manifest as the matter of being on the form of beings, so a nothing cannot make things happen. Allah is above all limitation and all individuation, and yet this happens by His Light. Allah reveals Himself in the objects in accordance with the essences of the things which He has created by His knowledge. They have these characteristics of knowing, seeing, willing, by His knowledge.

Allah, subhanahu wa ta'ala, has shown Himself in the objects in accordance with the essences of the things, hidden in His Essence and subsisting in His Attribute of knowledge. It is by His knowledge that He lets these things come into being. They are brought out by His Action: "Kun!" He only has to say to a thing, "Kun!" and it is.

The khalq, the created things come into created manifestation by the manifesting of Allah, subhanahu wa ta'ala, by His name Al-Khaliq. The Creator is an Attribute of the One Who is Reality, is Essence, is Haqq, high exalted above everything they could connect with Him. The famous Jami said: "Essences of the creatures are mirrors wherein Allah reflects Himself. Or, Allah's Being is the mirror wherein the essences reflect their forms." The Shaykh al-Akbar Ibn al-'Arabi said: "Allah is your mirror wherein you see yourself, and you are His mirror wherein He sees His own Names and their working."

Shaykh Ibn al-'Arabi says, "Were He not and were we not, what has happened would not have happened." Thus our existence is due to Him and His manifestation, His Tajalli is due to us. It is due to us that this manifestation takes place. He is the Rich, the Independent and we are the poor, the utterly dependent.

VI

May 1st 2004

I will just recapitulate the summing-up of the point we got to last week. We quoted Shaykh al-Akbar Ibn al-'Arabi as saying: "Were He not and were we not, what has happened would not have happened." There he is declaring the foundational reality in which we find ourselves. From it we derive that our existence is due to Him and His manifestation is due to us. Thus He is the Rich and Independent, and we are the poor and utterly dependent.

We summed up that Allah the Powerful, the Immutable, without change or multiplicity, without hulul – without embodiment in any form, or ittihad – without joining to anything, and without division, He manifests Himself by what we took as a technical term, al-'Ayan ath-Thabita, by His source-forms through His Attribute of light. The countless variety of source-forms that come into creation do not affect the unity of Allah and His being beyond them.

We have come to this key word which is 'Tajalli'. It is a Qur'anic term which means 'manifestation' or 'revelation', 'revealing of itself.' For there to be a Tajalli from Allah, subhanahu wa ta'ala, this requires a form. There cannot be a manifestation unless it becomes manifest so these forms are in the knowledge of Allah, but they have no intrinsic reality. Yet things do not come out of absolute nothingness, they come out of the nothing which is the zone of His knowledge of the forms which will manifest. We have to make this distinction.

To understand the nature of this manifesting we will look at Surat al-A'raf (7:143):

وَلَمَّا جَاءَ مُوسَىٰ لِمِيقَاتِنَا وَكَلَّمَهُ
رَبُّهُ قَالَ رَبِّ أَرِنِي أَنظُرْ إِلَيْكَ ۚ قَالَ لَن تَرَانِي وَلَٰكِنِ
انظُرْ إِلَى الْجَبَلِ فَإِنِ اسْتَقَرَّ مَكَانَهُ فَسَوْفَ تَرَانِي ۚ فَلَمَّا
تَجَلَّىٰ رَبُّهُ لِلْجَبَلِ جَعَلَهُ دَكًّا وَخَرَّ مُوسَىٰ صَعِقًا ۚ فَلَمَّا
أَفَاقَ قَالَ سُبْحَانَكَ تُبْتُ إِلَيْكَ وَأَنَا أَوَّلُ الْمُؤْمِنِينَ ﴿١٤٣﴾

VI

When Musa came into Our appointed time
and His Lord spoke to him,
he said, 'My Lord, show me Yourself
so that I may look at You!'
He said, 'You will not see me
but look at the mountain.
If it remains firm in its place,
then you will see Me.'
But when his Lord manifested Himself to the mountain,
He crushed it flat
and Musa fell unconscious to the ground.
When he regained consciousness he said,
'Glory be to You! I make tawba to You
and I am the first of the muminun.'

وَلَمَّا جَآءَ مُوسَىٰ لِمِيقَٰتِنَا

When Musa came into Our appointed time.

Look at how Allah surrounds the whole event, how He is the author of the event. It is an unfolding in itself of the point at which, as it were, the fixing of the Nabawiyya of Sayyiduna Musa takes place. 'Our appointed time' is Allah's appointment of him as a Messenger.

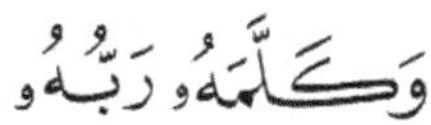

His Lord spoke to him

– Allah spoke to Sayyiduna Musa because this is part of the Maqam of the Messengers, that they are spoken to by Allah, subhanahu wa ta'ala.

قَالَ رَبِّ أَرِنِيٓ

He said, 'My Lord, show me Yourself!'

What is amazing is that there are these things in the Qur'an, and there are these ignorant, untaught 'ulama who have not been taught to reflect on the nature of Tawhid, and have not been able to confront that Sayyiduna Musa says: "My Lord, show me Yourself." This is what is called the Maqam al-Uns, the Station of Intimacy. In an intimacy with his Lord he speaks freely to Him. You will also find in all the recounting of the Mi'raj this intimacy with which Rasul, sallallahu 'alayhi wa sallam, speaks openly to his Lord. "My Lord, show me Yourself so that I may look at You." This is the Station of Intimacy, of love. The lover wants to look on the Face of the Beloved.

قَالَ لَن تَرَىٰنِي وَلَٰكِنِ ٱنظُرْ إِلَى ٱلْجَبَلِ

Allah, subhanahu wa ta'ala, says: "You will not see Me," and remember this in what we are coming to later – then He takes him into the station of Ma'rifa. He says: "But look at the mountain." The mountain is the most unarguable evidence of the khalq, of the created, it is solid rock.

فَإِنِ ٱسْتَقَرَّ مَكَانَهُۥ فَسَوْفَ تَرَىٰنِي

"If it remains firm in its place then You will see Me." He has asked for this to happen and Allah, subhanahu wa ta'ala, orders him to look at the mountain, at the created form.

فَلَمَّا تَجَلَّىٰ رَبُّهُۥ لِلْجَبَلِ جَعَلَهُۥ دَكًّا

"But when His Lord manifested Himself," when His Lord made this Tajalli, which is the word we have been looking at – "When His Lord manifested Himself to the mountain He crushed it flat."

This event was the illumination, the opening, the fatiha of Sayyiduna Musa, 'alayhi salam. What did it mean? From the outside we can say this: the mountain was still there but Allah, subhanahu wa ta'ala, had taken the form from the mountain so that all that was left was the dust. "Huwal-Awwalu wal-Akhiru, wadh-Dhahiru wal-Batin." Sayyiduna Musa realised that Allah is the Creator of the Dhahir and that He had removed the source-form which Allah had in His knowledge, so the thing was reduced to dust. It did not disappear, it was not magic, but the form was gone. He realised that all the projections of the created universe are themselves manifestations of Allah, subhanahu wa ta'ala. So when Allah manifested to the mountain He crushed it flat.

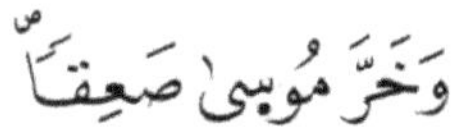

And Musa fell unconscious to the ground.

This is taken among the teachers of Tasawwuf to be an open description of what the Sufis call 'fana fillah'. Sayyiduna Musa was annihilated in this knowledge of Allah's revelation. Moulay al-'Arabi ad-Darqawi said: "If the world disappears, Allah has to appear." Of course Allah is not compelled to anything, but what he meant was that in the wisdom of how He has set up existence, if the world disappears, Allah has to appear because He is the Haqq. When the Tajalliyat of the solid forms vanish, then Allah is manifest. Allah says in Surat an-Nur (24:35):

ٱللَّهُ نُورُ ٱلسَّمَٰوَٰتِ وَٱلْأَرْضِ

Allah is the Light of the heavens and the earth.

Then Sayyiduna Musa returns to consciousness. This next part of the ayat, in the language of the Sufis, is 'baqa billah'. He does not return exalted, thinking that he has some secret knowledge. He returns completely, utterly reduced to being the first of the muminun and he says:

سُبْحَٰنَكَ

"Glory be to You." First he exalts Allah, subhanahu wa ta'ala, he makes tasbih. Then he makes tawba:

تُبْتُ إِلَيْكَ

I make tawba to You.

He is the Messenger of Allah, subhanahu wa ta'ala, and he makes tawba to Allah, he asks forgiveness. He even asks forgiveness for his adab that he should have asked that he could have the vision of Allah.

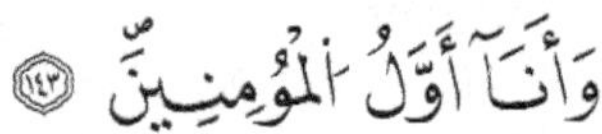

I am the first of the muminun.

This is the declaration of Sayyiduna Musa that he has accepted the destiny of being the Messenger of Allah, subhanahu wa ta'ala. In saying, "I am the first of the muminun," he is saying 'I have taken on this task you have given me. I am the Messenger of Allah.' All this is in this event of this Tajalli from the Essence of Allah, subhanahu wa ta'ala.

We will go now to the Diwan of Shaykh Muhammad ibn al-Habib, rahimahullah, to the qasida called The Buraq of the Tariq. Our Shaykh says:

وَالحَقُّ لا يُرَى فِي غَيْرِ مَظْهَرٍ　　لأَحَـدٍ مِـنْ مَلَكٍ أَوْ بَشَرِ
فَالمَظْهَرُ الأَوَّلُ نُـورُ أَحْمَدا　　عَلَيْهِ أَفْضَلُ الصَّلاةِ سَرْمَدا

The Haqq can only be seen in manifestation,
whether by an angel or a mortal man.

The first manifestation of the light
is the light of Ahmad,
may the most excellent of blessings
be upon him eternally.

Now we go to the Lesser Qasida where our Shaykh says:

وَلَيْسَ يُرى الرَّحْمانُ إلاَّ فِي مَظْهَرٍ　　كَعَرْشٍ وَكُرْسِيٍّ ولَـوْحٍ وَسِدْرَةِ

The Merciful is only to be seen in manifestations like
the Throne, the Footstool, the Tablet or the Lote-Tree.

Again, what is being said in the Diwan is being echoed from what we have found in the Qur'an. The Tajalli comes but only allowing the creature to see that the manifestation of the Essence is the manifestation of the power of Allah, subhanahu wa ta'ala, in these forms which are the limit-forms of creational knowledge.

These two things have come together which we looked at at the beginning and established ruthlessly as separate. We have on the one hand this term of the mutakallimun, of the Sufis, which is the 'Tanzih Mutlaq'. This is absolute transcendence. 'Tanzih' is that nothing can be associated with Allah, subhanahu wa ta'ala. At the same time we have Tashbih, which is that there is an imminence, a Presence of Allah, subhanahu wa ta'ala, in manifestation. They are created forms but as we saw earlier, "We have created everything bil-Haqq," they are not illusion.

Shaykh al-Akbar said very beautifully, "If you assert only Tanzih," which is like the wahhabis, that He is above all and has absolutely no connection with the creation at all, "you limit Allah." Because you are still left with this enormous creation. "If you assert only Tashbih," in other words, like the pantheists who say that Allah is in the universe, in all the stuff, "then you define Him." So if you exalt Him above the creation you limit Him, and if you declare He is in it, you define Him. "But if you assert both, you follow the right course and you are a leader and master in Ma'rifa."

The Dhat of Allah, the Essence of Allah, the Haqq, is existent. The dhat, the essences of the created things are non-existent but we have established that when we say 'non-existence' it is a relative non-existence because nothing can come out of nothing. It comes out of what is in the knowledge of Allah, subhanahu wa ta'ala, without diminishing or being connected to it.

Thus from the point of view of essences, otherness is predicated from the beginning to the end. All the essences of the created things are masiwallah, other-than-Allah. The known of Allah, from eternity, is still other-than-Allah. They are knowledges, but they are not the 'He-ness' of Him. The Essence is still immutable, untouched. These known things are known in His knowledge just as, to take a metaphor, you can know about someone somewhere and visualise them, but it does not diminish you or add to you. There are signs in yourself and on the horizon if you only understand. The creation is not connected to Allah, it is utterly dependent on Allah. Without Him it cannot be and He is independent of everything.

From the point of view of the essences, otherness is real. From the point of view of Existence, of Being, of the Divine – identity is real. Surat al-Ikhlas:

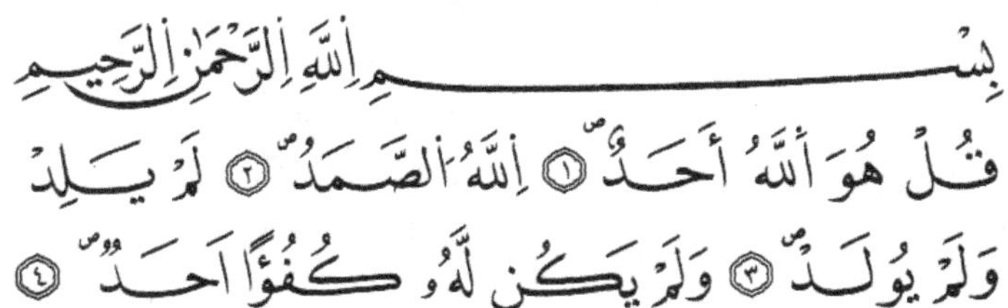

In the name of Allah, All-Merciful, Most Merciful

"Say: 'He is Allah, Absolute Oneness,
Allah, the Everlasting Sustainer of all.
He has not given birth and was not born.
And no one is comparable to Him.'"

The existence of the Haqq is nothing but the existence of the created beings. That is, the One is revealing Itself in the forms of the essences of the created things. Otherness and identity. The oneness of Allah and the otherness of all the created things. We understand with a double knowledge this Tawhid which is One.

Shah Kamaluddin said: "To soar into the realms of Ma'rifa, develop the two wings of identity and otherness." The created things are other-than-Allah and Allah has identity with a knowledge that encompasses all the created things.

We have come to four terms which will clear this up for us. The one who sees only the phenomenal, the created stuff, otherness, is veiled. He is called mahjoub. He who identifies the phenomenal with the Haqq, the one who says: "God is in the world, He is actually the world," is an illusionist. He is called maghzoub. He who is intoxicated with the wine of unity, who says: "There is only Allah!" is drunk with Allah. He is an absorbtionist absorbed in the majesty of Allah, and is called majdhoub. But he who distinguishes between otherness, the creation, and identity, the Creator, is loved by Him. He is mahboub.

So you have four – the mahjoub, the maghzoub, the majdhoub and the mahboub. The first sees only otherness and he is veiled, mahjoub. He is a materialist. The one who identifies the phenomena with the haqq is a maghzoub. The one who is intoxicated with the wine of His unity, he is absorbed in the Divine and is an absorbtionist and is majdhoub. But the one who distinguishes between otherness and identity is loved by Him and is mahboub. These are the four states of knowledge.

The first one is kufr itself. The other two are those who have been led astray, and the one who is on the Sirat al-Mustaqim is the one who distinguishes between otherness and identity.

To see this in its clearest form we will go to Surat ar-Rahman (55:19-21).

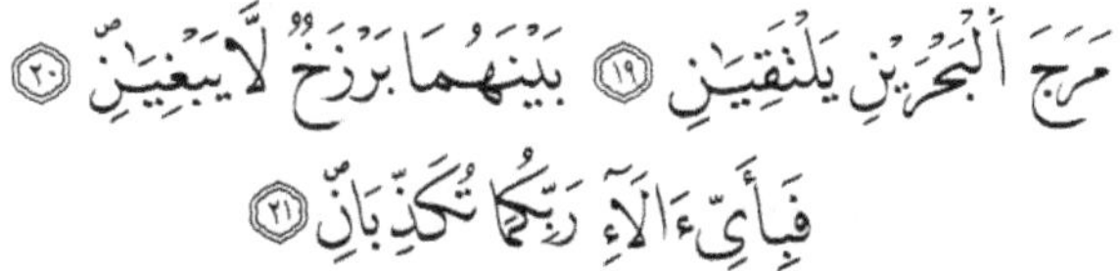

He has let loose the two seas, converging together,
with a barrier between them
they do not break through.
So which of your Lord's blessings
do you both then deny?

This is the summing up of this matter. Allah, subhanahu wa ta'ala, has set up existence with these two seas. They come together, but there is a barrier between them which does not break. Allah is the Rabb and the slave is the slave. Allah is the Creator and the creation is the creation. Until you say these two things you do not have a pure Tawhid. Then Allah, subhanahu wa ta'ala, asks:

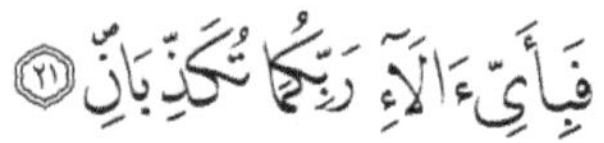

So which of your Lord's blessings
do you both then deny?

Do you deny the blessings of His being exalted above the creation, or do you deny the blessings of this enormous universe that He has made for us? This is the true understanding of Tawhid and it is embedded in this blessed ayat of Surat ar-Rahman.

HADRA

We make du'a to Allah, subhanahu wa ta'ala, to make from among this gathering of people the Awliya and salihun who will take the message of Islam through the whole of this continent. We ask Allah, subhanahu wa ta'ala, that by the people of this gathering the Deen of Islam will stretch from the south and raise its hand up to the north to restore Islam to the Berber and Arab people.

We ask Allah, subhanahu wa ta'ala, to give a fatiha to all the people of this gathering, and give them a fatiha for their own ruhani knowledge and for their actions in the world. We ask Allah, subhanahu wa ta'ala, to give light and strength and inspiration to all the people gathered here.

We ask Allah, subhanahu wa ta'ala, to let love grow in

the hearts of the fuqara. We ask Allah, subhanahu wa ta'ala, to make this a group of people worthy of the company of the Sahaba. We ask Allah, subhanahu wa ta'ala, to make them the Sahaba of their time. We ask Allah, subhanahu wa ta'ala, to raise this Tariqa up to be a light for the whole of Africa.

سُبْحَٰنَ رَبِّكَ رَبِّ ٱلْعِزَّةِ عَمَّا يَصِفُونَ ﴿١٨٠﴾
وَسَلَٰمٌ عَلَى ٱلْمُرْسَلِينَ ﴿١٨١﴾ وَٱلْحَمْدُ لِلَّهِ رَبِّ ٱلْعَٰلَمِينَ ﴿١٨٢﴾

VII

May 8th 2004

We have been going step by step in an unfolding of something. When you have assimilated all of this you will be among the knowers of Allah, subhanahu wa ta'ala. You will be among the people of knowledge and you will have entered into an understanding of Tawhid which is the Tawhid of the elite.

There is the Tawhid of the common people, the Tawhid of the elite, and there is the Tawhid of the elect of the elite. You have to grasp each stage of the way we have been going as each stage is an unfolding which will take you to another station of understanding and knowledge.

We were looking at how we can understand Allah the Creator, and creation. We looked at how the things come into being. We confirmed the oneness of Allah and at the same time we recognised that the created things were made bil-Haqq, by the Truth. We saw that there has to be a double understanding of Allah as the Outward and the Inward, and His relationship to the creation.

Now we are going to look at two terms which are, as it were, in the courtesy of how we may talk about Allah, subhanahu wa ta'ala. They are called Tanzih and Tashbih, and they are opposites.

Tanzih is exaltation. Allah is exalted above everything that can be associated with Him. Tanzih is disconnection. Allah is disconnected from the forms. Tashbih is when there are modes of speaking about Allah, subhanahu wa ta'ala, which seem to imply that He has form in the world of forms in time. We have to understand how this is so that we have a proper understanding of it.

Everything we have done so far has been founded on the teachings of Al-Ash'ari. He is a kind of defence system to prevent the rationalists and philosophers breaking down the barriers of adab and courtesy to the understanding of the Divine, and to prevent the reduction of our understanding of the Divine to a level of thought, to ideas and philosophy.

The Sufis go further. They do not negate Al-Ash'ari, in fact it is necessary to understand him because he is the one who speaks about the Acts, the Attributes and the

Essence of Allah, subhanahu wa ta'ala. Now we are going to go past that, we are going to vault over it without denying it in any way, to arrive at an understanding of these two terms which you might say are 'connection' and 'disconnection' – a way of speaking about Allah that appears in the Qur'an which seems to connect Him to the forms, and disconnecting Allah from the forms. We are going to do this in such a manner that we arrive at a knowledge of Allah, subhanahu wa ta'ala, in which there is no iota of association of Allah with anything.

We are going to look at Tashbih, this connection of Allah, subhanahu wa ta'ala, to created forms. We go first to Surat an-Najm (53:8-9):

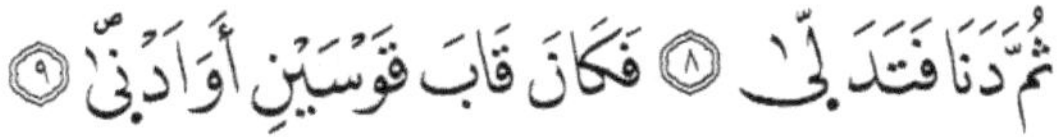

Then he drew near and hung suspended.
He was two bow-lengths away
or even closer.

Here we have a statement in the Qur'an of Rasul, sallallahu 'alayhi wa sallam, drawing near and being two bow-lengths away or even closer, meaning he was two bow-lengths away from Allah, subhanahu wa ta'ala. This statement flies in the face of all that we have been looking at because first of all it implies that this nearness is an actual, physical drawing near in this apparent proximity which implies space and time.

To understand this we must look at this statement of "two bow-lengths or even closer." We know that the Arab kings in the old days would let those brought nearest to them only approach to the length of two bows. That was as near the subject could approach the ruler. Intellectual proof which we have already established negates limit and distance from Allah so we have to find out how we are going to understand this statement.

You must know that that sect in Arabia, which has destroyed great swathes of the Deen and great swathes of the Muslims, has taught for some considerable time that for them this was a physical reality. The famous Ibn Batutta tells that he heard Ibn Taymiyya talking, astaghfirullah, about Allah, subhanahu wa ta'ala, descending from the Throne, "As I descend from this mimbar." In other words, they are anthropomorphists. They see the Divine as a being and an entity, and this is what is taught in Arabia where people are blowing everybody up including themselves.

Let us look at this. The Qur'an is Mubin. It is a Clear Qur'an which has been revealed in a clear Arabic. Remember that the Arabic language was prepared for the Qur'an, the Qur'an was not prepared to fit into the Arabic language. Allah, subhanahu wa ta'ala, prepared the Arabic language over centuries, took it to a point of fineness, refined it, extended it, made it more precise, then He gave to the Quraish tribe the gift of the best Arabic tongue. Then from the Quraish He gave to one family the exact pronunciation so that the Rasul, sallallahu 'alayhi wa sallam, said about his family: "We have been given the Dhad." They are the one family who were given the pure pronunciation of the letter Dhad.

So the language was perfected in his family so that at the time the Revelation came it was in this pure Arabic. So specific is it that Allah then permitted it to stretch over different readings so that there would be no ambiguity in it. At the same time it would be like one diamond that has different facets, so light would come from different ways, so that different readings illuminate the Qur'an in different ways, without them contradicting what was intended in the message of the Qur'an.

Rasul, sallallahu 'alayhi wa sallam, not only spoke it in this perfect family Arabic, he also spoke it in what you might call dialects, so that his followers could understand.

In Arabic there are four classes of phrase. If you look at the books of Arabic grammar like the famous Ajrumiyya and so on, you find for example that the great Sufi of Morocco, Shaykh Ibn 'Ajiba, has written a Sufic commentary on the Ajrumiyya, giving a different spiritual meaning and emphasis to every possible grammatical construct. The language is very formal and structured and can be appreciated in this way.

In Arabic there are four classes of phrase, of expression. There is a 'clear phrase': "The sea, key, scissors." There are 'indicated phrases' which have an agreed definition: if you say, "Man," we all know what that means, if you say, "Woman," or "Bird," we know what that means. It is an indicated phrase which represents some genus of which all are the same.

Then there are 'shared phrases' which have two meanings. For example, the word 'ayn in Arabic means 'eye', and it also means a 'spring.' Insan means 'man' and it also means the 'pupil of the eye.' This particular shared phrase is of vital importance to the way of speaking which is used by Shaykh al-Akbar because he sees a very important meaning in the fact that insan represents man and it also represents the pupil of the eye. So the shared phrase has two meanings at the same time.

Then we have the 'synonym phrase'. For example, the different words for lion like asad and hizaba, or for sword like sayf and husam – different words meaning the same thing.

In Arabic these four are defined as the four matrices. They are to language what the hot, the cold, the wet and the dry are to nature – they are fundamental. From these come other expressions: the simile, the metaphor, and transmitted phrases, phrases that are passed down.

If you take the simile, this sounds like something which is different from the four matrices. If you say something is "like light," it is applied to the known. But 'like light' is with the eye in revealing the sensory object which is seen. 'Like light' also means that the eye is able to see the thing it sees because you cannot say, "like light" if you are not able to see the object by the light. Then you say that knowledge is called light. For this process to happen you have a knowledge, and then this knowledge is called light so it becomes the third matrix, it becomes the shared phrase. All phrases move towards one of these four matrices.

'Like light' is a simile because in fact it moves to the shared phrase and means two things at once. Once you say, "This is like light," you have given two meanings at the same time. You cannot say, "Like light" without saying therefore that it is illuminating and therefore it is knowledge. So the understanding of it and the seeing of it are not disconnected but connected. Your grasping 'like light' is also your recognition of something. If you make a simile it is 'like light' but your knowing what is meant by 'like light' is knowledge, so it is both 'like light' and a knowledge which comes from this.

The 'Arif recognises what the Divine Presence demands: purity, disconnection and negation of likeness. These are not veiled by reports of Allah using the tools of limitation by time, direction and place. So the meaning – because we know that Allah is disconnected from everything – moves from one to the other so that we go back to the ayat: "Then he drew near and hung suspended. He was two bow-lengths away or even closer." But Allah is pure, disconnected and has no likeness.

The meaning moves from the report to the reality. It moves from the Mulk to the Malakut, it moves from the kingdom of forms to the Unseen. Let us be patient. A slave-girl was brought to the Rasul, sallallahu 'alayhi wa sallam, and they said about her, "This slave-girl is mushrik, she is connecting things to Allah." Rasul said, "Bring her to me!" And he said to the girl, "Where is Allah?" and the slave-girl pointed to the sky. The Messenger had better knowledge of Allah than her yet he affirmed her belief, and Allah has better knowledge of

Himself, disconnected from all forms.

Rasul, sallallahu 'alayhi wa sallam, knew that "Where is Allah?" is a question you cannot ask, and she gave an answer which on the face of it, you cannot give. But she pointed to the sky which is undifferentiated, it has no form, it is just blue and Rasul said, "She is mumin."

We go to Surat al-Mulk (67:16-17):

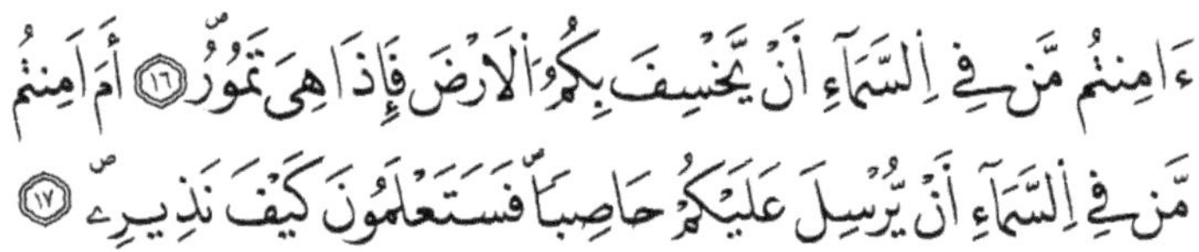

Do you feel secure against Him Who is in heaven
causing the earth to swallow you up
when suddenly it rocks from side to side?
Or do you feel secure against Him Who is in heaven
releasing against you a sudden squall of stones,
so that you will know how true My warning was?

Rasul, sallallahu 'alayhi wa sallam, asked, "Where is Allah?" and the girl pointed to heaven and he said that her Iman was correct. In Qur'an Allah says: "Do you feel secure against Him Who is in heaven," which is a way of speaking which indicates the Divine Reality. It goes from the statement to the meaning of it and these two are not disconnected, they are one reality in the intellect of the 'Arif.

Let us go to Surat Ta Ha (20:1-5):

VII

بِسۡمِ ٱللَّهِ ٱلرَّحۡمَٰنِ ٱلرَّحِيمِ

طه ﴿١﴾ مَآ أَنزَلۡنَا عَلَيۡكَ ٱلۡقُرۡءَانَ لِتَشۡقَىٰٓ ﴿٢﴾ إِلَّا تَذۡكِرَةٗ
لِّمَن يَخۡشَىٰ ﴿٣﴾ تَنزِيلٗا مِّمَّنۡ خَلَقَ ٱلۡأَرۡضَ وَٱلسَّمَٰوَٰتِ ٱلۡعُلَى ﴿٤﴾
ٱلرَّحۡمَٰنُ عَلَى ٱلۡعَرۡشِ ٱسۡتَوَىٰ ﴿٥﴾

In the name of Allah, All-Merciful, Most Merciful

Ta Ha
We did not send down the Qur'an to you
to make you miserable

You could also take that as an evidence that Allah did not send down the Qur'an for people to become Shi'a because it makes them miserable to have to believe all the terrible things they have to believe in! So:

Ta Ha
We did not send down the Qur'an to you
to make you miserable,
but only as a reminder for those who have fear,
a Revelation from Him Who created
the earth and the high heavens,
the All-Merciful,
established firmly upon the Throne.

Now we go to Surat al-Mujadala (58:7):

أَلَمْ تَرَ أَنَّ اللَّهَ يَعْلَمُ مَا فِي السَّمَاوَاتِ وَمَا فِي الْأَرْضِ مَا يَكُونُ مِن نَّجْوَىٰ
ثَلَاثَةٍ إِلَّا هُوَ رَابِعُهُمْ وَلَا خَمْسَةٍ إِلَّا هُوَ سَادِسُهُمْ وَلَا أَدْنَىٰ مِن
ذَٰلِكَ وَلَا أَكْثَرَ إِلَّا هُوَ مَعَهُمْ أَيْنَ مَا كَانُوا ثُمَّ يُنَبِّئُهُم بِمَا عَمِلُوا يَوْمَ
الْقِيَامَةِ إِنَّ اللَّهَ بِكُلِّ شَيْءٍ عَلِيمٌ ﴿٧﴾

Do you not see that Allah knows
what is in the heavens and on the earth?
Three men cannot confer together secretly
without Him being the fourth of them,
or five without Him being the sixth of them,
or fewer than that or more
without Him being with them wherever they are.
Then He will inform them on the Day of Rising
of what they did.
Allah has knowledge of all things.

Again, Allah, subhanahu wa ta'ala, is explaining how He is with the creatures and He is involving space and time and presence and number, so that He is one of number – this is Allah Who is One and nothing can be associated with Him. Allah says: "Three men cannot confer together secretly without Him being the fourth of them, or five without Him being the sixth of them, or fewer than that or more." It is extended to say that whatever number it is, He is able to take this condition of His knowledge to be the truth of the matter. Thus place does not prevent Him being in the place, and number does not prevent Him adding to that number by His being there, and Allah has knowledge of all things.

We confirm that Allah, subhanahu wa ta'ala, created times, places, directions, phrases, words, the one who speaks them, and the in-time creatures who are addressed. This is Allah's creation. But the 'Arif knows that when the connective tools of phrase are applied to the Real they have an aspect other than connection or resemblance. So the connection cannot be the affair, and the resemblance cannot be the affair.

There is a group of people who are confronted with these astonishing statements in the Qur'an who neither connect, nor anthropomorphise, nor say, "This is like a man, this is actually how it is," and they do not put one foot into the zone of ta'wil. Ta'wil is when you interpret things saying, "Well, it is in a special way," and you give a kind of secret meaning to it. For example the relationship of the man to the ghost – you cannot use ta'wil to deal with this matter. This group of people do not use ta'wil, they say, "I do not know."

A single sentence – "I do not know," but we avoid letting it be on Him by connection since Allah, subhanahu wa ta'ala, has said in Surat Ash-Shura (42:11):

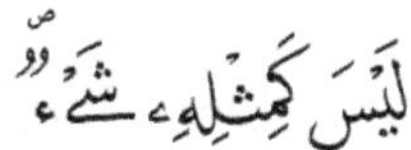

Nothing is like Him.

Faced with this the 'Arif says: "I do not know," because, "Nothing is like Him." The 'Arifin are thus free of ta'wil because they will not make the statement into a hidden meaning, or interpret it in a secret way, and they are free of tatil – the denial of Attributes. They will not deny Attributes of power, that He would act and He would do if He so wanted. This group empty their hearts of thought and speculation and they say: "We have gained in ourselves esteem for the Haqq. May His Majesty be exalted."

Therefore we cannot reach Ma'rifa by fine reflection and investigation. At this point the elite 'Arifin suspect the mutakallimun, the people of teaching and intellect, and they suspect the muhadithun who even produce texts to back up this matter. So they have to move, they have to travel on the path, and this is Tariqa as-Sufiyya.

They have to move otherwise they would be munafiqun, having bad thoughts about the 'ulama! They have to free the heart from logical speculation. They have to sit with Allah in dhikr on what Muhiyuddin Ibn al-'Arabi called the Carpet of Adab, and in muraqaba, watching their own hearts.

Allah takes charge of our instruction by unveiling and Ma'rifa, and so they enter the hal of these ayats we will now look at. Surat al-Anfal (8:29):

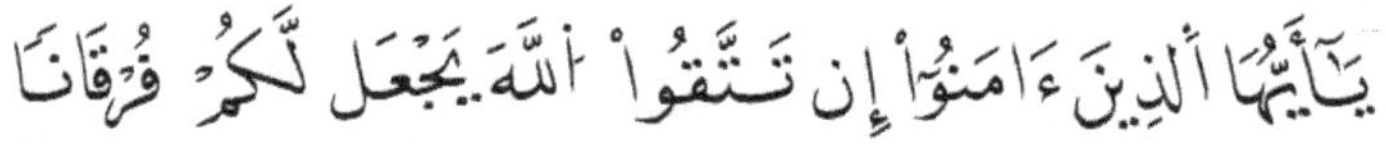

You who have Iman! If you have taqwa of Allah,
He will give you discrimination.

In other words, of these ayats, of this Revelation of Allah speaking of Himself in a matter that seems to involve intimeness, presence, movement and so on, if you who have Iman have taqwa of Allah, awe and fear of Allah, He will give discrimination.

Now we will go to Surat al-Baqara (2:281), at the end of this long ayat:

وَاتَّقُواْ اللَّهَ وَيُعَلِّمُكُمُ اللَّهُ

Have taqwa of Allah and Allah will give you knowledge.

What is required for knowledge of Allah is not ratiocination, is not reflection, is not philosophy, is not programme – what is necessary is to fear Allah and have taqwa of Allah, to be careful with Allah, and "Allah will give you knowledge." The Arabic is so beautiful – 'yu'allimukum Allah', it is like, 'you will be knowledged'!

These ayats we are looking at are progressive: "Have taqwa of Allah and He will give you discrimination," "Have taqwa of Allah and Allah will give you knowledge," and now Surat Ta Ha (20:114), the very last line of the ayat:

وَقُل رَّبِّ زِدْنِي عِلْمًا ﴿١١٤﴾

And say, 'My Lord, increase me in knowledge.'

"Have taqwa of Allah and Allah will give you knowledge." Now you reach that point where you become active and you say, "My Lord, increase me in knowledge." Give it to me! This is another step. You are able to ask for it, you have not become passive, and this is what is called in the language of Tasawwuf, himma. You want this thing, you are demanding it, you are insisting on it.

رَّبِّ زِدْنِي عِلْمًا ﴿١١٤﴾

My Lord, increase me in knowledge.

This is the active tense. This is the man moving into knowledge, and entering the hal of this ayat is your du'a to Allah, subhanahu wa ta'ala.

We finish with Surat al-Kahf (18:65):

فَوَجَدَا عَبْدًا مِّنْ عِبَادِنَآ ءَاتَيْنَٰهُ رَحْمَةً مِّنْ عِندِنَا
وَعَلَّمْنَٰهُ مِن لَّدُنَّا عِلْمًا ﴿٦٥﴾

They found a slave of Ours
whom We had granted mercy from Us
and whom We had also given knowledge direct from Us.

This is to say that the mercy which was granted to the slave was the Khatm of the destiny. Allah had decreed that this person would be 'Arif because it is not by your choosing, it is by His choosing because He is the Doer. The first thing you have to understand for this man to be this man:

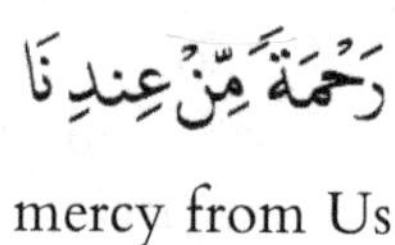

mercy from Us

– the mercy that Allah gave to the slave was a good seal on his destiny. He destined him for this knowledge. That is why the du'a of the mumin is, "O Allah, give me an Iman that is lasting," because you want your Iman to continue throughout your life so that, like the wine in the bottle, it becomes richer although nothing more enters the bottle. The bottle remains, and what is in it slowly changes its quality becoming stronger and richer. This is the Khatm of the destiny.

The second part of the ayat is:

$$وَعَلَّمْنَٰهُ مِن لَّدُنَّا عِلْمًا ۝$$

And whom We had also given knowledge direct from Us.

This is the path of the people who have this pure Tanzih of associating nothing with Allah. Surat Ash-Shura (42:11):

$$لَيْسَ كَمِثْلِهِۦ شَيْءٌ$$

Nothing is like Him, as we mentioned from Qur'an earlier. With this you come out of the circle of the people who say, "If He says, 'He sat on the Throne' then He sat on the Throne," which is ignorance. And you come out from the philosophers' position who say, "It is a metaphor. It is as if He sat on the Throne but He did not really sit on the Throne."

We take the Arabic language and say No. The joined phrase makes us see that this tells us that. There is no metaphor. There is structurally no such thing in Arabic grammar as a simile, it is the joined phrase. Thus if it says this, it is this. It is both of these things. The philosophers say, "You must not say that He sat on the Throne because that would be to connect Him to forms, so it is a metaphor and it is not real." But it is neither of these things.

The pure Tanzih is that it cannot be approached in this way. Imam Malik, radiyallahu 'anhu, said, "The sitting on the Throne is known. The way is not known, and to question it is bida'." In other words, it is something the understanding of which can only be arrived at on the Carpet of Adab in dhikr and in muraqaba. Then Allah will unveil for you these states, and then Allah, subhanahu wa ta'ala, will say to you: "Draw near."

HADRA

We ask Allah, subhanahu wa ta'ala, to confound all the enemies of Islam. We ask Allah, subhanahu wa ta'ala, by the baraka that He has given to the Du'a an-Nasiri that within all our hearts it should be answered by the angels in following the supplications in it.

We ask Allah, subhanahu wa ta'ala, to confound and confuse the enemies of Islam. We ask Allah, subhanahu wa ta'ala, to scatter the remnants of christianity, judaism and buddhism and all the false religions on the earth. We ask Allah, subhanahu wa ta'ala, to raise up and exalt Islam above what the Arabs have done to it. We ask Allah, subhanahu wa ta'ala, to let the Arabs return to Islam by Your Mercy.

VII

We ask Allah, subhanahu wa ta'ala, to establish the Deen all over the land of India and we ask Allah, subhanahu wa ta'ala, to confound its enemies. We ask Allah, subhanahu wa ta'ala, to give victory to the Muslims. We ask Allah, subhanahu wa ta'ala, to give the leadership of the Muslims from among the community of the dhakirun.

VIII

May 22nd 2004

Each week we have been pursuing a path to gaining a stronger and deeper knowledge of Tawhid. We have emphasised through all this that there is a dimension of this knowledge which is in itself the reality of your fear of Allah, subhanahu wa ta'ala. "Fear Allah and He will give you knowledge."

It is very important that you remember during all of this that this is something to be approached by reflection and by inwardly achieving states and arriving at certain stations. There is the fulfilment of the true knowledge of Tawhid which is, in the language of the Sufis, the 'Tajrid of Tawhid'. This is the stripping away of your consciousness of self before the Presence of Allah, subhanahu wa ta'ala.

We are now going to look at something which may seem a little complicated but it is not. Be patient, and just let the first stage of it flow over you, so to speak. We are going to look at a technical framework, and you must understand that we are now speaking as Muslims sitting in the mosque, talking about Allah, subhanahu wa ta'ala, and there is not anything in this that is similar to the way we talk about objects and things in the world.

We are trying to get at an understanding of Tawhid which also has in it this adab without which there is no path to this understanding. It is edged in with all kinds of conditions and inhibitions to prevent you having a wrong kind of thinking about Allah, subhanahu wa ta'ala, because these are the deviations and the things which anger Allah that are referred to in the Fatiha.

We are going to look at something in this technical language which you must all know, because you must go into the world with a secure Tawhid which cannot be shaken and which cannot be swept away by modern innovations, or by philosophy. It is not the proper business of philosophy. This term is called 'Tanazzulat'. Tanazzulat is like the unfolding descent from the Essence of Allah, subhanahu wa ta'ala, into the process by which He makes the creation. Again, bear in mind the detailed care with which we have confirmed that Allah is exalted above anything associated with Him and that He is not connected to anything, He is not dependent on anything, He has not come from anything and no thing has come out from Him.

We are going to describe the amazing process which results in our being here and results in the enormous vast creation of the universe of which He is the sole Creator, and exalted above it. We could say that it is something in reality but the description does not fit it, or it is something in description and this does not attain to the reality of it.

This descent is called the Tanazzulat as-Sita, the six-staged descent or unfolding of these stages by which we are able to understand the amazing reality of Allah, Creator of the universe. Shaykh Muhiyuddin Ibn al-'Arabi said: "You are not going to understand Allah, but you may reflect on the universe." It is by your reflection on the universe that you understand the majesty and power of Allah, subhanahu wa ta'ala.

This unfolding of the power and majesty of Allah, subhanahu wa ta'ala, is divided into six. Three of these ranks are utterly to do with Allah, and the other three are to do with how Allah manifests in the creation, the things to do with the world. The first are the 'Murati billahi', the Divine Ranks, which are three. Ahadiyat, Wahdat and Wahidiyat. These terms, which sound very forbidding to begin with, are all part of the enormous adab of those men who have been given the gift of unveiling by Allah, subhanahu wa ta'ala, who have come back from that illumination to speak about Allah in a way which fills us with awe and increases our fear of Allah, subhanahu wa ta'ala.

The first stage is Ahadiyat. This represents the Essence. The Essence is pure, disconnected from all forms and indeterminate. It is Allah in His unique Oneness, with nothing associated with Him, and with vast and tremendous powers hidden in this Oneness. It is also called the 'Mist' because someone asked the Rasul, sallallahu 'alayhi wa sallam: "Where was Allah before the creation of the world?" which is not a correct question, but Rasul, sallallahu 'alayhi wa sallam, said, "He was in the 'Amma', the Mist." In other words, it is unknowable. This is a term which we will come to in more detail in a moment.

So Ahadiyat is the Essence. Wahdat is the Unity. These are all ways of speaking about Allah, subhanahu wa ta'ala. We have not yet looked at the manifestation of the creation. The third term is Wahidiyat which is Unity which has in it the knowledge of plurality – Allah's knowledge that there can be the many myriad things.

The worldly ranks are called the Murati bil-Kawni, the ranks of the created forms. These are three: Ruh – which is the spirit, Mithal – which is the likenesses, the metaphoric capacity for form to take place, and Jism which is the body itself. These are the six ranks and then below this comes Insan, man.

We are going to look at this in detail. After Ahadiyat which is Essence, you have from Wahdat to Wahidiyat manifestation, not yet in the creation, but in Allah's, subhanahu wa ta'ala, knowledge of these potentials of His own majesty. From the ruh to the mithal, to the jism to the insan – the spirit to the likenesses, to the body to man – these are the external manifestations. These are when this enormous majestic power of Allah unfolds itself in the creation of the forms.

We will look at Ahadiyat. Ahadiyat is the absolute Being of Allah, unknown and unknowable. It is what Rasul, sallallahu 'alayhi wa sallam, warned people not to contemplate because it could destroy them, because it is not possible. Sayyiduna Abu Bakr as-Siddiq, radiyallahu 'anhu, made the famous statement on it which is used and referred to by all the Sufis and considered the final statement about it: "Your incapacity to know is all that you can know." Shaykh Ibn al-'Arabi said that this tremendous statement was not a negative statement, it was illumination. To know that you do not know is a kind of knowing. This is the adab on which this matter is dealt with.

The great Sufi, Jili said: "The Essence means the absolute dropping of all modes, all adjuncts, all relations, all aspects." In other words, it is the Creator before one talks of Him as the Creator. It is the Almighty in His Essence, the Dhat of Allah which in Qur'an is the Wajh, the Face, face being the indicator of the essence of the person.

We will look at Surat Al 'Imran (3:28 and 30), which we have looked at before and which we have to look at again in order that we are correct in our adab about understanding the Essence of Allah, subhanahu wa ta'ala, and which defines the understanding we have of Allah:

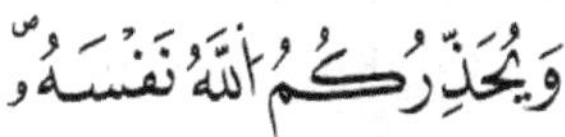

Allah advises you to be afraid of Him.

This is the Qur'anic injunction which contains the same

message. The being afraid of Allah and the being aware of Him – you cannot go beyond this understanding of Him, you cannot contemplate the Essence, you cannot understand the Essence and you cannot know the Essence. At this point He is hidden, He is unknown, unknowable, all His power is hidden. It is the unattainable absolute which is the Ahad of Allah, subhanahu wa ta'ala.

The Sufis have given this different names because they are so anxious that it has to be preserved before they contemplate the astonishing reality which is His creation. The Sufis have called this the Ghayb al-Ghuyub – the Unseen of the Unseen, and they have called it the 'Ayn al-Mutlaq – Absolute Essence. A very beautiful name the Sufis of the East have given it, which is in Hujwiri, is 'Aynal-Kafur – the Source of Camphor. Whatever enters into camphor becomes camphor, it has not any otherness. This is a beautiful and poetic expression for this absolute nature of Allah. That is the first stage of this Tanazzulat.

The second stage is Wahdat. The 'Arif recognises that Allah is One, knows Himself, is aware of all His potentialities and that He alone exists and has the power of manifestation. This is the first determination. The Sufis name it Al-Haqiqat al-Muhammadiya. We will look into this and find that this is a pure statement and does not contain any wrong thinking, but has to be understood.

So this second unfolding of Allah's power that we are able to understand is called Wahdat, Unity. These are pure potentialities of the Essence without any implied multiplicity. We are not talking yet about multiplicity, about creation, we are still within an understanding of the Divine Reality. We recognise four aspects: Wujud – which is existence, 'Ilm – which is knowledge, Nur – which is light, and Shuhud – which is witnessing.

Then we are able to say: Allah exists, knows His Being, His Attributes and His Actions. He is self-revealing and self-manifest. He witnesses His own Being, because the knowledge is in His witnessing of His own Being. All this is Essence itself. Identical with it, it does not proceed from the Essence and it is not prior to the Essence, thus it is Essence. Therefore Essence itself is Existence, Existent, and conscious of its existence. Essence itself is Knowledge, the Knower and the Known. Essence itself is the Light, the Lighter and the Lighted, and is itself Observance, Observer and Observed. We are still not talking about the creation but about how Allah is.

This stage of our understanding of Allah's Essence, in fact, contains all the Attributes of the Divine and the worldly Names, and all the created things destined for the creation, as the whole is included in the inwardness of the Essence. The knowledge of it, the existence of it, the light – and by that light that it is self-observing. The metaphor of this is that the whole date tree is hidden in the date stone – it is not there, but the whole tree is there.

The Sufis name this Tajalli al-Awwal – the first manifestation. It is the first emergence, as it were, for us to have a sort of knowledge about Allah, subhanahu wa ta'ala. They call it Wujud al-Awwal, the first existence.

Jawhar al-Awwal – the first jewel form. But the great Sufis have named this station of the speaking about Allah, subhanahu wa ta'ala, "Al-Haqiqat al-Muhammadiya."

This is because the human manifestation is above that of the things in the creation. So he, sallallahu 'alayhi wa sallam, is the highest manifestation among men. Follow this carefully to the end because it could look like something that we cannot accept, and this is not possible. Rasul, sallallahu 'alayhi wa sallam, said, "I am the first of the sons of Adam," and we also have that he is the last of the Messengers, he is the Seal of the Messengers.

To understand this the Sufis say that the materialists say that the function of the fruit is to produce the tree. But the 'Arifin say that the reality of the tree is that it is the fruit which is intended. Rasul, sallallahu 'alayhi wa sallam, is intended with the whole creation because he is the perfect manifestation of man in his being the first of the ones who praise Allah, and he recognises His Attributes and His Power and is able to bear the Message that is sent to him from Allah, subhanahu wa ta'ala.

We have to understand that the dhat, the essence of Muhammad, is not the Haqiqat al-Muhammadiya. The Haqiqat al-Muhammadiya belongs to the Knower and Allah is the Knower. The dhat of the Messenger is what is known. The 'abd is not the Rabb, the slave is not the Lord. His dhat is that of the slave, but his Haqiqat, his reality is with Allah. There is no association.

So what is called the Haqiqat al-Muhammadiya is not

the essence of the Rasul, sallallahu 'alayhi wa sallam, because this would be shirk and it would be kufr.

We go to Surat al-Ma'ida (85:17 and 18). This explains exactly what we mean:

لَقَدْ كَفَرَ ٱلَّذِينَ قَالُوٓا۟
إِنَّ ٱللَّهَ هُوَ ٱلْمَسِيحُ ٱبْنُ
مَرْيَمَ ۚ قُلْ فَمَن يَمْلِكُ مِنَ ٱللَّهِ شَيْـًٔا إِنْ أَرَادَ أَن
يُهْلِكَ ٱلْمَسِيحَ ٱبْنَ مَرْيَمَ وَأُمَّهُۥ وَمَن فِى ٱلْأَرْضِ
جَمِيعًا ۗ وَلِلَّهِ مُلْكُ ٱلسَّمَٰوَٰتِ وَٱلْأَرْضِ وَمَا بَيْنَهُمَا ۚ
يَخْلُقُ مَا يَشَآءُ ۚ وَٱللَّهُ عَلَىٰ كُلِّ شَىْءٍ قَدِيرٌ ﴿١٧﴾
وَقَالَتِ ٱلْيَهُودُ وَٱلنَّصَٰرَىٰ نَحْنُ أَبْنَٰٓؤُا۟ ٱللَّهِ وَأَحِبَّٰٓؤُهُۥ ۚ قُلْ
فَلِمَ يُعَذِّبُكُم بِذُنُوبِكُم ۖ بَلْ أَنتُم بَشَرٌ مِّمَّنْ خَلَقَ ۚ يَغْفِرُ لِمَن
يَشَآءُ وَيُعَذِّبُ مَن يَشَآءُ ۚ وَلِلَّهِ مُلْكُ ٱلسَّمَٰوَٰتِ وَٱلْأَرْضِ
وَمَا بَيْنَهُمَا ۖ وَإِلَيْهِ ٱلْمَصِيرُ ﴿١٨﴾

Those who say, 'Allah is the Messiah,
son of Maryam,' are kafir.
Say: 'Who possesses any power at all over Allah
if He desires to destroy the Messiah, son of Maryam,
and his mother, and everyone else on earth?'
The kingdom of the heavens and the earth
and everything between them

belongs to Allah.
He creates whatever He wills.
Allah has power over all things.

The jews and christians say,
'We are Allah's children and His loved ones.'
Say: 'Why, then, does He punish you
for your wrong actions?
No, you are merely human beings
among those He has created.
He forgives whomever He wills
and He punishes whomever He wills.
The kingdom of the heavens and the earth
and everything between them belongs to Allah.
He is our final destination.'

Here we have the explanation of how what is being said does not have any shred or implication of identification, of joining or linkage, of connection between the presence of Rasul, sallallahu 'alayhi wa sallam, and the Essence and the Reality of Allah, subhanahu wa ta'ala.

"Those who say, 'Allah is the Messiah, son of Maryam,' are kafir." So much for all these calls for the Muslims to have 'dialogue' with the christians! All we need to do is to put that in an envelope and send it to them.

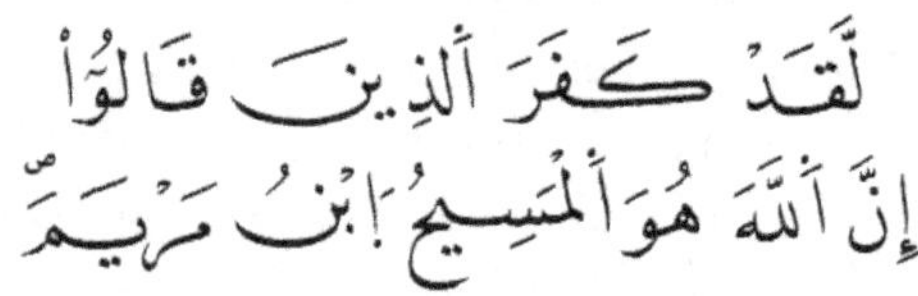

Those who say, 'Allah is the Messiah,
son of Maryam,' are kafir.

These are Allah's words.

قُلْ فَمَن يَمْلِكُ مِنَ ٱللَّهِ شَيْـًٔا إِنْ أَرَادَ أَن
يُهْلِكَ ٱلْمَسِيحَ ٱبْنَ مَرْيَمَ وَأُمَّهُۥ وَمَن فِى ٱلْأَرْضِ
جَمِيعًا ۗ وَلِلَّهِ مُلْكُ ٱلسَّمَٰوَٰتِ وَٱلْأَرْضِ وَمَا بَيْنَهُمَا ۚ
يَخْلُقُ مَا يَشَآءُ ۚ وَٱللَّهُ عَلَىٰ كُلِّ شَىْءٍ قَدِيرٌ ﴿١٧﴾
وَقَالَتِ ٱلْيَهُودُ وَٱلنَّصَٰرَىٰ نَحْنُ أَبْنَٰٓؤُا۟ ٱللَّهِ وَأَحِبَّٰٓؤُهُۥ ۚ قُلْ
فَلِمَ يُعَذِّبُكُم بِذُنُوبِكُم ۖ بَلْ أَنتُم بَشَرٌ مِّمَّنْ خَلَقَ ۚ يَغْفِرُ لِمَن
يَشَآءُ وَيُعَذِّبُ مَن يَشَآءُ ۚ وَلِلَّهِ مُلْكُ ٱلسَّمَٰوَٰتِ وَٱلْأَرْضِ
وَمَا بَيْنَهُمَا ۖ وَإِلَيْهِ ٱلْمَصِيرُ ﴿١٨﴾

Say: 'Who possesses any power at all over Allah
if He desires to destroy the Messiah, son of Maryam,
and his mother, and everyone else on earth?'
The kingdom of the heavens and the earth
and everything between them belongs to Allah.
He creates whatever He wills.
Allah has power over all things.

The jews and christians say,
'We are Allah's children and His loved ones.'
Say: 'Why, then, does He punish you
for your wrong actions?

No, you are merely human beings
among those He has created.
He forgives whomever He wills
and He punishes whomever He wills.
The kingdom of the heavens and the earth
and everything between them belongs to Allah.
He is our final destination.'

Sometimes this stage of unfolding of Allah's majesty and power is called Nuri Muhammadi. If we look at the Diwan of Shaykh Muhammad ibn al-Habib, radiyallahu 'anhu, and the Wird which we have just recited:

اللهم صل وسلم بأنواع كمالاتك في جميع تجلياتك على سيدنا و
مولانا محمد أول الأنوار الفائضة من بحور عظمة الذات

"The first of the lights emanating from the oceans of the sublimity of the Essence." That is a reference to the Nuri Muhammad, the Haqiqat al-Muhammadiya. It is very important for the one who takes the journey of Ma'rifa to understand this aspect of the Divinity.

We will see later when we look at the Diwan where Shaykh Muhammad ibn al-Habib, radiyallahu 'anhu, gives his definition of Tawhid and defines how part of Tawhid is contained in proper knowledge of Rasul, sallallahu 'alayhi wa sallam. Again, this is not in any way to deify him yet to recognise his high spiritual place. Remember the very important thing which Mawlana Rumi said about Abu Jahl: when he looked he did not see the Rasul but the son of 'Abdullah. There is a spiritual rank which is not the property of Rasul, sallallahu 'alayhi wa sallam, but that a light has been put into him which gives him the rank so that he said, "I am the first of the sons of Adam." He does not say that he is not one of the sons of Adam. Allah, subhanahu wa ta'ala, reminds us in Surat Al 'Imran, referring to the Prophet's future death (3:144-145):

وَمَا مُحَمَّدٌ إِلَّا رَسُولٌ
قَدْ خَلَتْ مِن قَبْلِهِ الرُّسُلُ أَفَإِيْن مَّاتَ أَوْ قُتِلَ انقَلَبْتُمْ
عَلَىٰ أَعْقَابِكُمْ وَمَن يَنقَلِبْ عَلَىٰ عَقِبَيْهِ فَلَن يَضُرَّ اللَّهَ شَيْئًا
وَسَيَجْزِي اللَّهُ الشَّاكِرِينَ ﴿١٤٤﴾ وَمَا كَانَ لِنَفْسٍ أَن
تَمُوتَ إِلَّا بِإِذْنِ اللَّهِ كِتَابًا مُّؤَجَّلًا

Muhammad is only a Messenger
and he has been preceded by other Messengers.
If he were to die or be killed,
would you turn on your heels?
Those who turn on their heels
do not harm Allah in any way.
Allah will recompense the thankful.
No self can die except with Allah's permission,
at a predetermined time.

So Allah's confirmation of this is the absolute impossibility for the Muslims to think about Rasul, sallallahu 'alayhi wa sallam, in that way. At the same time, in this modern age, we have had a denigration of Rasul, sallallahu 'alayhi wa sallam, and a bringing-down from his high position as the first of the sons of Adam and the Seal of the Messengers – by Egyptian scholars and the shayateen from Arabia who have been like Abu Jahl and have tried to say that he is merely the son of his father.

Without any shirk, without any kufr and without any crossing of this line that we will never, never cross, you have to recognise the high position which the Rasul, sallallahu 'alayhi wa sallam, has and the high position he has been given by Allah, subhanahu wa ta'ala, in the ayat of the Salat an-Nabiy (Surat al-Ahzab 56):

إِنَّ ٱللَّهَ وَمَلَٰٓئِكَتَهُۥ يُصَلُّونَ عَلَى ٱلنَّبِيِّۚ
يَٰٓأَيُّهَا ٱلَّذِينَ ءَامَنُواْ صَلُّواْ عَلَيۡهِ وَسَلِّمُواْ تَسۡلِيمًا ٥٦

Allah and His angels call down blessings on the Prophet.
You who have Iman! call down blessings on him
and ask for complete peace and safety for him.

To go back to this confirmation of Allah being exalted above everything, every form and every human being, Dhun-Nun al-Misri speaks of the Essence in this way:

علم ذات الحق جهل
تعريف حق المعرفة حيرة
إشارة المشير شرك

Knowledge of the Essence of the Haqq – ignorance.
Definition of the reality of Ma'rifa – bewilderment.
Indication by an indicator – shirk.

You cannot even make an ishara on this matter! Shirk. The line is drawn and the mouths are silent.

The poets of the Sufis use the Anqa', which is a mythological bird, to speak about the Essence, and one of them said, "Do not try to catch the Anqa', you will only be able to catch air." This is the knowledge of the Essence of Allah, subhanahu wa ta'ala. Inshallah we will continue with these six terms having done the first two of the three Divine ranks. Then we will move to the three worldly ranks, inshallah.

IX

May 29th 2004

We have been looking at the 'Tanazzulat as-Sita'. These stages are not in time or preceding the other, or following the other, but they are only in description. They are understood in their detail by the 'Arifin and they are also understood by the mutakallimun because they follow in a logical pattern what one may say about Allah, subhanahu wa ta'ala, with correct adab.

This Tanazzulat as-Sita is divided into three Murati bil-lahi, Divine ranks, and then the next three are the Murati bil-Kawni, the worldly ranks. In other words, the first three are what you can say about Allah, subhanahu wa ta'ala – their different aspects of Essence. We talked about Ahadiyat which is Essence – pure, disconnected from any forms and indeterminate, having no specificity of any kind. Then we came on Wahdat, which is unity and it is between Ahadiyat and Wahidiyat.

Wahdat is called in the language of the Sufis, Nuri Muhammadi, and is more generally called the Haqiqat al-Muhammadiya. Remember that we pointed out that this is not the essence of the Messenger, sallallahu 'alayhi wa sallam, which is different from his Haqiqat because the Messenger is a human being and cannot be associated in any way with the Divine as he is ordered to explain in the Qur'an itself.

Another name of this is the Tajalli al-Awwal, the first manifestation. Or Wujudi al-Awwal, the first existence, or the Jawhar al-Awwal, the first jewel. All this is within the Essence of Allah, subhanahu wa ta'ala.

After Wahdat, which is like a barzakh between Ahadiyat and Wahidiyat, we come to Wahidiyat. When the 'Arif reflects on the Dhat of Allah, of Allah possessing knowledge in detail – its Names, Attributes and source-forms with all the distinctions and aspects – this is called Wahidiyat. Now we can talk about Allah, subhanahu wa ta'ala, as possessing knowledge in detail in Himself, and His Names and Attributes and source-forms of all those knowledges which allow all the myriad forms in the universe to unfold and become manifest on the command of the 'Kun'. This is called Wahidiyat. So Ahadiyat is absoluteness in itself, and Wahidiyat is that with all its details.

Ahadiyat is absolute, Wahdat is implicit – that is why it is called the barzakh al-Kubra, the great divide in how we can understand Allah, subhanahu wa ta'ala, and Wahidiyat is explicit. It is Allah in His supremacy with all His Attributes and Names known to Himself and all His knowledge by which He will unfold, as He desires, the whole vast creation of the universe. These are three Divine Names but they are suppositional names, they are not actual, they have no reality – they are for us to understand.

Ahadiyat, Dhat, Essence without conditions. Ahadiyat is Surat al-Ikhlas:

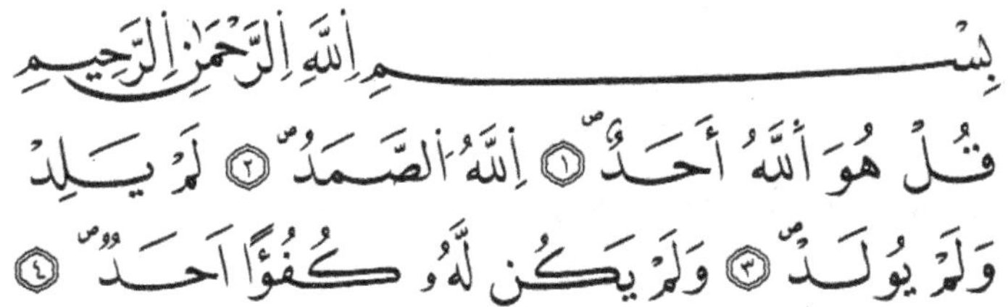

In the name of Allah, All-Merciful, Most Merciful
"Say: 'He is Allah, Absolute Oneness,
Allah, the Everlasting Sustainer of all.
He has not given birth and was not born.
And no one is comparable to Him.'"

The Ahad is Ahadiyat. Secondly Wahdat, the barzakh. This is unity but with potentiality. It is potential to have this vast unfolding of forms but still not determined, it is still not specified what Allah's unfolding will be.

Thirdly Wahidiyat, we would call the emergence of the Names. All this is within Allah's Divine Reality, not in the universe, not in the world of forms. It is the potential of His majesty – the emergence of the Names and the Attributes and what we called earlier the 'ayan ath-thabita, the source-forms. In other words, the form of the creature is in the knowledge of Allah, or the thing as He wishes it to be, before it is realised. Metaphorically it is the potter with the image of the pot before the pot is thrown, but there is no connection and the metaphor cannot be extended because Allah has no outsideness or insideness, or nearness or farness from His objects. Yet it is a metaphor of how the forms have to exist in His knowledge before they manifest and become the known to us.

For this we look at Surat al-Baqara (2:163):

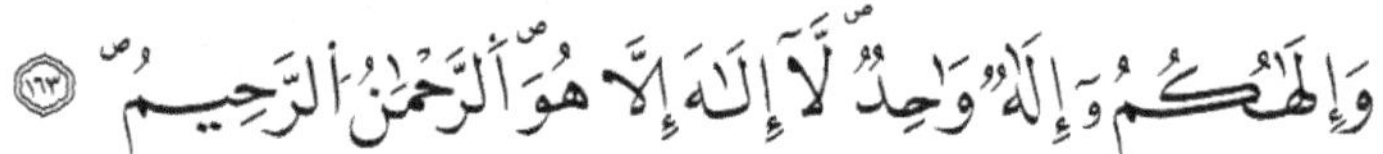

Your God is One God. There is no god but Him,
the All-Merciful, the Most Merciful.

Now we have the Ahad unfolding His Attributes. "Your God is One God. There is no god but Him," nothing is associated with Him so He is not connected to the world of forms, He is not connected to His creation in any way whatsoever. He is exalted above it, and He is "the All-Merciful, the Most Merciful." He has Rahman and He has Rahim. These are His Attributes, these are His qualities, this is Him showing Himself for what He is as the Lord of the Universe.

Here we have Essence and Attributes. Allah is One. This is the Ahadiyat which we have been looking at. "There is no god but Him," so the Wahdat, which we have said is everything in potential and is the Nuri Muhammad, still does not allow anything in that stage to be connected to Him. "The All-Merciful, the Most Merciful." Then He shows the splendour of His Attributes and the two dominant Attributes of His qualities are the Rahman and the Rahim which is why of course all but one of the surats of Qur'an begins with: "Bismillahi ar-Rahmani ar-Rahim." Bismillah – in the name of Allah, the Ahad, and the Rahman and the Rahim. In other words Qur'an puts Allah's Unity with His Attributes throughout.

This does not mean that there was Absolute which then became latent with powers and potentials and then became Existent. You must understand this because we are not saying that. This is a description for your clarity, and it is confirmed by the 'Arifin in their vision and their knowledge. It is a description which has not got time in it. It is not that He was this and then He was that. He is One, immutable and unchangeable always.

Rasul, sallallahu 'alayhi wa sallam, was asked, "Where was Allah before the creation?" and he replied, "Before the creation of the world, Allah was and there was nothing with Him." Imam Junayd confirmed this and made commentary on it by saying, "Is as He was."

The Names indicate the Essence along with its Attributes. In other words, when you are given the Attribute ar-Rahman, this is Allah, this is the Essence manifesting

Attribute. You cannot have the Attribute without the Essence so: Allahu Ahad, Allahu Samad. The Essence goes with the Name.

Shaykh al-Akbar tells of a Wali who was asked how he achieved his Ma'rifa and he replied, "By joining the opposite Attributes. The One Who Exalts and the One Who Brings Low." Also, Al-Awwalu wal-Akhiru, wadh-Dhahiru wal-Batin. So he joined these opposites because they are One, Allah is One, until he achieved his fana'.

With Wahidiyat emerge the four mother Attributes and they are: Hayy, 'Ilm, Irada and Qudra – life, knowledge, will and power. From these come all the Attributes of the hearing, the seeing and so on. From Allah as Al-'Alim comes the knowledge of the source-forms, the 'ayan ath-thabita. He knows that from this is the knowledge by which He knows how all the things will have form. Remember that we are saying that Allah is One in His Essence and in His Attributes and in His Acts because the form is not a static thing. Everything in the creation is alive. According to the Sufis, all the apparently inanimate things are also alive. This was something that they said from the time of Rasul, sallallahu 'alayhi wa sallam, but it was only confirmed by the scientists with nuclear science. The apparently dead matter was in fact moving enormously fast and was in motion and alive. This has always been the position of people of vision in Tasawwuf.

So from Al-'Alim comes the knowledge of the source-form. What we are saying is that the source-form is not a form in a static sense because for a living creature you cannot separate its form from its actions. The obvious example is a dog. The dog is not just a creature with four legs and a tail and a head – the essence of dog is that he hunts, he attaches to man and is loyal to man, he can turn on man, he is a guard, he is not clean – that is dog. So dog cannot be separated from dogness. Just as that is the case, so when we come to man. Allah creates the form of the man and also the history of the man, thus the whole man from the beginning of his coming into existence in the world until his death has been created by Allah, subhanahu wa ta'ala. Thus he will behave according to his form, he has no choice.

What the ignorant people call freedom is not what we understand by freedom. What we understand by complete freedom is complete 'ubudiyya, complete slavehood, because if you are completely the slave of Allah, subhanahu wa ta'ala, then you are liberated because you will move by Him, you will speak by Him, and so your actions will be by Him and pleasing to Him.

Shaykh Ibn al-'Arabi said about these source-forms, the 'ayan ath-thabita: "They never smell the odour of existence." You must understand that the forms on which things come into being have not got any existence. They are in the knowledge of Allah, subhanahu wa ta'ala. Then by the Command, 'Kun', He brings them into existence where they are not the 'ayan ath-thabita but the forms themselves. These 'ayan ath-thabita have no external existence, they are only subsistent in Knowledge. Every essence of a thing has a distinguishing nature or characteristic to distinguish it from other apparently similar forms.

In other words, each being is made on a particular form. That is why all of us are of the same genus but every single one of us is completely different. The finger-print is different, the hand-print is different, the eye – everything of each person is made on that particular form of Allah's Command. Thus the Attributes of Al-'Alim have endless possibilities. This is the form of the created beings, and we look for this in Surat al-Isra (17:84). This is a command on the Rasul, sallallahu 'alayhi wa sallam, therefore it is a direct education of the muminun:

قُلْ كُلٌّ يَعْمَلُ عَلَىٰ شَاكِلَتِهِۦ

The translation is, "Say: 'Each man acts according to his nature," but I am not satisfied with the translation of 'nature' because actually 'shakilat' is the 'form', the thing we have been talking about. So each man acts according to his 'ayn ath-thabita, to this form he had in the knowledge of Allah, subhanahu wa ta'ala, before he was ordered into existence by the Divine Command that brings things to life. And then:

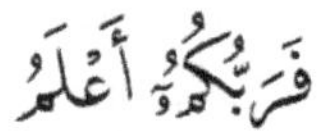

But your Lord knows best –

So here Allah, subhanahu wa ta'ala, speaks of Himself using the term Rabb. Very often in the Qur'an when the term Rabb is used, it is indicating Allah in His capacity, in that aspect of His Essence which manifests through the Attributes to make things happen in the world of forms in the created universe.

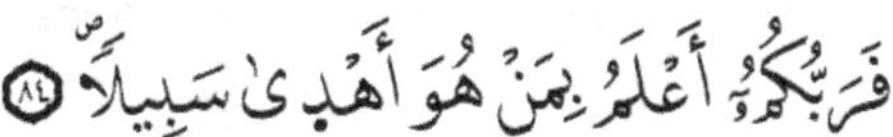

But your Lord knows best who is best guided on the path.

Allah knows best who is best guided on the path because the man has been made in that form that will put him on the path. This takes you to the wall of knowledge about the seal of the destiny. You cannot go beyond that knowledge because it is a knowledge that brings you to a complete halt. In other words, when you, by your choices, decide from inside the form that you have to do what you do, it reveals at that moment that Allah has chosen you to be mumin. Therefore you both choose to be mumin but also Allah, subhanahu wa ta'ala, because of His fore-knowledge and because of the nature of His design, had designed you to be mumin.

Beyond that you cannot go because your responsibility is not taken away. If you did not have a responsibility for the acts there would not have been the need for Prophets, for Qur'an, for the Books. You have an absolute responsibility before Allah for the destiny, and at the same time you are in fact acting out what He has designed you for.

What knowledge is, what wisdom is, is that the mumin wants to do what is pleasing to Allah because if He does what is pleasing to Allah it is because Allah has destined him to be one of those people who is pleasing to Him.

When you do act in a way that is pleasing to Allah you are not claiming, "I have done this, look! I have done what is pleasing to Allah," but, "He has put me on this path." The shakilat takes us to this knowledge.

The Tanazzulat then descends into its three worldly ranks which are ruh, mithal and jism. These in turn, in description only, take us to insan, to man. Again, these descents are not in space or time but are a way of understanding this incredible unfolding of the Divine Reality. In terms of the creation, when these Attributes have ordered into being the universe, and when the Throne of Allah has been set out in all its splendour, and the heavens have been created, and then the creatures have been created and the Khalif of Allah, subhanahu wa ta'ala, has been appointed, which is man, then you have ruh, mithal and jism. This is the spirit, mithal and body.

Mithal is that because certain things are like certain things you are able to understand these spiritual matters. You cannot understand them by reason, you cannot understand them except by glimpsing the likeness: "This is like that." You cannot say, "It is that," then, "Ah, you mean so and so," as if it were a real example. A mithal is not an example but a picture of something that makes it clear for you. This is a necessary dimension of the worldly condition.

If you are not able to interpret mithal then it is as though you are not a complete human being. To give you an example: in the medical profession, the psychiatrists' test that someone is insane, therefore not a full human being, is that they ask them a question like, "What does it mean if 'people in glass-houses should not throw stones'?" If the answer is, "Well, if you are in a glass house and you throw a stone you will break the window," then he is mad. If he is able to say, "It means you should not accuse the other when you are in the same situation," that means he understands the mithal.

If you cannot translate the mithal it is a sign of insanity because normal reason is actually based on something that is not reasonable, but is a faculty of the imagination to understand the situation the human being is in.

I will now take this exactly from Shaykh Muhiyuddin Ibn al-'Arabi's 'Fusus al-Hikam', 'The Seals of Wisdom', because it is so clear and so beautiful. He explains the position of man in the universe:

> "When Allah, subhanahu wa ta'ala, willed (He is using His Attribute of Will which is one of the Mother Attributes) that the source of His most beautiful Names, which are beyond enumeration, be seen, or you can equally say that He willed His source to be seen,"

– because if He wished that the source of His Attributes be seen, as the Attributes and the Essence are one, it meant that He wanted somehow to declare out His own Essence –

> "He willed that they be seen in a microcosmic being which contained the entire Command,

> having been endowed with existence, and through which His secret was manifested to Him."

He willed that the source of His most beautiful Names be seen in a microcosmic being which contained the entire Command, the entire universe, because every aspect of the universe is in man. Man is the microcosm of the macrocosm. He is the focal point of the whole thing, he is the end result, he is what is intended by the creation.

> "He willed that they be seen in a microcosmic being which contained the entire command, having been endowed with existence, and through which His secret was manifested to Him," for His delight. "For the vision that a thing has of itself through itself is not like a vision of itself in something else which acts like a mirror for it, so He manifests Himself to Himself in a form which is bestowed by the place in which He is seen. He would not appear thus without the existence of this place and His Tajalli to Himself in it.
>
> "Allah brought the entire universe into existence with the existence of a form fashioned without ruh, like an unpolished mirror. It is a matter of the Divine decree that He does not fashion a place but that it must receive the Divine ruh which is described as being 'blown into it' in Qur'an. This is none other than the obtaining of the predisposition of that fashioned form to re-

> ceive the overflowing, the perpetual Tajalli which has never ceased and which will never cease."

So he is saying that it was through man that Allah was able to see and contemplate Himself through the creation of this creature, but He has to blow the ruh into this creature so that the unpolished mirror could become polished and have light.

> "Then we must speak of the container. The container proceeds from none other than His most sacredly pure overflowing."

He is saying that the created creature, man, comes from the most sacred Essence of Allah, subhanahu wa ta'ala, and yet he is now, in the universe, the creature with a ruh.

> "So the whole affair has its beginning from Allah and its end is to Him and the whole affair will return to Him as it began from Him. Thus the command decreed the polishing of the mirror of the universe, and Adam was the very polishing of that mirror, and the ruh of that form.

> "Tajalli only comes from the Essence by means of the forms of predisposition of the one to whom the Tajalli is made," in other words, the container. The Tajalli from the Essence only comes because man has been created for this. He is predisposed to receive this event. "The one who receives the Tajalli will only see his own form in the mirror of the Real, and he will not

> see the Real for it is not possible to see Him."

Sayyiduna Musa, 'alayhi salam, said, "I want to see You," and Allah said, "You cannot see Me but look at the mountain," and the mountain crumbled to pieces and he then received this Divine knowledge by his own fana'.

> "At the same time he knows that he sees only his own form in it. It is like the mirror in the visible world – inasmuch as you see forms in it, or your own form, you do not see the mirror." If you look at the mirror you do not see the mirror, you see yourself. "At the same time you know that you see the forms or your form only by virtue of the mirror. Allah manifests this as a mithal," this is an essential part of the human creature, "appropriate to the Tajalli of His Essence, so that the one receiving the Tajalli knows that he does not see Him."

Thus when Allah manifests to him he does not see Him, he sees himself. "Man 'arafa nafsahu fa qad 'arafa Rabbah." He who knows himself knows his Lord.

> "There is no mithal nearer and more appropriate to vision and Tajalli than this, so try in yourself when you see the form in the mirror to see the body of the mirror as well – you will never do it. If you wish to taste of this, then experience the limit beyond which there is no higher limit possible in respect to the creature. Neither aspire, nor tire yourself in going beyond this

> degree for in principle there is only pure non-existence after it. Allah is then your mirror in which you see yourself, and you are His mirror in which He sees His Names."

This returns us to our primary understanding of the difference between the Divine Essence and the essences of created things. We look at the Diwan of Shaykh Muhammad ibn al-Habib, radiyallahu 'anhu, in the qasida 'Withdrawal from all that is other-than-Allah':

رُوحِي تُحَدِّثُنِي بِأَنَّ حَقِيقَتِي   نُورُ الإِلَهِ فَلا تَرَى إِلاَّهُ
لَوْ لَمْ أَكُنْ نُوراً لَكُنْتُ سِواهُ   إِنَّ السِّوَا عَدَمٌ فَلا تَرْضاهُ
وَإِذا نَظَرْتَ بِعَيْنِ سِرِّكَ لَمْ تَجِدْ   غَيْرَ الإِلَهِ فِي أَرْضِهِ وَسَماهُ
لَكِنْ تَوَهُّمُ غَيْرِهِ يَخْفَى بِهِ   فَانْبُذْ هَواكَ إِذا أَرَدْتَ تَراهُ

My ruh speaks to me and says,
"My Haqiqat is the Light of Allah,
so look to no-one except Him.

If I were not a light I would be other-than-Him.
Indeed otherness is nothingness
so do not be content with it.

If you look with the eye of your Secret," the inner eye,
"you will not find a trace of other-than-Allah
in either earth or heaven.

But the illusion of other-than-Him hides Him.
So combat your desires if you wish to see Him."

In other words, rise above this nafs that insists on the reality of things and does not realise the secret which is that if you look with the eye of your Secret you will not find anything that is other-than-Allah.

Thus from the stand-point of created forms everything is masiwallah. From the point of view of the forms brought into existence everything is other-than-Allah. But from the inward aspect, all things are His from before-time and after it. "If I were not a light I would be other-than-Him. Otherness is nothingness so do not be content with it. If you look with the eye of your Secret you will not find a trace of other-than-Allah in either earth or heaven."

We will now look at Surat an-Nahl (16:96) for the final clarification of this matter, confirming what I have said. This ayat is astonishing:

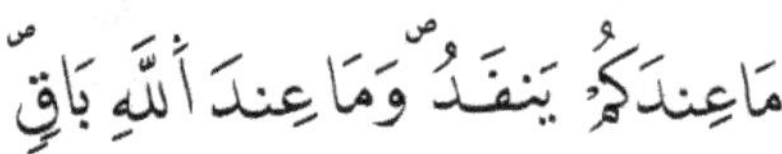

What is with you runs out,
but what is with Allah goes on forever.

There is an in-time aspect of you which runs out and then that is it, finished and gone. But in the secret, what is with Allah goes on forever. The reality is that the Essence is present so you are in the knowledge of Allah. You have come into the creation and He is the Knower, and then when you are finished you return to Him, there is the Judgment Day and all the unfolding of the secrets of the Malakut. You go from the Mulk to the Malakut to the Jabarut to the meeting with the Essence because you have been known to Allah, subhanahu wa ta'ala, before the creation of the world.

In Qur'an we know very well the ayat where Allah orders all of mankind before the creation of the world in the Essence – in His knowledge, the 'Alim – and says to them, in Surat al-A'raf (7:172):

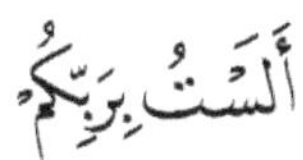

Am I not your Lord?

and all the human creatures say,

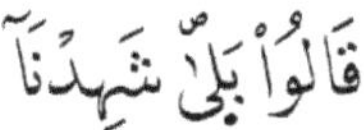

We testify that indeed You are!

Then Allah, by the Command, puts them into the world in their time and in their place, and Allah says in Surat al-'Ankabut (29:2):

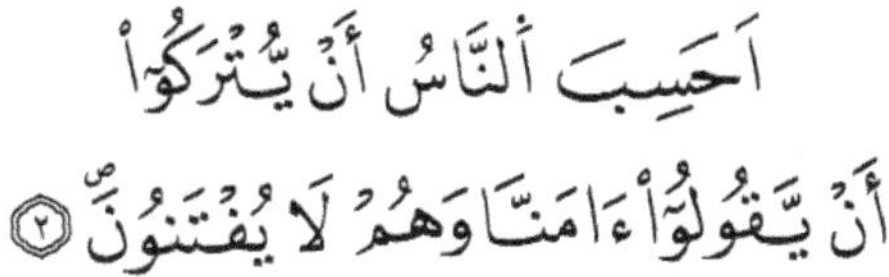

Do people imagine that they will be left to say,
'We have iman,' and will not be tested?

So they are tested and you see who are this and you see who are that. You see who are the muminun and you see who are the kafirun, and you see in between who are the munafiqun. Then they will be gathered to Allah, subhanahu wa ta'ala.

"What is with you runs out but what is with Allah goes on forever." "What is with you runs out," ends with the washing of the body and the funeral prayer. "What is with Allah goes on forever," is the fulfilment of the meaning of the life when the form of the life has been returned to its Owner in the earth and the phosphates have gone to the phosphates and the potassium has gone to the potassium and the minerals have returned to the earth. Then what is with Allah goes on forever, some for the Fire and some for the Garden. Allah, subhanahu wa ta'ala, says: "I send some to the Fire and I do not care, I send some to the Garden and I do not care," because this is part of the Divine unfolding of the Essence of Allah, subhanahu wa ta'ala, and this is the reality of the Haqq and this is the One Whom we worship and we associate nothing with Him.

Fatiha.

Reflection

from the Diwan of Shaykh Muhammad ibn al-Habib

رائِيَّةُ التَّفْكِيرِ

تَفَكَّرْ جَمِيلَ الصُّنْعِ فِي الْبَرِّ والبَحْرِ   وَجُلْ فِي صِفاتِ اللهِ فِي السِّرِّ وَالجَهْرِ
وَفِي النَّفْسِ والآفــاقِ أَعْظَمُ شاهِدٍ   عَلى كَمالاتِ اللهِ مِنْ غَيْرِ مـا حَصْرِ
فَلَوْ جُلْتَ فِي الأَجْسامِ مَعْ حُسْنِ شَكْلِها   وَتَنْظِيمِها تَنْظِيـمَ خَيْـطٍ مِـنَ الدُّرِّ
وَجُلْتَ فِي أَسْرارِ اللِّسانِ وَنُطْقِــهِ   وَتَعْبِيرِهِ عَمَّـا تُكِنُّــهُ فِي الصَّدْرِ
وَجُلْتَ فِي أَسْرارِ الجَوارِحِ كُلِّهــا   وَتَسْتَخِيرِها لِلْقَلْبِ مِنْ غَيْرِ ما عُسْرِ
وَجُلْتَ فِي تَقْلِيبِ القُلُوبِ لِطاعَــةٍ   وَفِي بَعْضِ أَحْيانٍ لِمَعْصِيَــةٍ تَسْرِي
وَجُلْتَ فِي أَرْضٍ مَــعْ تَنَوُّعِ نَبْتِهــا   وَكَثْرَةِ ما فِيها مِــنَ السَّهْلِ وَالوَعْرِ
وَجُلْتَ فِي أَسْرارِ البِحارِ وَحُوتِهــا   وَكَثْرَةِ أَمْــواجٍ لَهــا حاجِزٌ قَهْرِ
وَجُلْــتَ فِي أَسْرارِ الرِّياحِ وَجَلْبِها   لِغَيْمٍ وَسُحْبٍ قَدْ أَسالَتْ مِنَ القَطْرِ
وَجُلْتَ فِي أَسْرارِ السَّمَواتِ كُلِّهــا   وَعَرْشٍ وَكُرْسِيٍّ وَرُوحٍ مِنَ الأَمْرِ
عَقَدْتَ عَلى التَّوْحِيدِ عَقْــدَ مُصَمِّمٍ   وَحُلْتَ عَنِ الأَوْهامِ وَالشَّكِّ وَالغَيْرِ
وَقُلْتَ إلاهِي أَنْتَ سُؤْلِــي وَمَطْلَبِي   وَحِصْنِي مِنَ الأَسْواءِ وَالضَّيْمِ وَالمَكْرِ
وَأَنْتَ رَجاءِي فِي قَضاءِ حَوائِجِــي   وَأَنْتَ الذِي تُنْجِي مِنَ السُّوءِ وَالشَّرِّ
وَأَنْتَ الرَّحِيمُ المُسْتَجِيبُ لِمَنْ دَعاكْ   وَأَنْتَ الذِي تُغْنِي الفَقِيرَ عَنِ الفَقْرِ
إِلَيْكَ رَفَعْــتُ يــا رَفِيــعُ مَطالِبِي   فَعَجِّلْ بِفَتْحٍ يا إِلاهِــي مَــعَ السِّرِّ
بِجاهِ الذِي يُرْجَى يَوْمَ الكَرْبِ وَالعَنا   وَيَوْمَ وُرُودِ النَّاسِ لِمَوْقِــفِ الحَشْرِ
عَلَيْهِ صَلاةُ اللهِ مــا جــالَ عارِفٌ   فِي أَنْوارِ ذاتِــهِ لَــدَى كُلِّ مَظْهَرِ
وَآلِهِ وَالأَصْحابِ مَــعْ كُــلِّ تَابِعٍ   لِسُنَّتِهِ الغَــرَّاءِ فِي النَّهْــيِ وَالأَمْرِ

Reflect upon the beauty of the way in which both the land and sea are made, and contemplate the Attributes of Allah outwardly and secretly.

The greatest evidence of the limitless perfections of Allah can be found both deep within the self and on the distant horizon.

If you were to reflect on physical bodies and their marvellous forms and how they are arranged with great precision, like a string of pearls,

And if you were to reflect on the secrets of the tongue and its capacity for speech, and how it articulates and conveys what you conceal in your breast,

And if you were to reflect on the secrets of all the limbs and how easily they are subject to the heart's command,

And if you were to reflect on how the hearts are moved to obey Allah and how at other times they move darkly to disobedience,

And if you were to reflect on the earth and the diversity of its plants and the great varieties of smooth and rugged land in it,

And if you were to reflect on the secrets of the oceans and all their fish, and their endless waves held back by an unconquerable barrier,

And if you were to reflect on the secrets of the many

winds and how they bring the mist, fog and clouds which release the rain,

And if you were to reflect on all the secrets of the heavens – the Throne and the Footstool and the spirit sent by the Command –

Then you would accept the reality of Tawhid with all your being, and you would turn away from illusions, uncertainty and otherness,

And you would say, "My God, You are my desire, my goal and my impregnable fortress against evil, injustice and deceit.

You are the One I hope will provide for all my needs, and You are the One Who rescues us from all evil and wickedness.

You are the Compassionate, the One Who answers all who call on You. And you are the One Who enriches the poverty of the faqir.

It is to You, O Exalted, that I have raised all my request, so swiftly bring me the Opening, the rescue and the secret, O my God."

By the rank of the one in whom we hope on the day of distress and grief – that terrible day when people come to the Place of Gathering –

May Allah's blessings by upon him as long as there is an

'Arif who reflects on the lights of His Essence in every manifestation,

And upon his family and Companions and everyone who follows his excellent Sunna in all its prohibitions and commands.

HADRA

We ask Allah, subhanahu wa ta'ala, to keep us in the company of the 'Arifin. We ask Allah, subhanahu wa ta'ala, to let the people of this dhikr spread out through the whole of Africa and take the Deen to all of Africa. We ask Allah, subhanahu wa ta'ala, to give to Africa the Deen of Islam that has been rejected by the Arabs. We ask Allah, subhanahu wa ta'ala, to give baraka to the people of this room.

We ask Allah, subhanahu wa ta'ala, to make the people of this room people of baraka, people of wisdom and people of teaching. We ask Allah, subhanahu wa ta'ala, to give benefit to all the people who see the fuqara and meet the fuqara so that they love them and respect them.

THE BOOK

OF

HUBB

(LOVE OF THE DIVINE)

Seven Discourses
given between July 21st
and September 1st 2007
at Masjid al-Mansoor,
Constantia, Cape Town

I

July 21st 2007

The Three Foundational Terms of Love

I would like, inshallah, over the next few gatherings of Dhikr to look at some of the technical language of Tasawwuf, and some of the framework of the Suluk of the Sufi on his Path.

Tonight we will make an introduction to it by discussing three terms, and then, properly speaking, we would begin looking at the Ten Stages of Love as it is defined by the great Sufis and 'Arifin in Islam.

There are three terms I want you to become acquainted with. The first is Mahabba, which is affection. Mahabba derives from the root word Hubb. Hubb is, in its root meaning, a seed. It is a seed which lies embedded in the ground and while the rain comes on it, it does not move. The sun comes on it and it does not move. The winter comes on it and the summer comes on it, and there is no change in it. Once that not-changing is established so that the summer and the winter are the same for it, and the rain and the sun are the same for it, at a certain moment it is ready to sprout, and from it come the green shoots and the leaves and the fruit.

This affection does not change. Absence or presence, pain or pleasure become the same. So when the time comes it begins to sprout with its life. The Sufis say that this word Hubb has two letters: Ha and Ba. Ha is the last letter of Ruh – spirit, and Ba is the first letter of Badan – body. So it is said that Hubb is where these two come together – the Ruh and the body, and between these two letters, separating them, there is a Barzakh which is love. It is something that comes between the incompatibility and the 'un-meetability' of Ruh and body.

The other term we shall look at is 'Ishq. 'Ishq appears in many Diwans and much of the literature of the Sufis, and in the writings of the great scholars of Tasawwuf. 'Ishq derives from 'Ashiqa, and 'Ashiqa is also a term used for a creeper, whose other name in Arabic is Liblab. The creeper grows and entwines itself around a tree and slowly, slowly it covers all its branches and it takes from the tree its leaves and its fruit until the leaves turn yellow, and it completely destroys the tree until it becomes the tree. 'Ishq is this term for ardent love, and it is one of the key terms of Tasawwuf.

We are going to look at Ten Stages of Love, and prior to the Ten Stages we have what is called Muwafaqa. Muwafaqa is Compatibility. Imam al-Ghazali says that Muwafaqa is the prior condition of the Path of Love. In other words, you have to be compatible with it. It suits you. This is part of the secret of the Khatam, of the Destiny. The Destiny is a hidden thing, but at the same time it of course manifests through events – the event of the person and the event of the action. Allah says in Surat as-Saffat (37:96):

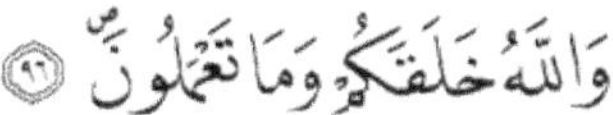

Allah is the Creator of you and your actions.

So it is a secret of the Destiny which is hidden even in the genetic pattern of the individual. For example, Sayyiduna Yusuf, 'alayhi salam, and his brothers are from the same father, and yet they are not the same. There is something in Yusuf which makes him beloved by Allah, subhanahu wa ta'ala.

The sign of Muwafaqa on the person, according to Imam al-Ghazali, is that they love with the Love of Allah, and they hate with the Hatred of Allah. This is the command of Rasul, sallallahu 'alayhi wa sallam, who said, "O Allah! With those You hate I have put an enmity between them and I." So you love what Allah loves and you hate what Allah hates. This means that already you have this Compatibility, because in this very first stage you are ready for the encounter with Allah, subhanahu wa ta'ala, with illumination, with entering into states and establishing yourself in Stations by your knowledge of Allah, subhanahu wa ta'ala – because you are established in being compatible. You love what He loves, and you hate what He hates.

These are the beginning terms which will allow us to look at the Ten Stages of Love: Mahabba, which transforms into 'Ishq in its extreme ardent love, and underlying it is Muwafaqa – Compatibility. Inshallah, with these as our guide-posts we will look at these subjects further.

II

JULY 28TH 2007

THE SEVEN ASPECTS OF ALLAH'S LOVE FOR THE MUSLIMS

I said that we were going to look at the meanings of Mahabba, of Love, inside this terminology of Tasawwuf. It is very important that you understand that the things we are going to look at, which are very exalted and have very fine and subtle meanings, are absolutely grounded in the Qur'an and in fundamental Islamic thinking. Before we actually approach this specific terminology, we are going to look at how love is spoken of by Allah, subhanahu wa ta'ala, in the Qur'an.

The first thing we find out is that love is Maqam Ilahi – it is a Divine Station. Let us look at Surat al-Ma'ida (5:54):

يَـٰٓأَيُّهَا ٱلَّذِينَ ءَامَنُوا۟ مَن يَرْتَدِدْ مِنكُمْ عَن دِينِهِۦ
فَسَوْفَ يَاتِي ٱللَّهُ بِقَوْمٍ يُحِبُّهُمْ وَيُحِبُّونَهُۥٓ أَذِلَّةٍ عَلَى ٱلْمُؤْمِنِينَ
أَعِزَّةٍ عَلَى ٱلْكَـٰفِرِينَ يُجَـٰهِدُونَ فِي سَبِيلِ ٱللَّهِ وَلَا يَخَافُونَ لَوْمَةَ لَآئِمٍ

You who have Iman!
If any of you renounce your Deen,
Allah will bring forward a people
whom He loves and who love Him,
humble to the Muminun,
fierce to the kafirun,
who strive in the Way of Allah
and do not fear the blame of any censurer.

This is what we call the Divine Contract. This love is both a Divine Station and it is a Divine Contract. This is something that is laid out for all the human creatures in creation to respond to or to negate. Let us look at the famous Ayat in Surat adh-Dhariyat (51:56):

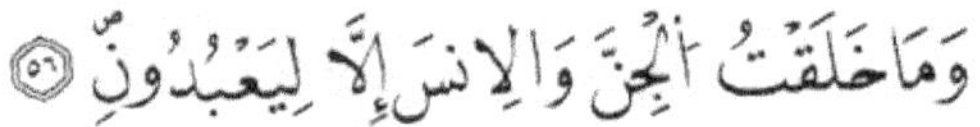

I only created jinn and man to worship Me.

The Arabic term here is 'liya'budun' from the root verb 'Abada, which means 'worship', although the translation is never exact. 'Abud is a very interesting term because it is of the nature of slavehood. "I only created jinn and man to make this 'Abud of Me." The slaveness is what they are for. In a sense it could be said, "I have created jinn and man to be slaves for Me." This slaveness is worship of Allah. It is not just Salat but the whole process of adoring Allah and obeying Allah. Imam al-Ghazali was asked, "Why is it seven Tawaf? Why is it forty nine stones for the stoning of the shaytan?" He replied, "There is no 'Why?'" That is the 'Ubudiyya. That is the slavehood. You have been told to do it, so you do it! The wisdom is in your doing it, because you have been told to do it.

The human creature was created for the process of adoration of Allah. At the heart of adoration and the fulfilment of adoration is what love itself is. Love is not poetry. Love is submerging yourself in the Beloved. This is what mankind is created for. The human being is created for this adoration and obedience to Allah, subhanahu wa ta'ala. If he does not do it, it is because he is sick or he is in loss. Allah, subhanahu wa ta'ala, says in Surat al-Asr (103:2):

Man is in loss.

What is the loss of man? It is like when you cut off the electric power – man has got cut off from the current of what life is, so that he becomes a disturbed creature because he is not doing what he was made for.

If you have a race-horse and you do not race it, it becomes a sick, heavy, fat animal, but if you race it then it is a race-horse. Equally, man is made for this worship and if he does not do it he is in loss, he is in this Khusr. Then we find that this position of man links him with the whole of creation. Let us look at Surat al-Isra' (17:44). Here we find out that this worship is a cosmic event. Allah says:

يُسَبِّحُ لَهُ السَّمَٰوَٰتُ السَّبْعُ وَالْأَرْضُ وَمَن فِيهِنَّ
وَإِن مِّن شَيْءٍ إِلَّا يُسَبِّحُ بِحَمْدِهِ وَلَٰكِن لَّا تَفْقَهُونَ تَسْبِيحَهُمْ
إِنَّهُ كَانَ حَلِيمًا غَفُورًا ﴿٤٤﴾

The seven heavens and the earth
and everyone in them glorify Him.
There is nothing which does not glorify Him with praise
but you do not understand their glorification.
He is All-Forbearing, Ever-Forgiving.

This is a blessed Ayat. What it means is that now we are finding out that this thing for which man was created puts him into a process which is completely cosmic because the heavens and earth, and everyone in them – everything is making this glorification, this adoration of Allah, subhanahu wa ta'ala. Thus the fundamental nature of this Love is an actual cosmic, dynamic force that Allah has put into the creation to glorify Him. For further confirmation of this we will look at Surat an-Nur: (24:40):

أَلَمْ تَرَ أَنَّ اللَّهَ يُسَبِّحُ لَهُ مَن فِي السَّمَٰوَٰتِ وَالْأَرْضِ
وَالطَّيْرُ صَٰٓفَّٰتٍ كُلٌّ قَدْ عَلِمَ صَلَاتَهُ وَتَسْبِيحَهُ
وَاللَّهُ عَلِيمٌ بِمَا يَفْعَلُونَ ﴿٤١﴾

Do you not see that everyone
in the heavens and earth glorifies Allah,
as do the birds with their outspread wings?

Each one knows its prayer and glorification.
Allah knows what they do.

This means that everything is glorifying Allah. We know that the Rasul, sallallahu 'alayhi wa sallam, in certain Ruhani states addressed inanimate objects, am I not correct? He spoke to the stones, so he understood that even the stones were glorifying Allah when he addressed them. Everything is glorifying Allah, "As do the birds with their outspread wings." If the bird is glorifying Allah by outspread wings in its supreme act which is flying, the human creature, as we shall find out, is glorifying Allah by those actions which are pleasing to Allah, subhanahu wa ta'ala.

For the final completion of this we go to Surat al-Hajj (22:18). Here we find a wonderful Ayat. We shall omit the last part of the Ayat because it is not in reference to what we are looking at.

أَلَمْ تَرَ أَنَّ ٱللَّهَ يَسْجُدُ لَهُۥ
مَن فِى ٱلسَّمَٰوَٰتِ وَمَن فِى ٱلْأَرْضِ وَٱلشَّمْسُ وَٱلْقَمَرُ
وَٱلنُّجُومُ وَٱلْجِبَالُ وَٱلشَّجَرُ وَٱلدَّوَآبُّ وَكَثِيرٌ مِّنَ ٱلنَّاسِ

Do you not see that everyone in the heavens
and everyone on the earth
prostrates to Allah,
and the sun and moon and stars
and the mountains, trees and beasts
and many of mankind?

Here we get the first indication that with the human beings there is a different reality, and we find this in the last phrase:

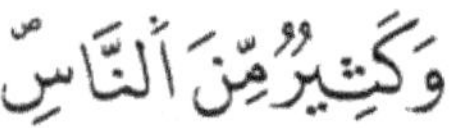

Many of mankind.

Allah has made the nature of the human creature such that he can take this path or take this other path. If he did not have that possibility, the one who does take the right path would not be able to fulfil his action of submitting, when in fact he could 'not submit'. This is the glory of the human condition, and also the terror of the human condition.

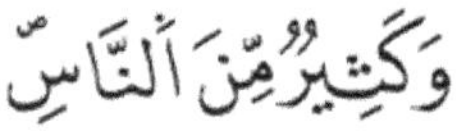

Many of mankind.

That is the Muslims.

We have been looking at this Divine Contract which Allah has made with the whole of creation, and in particular with mankind. To complete this we look at Surat an-Nahl (16:48-50):

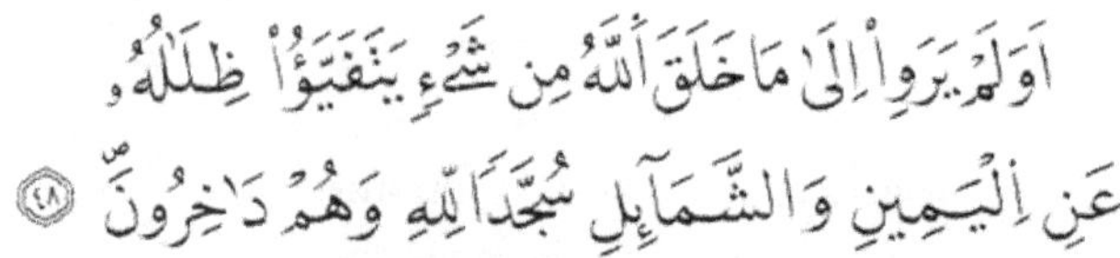

II

وَلِلَّهِ يَسْجُدُ مَا فِي السَّمَاوَاتِ وَمَا فِي الْأَرْضِ مِن دَابَّةٍ وَالْمَلَائِكَةُ
وَهُمْ لَا يَسْتَكْبِرُونَ ﴿٤٩﴾ يَخَافُونَ رَبَّهُم مِّن فَوْقِهِمْ
وَيَفْعَلُونَ مَا يُؤْمَرُونَ ۩ ﴿٥٠﴾

Do they not see the things Allah has created,
casting their shadows to the right and to the left,
prostrating themselves before Allah
in complete humility?

Everything in the heavens
and every creature on the earth
prostrates to Allah, as do the Angels.
They are not puffed up with pride.

They fear their Lord above them
and do everything they are ordered to do.

Here we have another dimension. We find out that in the fulfilling of this contract, there is fear of Allah and obedience to Allah – doing everything we are ordered to do. This is that element which is the delight of Allah and the completion of the Contract.

Now we shall look at seven elements of this love. We are now looking at this Contract in relation to man. We find that the Divine Contract links to the Prophetic Contract which Allah, subhanahu wa ta'ala, has with His Messenger. That Prophetic Contract links to the Muslims' Contract because the Muslims' Contract goes to Rasul, sallallahu 'alayhi wa sallam. His contract with Allah, which is on a much higher level, illuminates and guides the Muslims to fulfil theirs.

The first aspect of Love is love of the Prophet. It is about Allah's love of Rasul, sallallahu 'alayhi wa sallam, and the Muslims' love of him from below to his highest of stations. So we look at Surat Al 'Imran (4:31-32). This is the link between Allah, subhanahu wa ta'ala, and the Rasul, sallallahu 'alayhi wa sallam – 'link' in terms of course – because nothing is associated with Allah – in terms of this wisdom unfolding itself, and the guidance to the Muslim, how he too can have this highest possible state of love with Allah, subhanahu wa ta'ala.

قُلْ إِن كُنتُمْ تُحِبُّونَ ٱللَّهَ فَٱتَّبِعُونِى
يُحْبِبْكُمُ ٱللَّهُ وَيَغْفِرْ لَكُمْ ذُنُوبَكُمْ ۗ وَٱللَّهُ غَفُورٌ رَّحِيمٌ ﴿٣١﴾ قُلْ أَطِيعُوا۟
ٱللَّهَ وَٱلرَّسُولَ ۖ فَإِن تَوَلَّوْا۟ فَإِنَّ ٱللَّهَ لَا يُحِبُّ ٱلْكَٰفِرِينَ ﴿٣٢﴾

Say, "If you love Allah, then follow me
and Allah will love you and forgive you
for your wrong actions.
Allah is Ever-Forgiving, Most Merciful."

Say, "Obey Allah and the Messenger."
Then if they turn away,
Allah does not love the kafirun.

Here you see the linkage, here you see the Path that is the Sirat al-Mustaqim laid out, and it is the path of love. Allah commands the Messenger to tell the Muminun how they can go on this exalted Path of love. Allah, subhanahu wa ta'ala, is saying to Rasul, sallallahu 'alayhi wa sallam, "Tell them: 'If you LOVE Allah, then follow me.'" This is the message you are delivering. This is what the Revelation is. This is what the event of Qur'an is.

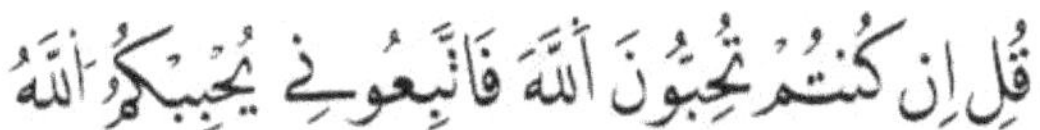

Say, "If you love Allah, then follow me
and Allah will love you," [...]

And now you get the linkage:

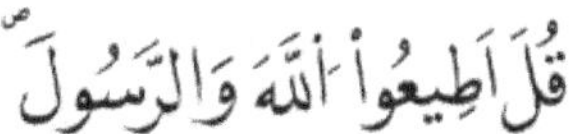

Say, "Obey Allah and the Messenger."

So the key is put into our hands: from Allah, the Message to Rasul, and from Rasul the Message to the Muslims is that for this love, the key is "Obey Allah and the Messenger." There is tremendous wisdom is these two Ayats, and tremendous secrets in these two Ayats.

Now we are given a secret of this connection between Rasul, sallallahu 'alayhi wa sallam, and the Muslims. We go to Surat al-Insan (76:29-30). This goes back to what I have just been saying. What we find is that Allah has given us this

Message, but you might also say that this is part of the warning:

This truly is a Reminder,
so whoever wills
should take the Way towards his Lord.

But you will not will unless Allah wills.
Allah is All-Knowing, All-Wise.

"Whoever wills should take the Way towards his Lord." Allah then gives the secret openly in the Qur'an: "But you will not will unless Allah wills." It will not happen unless you will it, but you will not will it unless He has willed that you will it. This is the great golden door that invites you into the knowledge of Tasawwuf. The second song of Shaykh Ibn al-'Arabi in his Diwan is a meditation on this matter. You have to will it, but the moment you will it, it is because He willed that you will it.

So an obedience to Allah is like you click into harmony with the birds and the beasts and the mountains and the stars because they have all submitted to be that which they are. You are not what you are until you submit and then your fullness is realised. When you will it, there is the knowledge that goes with that, which is that He willed you to be the one who would will it. This is why it is called "the Way towards his Lord."

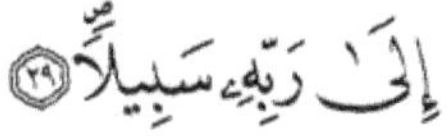

Now we turn to Surat at-Takwir. These are astonishing Ayats. You must realise how tremendous the Qur'an is. The most awesome thing about the Qur'an is not its beauty and it is not that it happened at all, but given that it is beautiful and that it happened, what is amazing about the Qur'an is that Allah speaks many, many secrets of existence, openly, that were not known or understood until they were given to Rasul, sallallahu 'alayhi wa sallam, to tell to the Muslims. Again, here we find this lifting of veils that had covered mankind way back from the time of the last Prophet before him. Allah, subhanahu wa ta'ala, says in Surat at-Takwir (81:26-29):

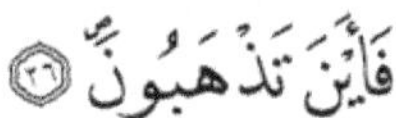

So where, then, are you going?

This is what nowadays you would term an existential question.

إِنْ هُوَ إِلَّا ذِكْرٌ لِّلْعَالَمِينَ ﴿٢٧﴾ لِمَن شَاءَ مِنكُمْ أَن يَسْتَقِيمَ ﴿٢٨﴾

It is nothing but a Reminder to all the worlds,
to whomever among you wishes to go straight.

Not everybody wants to go straight. Some people get hit back into being straight. Some people reject it and will never go straight –

وَمَا تَشَآءُونَ إِلَّآ أَن يَشَآءَ ٱللَّهُ رَبُّ ٱلْعَٰلَمِينَ ﴿٢٩﴾

But you will not will unless Allah wills,
the Lord of all the Worlds.

This is the absolute core of the Qur'an, this is absolutely the heart of the matter. This is why when you turn on the television they talk about 'Islamic this' and 'Islamic that', but it has nothing to do with Islam! THIS is the Divine Contract, and this is Allah's address to the human creatures. "So where, then, are you going? It is nothing but a Reminder to all the worlds, to whomever among you wishes to go straight." Remember that the Divine Contract from Allah to the Rasul, sallallahu 'alayhi wa sallam, is that he just deliver the Message – finished! That is all he has to do. Allah tells him that all he has to do is deliver the Message, is that not correct?

"It is nothing but a Reminder to all the worlds, to whomever among you wishes to go straight." The Sufis call this the Ayat of Tariqa. This is the Ayat that clicks in the heart of the Muslim who says, "I want to be one of the people of this Sirat al-Mustaqim." So the first step on the Tariqa is that your wanting it is because Allah wants it.

All that completes this picture of the relationship of love of the Prophet, linking the Divine Contract to the Prophetic Contract to the Muslims' Contract. The second and third aspects of love, after the love of the Prophet, are for the Tawwabun – the repentant, and the Mutatahhirun – the ones who purify themselves. So we look for these two qualities, the ones of repentance and the ones of purification, in Surat al-Baqara (2:222). The Ayat in its main part is about menstruation and purification, but then Allah takes it to another level and says:

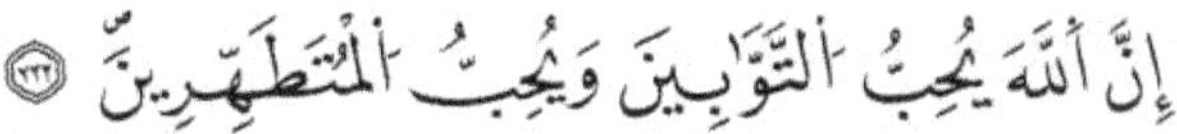

Allah loves those who turn back from wrongdoing
and He loves those who purify themselves.

Again, we have two aspects of this love in this Contract from Allah to the creatures. Allah loves those who make Tawba from their wrong actions and Allah loves those who purify themselves.

The fourth aspect of this love of Allah is for the Sabirun – the patient. We find this in Surat Sâd (38), at the end of Ayat 43:

We found him steadfast.
What an excellent slave!
He truly turned to his Lord.

We find Allah's delight with the Sabirun, the people of patience. Hajj 'Abdalhaqq likes to translate Sabirun as 'steadfast', although I prefer 'patient' – but of course the nature of the patient ones is that they hold on, and in that sense he is correct. "We found him steadfast" – we found him patient, we found him holding on. "What an excellent slave! He truly turned to his Lord." So here is the one whom Allah loves. The one who held on, who was patient, and who turned to his Lord.

The fifth aspect of love that Allah has for His creatures is revealed in Surat Ibrahim (14:7):

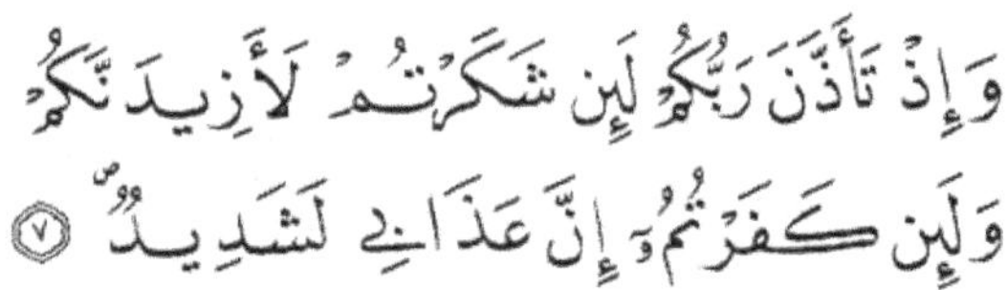

And when your Lord announced:
"If you are grateful, I will certainly give you increase,
but if you are ungrateful, My punishment is severe."

Here we have that Allah loves the people of gratefulness and thanks, the Shakirun. Here Allah has indicated that the reward for this gratefulness is increase, and increase is the gift of the Beloved to the Lover.

The Sixth aspect of Allah's love is for the people of Ihsan – the Muhsinun. We will look in Surat al-Baqara (2:195):

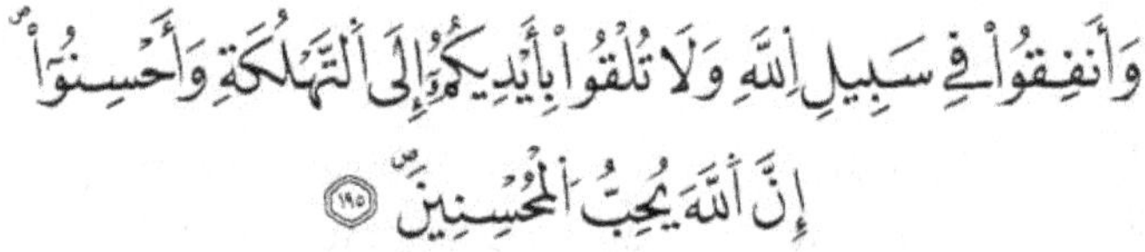

Spend in the Way of Allah.
Do not cast yourselves into destruction.
And do good: Allah loves good-doers.

So Allah loves the good-doers, the Muhsinun. It is interesting that the translator has translated it as "people who do good," but let us look at this Muhsin. He is the one of Ihsan. In the first Hadith from the collection of Imam Muslim, the Angel Jibril questions the Rasul, sallallahu 'alayhi wa sallam, about his Deen and says: "What is Islam?" "What is Iman?" Then he says: "What is Ihsan?" and the answer of Rasul, sallallahu 'alayhi wa sallam, which you all know, is: "To worship Allah as if you saw Him, and while you do not see Him, know that He sees you." So Ihsan is a knowledge that Allah sees you.

This opens a door into the Suluk of Tasawwuf, it opens a door through the Wird As-Sahl. The Wird As-Sahl is derived from the Qur'an:

الله معي الله ناظر إلي الله شاهد علي

Allah is with me, Allah sees me,
Allah is the Witness of my acts.

So the one of Ihsan is the one who most importantly knows that Allah sees him. Knowing that he is seen by Allah turns the subject into the object, and that is the real middle of the Path for the Sufi. He is not the observer, but the observed. This was the Wird that was given to Sahl at-Tustari which gave him the fatiha for his Fana'. Allah witnesses you. This is the Muhsin.

The seventh and final aspect of this is in Surat as-Saff (61:4). This is very interesting because it is the last of the group of people whom Allah loves:

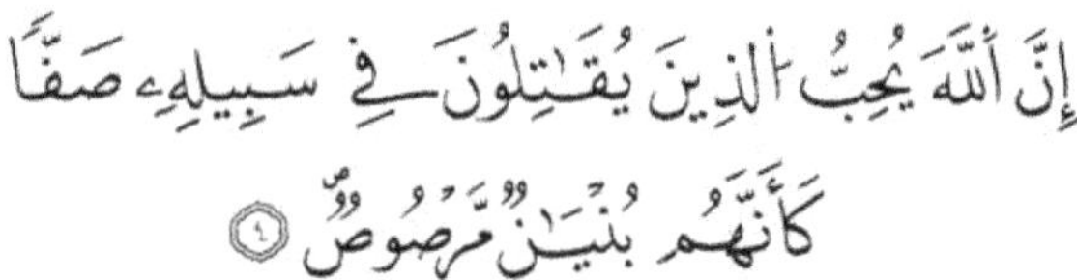

Allah loves those who fight in His Way in ranks
like well-built walls.

We should take note of this, because today there are many people doing things which we know are against the Shari'at yet they are held up as "Shahids who are dying in the Way of Allah." They cannot be such, because they have not fulfilled what Allah has told them in the Qur'an. "Allah loves those who fight" – this Arabic word for fight is from the verb 'Qatala', which is not some poetic thing like the modernists who want to make everything to do with Jihad a psychological thing – Qatala is to cut, it is to fight.

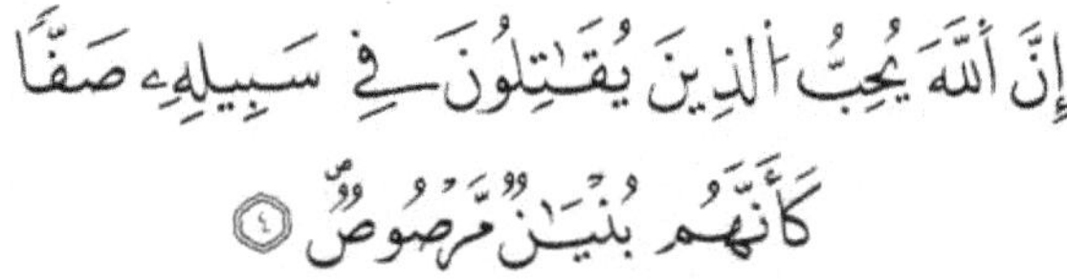

Allah loves those who fight in His Way in ranks
like well-built walls.

So Allah loves those who fight in His Sabil, in His Way. You will find in other Ayats "Jihad fisabilillah" – Jihad in the Way of Allah. But He tells us here that it is in 'ranks'. What does that mean? It means it is an army. It is not a man tying dynamite to his belly and going out in the dark and committing suicide. It is men who take their strength from the ones on either side of them. They are "like well-built walls," and a well-built wall is made of stones which take their strength from the stones on either side. THIS is fighting in the Way of Allah, and for the cause of Allah – not to defeat a nation, not to recover territory, but in the Way of Allah, and the Way of Allah is to establish the Deen.

You cannot establish the Deen unless you are taking it with you. This is the Deen. The one who fights this Way is bringing the Deen. When the forces of Sayyiduna 'Umar ibn al-Khattab, radiyallahu 'anhu, spread through this enormous area in his life-time, this is how he did it, with men fighting in ranks. When they entered the place, you then saw this power of the Amir and the power of the Muslims. So wherever they went people accepted Islam. They did not accept it because of some 'Alim coming with rational explanations about what good sense it all made, they accepted it because these men were superior to them, they were dynamic, they came with life, they came with law, they came with worship, they came with medicine, they came with science – they came with the whole science. And they fought like that too because they fought scientifically.

Jihad fisabilillah has rules, and one of the first rules which these ignorant people do not even know, is that the Sahaba were forbidden to fight if they were outnumbered by more than two to one. So how could they declare war on the United States of America, as if that were a valid thing for Muslims to do? They are completely overwhelmed and outnumbered! The Sahaba used to say, "Oh, we have nostalgia for the time of Badr, when we were grossly outnumbered! The order came down that we were not to fight if we are outnumbered more than two to one, and so we do not fight like that anymore." These ignorant modern people do not know these things because they do not know the Deen. If they had victory, who would take the victory? The one who would say, "Well, I got my son to blow himself up so now I am in charge!"? Whereas if it had been a victory fisabilillah, the man would say, "My father fought and died fisabilillah, and now I want to establish the Deen, and this is how I will do it."

This is the final aspect of the seven aspects of Allah's love for the Muslims. Inshallah, at our next gathering we will begin on the teachings of Shaykh Nasirud-Din, the Chiraghi of Delhi.

III

August 4th 2007

The Four Principal Categories of Love

We are now taking another step in our examination of the subject of Divine Love, the love of the Divine. We are going deeper in, and we are going to look at four categories of Love. Of these four categories, the Ahwal – the spiritual states of each are not shared by the others. Each has its own distinct imprint on the self of the Faqir.

The first of the four categories has two aspects. This first category is called Al-Hawa. Al-Hawa is the sudden passion of love, or the falling in love. The first meaning of this is what comes into the heart from the Ghayb, from the Hidden, and bursts into the Shahada, onto the outward appearance. For this we look to Qur'an, and we shall look at Surat an-Najm (53:1):

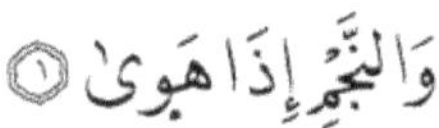

By the star when it descends

We find that 'descends' is this term itself – Hawa. The verb is Ha-wi-ya, the future is Ya-h-wa, the noun is Ha-wa and Hawa means 'to fall in love'. From the same root comes the noun Huwiy which means 'to fall'. What we are saying is that this love is something that falls into the heart.

This falling into the heart is by one or more of three events. The first event is Nadhar, which is the glance. Thus the first thing that will make this plunge into the heart and cause this havoc is the glance. The glance is the thing that awakens the Faqir to this yearning and love of Allah, subhanahu wa ta'ala. This involves the subtlest and finest aspects of transmission in Tasawwuf, between the Shaykh and the serious Murid, and between the seeker and Wilayat. It is by the encounter with the Wali of Allah – and he may not know he is a Wali of Allah, but by his glance the seeker will be affected.

The second event is Sama' which as you know means 'hearing'. The Faqir hears news of the Beloved in the Diwan of the Shaykh. He hears news of the Beloved in these great, sublime writings of the people of Tasawwuf, or by hearing it in the way that the recitation of Qur'an affects his heart and the click happens, and there falls into his heart this awakening of love.

The third event which makes this falling into the heart is

Ihsan. That is when the seeker encounters noble action, encounters someone acting with nobility, with excellence which touches the heart and awakens the heart. Remember, the definition of Ihsan is in the famous Hadith which opens the collection of Imam Muslim, where Rasul, sallallahu 'alayhi wa sallam, was questioned by the Angel Jibril: "What is Islam?" "What is Iman?" "What is Ihsan?" The answer to "What is Ihsan?" was: "To worship Allah as if you saw Him, and while you do not see Him, know that He sees you." This knowledge is the essence of this quality of Ihsan. So it is in the encounter with the one who embodies this Ihsan. It could be a noble outward action but it tends to be this Ihsan which awakens love, it is the encounter with someone who embodies this conscious awareness that they are being watched by Allah, subhanahu wa ta'ala.

Now it becomes very profound so we must concentrate. The second aspect of Al-Hawa is that the passion must conform to the revealed Shari'at. For this we go to Surat Sâd 38, and the first half of Ayat 26:

يَٰدَاوُۥدُ إِنَّا جَعَلْنَٰكَ خَلِيفَةً فِى ٱلْأَرْضِ فَٱحْكُم بَيْنَ ٱلنَّاسِ بِٱلْحَقِّ
وَلَا تَتَّبِعِ ٱلْهَوَىٰ فَيُضِلَّكَ عَن سَبِيلِ ٱللَّهِ

"Dawud! We have made you a Khalif on the earth,
so judge between people with truth
and do not follow your own desires,
letting them misguide you from the Way of Allah."

"Dawud! We have made you a Khalif on the earth, so judge

between people with truth" – with truth is 'bil-haqq' – "and do not follow your own desires," – here we have the term Hawa. "Do not follow your own desires, letting them misguide you from the Way of Allah." Now concentrate, as this is very important. We can say, by Ishara, that this Ayat is saying: "Do not follow the movement of your love, but be the object of My, subhanahu wa ta'ala, love, for this is the rule I have laid down." Do you follow? Do you see what this means? If the impulse of the love comes from your consciousness, it can go astray. Look at the Ayat again:

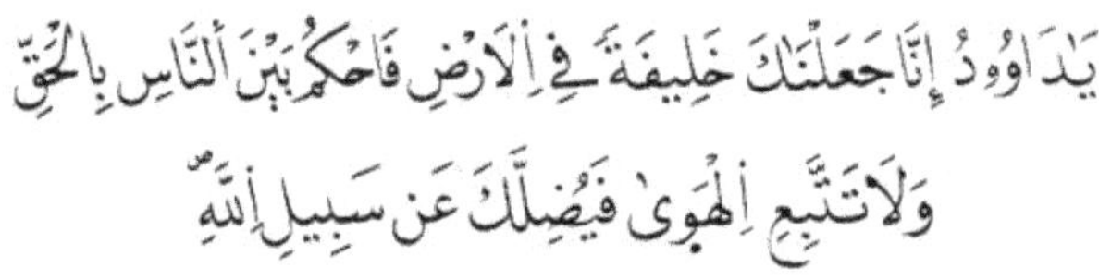

So we oppose bil-haqq to "Do not be led away from the Sabil of Allah."

Now we come to the second of the four principle categories which is Al-Hubb. You could take Al-Hubb to mean Purified Love. When the turbulence of love, for all its attachments is purified, and the sediments – which are those things which are attached to Ma-siwallah, other than Allah – fall to the bottom of the glass, then the liquid is pure. The famous sentence of Imam al-Junayd, speaking of Ma'rifa, was: "The clarity of the Wine of Ma'rifa is the clarity of the glass." As it was clear, that was the Ma'rifa. For this we go to the Diwan of Shaykh Muhammad ibn al-Habib, rahimahullah, and his Qasida 'The Manifestation of the Essence.' We shall look at the opening lines of it:

III

أَشَمْسٌ بَدا مِنْ عالَمِ الغَيْبِ ضَوْؤُها
أَمِ انْكَشَفَتْ عَنْ ذاتِ لَيْلَى سُتُورُها

نَعَمْ تِلْكَ لَيْلَى قَـدْ أَباحَتْ بِحُبِّها
لِخِـلٍّ لَهـا لَمَّا تَزايَـدَ شَوْقُها

فَأَضْحَى أَسِيراً فِي مُـرادِ غَرامِها
وَنادَتْ لَهُ الأَشْواقُ هَذِي كُؤُوسُها

فَما بَرِحَـتْ حَتَّى سَقَتْهُ بِكَأْسِها
فَلا لَوْمَ فَاشْرَبْ فَالشَّرابُ حَدِيثُها

وَما هِـيَ إِلاَّ حَضْرَةُ الحَقِّ وَحْدَها
تَجَلَّـتْ بِأَشْكـالِ تَلَـوَّنَ نُورُها

Has the light of the sun appeared
from the world of the Unseen,
or have the veils of Layla been lifted from Her Essence?

Yes, the longing of Layla for Her beloved friend
has grown until She revealed Her love.

So that he has become a captive of Her ardent desire
and the longings which are Her goblets called out to him.

She did not leave until She had given him

a drink from Her goblet. There is no blame. Drink –
for the wine is Her speech.

And She is none but the Presence of the Truth, alone,
Who manifests Herself with forms whose every light is
different.

Now we will look also to Shaykh al-Fayturi, rahimahullah,
and the Fifth Qasida in his Diwan. He says:

أُتْرُكْ يَـا مُرِيدْ نَفْسَكْ ما تُرِيدْ

إِن رُمْتَ المَزِيدْ مِنْ أَسْرَارِ اللهْ

أُدْخُلِ الطَّرِيقْ وَالــزَمِ الرَّفِيقْ

يُسْقِيكَ العَتِيقْ مِــنْ خَمْرَةِ اللهْ

يُعْطِيكَ الحَبِيبْ سِرَّهُ العَجِيبْ

هِمْ بِـــهِ وَغِبْ فِي أَنْوَارِ اللهْ

ذَابَتِ الأَشْبَاحْ لَمَّا حِبِّي بَــاحْ

بِإِسْمِ الفَتَـــاحْ (لِمُرِيدِ اللهْ)

دَارَتِ الأَقْدَاحْ (بَيْنَنَا يَا صَاحْ)

فَاحَ السِّرُّ فَاحْ مِنْ مِشْكَاةِ اللهْ

أَدْنَ لَدُنِ الرَّاحْ شُرْبُهُ مُبَاحْ

بِـــهِ حَقًّا تَرْتَاحْ تَرَى وَجْهُ اللهْ

III

O Murid! Abandon your self and what it wants
if you desire increase from the secrets of Allah!

Enter the Path and cling to the friend.
He will give you an ancient vintage
of the wine of Allah to drink.

The Beloved will give you His wondrous secret.
Thirst with love for Him,
and withdraw into the lights of Allah.

The forms melted away when my Beloved divulged the
name of opening for the one who desires Allah.

The cups went round among us, O friend,
the secret diffused a fragrant scent from the niche of Allah.

Draw near to the wine-jug of joy. Its drink is permitted!
Truly, you will be pleased with it –
you will see the Face of Allah!

Now you are beginning to sec that in the Diwans, the Shaykhs are using a language which is common to them. Both Shaykh Muhammad ibn al-Habib and Shaykh al-Fayturi, rahimahumallah, use these terms, but one must understand that they have a shifting meaning, they are not fixed. In the first Qasida Shaykh Muhammad ibn al-Habib refers to the famous story of Layla and Majnun which is THE most common and most known and used – not metaphor, but imaging of this affair of love between Layla and Majnun.

Layla also means 'night' and Majnun means 'mad', so this indicates one who is completely intoxicated with love, mad with love. Layla – the use of the 'she', the feminine in grammatical usage is because it is used for the Essence of Allah, subhanahu wa ta'ala. So when they refer to Layla, they are referring to the Dhat of Allah, subhanahu wa ta'ala. This particular reference is to the Essence of Allah, and the impact of the Essence unveiling itself, of Layla unveiling Herself, is what obliterates Majnun and destroys him. This is the language of Tasawwuf, of Fana' fillah.

At the same time there is this offering of the drink, and you will see the imagery of the cup, or the goblet, and the wine, and the merging of these two. The poems begin to cross these pictures in your mind in order to take you to a further bewilderment in your own spiritual condition.

Thus, all this that we have just seen in these two Diwans is about the purification of love, of love becoming Hubb – losing all its connection with Ghayr. We are finding in the Qur'an a clear indication of this differential between the one who has tasted this wine, and those who have not. We look at Surat al-Baqara, and the first part of Ayat 165.

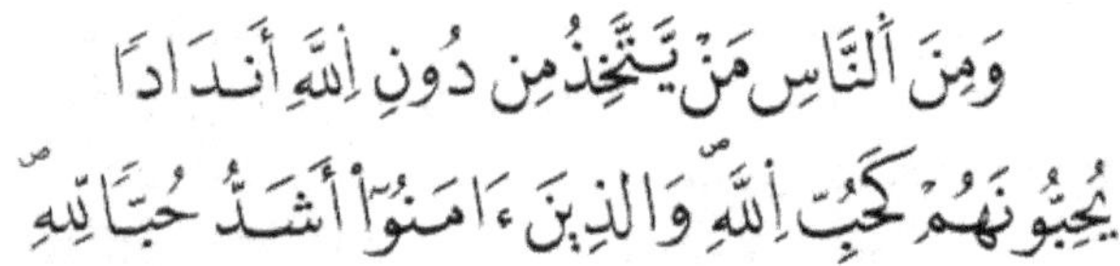

Some people set up equals to Allah,
loving them as they should love Allah.
But those who have Iman have greater love for Allah.

"Some people set up equals to Allah, loving them as they should love Allah." In other words, they love what is in this world, they love what is Ghayr. "But those who have Iman have greater love for Allah." These are the ones who drink the wine.

وَالَّذِينَ ءَامَنُوٓاْ أَشَدُّ حُبًّا لِّلَّهِ

This is very important. We see a distinction between the people who set up equals to Allah, loving them as they should love Allah, and those who have Iman and thus have greater love for Allah. Now keep that place in the Qur'an while we go to Surat Al 'Imran (3:10):

إِنَّ الَّذِينَ كَفَرُوا لَن تُغْنِىَ عَنْهُمْ
أَمْوَٰلُهُمْ وَلَآ أَوْلَٰدُهُم مِّنَ اللَّهِ شَيْـًٔا

As for those who are kafir, their wealth and children
will not help them against Allah in any way.

This is a devastating statement. The ones who are kafir are those who do not worship Allah and who do not obey Allah, yet what they do have is love for their wealth and for their children. But Allah says that is no use. Now go back to Surat al-Baqara (2:165):

وَالَّذِينَ ءَامَنُوٓاْ أَشَدُّ حُبًّا لِّلَّهِ

But those who have Iman have greater love for Allah.

Their love for Allah dominates whatever love they have in this world, in the Dunya. This balance has to be achieved in order that you can get any value and meaning out of life. You HAVE to change the balance. You have to fix in yourselves that this love for Allah dominates all the aspects of Dunya.

The third category is Al-'Ishq, which is Excessive Love. This we will, inshallah, look at in enormous detail but we will break it down very scientifically so that you can understand it. It is passion. We have to be like the doctor who examines it clinically and who understands it without any turbulence in the examination. We must look at it and understand it very well. This will be the next stage of our examination.

The fourth aspect of love, the completion of our four-part definition, is Al-Wadd, which is Loyalty in Love. It is fixed, it is the fixity of love. It does not wobble or shake. It is what we call 'constancy' – Thabat al-Hubb. This is very important because here, in the Qur'an, is the importance of Al-Wadd, of this fixity of love. It is explained in these Ayats, setting the Lovers apart from the other slaves of Allah, subhanahu wa ta'ala. Look at Surat Maryam (19:93-96):

إِن كُلُّ مَن فِي ٱلسَّمَٰوَٰتِ وَٱلْأَرْضِ
إِلَّآ ءَاتِي ٱلرَّحْمَٰنِ عَبْدًا ﴿٩٣﴾ لَّقَدْ أَحْصَىٰهُمْ وَعَدَّهُمْ عَدًّا ﴿٩٤﴾
وَكُلُّهُمْ ءَاتِيهِ يَوْمَ ٱلْقِيَٰمَةِ فَرْدًا ﴿٩٥﴾
إِنَّ ٱلَّذِينَ ءَامَنُوا۟ وَعَمِلُوا۟ ٱلصَّٰلِحَٰتِ سَيَجْعَلُ لَهُمُ ٱلرَّحْمَٰنُ وُدًّا ﴿٩٦﴾

There is no one in the heavens and earth
who will not come to the All-Merciful as a slave.
He has counted them and numbered them precisely.
Each of them will come to Him on the Day of Rising
all alone.
As for those who have Iman and do right actions,
the All-Merciful will bestow His love on them.

"As for those who have Iman and do right actions, the All-Merciful will bestow His love on them." So you see that on the Last Day, Allah puts in a different category the Lovers of Allah, subhanahu wa ta'ala. This is the pre-determined and desired state of the Fuqara.

IV

AUGUST 11TH 2007

THE FOUR CONDITIONS OF THE LOVER

We are continuing with what we have been studying over the last few weeks. We are now going to come to the Four Conditions of the Lover. The Tajalliyat al-Haqq to the Gnostic Lovers is what the Sufis call Manassat al-A'ras – In the bridal chamber of the Lovers. The Tajalliyat confer on the Lover the Attributes of Love, and they are four.

The First Condition of the Lover is Maqtul – To be Slain. It is from the Wedding Throne of this Tajalli that the Lover is invested with this condition of being the slaughtered creature, given that he is composed of a natural sub-structure, Tabi'a, and a spirit – he consists of a material substance and a Ruhani reality.

It was said by one of the poets, "The spirit is light, nature is dark. Now, these are an antimony in the creature." There is a contradiction in the human creature between these two aspects. Two realities oppose and exclude each other and each claims a unique status. Thus to claim Shari'at without Haqiqat, or Haqiqat without Shari'at is to remain a dualist. The Lover does not escape this rule.

If the natural aspect dominates, his condition – Haykal, is darkened so that he loves Allah through the creatures, so that the light progressively penetrates the darkness. We shall look to the Qur'an and at Surat YaSin (36:37-38):

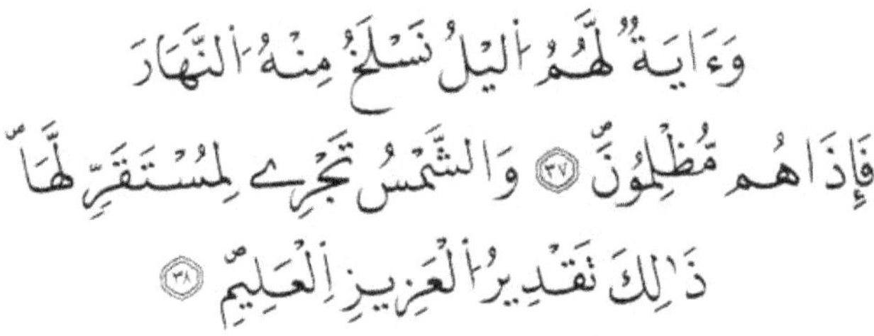

A Sign for them is the night:
We peel the day away from it
and there they are in darkness.
And the sun runs to its resting place.
That is the decree of the Almighty, the All-Knowing.

The day in this Ayat represents the light, so that on the horizon is the metaphor for what is taking place inside the self. This is to love Allah for the favours He gives you – these coming like provisions at the hand of others. There is a love that is a love for the creatures, for the created beings, but it is because you love the One who provides for you. In that loving, the Giver is Allah, subhanahu wa ta'ala. The Provider is Allah, but the ordinary person loves the creature who is the giving one. So this is, as it were, the first condition of love which is mixed. But, if the natural dominates the creature then there is conflict which leads to death. If the Ruhani dominates the creature then he would die Shahid, alive in Allah.

Thus, in the person and their journey through life there is a dominance of Ruhani energies, or there is a dominance of darkness from his animal nature. The Lover is slaughtered in the world, even if he is not aware of it. If he does not die one way he will die the other, but it is the process of love that will bring about this end. Now we come to the second condition.

The Second Condition of the Lover is Talif – To be Mentally Thrown Off Course, to be confused. Allah has created the Lover by His two Names, Adh-Dhahir and Al-Batin. As we have said, there are these two aspects in man, of a physical nature and of a Ruhani nature. So Allah has created the Lover to form a creature that is manifest and hidden. The human creature has a manifest dimension and a hidden dimension. He places reason within the creature so that he may discriminate and keep an equilibrium in his self. Also, he has to keep an equilibrium in the cosmos. Remember Surat Fatir (35:39):

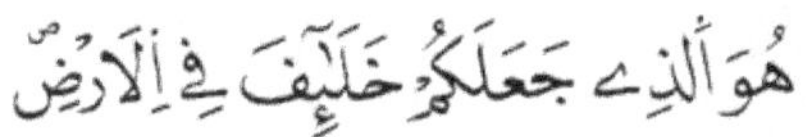

It is He who made you Khalifs on the earth.

Allah has made the human creature responsible for the whole planet. All this thing that the kuffar are now talking about, about the disorder on the planet, has been created by man – he has this responsibility yet he has not carried it out. He has handed it over for money and for wealth. It is man's job to keep an equilibrium in the cosmos and an equilibrium in himself, and he has been given reason in order to see that these two aspects of himself have got balance. Of course, the Shari'at is the guide to a behaviour which will allow a possibility of a Ruhani illumination.

So it is possible to love Allah through the creatures to sustain equilibrium. Yet, Allah has unveiled to the Lover His Name in Surat ash-Shura (42:11):

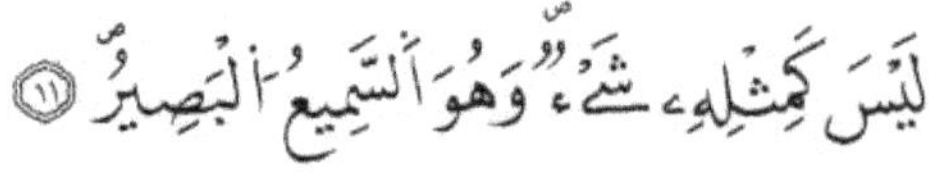

Nothing is like Him.
He is the All-Hearing, the All-Seeing.

Look at this devastating situation. I have commented on this at length in 'The Book of Tawhid'. "Nothing is like Him. He is the All-Hearing, the All-Seeing." Thus Allah unveils Himself to the Lover by His Name 'Nothing is like Him'. Allah shows him that He is not like anything. This is the confusion. This is the turbulence into which the human creature is set, when knowledge hits him. Here he is with love that is going out here and going out there and suddenly the Creator says, "Nothing is like Him," and then this leaves the Lover disoriented. This then reveals to him that he can never measure the force of things, especially since He, Allah, has added after this: "He is the All-Hearing, the All-Seeing." This is the situation he finds himself in – that Allah has revealed His Names: The Hearer and The Seer.

Thus since the affair itself is Allah's affair, the Lover is thrown off the life-project. He has his life-project, he has the other creatures, and suddenly he discovers this devastating thing which is that Allah is not like any of the things. This is the throwing-off of the life-project. The life-project is thrown into crisis by this devastating discovery which is the heart of Tawhid.

This is the proper derangement of the Lover. This apparent dislocation is in fact the awakening of the spiritual Ruhani capacity to love Allah. It is not a disobedience of the Shari'at, but a rejection of the all-demanding project of the Dunya, because suddenly, to reach out to Love of Allah means this project of the Dunya is dislocated as Allah is not like any of it! He is not like any thing!

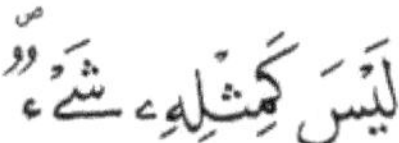

The Third Condition of the Lover is 'To be On the Way'. It is to be on the Way towards Allah by His Names. He has to affront this turbulence in him, this awakening love that comes by this crack in the material consciousness. He must approach Allah by his Names. Allah manifests to the Lover both by the names of the creatures – the Kawn – as by the Divine Names, as He explains in Surat al-Baqara (2:31):

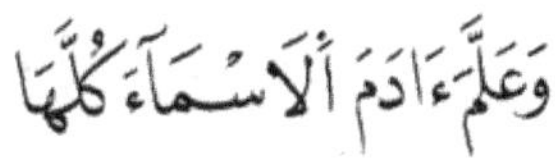

He taught Adam the names of all things.

So his faculty that allows him to know the names of the creatures is itself a Divine unveiling. Allah manifests to the Lover both by the names of the creatures – the Kawn – as by the Divine Names. The Lover sees the Tajalliyat of the names of the creatures by their attributes, as receiving a Divine descent. In other words, he sees that the creature is hearing, seeing and knowing – all the mother attributes that we have totally given to Allah and nothing is like Him, and then he still sees that the creatures have these borrowed in-time attributes of Allah, Who is beyond-time. So he finds that all this love he had for the creatures is actually because in them he perceives the Names. They have these attributes by Divine descent, yet by an unknown perspective, otherwise you would identify Allah, astaghfirullah, with the creation which is not possible because "Nothing is like Him." You recognise that by a Divine descent onto the creature there are these in-time borrowed attributes which belong to Allah.

Then he sees that he has an in-time appropriation of Divine Names and they become apparent by character – Takhalluq. He sees the signs in himself and in creation. Surat al-Fussilat (41:53-54):

سَنُرِيهِمْ ءَايَٰتِنَا فِى ٱلْءَافَاقِ وَفِىٓ أَنفُسِهِمْ حَتَّىٰ يَتَبَيَّنَ لَهُمْ أَنَّهُ ٱلْحَقُّ ۗ أَوَلَمْ يَكْفِ بِرَبِّكَ أَنَّهُ عَلَىٰ كُلِّ شَىْءٍ شَهِيدٌ ۞ أَلَآ إِنَّهُمْ فِى مِرْيَةٍ مِّن لِّقَآءِ رَبِّهِمْ ۗ أَلَآ إِنَّهُ بِكُلِّ شَىْءٍ مُّحِيطٌۢ ۞

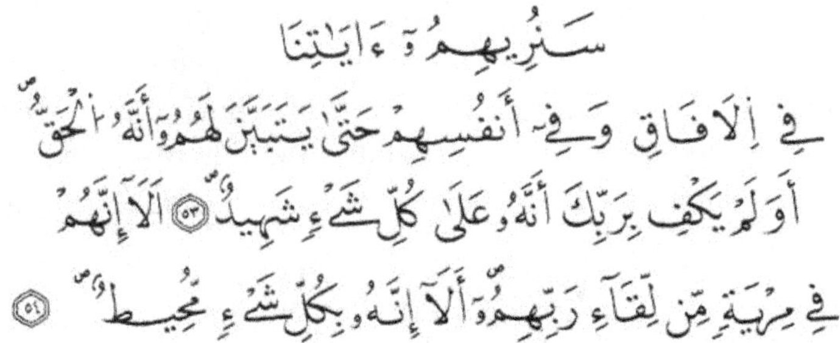

We will show them Our Signs on the horizon
and within themselves
until it is clear to them that it is the truth.
Is it not enough for your Lord
that He is a witness of everything?

What! Are they in doubt
about the meeting with their Lord?
What! Does He not encompass all things?

He sees the signs in himself and in creation, so he is recognising the manifestation of the Names in the creation without making any association between the things and the Divine Reality.

Now we go to the Diwan of Shaykh Muhammad ibn al-Habib, rahimahullah, and 'The Greater Qasida' which is at the beginning. We shall look at a section in the middle of this Qasida:

فَأَسْمَاءُ رَبِّ الْعَرْشِ قَدْ عَمَّ نُورُها　　بأجزائِهَا ما بَيْنَ خــافٍ وَشُهْرَةِ
فَلَوْ جُلْتَ فِي المِياهِ مَعْ أُصْلِ نَشْئِها　　وَتَرْيبَـةِ الأَشْياء مِنْهــا بِحِكْمَةِ
حَكَمْتَ بِعَجْزِ الكُلِّ عَنْ دَرْكِ سِرِّها　　وَبُحْتَ بِتَخْصِيصِ الإلَـهِ بِقُدرَةِ
وَأَطْلِقْ عِنــانَ الفِكْرِ عِنْدَ جِبالِها　　تَجِدْها هِيَ الأَوْتادُ مِنْ غَيْرِ مِرْيَةِ
وَما حَوَتِ الأَزْهارُ مِنْ حُسْنِ مَنْظَرٍ　　وَكَثْرَةِ تَنْوِيــعِ الثِّمــارِ البَدِيعَةِ
وَما أَظْهَرَتْ مِنْ كُلِّ شَيءٍ يُرى بِها　　وَكُلٌّ أَتى مِــنْ عَيْنِ عِـزٍّ وَسَطْوَةِ
فَشاهِــدْ جَمالَ الحَقِّ عِنْدَ لِحاظِها　　وَإِيَّــاكَ تَنْكِيفــاً عَلى أَدْنَــى ذَرَّةِ
فَمــا قامَــتِ الأَشْياءُ إِلاَّ بِرَبِّها　　فَيــا حَــيُّ يــا قَيُّومُ أَبْلَغُ حُجَّةِ

For the light of the Names of the Lord of the Throne
Extends throughout all its known and hidden parts.

If you were to reflect on the oceans and their origin,
And how wisdom is learned through studying them,

Then you would know
that no-one is capable of grasping its secret
And you would affirm that power belongs to Allah alone.

Let your thoughts flow freely regarding its mountains
And you will find that they are the pegs without a doubt.

Look at the beauty of the appearance of the flowers,
And the marvellous variety of different fruits.

Look at every visible manifestation!
It all gushes from the fount of energy and power.

Consider all this and then see the beauty of the truth.
Take care – you cannot despise even the lowest atom.

Things have no existence except through their Lord.
O Living! O Eternal! Your own most eloquent proof!

Thus the entire universe is constituted by the totality of the Divine Names. All, that is except for the name of the human creature which is 'Abd – slave. So on his journey he recognises that he has all along been in error. He has distinguished and set apart the Lover from the Beloved. Abu Yazid told of what happened to him when he arrived at the end of his journey in his narration: "Allah approached me by something that was not part of me, that did not belong to me." When he relinquished what did not belong to him, that is his slavehood, he was of course annihilated – "Nothing is like him."

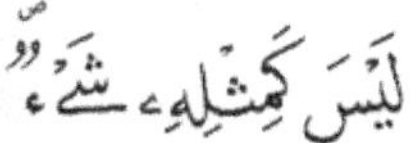

So he had to disappear. He tells that a voice said to him in the cave, "Who is within?" And he replied, "Abu Yazid." The voice said, "Know then that I cannot enter, for where I am there can be no other." This was what the Sufis call the Fana', the annihilation of Abu Yazid in the Tajalliyat of the Essence of Allah, subhanahu wa ta'ala.

The Fourth Condition of the Lover is Tayyar – To be Mobile like a Bird. The Lover looks on his names, his borrowed attributes, he looks on these qualities that he has from Allah, subhanahu wa ta'ala, and he looks on the collection of these Names by which we exist: the knowing, the hearing, the seeing, the willing and so on, and he looks on that as his nest – Wikar. Once he realises that this is not how it is, he flies out from his own nest. He then moves by Allah, sustained by His Names. He flies to the Owner of the Names, to the zone of knowledges. Surat ar-Rahman (55:29):

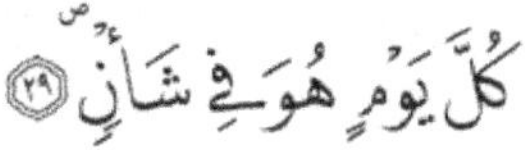

Every day He is engaged in some affair.

Every day He, Allah, subhanahu wa ta'ala, is engaged in some affair. It is by the wisdom of this Ayat that he flies to the Owner of the Names to the zone of knowledges which is in this "Every day He is engaged in some affair." Shaykh Zarruq had been for years in the desert with a Shaykh, when he was suddenly told by his Shaykh, "Now you are finished, go!" Shaykh Zarruq said to the Muqaddam, "But there is something I wanted from him and I have not got it – don't make me go!" But the Muqaddam insisted, "You must go!" and led him to the door of the Zawiyya and shut the gates against him. He was faced with the desert and felt he had nothing. He banged on the door of the Zawiyya and the Muqaddam opened it and he exclaimed, "Please! I cannot go, I am not ready. Tell the Shaykh to give me something that will last me all my life!" The Muqaddam went back to the Shaykh and returned with this poem which is very famous to all the Sufis:

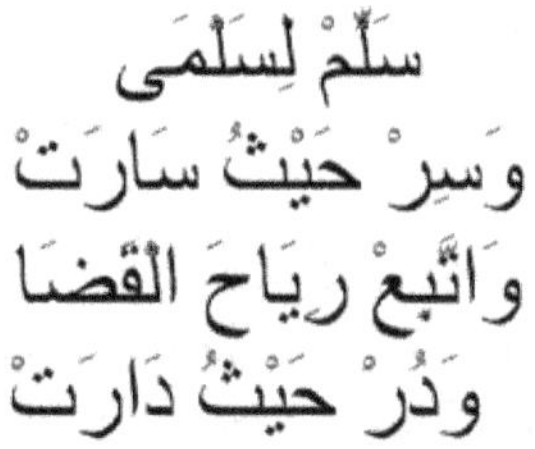

Submit to Salma,
Go where she goes.
Follow the winds of Destiny,
Turn wherever they turn.

Salma is a woman's name and it is used in the language of the Sufis to represent the Essence of Allah.

Thus the Lover of Allah goes from one day to the next,

from one action to the next, from one Hal to the next. In this way he is sustained in the Hadrat of contemplation of Allah, subhanahu wa ta'ala.

Now we shall comment on the Ten Stages of Love, from Shaykh Nasirud-Din, the Chiraghi of Delhi.

The First Stage is 'Ulfa – Attachment. It has five phases. The first is Qul. The word of Allah, subhanahu wa ta'ala, is "Say": "Qul." We are familiar with this word:

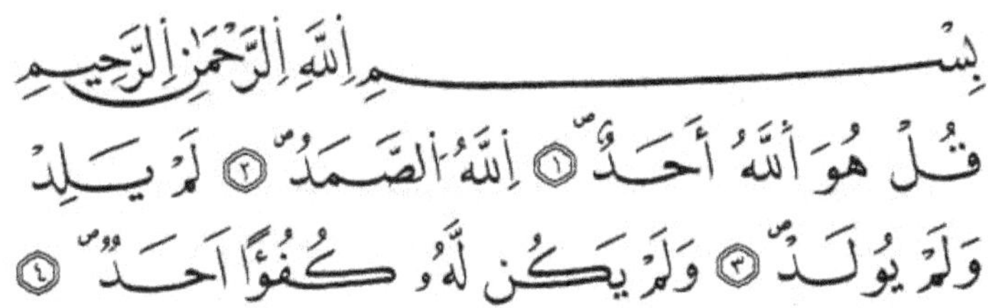

In the name of Allah, All-Merciful, Most Merciful
Say: "He is Allah, Absolute Oneness,
Allah, the Everlasting Sustainer of all.
He has not given birth and was not born.
And no one is comparable to Him."

This creates this attachment. It is this Qul, it is this news that is the beginning of the Lovers' Path.

The second phase is kitmani maylan – Keeping it Secret. He keeps secret to himself his love. One of the Sufis said, "The remedy for the pain is the pain."

The third phase is Timna – The Turbulence of Yearning for

Contact. The turbulence begins to stir the heart in wanting some indication, some light to come from Allah, subhanahu wa ta'ala.

The fourth phase is Ikhbar wa Istikhbar – you want news of Allah and you want Allah to recognise you. You want to be noticed in the Divine Presence.

The fifth phase is Tadarru' wa Tamalluq – Humility and Begging. Amir Khusran prayed to Allah: "I am dying, come and let me live!"

That is the First Stage. The Second Stage is Sadaqa – Sincerity. It has five phases. The first is 'Taking in the Troubles of Dunya as Gifts from the Beloved'. Here you see this turning upside down of the 'Arifin who see everything differently from all the other human beings. The Muslim who has knowledge sees things differently. That is that he takes the troubles of Dunya as gifts from the Beloved. In other words, he is not separating, he is not making a duality, he is not seeing a world of darkness and a world of light as though they were contrasts. He sees that all is from the Divine Lord.

The second phase is Ghayra – Jealousy. When I went to visit Shaykh Ibn al-Mashish in the Rif Mountains, my Shaykh asked me where I had been and I told him, and he said, "Shaykh Ibn al-Mashish had a very high station with Allah. It was Ghayra. He was jealous! Once he was making du'a in his cave," which was at the very top of the mountain and then you go down the side of the mountain where there is a cave where he had his Khalwa, "and a Faqir had climbed up the mountain to see him and he heard him making du'a and thought, 'If I listen to what he is saying I shall learn something!' but he was very shocked because as he got to the cave he heard Shaykh Ibn al-Mashish saying, 'O Allah, please make everybody go off the Sirat al-Mustaqim so that there is just You and me!'" This is called Ghayra, Jealousy – where the Love becomes so beyond the person's being.

The third phase is Ishtiaq – Ardour. That is when the Faqir begins to find in the Diwans a corroboration of something he is already beginning to feel which is: "What is life without You?" This is the beginning of the real Faqir: "Allah, I cannot live without Your Presence."

The fourth phase is Dhikri Mahbub – Dhikr of the Beloved. Rasul, sallallahu 'alayhi wa sallam, said, "A man lies hidden under his tongue." So the tongue of the 'Arif is supple with the Name of Allah, subhanahu wa ta'ala. "Hidden under the tongue" means the dhikr which is done by the 'Arif because he is remembering Allah in every situation.

The fifth phase is Tahayyur – Astonishment. Rasul, sallallahu 'alayhi wa sallam, made this du'a:

يا ربي زدني فيك تحيرا

"Oh Lord, increase me in astonishment about You."

The Third Stage is Mawadda – Friendship. We shall go to the Qur'an and look at Surat al-Mumtahana (60:7):

عَسَى ٱللَّهُ أَن يَجْعَلَ بَيْنَكُمْ وَبَيْنَ ٱلَّذِينَ عَادَيْتُم مِّنْهُم مَّوَدَّةً وَٱللَّهُ قَدِيرٌ وَٱللَّهُ غَفُورٌ رَّحِيمٌ ۝

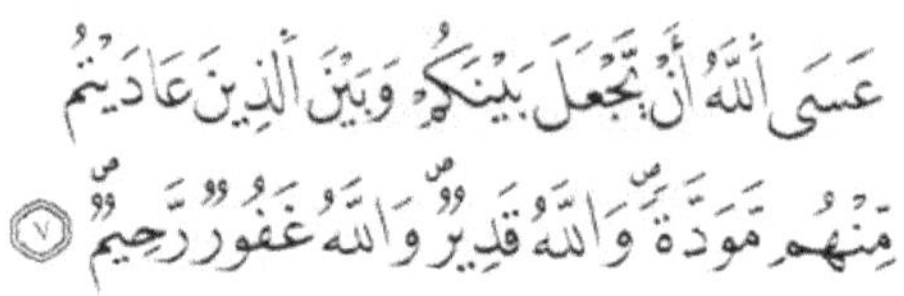

It may well be that Allah will restore the love
between you and those of them who are now your enemies.
Allah is All-Powerful.
Allah is Ever-Forgiving, Most Merciful.

The mark of this Muwadda is the Agitation of the Heart –
the Hijan al-Qalb, and it has five phases:

The first phase is Niyaha wa Idtirar – Bewailing and Agitation. The first aspect of this, the bewailing, is what you see
many times in the circle of Dhikr: a man dissolving into tears.
It is a Fatihah, it is a spiritual opening which makes him weep.

The second phase is The Shedding of Tears. Rasul, sallallahu
'alayhi wa sallam, prayed to Allah, "Bless us with a weeping
eye." So the weeping eye is again making possible lights to
manifest in the heart.

The third phase is Hasra – Regret. It is looking on the past
as wasted in its absence of the Beloved. Yet even that throws
you into deeper confusion because you know that without
that, the Path would not have led you to the present. So you
know that it was a gift from Allah, because the things which
kept you from Allah are also those things which brought
you to the Path of Allah. Again, you begin to recognise
Allah's Presence in every situation.

The fourth phase is Fikri Mahbub – Contemplating the

IV

Beloved. In the Diwan of Shaykh Muhammad ibn al-Habib, rahimahullah, you will find the Qasida entitled Reflection:

REFLECTION

تَفَكَّرْ جَمِيلَ الصُّنْعِ فِي الْبَرِّ وَالْبَحْرِ   وَجُلْ فِي صِفَاتِ اللهِ فِي السِّرِّ وَالْجَهْرِ

وَفِي النَّفْسِ وَالْآفَاقِ أَعْظَمُ شَاهِدٍ   عَلَى كَمَالَاتِ اللهِ مِنْ غَيْرِ مَا حَصْرِ

فَلَوْ جُلْتَ فِي الْأَجْسَامِ مَعْ حُسْنِ شَكْلِهَا   وَتَنْظِيمِهَا تَنْظِيمَ خَيْطٍ مِنَ الدُّرِّ

وَجُلْتَ فِي أَسْرَارِ اللِّسَانِ وَنُطْقِهِ   وَتَعْبِيرِهِ عَمَّا تُكِنُّهُ فِي الصَّدْرِ

وَجُلْتَ فِي أَسْرَارِ الْجَوَارِحِ كُلِّهَا   وَتَسْخِيرِهَا لِلْقَلْبِ مِنْ غَيْرِ مَا عُسْرِ

وَجُلْتَ فِي تَقْلِيبِ الْقُلُوبِ لِطَاعَةٍ   وَفِي بَعْضِ أَحْيَانٍ لِمَعْصِيَةٍ تَسْرِي

وَجُلْتَ فِي أَرْضٍ مَعْ تَنَوُّعِ نَبْتِهَا   وَكَثْرَةِ مَا فِيهَا مِنَ السَّهْلِ وَالْوَعْرِ

وَجُلْتَ فِي أَسْرَارِ الْبِحَارِ وَحُوتِهَا   وَكَثْرَةِ أَمْوَاجٍ لَهَا حَاجِزٌ قَهْرِ

وَجُلْتَ فِي أَسْرَارِ الرِّيَاحِ وَجَلْبِهَا   لِغَيْمٍ وَسُحْبٍ قَدْ أَسَالَتْ مِنَ الْقَطْرِ

وَجُلْتَ فِي أَسْرَارِ السَّمَوَاتِ كُلِّهَا   وَعَرْشٍ وَكُرْسِيٍّ وَرُوحٍ مِنَ الْأَمْرِ

عَقَدْتَ عَلَى التَّوْحِيدِ عَقْدَ مُصَمِّمٍ   وَحُلْتَ عَنِ الْأَوْهَامِ وَالشَّكِّ وَالْغَيْرِ

وَقُلْتَ إِلَاهِي أَنْتَ سُؤْلِي وَمَطْلَبِي   وَحِصْنِي مِنَ الْأَسْوَاءِ وَالضَّيْمِ وَالْمَكْرِ

وَأَنْتَ رَجَاءِي فِي قَضَاءِ حَوَائِجِي   وَأَنْتَ الَّذِي تُنْجِي مِنَ السُّوءِ وَالشَّرِّ

وَأَنْتَ الرَّحِيمُ الْمُسْتَجِيبُ لِمَنْ دَعَاكْ   وَأَنْتَ الَّذِي تُغْنِي الْفَقِيرَ عَنِ الْفَقْرِ

إِلَيْكَ رَفَعْتُ يَا رَفِيعُ مَطَالِبِي   فَعَجِّلْ بِفَتْحٍ يَا إِلَاهِي مَعَ السِّرِّ

بِجَاهِ الَّذِي يُرْجَى يَوْمَ الْكَرْبِ وَالْعَنَا   وَيَوْمَ وُرُودِ النَّاسِ لِمَوْقِفِ الْحَشْرِ

عَلَيْهِ صَلَاةُ اللهِ مَا جَالَ عَارِفٌ   فِي أَنْوَارِ ذَاتِهِ لَدَى كُلِّ مَظْهَرِ

وَآلِهِ وَالْأَصْحَابِ مَعْ كُلِّ تَابِعٍ   لِسُنَّتِهِ الْغَرَّاءِ فِي النَّهْيِ وَالْأَمْرِ

Reflect upon the beauty of the way in which
both the land and sea are made, and contemplate
the Attributes of Allah outwardly and secretly.

The greatest evidence of the limitless perfections of Allah
can be found both deep within the self
and on the distant horizon.

If you were to reflect on physical bodies
and their marvellous forms and how they are arranged
with great precision, like a string of pearls,

And if you were to reflect on the secrets of the tongue
and its capacity for speech, and how it articulates
and conveys what you conceal in your breast,

And if you were to reflect on the secrets of all the limbs
and how easily they are subject to the heart's command,

And if you were to reflect on how the hearts are moved
to obey Allah and how at other times they move darkly
to disobedience,

And if you were to reflect on the earth
and the diversity of its plants and the great varieties
of smooth and rugged land in it,

And if you were to reflect on the secrets of the oceans
and all their fish, and their endless waves held back
by an unconquerable barrier,

And if you were to reflect on the secrets

of the many winds and how they bring the mist,
fog and clouds which release the rain,

And if you were to reflect on all the secrets of the heavens
– the Throne and the Footstool
and the spirit sent by the Command –

Then you would accept the reality of Tawhid
with all your being, and you would turn away
from illusions, uncertainty and otherness,

And you would say, "My God, You are my desire,
my goal and my impregnable fortress against evil,
injustice and deceit.

You are the One I hope will provide for all my needs,
and You are the One Who rescues us from all evil
and wickedness.

You are the Compassionate, the One Who answers
all who call on You. And you are the One
Who enriches the poverty of the Faqir.

It is to You, O Exalted, that I have raised all my request,
so swiftly bring me the Opening, the rescue
and the secret, O my God."

By the rank of the one in whom we hope
on the day of distress and grief – that terrible day
when people come to the Place of Gathering –

May Allah's blessings be upon him

as long as there is an 'Arif who reflects on the lights
of His Essence in every manifestation,

And upon his family and Companions
and everyone who follows his excellent Sunna
in all its prohibitions and commands.

We remember of course that Rasul, sallallahu 'alayhi wa sallam, spoke about an hour of Fikr, of contemplation, of reflection, being better than 60 years of 'Ibada.

فِكْرَةُ سَاعَةٍ خَيْرٌ مِنْ عِبَادَةِ سِتِّيْنَ سَنَة

The fifth phase of Muwadda, of this Friendship with Allah, subhanahu wa ta'ala, is the Muraqabat al-Mahbub – Watching of the Beloved. It is the beginning of the Sufi in his calling on Allah, he is beginning to watch. That is in order to pass from his watching to his recognition, to his gnosis that he is watched.

الله معي الله ناظر إلي الله شاهد علي

Allah is with me, Allah sees me,
Allah is the Witness of my acts.

We shall stop here, and continue next week, inshallah.

V

AUGUST 18TH 2007

We were commenting on the Ten Stages of Love, and we now come to the Fourth of these Ten from Shaykh Nasirud-Din of Delhi. We have covered 'Ulfa, Sadaqa and Mawadda, and we now come to Hawa. Now that we are almost, as it were, halfway into this designation of our Shaykh from Delhi, I would like to preface this with something that will also help you to understand why our Muslim Community is in the state that it is in.

Tasawwuf has, over the last hundred years, been very savagely and brutally attacked from outside Islam. At the same time it has degenerated inside the Muslim Community among its own proponents and followers. You see, we all say it like a truism, but it is a Hikma that there cannot be Haqiqat without Shari'at. In that sense we could say that all the trouble of the Muslims has come from the abandonment of Shari'at. In these last days, in the last half of this century over, we have seen people try to turn, as it were, the Haqiqat into a kind of Shari'at so that they made the rules that apply to Shari'at as if they applied to Haqiqat. Thus you find, especially in the Subcontinent, but also in Morocco in the Maghrib, that because of the silsila of the Shaykhs, some people claim a kind of Wilayat because they are the grandson or the great-grandson or the great-great-grandson of a real Wali. This is like in Shari'at if there were a descent of family there would be inheritance. But there cannot be an inheritance by family in the Ma'rifa. Or as the Sufis say, the exception proves the rule. For example, we have two father and son Shuyukh in our Tariqa, Sidi 'Ali Wafa and Sidi Muhammad Wafa, but they are the exceptions, and also the two Fasis. But they are the exceptions which prove the rule.

At the same time, what is strange is that just as the people who are defending Tasawwuf have already betrayed it, the irony, or the inevitable result is that the people who claim that they want Shari'at, have also betrayed the Shari'at. You read about this in all the kafir media which tells you every day that there are these terrible people who want to impose what they call 'Shari'at Law', but this is not Deen of Islam. We want Shari'at, but the truth of the matter is that what is law, what carries with it judgment, and what carries with it in certain cases punishment – that is not the whole of the Shari'at. Ad-Deen al-Mu'amalat – The Deen is Behaviour. If you take out character and behaviour, you cannot have Deen, you cannot have Shari'at. We have seen it, because we have seen people who have not got correct behaviour or correct character imposing Hadd punishments on people out of the blue, out of nothing, out of nowhere, and it is a savagery and a cruelty of exceptional dimensions.

In that sense, to have Shari'at you have already admitted the basic and fundamental principle of Haqiqat, which is that Mu'amalat has an outward aspect – because the right action, the good action is visible, and is known and is recorded – but at the same time it has an aspect that is hidden because it cannot spring out of nothing. Otherwise it would be a hypocrisy. Is that not correct? So this is the dilemma in which we find ourselves.

Now, if you then erode the thing further – and this is where we come to something very strange – you find that people today, and I mean 'Ulama, I mean educated people, certainly from fifty years back, in my time as a Muslim, but probably back a bit further to the beginning of the twentieth century, have somehow accepted the idea – which is ironically not criticised or reformed or challenged by the so-called people who want Shari'at – that the financial system and the financial structures and the financial transactions which are today called Capitalism, are alright. This is something that cannot be explained rationally because if you challenge these people to their face they will nod and say to you, "Certainly, that is absolutely true," but they will continue in the procedures of that Capitalism which are a denial of the Deen of Islam and what Allah, subhanahu wa ta'ala, has ordered.

I have written in my writings about a certain change which took place in the world in the middle of the nineteenth century, and I am not the only person to make that observation. Christians have made it, humanists have made it, historians have made it, sociologists have made it – that is that somewhere, in the century before last, there was a kind of split, a crack in consciousness, and it is like, after that, a kind of defeat of the human creatures occurred, and it was done in the high effervescence of something that was called Humanism. But at the very point they were declaring humanism, people became subhuman and in that sense we are all subhuman. What is subhuman? It is that we have gone out of kilter, we have gone out of the pattern which, in the language of our 'Ulama, is called Deen al-Fitra.

The Fitra of the human being has been totally dislocated because the action of usury, the action of the fundamental motor of this social system actually cracks and breaks the Fitra. So people are no longer able to have the Deen which is Deen al-Fitra. Also, Deen al-Fitra is Deen al-Haqq, so you cannot have the Haqq, you cannot have Tasawwuf if you do not have this pattern of behaviour which means that in the transaction you are honest and act according to what has been commanded in the Book of Allah and by Rasul, sallallahu 'alayhi wa sallam, and the First Community of Madinah.

It is VERY important that we grasp this because what has to happen and will happen over the coming years of this new century, is there has to awaken a generation of men who want to taste that matter which is the subject of what we have been studying – that is Divine Love and passion and ecstasy for Allah, the Creator of the Universe. Without this, nothing can be achieved.

Properly speaking, the nihilist, suicidal terrorist is the blood brother of the capitalist million and billionaires. They are one. They are the two extremities and they meet. Where do they meet? They meet in having cut themselves off from ANY understanding that they have to obey Allah and obey the Messenger. They do not do this, and they cannot do it by charity, and they cannot do it by screaming Takbirs before they blow themselves up. They are exactly the same. As long as you have the one, you will have the other. They belong together, and they will continue together until a generation comes who wakes up and says, "I have still got some contact with my Fitra and I want to taste this matter." But when they taste this matter, it becomes the dominant factor of their lives. This is what the subject of Divine Love is that we have been examining.

The truth of the matter is: Islam is the religion of the sciences of Divine Love and Passion. That is true. It is not for a special lot of people, it is not a metaphoric condition – everything that you read about the Battle of Badr is that. It is that. It is everything you read about the Sahaba at the time of Rasul, sallallahu 'alayhi wa sallam, in Madinah. It is that.

Now we will look at the Fourth Stage which is Hawa – Passionate Desire. It is longing. Longing has to awaken in the Lover. This longing, this passionate desire has five phases. The first is Khudu – Humility. There is a very famous text of Moulay 'Abdalqadir al-Jilani, radiyallahu 'anhu, in which he wrote about his longing for the Presence of Allah, subhanahu wa ta'ala. The more he tried and the more he struggled, the less successful he was. Then he heard a voice say to him, "Go to the little door of humility." He said "I went to the little door of humility, and there I found only a few and I was able to enter."

The second phase is Ita'ati Mahbub – Obedient Devotion. That means that the worship of Allah, subhanahu wa ta'ala, the acts of 'Ibada become events of great emotional enrichment.

The third phase is Sabr – Patient Endurance. Our Shaykh says, "Patience calms the turbulence." To that he adds, "Because when water becomes still, it is like a mirror." So when the inner turbulence calms itself, it means that he is then able to gaze in the mirror and have direct vision.

The fourth phase is Tadarru – Supplication in Humility. This we find in Surat al-'Araf (7:205):

وَٱذْكُر رَّبَّكَ فِى نَفْسِكَ
تَضَرُّعًا وَخِيفَةً وَدُونَ ٱلْجَهْرِ مِنَ ٱلْقَوْلِ بِٱلْغُدُوِّ
وَٱلْءَاصَالِ وَلَا تَكُن مِّنَ ٱلْغَٰفِلِينَ ٢٠٥

Remember your Lord in yourself
humbly and fearfully,
without loudness of voice,
morning and evening.
Do not be one of the unaware.

The fifth phase of this passionate desire is Rida, which is, really, Resignation. This is a journey, this is a path, and in this path the end is always there, it is always present at every stage. What we are looking at is not a progressive thing with stage after stage after stage because these conditions and phases mingle and mix depending on the individual Lover in his search. Inside this turbulence are these conflicting aspects of humility – Endurance and Resignation.

Now we move to the Fifth Stage which is Shaghaf – Violent Affection. We are looking at this love as having a violent, explosive nature and we find this term in Surat Yusuf (12:30), in the famous story of the governor's wife. Remember that the language of Tasawwuf all comes from Qur'an.

وَقَالَ نِسْوَةٌ فِي الْمَدِينَةِ امْرَأَتُ الْعَزِيزِ تُرَاوِدُ فَتَاهَا عَن
نَّفْسِهِ قَدْ شَغَفَهَا حُبًّا إِنَّا لَنَرَاهَا فِي ضَلَالٍ مُّبِينٍ ٣٠

Some city women said, "The governor's wife
solicited her slave. He's fired her heart
with love. We see that she's the one to blame."

Here we find the term Shaghaf as being this explosive event as told in the story of Sayyiduna Yusuf, 'alayhi salam. This Shaghaf, this violent affection that cannot be stopped – for once it has happened it is out and there is nothing you can do about it – has five phases. Of course, the first phase, because we are talking about Divine Love, is Obedience to Allah's Commands. We go to Surat Hudd (11:112):

فَاسْتَقِمْ كَمَا أُمِرْتَ وَمَن تَابَ مَعَكَ وَلَا تَطْغَوْا
إِنَّهُ بِمَا تَعْمَلُونَ بَصِيرٌ ١١٢

Go straight as you have been commanded,
and also those who turn with you to Allah,
and do not exceed the bounds.
He sees what you do.

Remember, there is a recurrent aspect of these Ayats of Qur'an that we have found in which Allah reminds us that He is watching us. We are not watching for Allah. Allah is the Watcher, and He sees what you do. "Go straight as you have been commanded." What has been commanded? For the answer to this we go to Surat al-Muzzammil (73:7):

وَاذْكُرِ اسْمَ رَبِّكَ وَتَبَتَّلْ إِلَيْهِ تَبْتِيلاً ۞

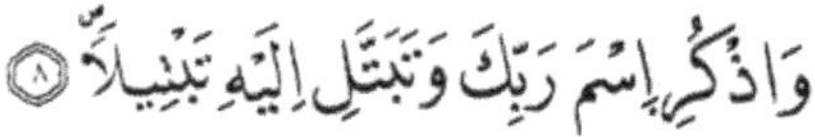

Remember the Name of your Lord,
and devote yourself to Him completely.

This is the whole of Tasawwuf. "Devote yourself to Him completely," means in your inward and in your outward actions.

The second phase is Guarding the Inward from Turning to Other. For this we go to the Diwan of Shaykh Muhammad ibn al-Habib, rahimahullah, to the Qasida entitled 'Withdrawal from All that is Other than Allah':

رُوحِي تُحَدِّثُنِي بِأَنَّ حَقِيقَتِي

نُورُ الإِلَـهِ فَلا تَـرَى إِلاَّهُ

لَوْ لَمْ أَكُـنْ نُوراً لَكُنْتُ سِواهُ

إِنَّ السِّوَا عَـدَمٌ فَـلا تَرْضاهُ

V

My ruh speaks to me and says,
"My haqiqat is the Light of Allah,
So look to no-one except Him.

If I were not a light I would be other-than-Him.
Indeed otherness is nothingness
so do not be content with it."

We look also at 'The Gifts of the Ism al-'Adham':

تَجَرَّدْ عَنِ الأَغْيـــارِ تَحْظَ بِقُرْبِهِ
وَتَرْقَ مَراقِي القَوْمِ فِي كُلِّ مَشْهَدِ

Free yourself from all that is other
and you will attain His nearness,
And you will rise to the ranks
of the People of every assembly.

This is The Guarding of the Inward from Turning to Other which is the beginning of taking on complete knowledge of Tawhid and to know that there is no 'other', that other is an illusion. This is very important because that is the turning point at which the Lover begins to view events differently.

The third phase is Muwafaqa, and we have met it before in the configuration of Imam al-Ghazali – Compatability. Compatability is defined as loving with the love of Allah and hating with the hatred of Allah.

The fourth phase of Shaghaf is Regard for the Friends of

Allah. This is defined in the famous Song of Abu Madyan al-Ghawth:

ما لذة العيش إلا صحبة الفقرا هم السلاطين و السادات والأمرا

متى أراهم و أنى لي برؤيتهم أو تسمع الأذن مني عنهم خبر

The pleasure of life is only in the company of the fuqara.
They are the Sultans, the masters, the princes.

When will I see them, where will I see them?
When will my ear have news of them?

This is the regard for the friends of Allah. Many commentaries have been written on this Song because of the importance of it. It is in respecting and having a high regard for the People, for the Lovers of Allah, that the Lover advances himself swiftly on the Path.

The fifth phase of this Violent Affection is To Conceal the Matters of Love. We go back to the Diwan, to the Qasida 'Fana' fillah' and the sixth, seventh and eighth couplets:

وَاذْكُرْ بِجِدٍّ وَصِدْقٍ   بَيْنَ يَدَيْ عَبِيدِ اللهْ
وَاكْتُمْ إِذا تَجَلَّى لَكَ   بِأَنْوارٍ مِنْ ذاتِ اللهْ
فَالغَيْرُ عِنْدَنا مُحالْ   فَالوُجُودُ الحَقُّ للهْ

Do Dhikr of Him with gravity and sincerity in the
presence of the slaves of Allah.

Hide (your awareness) when He is manifested to you
With lights from the Essence of Allah.

With us, other is impossible,
For existence is the Haqq of Allah.

"Other is impossible" – this is the pivotal point at which you view events differently. "Existence is the Haqq of Allah." When we look at these lines you must bear in mind what you have absorbed and that part of your understanding of this matter is that which I have explained in the series of discourses comprising 'The Book of Tawhid'. The ignorant and the kuffar think, "Ah, the Sufis are saying that God is the creation!" But we are not saying that, we are not pantheists, we are not saying that God is the creation because we have understood how Allah creates matter bil-Haqq, with the Truth. "With us, other is impossible for existence is the Haqq of Allah."

Now we come to the Sixth Stage which is Khulla – Exclusive Attachment to the Beloved. This is derived from Takhliya, which is emptying the heart, emptying the heart of all but the Beloved. It has five phases. The first phase is Mu'anada – Enmity. The Lover becomes ill-at-ease, and at a certain stage of his journey he becomes ill at ease with the company he used to keep because it does not measure up to this event which is happening inside him. He becomes afraid of their mockery, or of calling him away from the Path. We find this in Surat al-Hajj (22:52-54):

وَمَآ أَرْسَلْنَا مِن قَبْلِكَ مِن رَّسُولٍ
وَلَا نَبِيٍّ إِلَّآ إِذَا تَمَنَّىٰٓ أَلْقَى ٱلشَّيْطَٰنُ
فِىٓ أُمْنِيَّتِهِۦ فَيَنسَخُ ٱللَّهُ مَا يُلْقِى ٱلشَّيْطَٰنُ ثُمَّ يُحْكِمُ
ٱللَّهُ ءَايَٰتِهِۦ وَٱللَّهُ عَلِيمٌ حَكِيمٌ ﴿٥٢﴾ لِّيَجْعَلَ مَا يُلْقِى ٱلشَّيْطَٰنُ
فِتْنَةً لِّلَّذِينَ فِى قُلُوبِهِم مَّرَضٌ وَٱلْقَاسِيَةِ قُلُوبُهُمْ
وَإِنَّ ٱلظَّٰلِمِينَ لَفِى شِقَاقٍۭ بَعِيدٍ ﴿٥٣﴾ وَلِيَعْلَمَ ٱلَّذِينَ أُوتُوا۟
ٱلْعِلْمَ أَنَّهُ ٱلْحَقُّ مِن رَّبِّكَ فَيُؤْمِنُوا۟ بِهِۦ فَتُخْبِتَ لَهُۥ
قُلُوبُهُمْ وَإِنَّ ٱللَّهَ لَهَادِ ٱلَّذِينَ ءَامَنُوٓا۟
إِلَىٰ صِرَٰطٍ مُّسْتَقِيمٍ ﴿٥٤﴾

We did not send any Messenger or any Prophet before you
without Shaytan insinuating something into his recitation
while he was reciting.
But Allah revokes whatever Shaytan insinuates
and then Allah confirms His Signs –
Allah is All-Knowing, All-Wise –
so that He can make what Shaytan insinuates
a trial for those with sickness in their hearts
and for those whose hearts are hard –
the wrongdoers are entrenched in hostility –
and so that those who have been given knowledge
will know it is the truth from their Lord
and have Iman in it
and their hearts will be humbled to Him.
Allah guides those who have Iman to a straight path.

This is very important. This is very significant. What we find from this is that Shaytan has an anxiety precisely to prevent this love from completing itself in knowledge and wisdom.

The second phase is Sidq – Sincerity. Sidq is the badge of the Lovers. For this we go to Surat az-Zumar (39:33-35):

وَالَّذِي جَاءَ بِالصِّدْقِ وَصَدَّقَ بِهِ
أُولَٰئِكَ هُمُ الْمُتَّقُونَ ٣٣
لَهُم مَّا يَشَاءُونَ عِندَ رَبِّهِمْ ذَٰلِكَ جَزَاءُ الْمُحْسِنِينَ ٣٤
لِيُكَفِّرَ اللَّهُ عَنْهُمْ أَسْوَأَ الَّذِي عَمِلُوا وَيَجْزِيَهُمْ
أَجْرَهُم بِأَحْسَنِ الَّذِي كَانُوا يَعْمَلُونَ ٣٥

He who brings the genuine and he who confirms it –
those are the people who have Taqwa.

They will have anything they wish for with their Lord.
That is the recompense of the good-doers.
So that Allah may erase from them
the worst of what they did
and pay them their wages for the best of what they did.

"They will have anything they wish for with their Lord." To the people of the Path, this means Ma'rifa. "That is the recompense of the good-doers. So that Allah may erase from them the worst of what they did and pay them their wages for the best of what they did." This is the whole of the Path.

The third phase is Ishtihar – Making Love Public. This is the opposite of hiding. Earlier there was concealment, now there is a strengthening of the love by his making love public. This is the step beyond egotism. Why? Because it means he does not care about the others. He makes his love public. This is the sign of the great Lovers of Allah. Doing so brings with it difficulties. This is the phase in which difficulties come.

The next phase of this Exclusive Attachment is Shikwa – Complaint. The complaint is the opening to Tawhid. When the Lover complains to Allah, he takes the complaint to Him. The common people give thanks to Allah, and they make complaint about themselves, but the 'Arif takes his complaint to Allah as he takes his thanks to Allah. So we go to the blessed Ayat in Surat al-Anbiya (21:83):

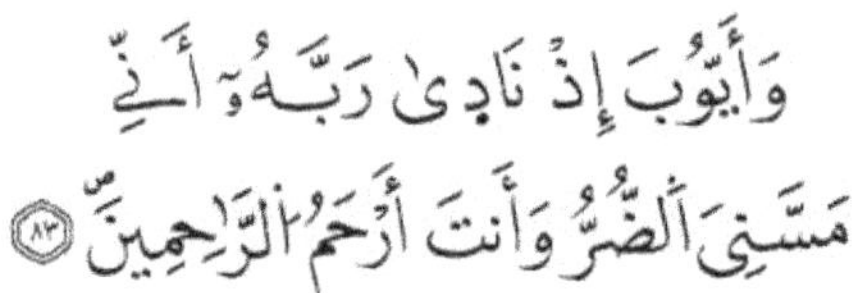

And Ayyub when he called out to his Lord,
"Great harm has afflicted me
and You are the Most Merciful of the merciful."

So Sayyiduna Ayyub, 'alayhi salam, connects something like the opposite of mercy and gives it back to the Giver, to Allah, subhanahu wa ta'ala, by His Name – The Most Merciful of the merciful.

For Allah's confirmation of this affair, we go to Surat Sad

(38:44), and the second half of the Ayat:

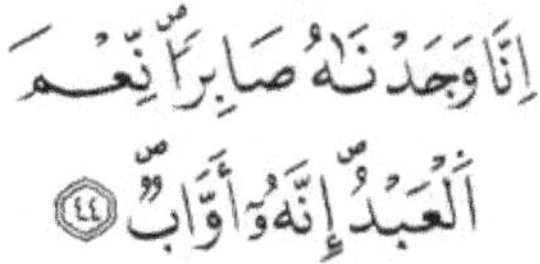

We found him steadfast.
What an excellent slave!
He truly turned to his Lord.

So the complaint of Sayyiduna Ayyub was pleasing to Allah, subhanahu wa ta'ala. It was the completion of Ayyub's Ma'rifa itself because it had to be taken back to Allah so that there was no duality.

The fifth phase of this Khulla is Huzn – Anguish. The Sufis say: "The anguished heart," the heart that is in anguish for Allah, "is the arena of coming bliss." That anguish is when the Lover knows that there is a coming bliss that will be the healing of the anguish.

This takes us to the Seventh Stage which is Mahabba – Increase of Affection. It is a sublime station. We find this in Surat al-Ma'ida (5:54):

يَـٰٓأَيُّهَا ٱلَّذِينَ ءَامَنُوا۟ مَن يَرْتَدَّ مِنكُمْ عَن دِينِهِۦ
فَسَوْفَ يَأْتِى ٱللَّهُ بِقَوْمٍ يُحِبُّهُمْ وَيُحِبُّونَهُۥٓ أَذِلَّةٍ عَلَى ٱلْمُؤْمِنِينَ
أَعِزَّةٍ عَلَى ٱلْكَـٰفِرِينَ يُجَـٰهِدُونَ فِى سَبِيلِ ٱللَّهِ وَلَا يَخَافُونَ لَوْمَةَ لَآئِمٍ
ذَٰلِكَ فَضْلُ ٱللَّهِ يُؤْتِيهِ مَن يَشَآءُ وَٱللَّهُ وَٰسِعٌ عَلِيمٌ ﴿٥٤﴾

You who have Iman! if any of you renounce your Deen,
Allah will bring forward a people
whom He loves and who love Him,
humble to the muminun, fierce to the kafirun,
who do Jihad in the Way of Allah
and do not fear the blame of any censurer.
That is the unbounded favour of Allah
which He gives to whomever He wills.
Allah is Boundless, All-Knowing.

We say that this is a sublime station because in this Ayat there is this very important phrase: "Whom He loves and who love Him." This makes the Shuyukh and the 'Arifin ask, "In this Ayat, who is the Lover and who is the Beloved?" In this situation they are the same.

Mahabba has five phases. The first phase is Husni Akhlaq – Good Behaviour in Private and Public, in Good Times and Bad. It is about 'amal, it is about behaviour. The Sufi is someone of a higher quality, he has a texture that brings life to everything around him because of the beauty of his behaviour. It is the stage of being active in the world, but already not of it. So the mark of the Sufi is that he IS active in the world but 'he' is not there, or rather, he is present in the world but not of it.

The second phase is Malamat wa Izhari Sukr wa Hayra – Risking Blame in Stages of Intoxication and Bewilderment. Now he is going so far that he is risking being blamed for not being sincere. Of course there is the hadith which relates to that where Rasul, sallallahu 'alayhi wa sallam, encourages people to "Do Dhikr until they say you are mad."

V

أَكْثِرُوا ذِكْرَ اللهِ حَتَّى يَقُولُوا مَجَانِينُ

Careless of blame he finally lets himself go into the realm of Ruhani drinking. This means that to reach that, you let yourself flow out and burst over in the singing of the Diwan, and in the Hadra you let yourself lose your self. You let go of the reins. For this we go to Surat al-Isra' (17:86-87). It is important that you understand that we are talking about risking blame in letting burst out of you your passion for Allah.

وَلَئِن شِئْنَا لَنَذْهَبَنَّ بِالَّذِيٓ
أَوْحَيْنَآ إِلَيْكَ ثُمَّ لَا تَجِدُ لَكَ بِهِۦ عَلَيْنَا وَكِيلًا ﴿٨٦﴾
إِلَّا رَحْمَةً مِّن رَّبِّكَ إِنَّ فَضْلَهُۥ كَانَ عَلَيْكَ كَبِيرًا ﴿٨٧﴾

If We wished We could take away
what We have revealed to you
and then you would not find any to guard you from Us –
but for a mercy from your Lord.
His favour to you is indeed immense.

This is the Divine ruling on the matter of unveiling from Him. What is true for the Prophets is true to a lesser degree for the Awliya and the 'Arifin. It is a Divine ruling. Again, everything is coming from Allah, subhanahu wa ta'ala. It is nothing to do with you. Allah's affair is descending on you. This is the indication on the Prophets, thus on the highest level of illumination, Sayyiduna Musa, 'alayhi salam, is told in Surat Ta Ha (20:41):

وَٱصْطَنَعْتُكَ لِنَفْسِى ﴿٤١﴾

I have chosen you for Myself.

This is the definition of the completion of Love, and of the contract of Love in Ma'rifa: "I have chosen you for Myself." Then he is warned in the famous Ayat of Surat al-A'raf (7:143):

وَلَمَّا جَآءَ مُوسَىٰ لِمِيقَٰتِنَا وَكَلَّمَهُۥ
رَبُّهُۥ قَالَ رَبِّ أَرِنِىٓ أَنظُرْ إِلَيْكَ قَالَ لَن تَرَىٰنِى وَلَٰكِنِ
ٱنظُرْ إِلَى ٱلْجَبَلِ فَإِنِ ٱسْتَقَرَّ مَكَانَهُۥ فَسَوْفَ تَرَىٰنِى فَلَمَّا
تَجَلَّىٰ رَبُّهُۥ لِلْجَبَلِ جَعَلَهُۥ دَكًّا وَخَرَّ مُوسَىٰ صَعِقًا فَلَمَّآ
أَفَاقَ قَالَ سُبْحَٰنَكَ تُبْتُ إِلَيْكَ وَأَنَا۠ أَوَّلُ ٱلْمُؤْمِنِينَ ﴿١٤٣﴾

When Musa came to Our appointed time
and his Lord spoke to him,
he said, "My Lord, show me Yourself
so that I may look at You!"
He said, "You will not see Me, but look at the mountain.
If it remains firm in its place, then you will see Me."
But when His Lord manifested Himself to the mountain,
He crushed it flat
and Musa fell unconscious to the ground.
When he regained consciousness he said,
"Glory be to You! I make Tawba to You
and I am the first of the Muminun!"

V

At this stage the affair of Ma'rifa is openly shown. From this the Sufis derive the Doctrine of Fana' fillah. Allah openly reveals the purpose of the human creature. So we go to Surat al-Baqara (2:30). Here Allah reveals the whole event, the whole business of what the human creature is.

وَإِذْ قَالَ رَبُّكَ لِلْمَلَٰٓئِكَةِ إِنِّي جَاعِلٌ فِي ٱلْأَرْضِ خَلِيفَةً قَالُوٓاْ
أَتَجْعَلُ فِيهَا مَن يُفْسِدُ فِيهَا وَيَسْفِكُ ٱلدِّمَآءَ وَنَحْنُ نُسَبِّحُ
بِحَمْدِكَ وَنُقَدِّسُ لَكَ قَالَ إِنِّيٓ أَعْلَمُ مَا لَا تَعْلَمُونَ ٣٠

When your Lord said to the angels,
"I am putting a khalif on the earth,"
they said, "Why put on it one
who will cause corruption on it and shed blood
when we glorify You with praise
and proclaim Your purity?"
He said, "I know what you do not know."

That is the instilling into this creature of the Khilafal knowledge. This question that was asked is the question asked by the people who deny this whole dimension which is the truth of Islam – they are in the same position as those Angels who asked this wrong question to Allah, subhanahu wa ta'ala.

The third phase is Mushahida-i Ghayb – Seeing the Unseen. The Shuyukh say that at this stage many heads fall into the dust. Yet Allah grants insights, inspirations and understandings. To remain secure at this stage of the proceedings, the model, as in all matters of Ma'rifa, is the Rasul, sallallahu 'alayhi wa sallam. We go to Surat an-Najm (53:17-18). Here Allah tells us about the Rasul, in this affair of Divine Knowledge:

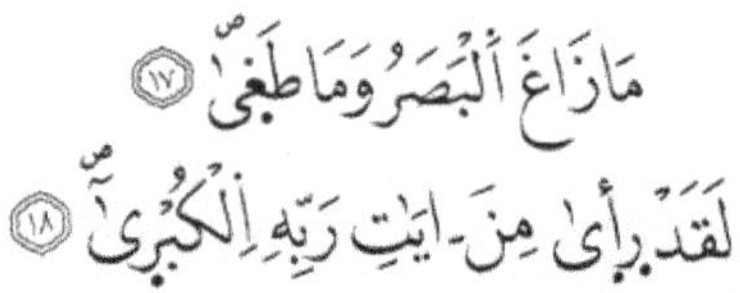

His eye did not waver nor did he look away.
He saw some of the Greatest Signs of his Lord.

This is the core of knowledge, as in Surat an-Najm (53:8-10):

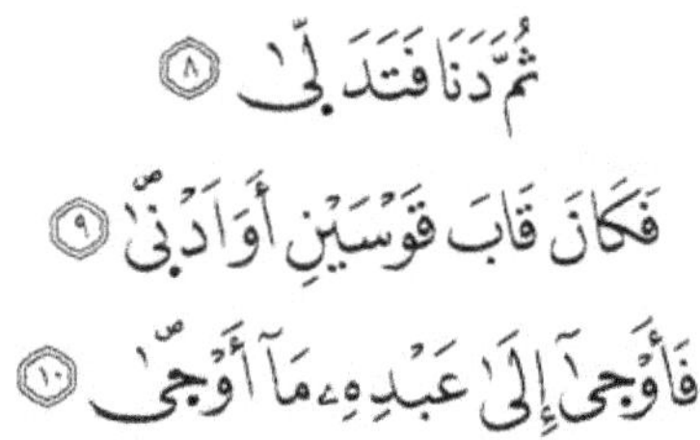

Then he drew near and hung suspended.
He was two bow-lengths away
or even closer.
Then He revealed to His slave what He revealed.

Look too, at the Qasida in the Diwan of Shaykh Muhammad ibn al-Habib – 'Withdrawal into the Perception of the Essence':

قَدْ بَــدا وَجْهُ الحَبِيبِ   لاحَ فِي وَقْتِ السَّحَرْ

نُورُهُ قَــدْ عَــمَّ قَلْبِي   فَسَجَــدْتُ بِانْكِسَارْ

قالَ لِي اِرْفَعْ وَاسْأَلْنِي   فَلَكُــمْ كُــلُّ وَطَرْ

قُلْتُ أَنْتَ أَنْتَ حَسْبِي   لَيْسَ لِي عَنْكَ اصْطِبارْ

قالَ عَبْدِي لَكَ بُشْرَى   فَتَنَعَّــمْ بِـــالنَّظَرْ

The Face of the Beloved appeared
And shone in the early dawn.

His light pervaded my heart,
So I prostrated myself in awe.

He said to me, "Rise! Ask of Me!
You will have whatever you desire."

I replied, "You. You are enough for me!
Away from You I cannot live!"

He said, "My slave, there is good news for you,
So enjoy the vision."

On the same theme, we find in the Qur'an, in the first line
of Ayat 45 in Surat al-Furqan (25:45):

أَلَمْ تَرَ إِلَىٰ رَبِّكَ كَيْفَ مَدَّ ٱلظِّلَّ

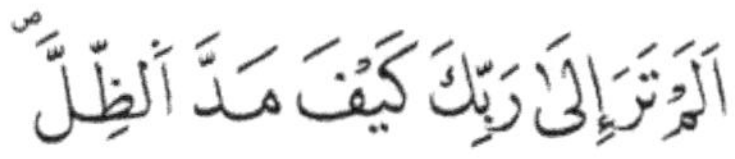

Have you not seen your Lord,
how He extends the shadows?

This is an astonishing Ayat. Whole books have been written by the Awliya on this. By Ishara, the great Sufis have taken the station to be indicated in the following Ayat of Surat al-Kahf (18:16):

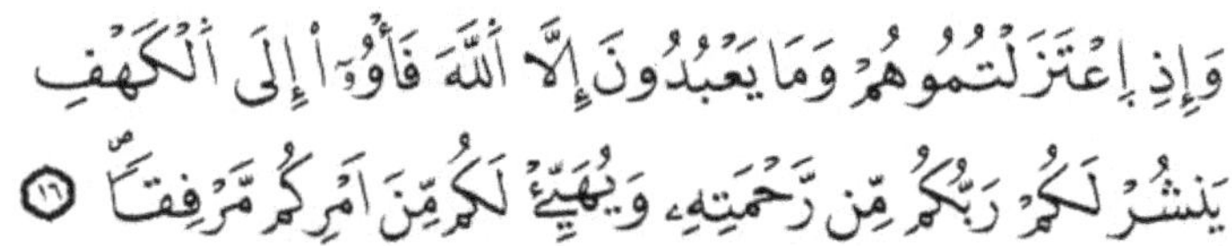

"When you have separated yourselves from them
and everything they worship except Allah,
take refuge in the cave
and your Lord will unfold His mercy to you
and open the way to the best for you in your situation."

Now you begin to see these Ayats with a new understanding. You have now learned the meaning of that phrase because we have learned that everything that is masiwallah has no reality. The Haqq is Allah. By Ishara, the Sufis have always read in this Ayat that to "take refuge in the cave" is to go into the heart, to take refuge in the heart, "and your Lord will unfold His mercy to you and open the way to the best for you in your situation." In other words, this action will produce the Fana' in Allah AND the Baqa' – the going-on-in-Allah, because then Allah will put you back in the world and you will be able to deal with everything.

The fourth phase of this is Arzu-i Mulukat – Desire for the

Meeting. This is the sign that the Lover is now the property of the Beloved. It is the Musan yearning for Ma'rifa. We look at Surat al-A'raf (7:143). It is the same Ayat we looked at earlier, but we will look at it again. This is becoming familiar to you now, and you see it now with a new understanding.

وَلَمَّا جَآءَ مُوسَىٰ لِمِيقَٰتِنَا وَكَلَّمَهُۥ
رَبُّهُۥ قَالَ رَبِّ أَرِنِىٓ أَنظُرْ إِلَيْكَ قَالَ لَن تَرَىٰنِى وَلَٰكِنِ
ٱنظُرْ إِلَى ٱلْجَبَلِ فَإِنِ ٱسْتَقَرَّ مَكَانَهُۥ فَسَوْفَ تَرَىٰنِى فَلَمَّا
تَجَلَّىٰ رَبُّهُۥ لِلْجَبَلِ جَعَلَهُۥ دَكًّا وَخَرَّ مُوسَىٰ صَعِقًا فَلَمَّآ
أَفَاقَ قَالَ سُبْحَٰنَكَ تُبْتُ إِلَيْكَ وَأَنَا۠ أَوَّلُ ٱلْمُؤْمِنِينَ ﴿١٤٣﴾

When Musa came to Our appointed time
and his Lord spoke to him,
he said, "My Lord, show me Yourself
so that I may look at You!"
He said, "You will not see Me,
but look at the mountain.
If it remains firm in its place,
then you will see Me."
But when His Lord manifested Himself to the mountain,
He crushed it flat
and Musa fell unconscious to the ground.
When he regained consciousness he said,
"Glory be to You! I make Tawba to You
and I am the first of the Muminun!"

The fifth phase is Istinas – Desire for Attachment. Desire then comes on the Lover to have this attachment to the Divine Experience. This manifests itself by the breaking of the contracts of Dunya. What that means is that the imposition and the demands and the necessities and the obligations of Dunya no longer matter to the heart of the Lover of Allah. The evidence of this – and this is the sign of the mature, experienced Sufi, the man who is strong on the Path – is that it is the same for him to stay as it is for him to go. It is the same for him to remain in his place or to go elsewhere. If there is a compulsion for him to go, and he says, "No, I am going to stay," he will do it from this inner state and condition which means that they are the same for him. If they are not the same for him, he will hold back until he has achieved that balance in himself.

The one who says, "No, because I have these important things to do," is of course blind, ignorant and lost, and only trouble will come on him because that itself is the contract of trouble. The contract of Dunya is the contract of trouble. Rasul, sallallahu 'alayhi wa sallam, has given many, many examples of this in famous recorded Hadith about the matter. Thus, being free to go and free to stay, being free to move and being free to be still – this is the mark of the Man. At this point you say that he is Rajul. These are the Rijalallah – those ones to whom these two are the same, because their only concern is what is pleasing to Allah, subhanahu wa ta'ala.

VI

AUGUST 25TH 2007

THREE MORE SPECIAL CONDITIONS OF THE LOVER

It is very important that you are absolutely still, apart from our looking up in the Ayats of Qur'an. We have been going into this matter for six weeks, and we are now going deeply into this subject of Love of Allah, subhanahu wa ta'ala.

Earlier on we gave Four Conditions of the Lover. I am interrupting the commentary of our Shaykh from Delhi, in order to add Three More Special Conditions of the Lover that are required. Next week, inshallah, we shall look at the final three Stages of our Shaykh from Delhi, in his summation.

So there are three more Special Conditions of the Lover. The First Condition is Ta'awwuh – To Sigh Deeply in Love of Allah, to give deep sighs of love. We look at Surat at-Tawba

(9:115), and the last line of the Ayat:

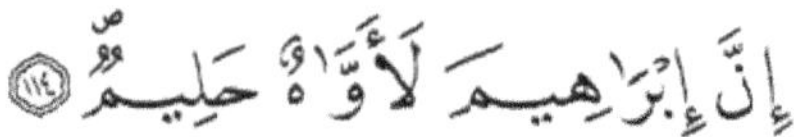

Ibrahim was tender-hearted and forbearing.

Our translation says, "tender-hearted," but in fact it is not really that. It is rather that he 'sighed deeply' with love of Allah, subhanahu wa ta'ala.

We now look at the matter of this sighing for love of Allah. Allah is qualified by His Name, Ar-Rahman which, let us say, has a breath, a breathing in – Nafas, and a breathing out – Naffasa, which gives His slaves. It is this breathing out that gives the creation the slaves. It is this Divine breathing out that gives the universe, by His Word: "Kun!" – "Be!" The Kun contains the breathing vowel and the interruptive consonants. This indicates the in-time, in-space bounded nature of all created things. This is also true of the Ha – the out-breath, and the 'A – the break of the Hamsa which is consonantal, it is a stop. These are the first guttural letters, or more precisely, they are the letters of the breast, being the consonantal model of the natural breathing out – Mutanaffis. This is the deep connection with the heart for they indicate the heart's activity with Ta'awwuh, with this, "Haaa," with this sighing deeply with love.

This is the meaning of the Imara, or the Hadra, among the Sufis. As the universe is created by the Kun, so all the letters are produced by the breathing out. Since Hadith Qudsi has taught us that the whole universe cannot contain Him, but the heart of the Mumin contains Him, it is from the breath which the heart releases that its source is in the Kun – the Breath of the Merciful.

It is the knowledge of this that awakens in the Lover a concern, desiring that the veiled humans could share this love, for Rasul, sallallahu 'alayhi wa sallam, has said, "The perfection of Iman in the Mumin is that he should love for his brother what he loves for himself." So the Lover of Allah also has a tumultuous concern that the people who are veiled should also have this love of Allah, subhanahu wa ta'ala.

Thus tenderness for the Beloved is one of the conditions of the Lover, which in turn awakens in them tenderness for the other human creatures who are veiled from this knowledge. Shafaqa.

The Second Condition is Istirah ila al-Kalam – To Seek Rest in the Words of his Beloved, and in the recitation which reminds of Him – Dhikr. Now we go to Qur'an and look at Surat al-Hijr (15:9):

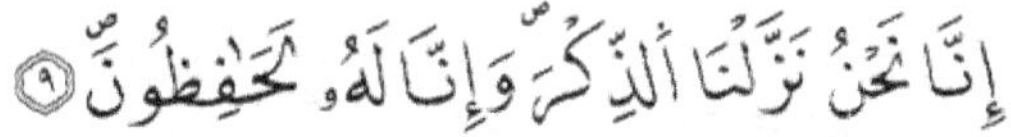

It is We Who have sent down the Reminder
and We Who will preserve it.

Here in this Ayat, the Word of Allah is named Dhikr – Reminder. By word of the command, "Kun!" – when the Kun brings the things into the creation – the human creature is transmuted and agitated through the passing from the condition of pure potentiality – 'Adm, to that of effective existence – Wujud, and is thus generated – Takawwana, he becomes living form, Kawn. It is this primal process which reverberates in the human creature when he hears the Sama', when he hears the spiritual music. The Dhikr, the Reminder, reminds of the Divine Command and this produces the Wajd – the ecstasy which is the subject of our study.

So the Dhikr connects him to knowing that he is the result of the "Kun!" He is the result of a Divine Command, for as the Kun is also the known Dhikr which is the Message and Command of the Beloved, so the Wajd, the ecstasy, is also the original Hubb, the original Love of the Beloved.

The Wajd is also the original Hubb, the original Love of the Beloved, which in turn is the Shawq – the Yearning and Longing of the Lover. Do you see? This dynamic is set in motion from the in-time creature to a beyond-time reality of Allah, subhanahu wa ta'ala, in His ordering the universe and His ordering us into existence one by one.

The Lover seeks rest in the Words, all the Words, of the Beloved. The Qur'an has Words of the Beloved and about the Beloved. Thus we can see where Allah gives Revelation to the Rasul, sallallahu 'alayhi wa sallam, and indicates His guidance to the kuffar. But at the same time, they are healing words to the Messenger, sallallahu 'alayhi wa sallam, and at the same time, healing words to the listening Mumin. Thus when the Ayat is revealed about a particular thing, it also brings with it a healing for the Rasul, sallallahu 'alayhi wa sallam, because it is a Word from his Lord. Surat Ya Sin (36:58):

سَلَٰمٌ قَوْلًا مِّن رَّبٍّ رَّحِيمٍ ٥٨

'Peace!'
A word from a Merciful Lord.

So also it has a healing to the Mumin who listens to the recitation of the Qur'an over a thousand years later. Look at Surat at-Tawba (9:6):

وَإِنْ أَحَدٌ مِّنَ ٱلْمُشْرِكِينَ ٱسْتَجَارَكَ فَأَجِرْهُ حَتَّىٰ يَسْمَعَ كَلَٰمَ
ٱللَّهِ ثُمَّ أَبْلِغْهُ مَأْمَنَهُۥ ذَٰلِكَ بِأَنَّهُمْ قَوْمٌ لَّا يَعْلَمُونَ ٦

If any of the mushrikun ask you for protection,
give them protection
until they have heard the Words of Allah.
Then convey them to a place where they are safe.
That is because they are a people who do not know.

This Ayat has these elements in it. It has an instruction about the relationship of the mushrikun to the Revelation, to the Words of Allah. That, in itself, being the Word of Allah, is what fills the heart of the Rasul, sallallahu 'alayhi wa sallam, because it has descended into his heart to reveal this Ayat. It is that Ayat, which is an instruction about the mushrikun, and which is the filling the heart of Rasul, sallallahu 'alayhi wa sallam, which also affects the heart of the Mumin when he hears Qur'an recited. Do you see the dimensions of reality involved in the Divine Revelation?

This Ayat also shows the meaning of the Hadith where Rasul, sallallahu 'alayhi wa sallam, said, "Every Ayat has an outward, an inward, and an 'Urf – a look-out post." We take that in a Ruhani sense. Every Ayat has an outward, an inward, and a Ruhani source. So we would say that the outward of the Ayat is the instruction concerning how Rasul, sallallahu 'alayhi wa sallam, is to deal with the mushrikun. At the same time, its inward is that it is illumination for Rasul, sallallahu 'alayhi wa sallam, in its coming from his heart and onto his tongue, from the Angel Jibril, 'alayhi salam. The 'Urf, the look-out post, is that it enters into the heart of the Mumin and affects him so that he can see in it also: "Give them protection until they have heard the Words of Allah. Then convey them to a place where they are safe." So when we hear it, it conveys us to that place which is safe, safe from our inward Shirk – and that place is in the Hadrat ar-Rabbani.

Now we come to the Third of these Conditions of the Lover – Ithar. Preference. It is 'To Prefer the Beloved to every other Company'. This preference of the Lover for the Beloved is explained by the reality that each element of the universe holds a place in man to whom it has been confided, and which must be restored. These deposits for which he is responsible are of a considerable number and their restitution is linked to the precise moments each one possesses his particular deposit.

Let me explain. Man has been placed in charge of the world and is answerable for it, for he is its purpose, its summit, and its master. Let us look at this. Abu Talib al-Makki, who was the first of the great Sufic writers of the science of Tasawwuf, in his famous book, 'Qut al-Qulub', indicates this cosmic trust, explaining this matter which I have just said:

> The celestial sphere runs its course thanks to the breaths of man – Anfas, or to be more precise, thanks to the breath of all the creatures that breathe. For the ultimate end of the universal manifestation, which is especially man, is realised by the Dhikr, or invoked breath, given that the heavenly sphere – the Fulk, takes its movement from the actual motion of the breath of Dhikr and cannot be disassociated from it in any way. This is why the world does not cease to be intimately associated with man.

Let us look at Qur'an, Surat al-Jumu'a (61:1):

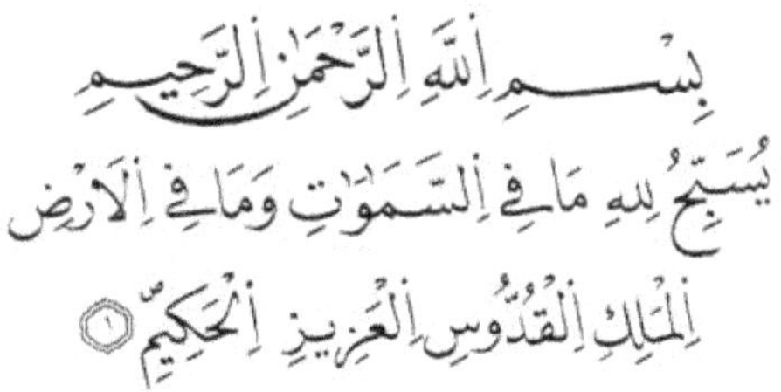

In the name of Allah, All-Merciful, Most Merciful
Everything in the heavens
and everything in the earth glorifies Allah,
the King, the All-Pure, the Almighty, the All-Wise.

With this knowledge that the Lovers have, they know that the whole universe is contained in them! The famous poem of Mawlay 'Abdalqadir al-Jilani, describing Ma'rifa, said, "Here is a strange thing: the boat is in the ocean, and now the ocean is in the boat." The creature is in the cosmos, and now the whole cosmos is in him!

Charged with the whole world, the Lovers look lovingly to Him in His nearness and His farness, preferring Him to the changing world. We look at Surat al-Hadid (57:4):

هُوَ ٱلَّذِي خَلَقَ ٱلسَّمَٰوَٰتِ وَٱلْأَرْضَ فِي سِتَّةِ أَيَّامٍ ثُمَّ ٱسْتَوَىٰ عَلَى
ٱلْعَرْشِ يَعْلَمُ مَا يَلِجُ فِي ٱلْأَرْضِ وَمَا يَخْرُجُ مِنْهَا وَمَا يَنزِلُ مِنَ ٱلسَّمَآءِ
وَمَا يَعْرُجُ فِيهَا وَهُوَ مَعَكُمْ أَيْنَ مَا كُنتُمْ وَٱللَّهُ بِمَا تَعْمَلُونَ بَصِيرٌ ﴿٤﴾

It is He Who created the heavens and the earth in six days,
then established Himself firmly on the Throne.
He knows what goes into the earth
and what comes out of it,
what comes down from heaven and what goes up into it.
He is with you wherever you are – Allah sees what you do.

One of the great Sufis, Sahl at-Tustari, was asked, "What is the maintenance of the created world?" What holds up, what sustains, what maintains the created forms? He said, "Allah." They said, "We want to know what makes life appear." He said, "Allah." He only saw Allah. When he realised that they could not understand, he qualified his answer. He said:

> Leave the dwellings to the Builder. If Allah wants, He will bring them to life but if He wants, He will devastate them. He does not enter into the condition of the subtle human entity to associate with this bodily

> residence, unless it dedicates itself to the works of the Beloved, the works that the Beloved has imposed on him – He Who is the Life itself and the Existence of this subtle entity. Whatever dwelling He has assigned to Himself, there He resides, there He dwells.

The Lover, therefore, is Allah, who has chosen man and preferred him to all the created beings, making him His Beloved.

So we now see that the thing is actually reversed. We started this journey seeing ourselves as the Lovers longing for the Beloved, and we discover that the Lover is Allah, because He has chosen man and preferred him to all the creatures. He has chosen man for His Company. Look at Surat al-Baqara (2:29), and the first two lines of this Ayat:

When your Lord said to the Angels,
"I am putting a Khalif on the earth."

This is the indication of the position of man. "I am putting a Khalif on the earth." Khalif, in the Arabic meaning of the word, is 'the one who stands in, in the absence of the King.' So it is as though Allah is saying, "I am putting My representative on the earth." It is this intimacy of elevation and ennoblement that is the true nature of the human creature.

From what follows in this part of Qur'an, with the discourse between Sayyiduna Adam and the Angels, is that Allah has placed man higher than the Angels. The one aspect of this Ma'rifa is this discovering that you have this high elected position with Allah, subhanahu wa ta'ala. You are His Khalif on the earth.

This takes us to the last recorded words of Rasul, sallallahu 'alayhi wa sallam, which our Imam mentioned last Jumu'a:

To the Highest Companion.

"To the Highest Companion" – to Allah, subhanahu wa ta'ala. This is the beloved going to the Lover, to Allah, subhanahu wa ta'ala. This is the Path of Ma'rifa, and its best model is Rasul, sallallahu 'alayhi wa sallam.

VII

SEPTEMBER 1ST 2007

This is the final session of our study on the subject of Hubb, of Love. We were looking at the Ten Stages of Love as defined by our Shaykh from Delhi, and we stopped at the Seventh, and then we looked at Three More Conditions necessary for the Lover.

Now we take up the last three of the Ten Stages, and we are now therefore at the Eighth Stage, which is Hubb itself – Love. This is what uproots the Tree of Life. Iman cannot be secured without love. We look at Surat al-Baqara (2:164):

وَالَّذِينَ ءَامَنُوٓا۟ أَشَدُّ حُبًّا لِّلَّهِ

But those who have Iman have greater love for Allah.

This is the confirmation of what I have just said. I would just re-iterate to you that every step of the way we have taken on the study of this Sufic science of Love, has been accompanied and backed up, and explained and supported directly from the Qur'an. We have said that Iman cannot be secured without love, and we find in Surat al-Baqara these lines:

وَالَّذِينَ ءَامَنُوٓا۟ أَشَدُّ حُبًّا لِّلَّهِ

But those who have Iman have greater love for Allah.

This happens now with a new knowledge. It is not in the doing of the Lover, but in the gift of the Beloved. We go to Surat al-Baqara again (2:245), and the last two lines:

وَاللَّهُ يُؤْتِي مُلْكَهُۥ مَن يَشَآءُ
وَاللَّهُ وَاسِعٌ عَلِيمٌ ٢٤٧

Allah gives kingship to anyone He wills.
Allah is All-Encompassing, All-Knowing.

Hubb has five phases. The First is Fuqdan-i Qalb – To Lose one's Heart. It has been dislocated from satisfaction in the Dunya. This is the essential event. This is the crack that in fact makes possible the lights that comes from Love. The heart is dislocated from being satisfied with the Dunya, not from being against Dunya, not desiring Dunya, but dislocated from satisfaction in the Dunya. This means that whatever it gets, that is not enough, that is not it, and the person remains restless, however successful, however fulfilling to other people their Dunya would seem on observing them. At that stage, the Lover cannot live without the Tavern of the Wine.

The Second Phase of Hubb is Ta'assuf – Grief. Its condition is defined in Surat Yusuf (12:84). This is one of the vital phases of this Hubb, being the grief which is expressed in this Ayat.

وَتَوَلَّىٰ عَنْهُمْ وَقَالَ يَٰأَسَفَىٰ عَلَىٰ يُوسُفَ
وَٱبْيَضَّتْ عَيْنَاهُ مِنَ ٱلْحُزْنِ فَهُوَ كَظِيمٌ ﴿٨٤﴾

He turned himself away from them and said,
"What anguish is my sorrow for Yusuf!"
And then his eyes turned white from hidden grief.

The third phase is Wajd – Ecstasy. The whole cosmos becomes constricted and contained, and the Lover flies out beyond it. So we look now at 'The Greater Qasida' of Shaykh Muhammad ibn al-Habib, rahimahullah:

فَلَوْ عَـرَفَ الإنْسانُ قِيمَـةَ قَلْبِهِ   لأنْفَـقَ كُلَّ الكُلِّ مِـنْ غَيْرِ فَتْرَةِ
وَلَـوْ أَدْرَكَ الإنْسانُ لَـذَّةَ سِرِّهِ   لَقـارَنَ أَنْفاسَ الخُـرُوجِ بِعَبْرَةِ
وَطارَ مِنَ الجِسْمِ الذِي صارَ قَفْصَهُ   بِأَجْنِحَـةِ الأَفْكـارِ مُنْتَهى سِدْرَةِ
وَجالَ نَواحِي العَرْشِ وَالكُرْسيِّ الذِي   تَضاءَلَتِ الأَجْـرامُ عَنْـهُ كَحَلْقَةِ

For a man would not hesitate to spend all he had
– if he only understood the secret of his own heart.

If a man could but grasp the bliss of his secret
he would shed a tear with every breath he breathed.

Then, his body become his cage, he would fly from it
with the wings of contemplation to the Furthest Lote-tree.

He would freely roam around the Throne and the Footstool
which make the heavenly bodies appear like a small ring.

You must understand that this is a specific, exact description of the experience of the person in Khalwa. This is EXACTLY what he will experience.

The fourth phase is Bi-Sabri – Impatience. This is the penultimate stage of restlessness. Love and patience are two antonyms. One of the Sufis said, "Between love and patience lie a thousand miles."

The fifth phase is Sianat – Safety. Only in this stage does the mention of the Beloved bring respite. We look at the Second Qasida in the Diwan of Shaykh al-Fayturi, rahimahullah:

أَضْرَمَتْ نَارُ الهَوَاى لَدَعَتْ قَلْبِي انْكَوى
لَنْ تَذَرْ فيه السِّوَى عَـادَ مَرْعِي لأَصْلِي
خِلِّي ظَاهِرْ في مَجْلاهْ أَضاءَ الكَوْنَ سَناهْ
ظَهَرَتْ شَمْسُ بَهاهْ مـــا أَبْدَعُ التَّجَلِّي
فَهُوَ سِرُّ الوُجُودْ هُـــوَ الشَّاهِدْ والمَشْهُودْ
إِلَيْهِ الأَمْرُ يَعُـــودُ هُـــوَ مُرْشِدُ الكُلِّ

The fire of passion was kindled and it called my heart:
Be burned!
It will not leave other in it,
so it became a branch of my root.

My close Friend is outwardly manifest
in His place of Tajalli.
The cosmos illuminated His radiance.
The sun of His splendour appeared –
how marvellous the Tajalli is!

He is the secret of existence.
He is the Witness and the Witnessed.
The command returns to Him. He is the guide of all.

We go now from the Eighth to the Ninth Stage of Love, which is Taim – Enslavement. At this stage the manacles of humiliation and submission are put round the neck of the Lover, and his feet are bound by the chains of slavery. It has five phases.

The first phase is Tafarrud – Isolation. This is the station of isolation prior to the meeting of the Beloved and its Secret. Now love, Lover and Beloved become one. The end of duality is the end of the separated self. The union with the Beloved is the disappearance of the Lover. Here the kuffar accuse the Sufis of 'joining' and connecting, but the Doctrine of Fana' fillah is itself an 'Ashari position. The Diwan of Shaykh Muhammad ibn al-Habib explains in the Qasida 'The Gifts of the Ism al-'Adham':

وَمَـا نَالَ عِـزّاً غَيْرُ مُنْفَـرِدٍ بِـهِ

تَحَلَّى بِما يُرْضِيهِ مَعْ كَثْرَةِ الحَمْدِ

فَما زَالَ يَرْقَـــى فِي مَهامِهِ ذاتِهِ

وَيَفْنَـى فَنَاءً لَيْسَ فِيهِ سِوَى الفَقْدِ

Power is only given to the one isolated with Him,
And who, through much praise, pleases Him.

Thus he will rise, crossing the deserts of His Essence, until
His Fana' enters a Fana', one that has nothing in it but loss.

This we find in the Qur'an, in Surat ar-Rahman (55:24-25):

كُلُّ مَنْ عَلَيْهَا فَانٍ ۝

وَيَبْقَىٰ وَجْهُ رَبِّكَ ذُو ٱلْجَلَٰلِ وَٱلْإِكْرَامِ ۝

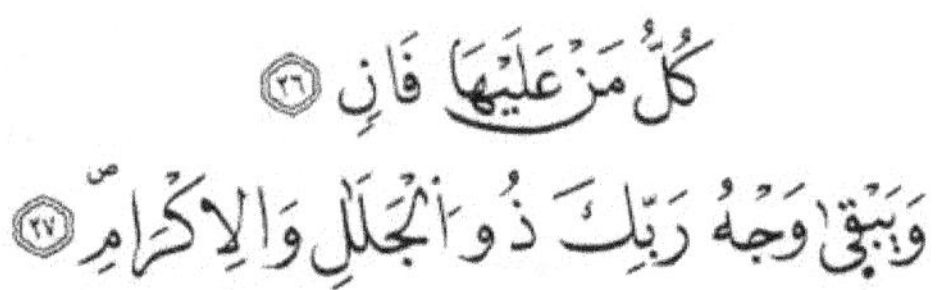

Everyone on it will pass away;
but the Face of your Lord will remain,
Master of Majesty and Generosity.

So you see how this is exactly what the Shaykh has said in
his Diwan. When the Lover enters Fana', then, as in that
Ayat, he passes away, but there remains the Face of Allah,
subhanahu wa ta'ala.

The second phase of this Enslavement is Istitar – Concealment. It is at this stage that Allah gives reward to His Lover

with secrets in accord with his Wilayat. Its highest aspect is shown between Allah and His Messenger, sallallahu 'alayhi wa sallam, on the Mi'raj. So we shall look at Surat an-Najm (53:10), which is in relation to the Rasul, sallallahu 'alayhi wa sallam:

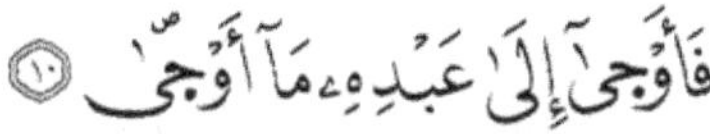

Then He revealed to His slave what He revealed.

The term is Wahy, and that is very important to understand, because Wahy is 'Showing'. Wahy is the word used for Revelation, but the Revelation is to show it. It is Allah showing secrets to the Rasul, sallallahu 'alayhi wa sallam.

"Then He revealed to His slave what He revealed." Some say these are indicated in the isolated letters of the Qur'an: Alif, Lam, Mim and Kaf, Ha, Ya, 'Ayn, Sad, and so on, but Allahu 'Alim, we do not ever indicate meanings to these letters.

The third phase is Badhl-i Ruh – To Stake one's Life. With this aspect of Hubb comes the understanding that nothing matters anymore. Nothing in the world matters. This is the essence of Love because once you have this with Allah, nothing matters, that's it! The Lover is free.

Because from this come the next two phases which are Khawf and Raja' – Fear and Hope. These two are the dialectic of Love. Iman is between the two. You will find also that there are Hadith to that effect. Shaykh Muhammad ibn al-Habib instructs in his Diwan in the Qasida of 'Purification':

وَلا بُدَّ مِنْ نَعْلَيْنِ خَوْفٍ مَـعَ الرَّجَى
وَعُكَّازِ إيقانٍ وَزادٍ مِـنَ التَّقْوَى

Put on the twin sandals of Khawf and Raja',
Take the staff of Yaqin and a store of Taqwa.

This is a fundamental knowledge that the Faqir has taken from the very beginning of his journey, because of his taking this counsel in this Song, in order to reach the highest Ma'rifa.

This takes us to the Tenth and final Stage of Love which is Walah – Bewilderment. In distance it is torment, in proximity it is bewilderment. The Sufi cries out:

If I see You, I lose my life!
If I do not see You, how can I live?
I face a strange dilemma!
Should I lose my life –
or should I abstain from seeing You?

This is Walah. It has five phases. The first phase is Ibtihal – Supplication. The Lover begs only for the Beloved. We look now at the Diwan of Shaykh Muhammad ibn al-Habib, and 'Withdrawal into the Perception of the Essence':

قَدْ بَـدا وَجْهُ الحَبيبِ　　لاحَ فِي وَقْتِ السَّحَرْ
نُورُهُ قَـدْ عَـمَّ قَلْبِي　　فَسَجَـدْتُ بِانْكِسارْ
قالَ لِي اِرْفَعْ وَاسْأَلَنِّي　　فَلَكُـمْ كُـلُّ وَطَرْ
قُلْتُ أَنْتَ أَنْتَ حَسْبِي　　لَيْسَ لِي عَنْكَ اصْطِبارْ

The Face of the Beloved appeared
And shone in the early dawn.

His light pervaded my heart,
So I prostrated myself in awe.

He said to me, "Rise! Ask of Me!
You will have whatever you desire."

I replied, "You. You are enough for me!
Away from You I cannot live!"

Now we come to the second phase which is Shurb – Drinking the Wine of Love. Shaykh al-Fayturi tells in his Diwan, in his Second Song:

نَظَرْتُ خَلْفَ السِّتَارْ ما لاَ تُدْرِكُ الأَبْصارْ
غِبْتُ فِي بَحْرِ الأَنْوارْ صارَ بَعْضِي كُلِّي
دارَتْ كُؤُوسُ الطَّارِيقْ أُدْنُ مِنِّي يا رَفِيقْ
نُسْقِيكَ خَمْرٌ عَتِيقْ نُحْظَى بِرُوحِ الكُلِّ

I looked behind the veil at what the eyes do not perceive,
I withdrew into the sea of lights –
Part of me became all of me.

The goblets of the Path were passed around:
"Come near Me, My friend!
We will let you drink an ancient wine –
You will obtain the joy of all!"

He tells also in his Fourth Song:

شَرِبْتُ بِالأَقْداحْ مِنْ دَنْداتِ الرَّاحْ
فَاهْتَزَتِ الأَشْبَــــاحْ طَرَبــــاً بِاللهْ

I drank cups from wine-jars of joy
And so the forms quivered out of rapture with Allah.

Also in the Fifth Song of Shaykh al-Fayturi we find:

أَدْنَ لَدُنِ الرَّاحْ شُرْبُهُ مُباحْ
بِــــهِ حَقّاً تَرْتَاحْ تَرَى وَجْهُ اللهْ

Draw near to the wine-jug of joy.
Its drink is permitted!
Truly you will be pleased with it –
You will see the Face of Allah!

Now let us look again at the Diwan of Shaykh Muhammad ibn al-Habib, and his Qasida 'The Robe of Nearness' – Qad Kasana:

وَسَقانا الحَبيبُ شُرْبَـــةَ حُبٍّ
قَدْ أَزالَتْ سِوَى الحَبيبِ اضْطِرارا
وَشَهِدْنا الأَكْوانَ مَحْضَ هَبـاءٍ
وَرَأَيْنا الأَنْـــوارَ تَبْـــدُو جِهارا

The Beloved gave us a draught of pure love to drink
Which forced all but the Beloved to disappear.

We saw the whole creation as mere floating specks of dust:
We saw the lights appear, openly and clearly.

The third phase is Sukr – Intoxication. Here Shaykh al-Fayturi declares in his Diwan, in the Third Song:

مَوْتي وُجُودِي غَيْبي شُهُودِي
فَالْجُودُ جُـــودِي والحَيْرَهْ تَمْتَمْ

My death is my existence,
my withdrawal is my witnessing –
So generosity is my generosity and confusion stutters.

The intoxication makes him say that his death is his existence, and his withdrawal is his witnessing, and the generosity is his generosity, and confusion stutters because he cannot make sense of it, it is so intoxicating.

The fourth phase of this Walah is Idtirab wa Bikhudi – Distraction and Selflessness. One of the Sufis was alone, sobbing, and he cried out, "Fire! Fire!" People rushed to him and saw no fire. "What is on fire?" they asked. The Lover beat his breast and he recited this Ayat of Qur'an. Surat al-Humaza (104:6-7):

نَـارُ ٱللَّهِ ٱلْمُوقَـدَةُ ۝

ٱلَّتِي تَطَّـلِعُ عَلَى ٱلْأَفْـِدَةِ ۝

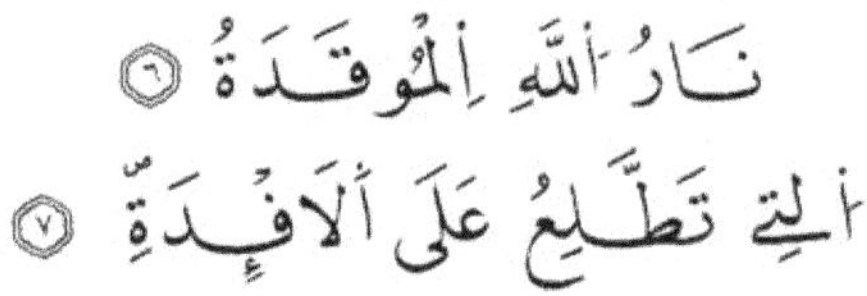

The kindled Fire of Allah
reaching right into the heart.

The fifth and final phase is Talaf – Destruction. Shaykh Muhammad ibn al-Habib explains in his Diwan, in 'The Gifts of the Ism al-'Adham':

فَما زالَ يَرْقَـى فِي مَهامِهِ ذاتِهِ

وَيَفْنَـى فَناءً لَيْسَ فِيهِ سِوَى الفَقْدِ

فَإِنْ رُدَّ لِلآثَـارِ جَـاءَ بِحُلَّـةٍ

تُـنادِي عَلَيْـهِ بِالوِلايَـةِ وَالمَجْدِ

Thus he will rise, crossing the deserts of His Essence,
Until his Fana' enters a Fana',
one that has nothing in it but loss.

If he returns to the traces of existence,
he brings a Robe of Honour
which proclaims his Wilaya and glory.

At that point, the annihilation of the presence of the experiencing Lover, in the wiping out even of his knowledge that he is obliterated, the affair of love, from the science of Sufism, from the laws of the secret transaction, the vanished Lover may return. Our Shaykh has explained in 'The Robe of Nearness':

وَرَجَعْنا لِلْخَلْـقِ بَعْـدَ انْمِحاقٍ
وَفَناءٍ فِي خَمْـرَةٍ تُعْطِي نُورا
فَبِفَضْـلٍ مِـنَ الإلَـٰـهِ بَقِينا
وَكَتَمْنا الذِي نُحِـبُّ اصْطِبارا

After having been effaced by Fana'
In a light-giving wine, we returned to creation.

By a pure gift from Allah we were given Baqa',
And so, with patience, we concealed the One we love.

At that stage, we have really reached the end of the Shaykh of Delhi's description of Love, and we now discover beyond it a whole other reality which is Baqa' billah. Baqa', properly speaking, in Ruhani terms, is the beginning of the Deen and its transmission. Our Master is the Master of the Mi'raj, of the Night Journey. What is the result of the Night Journey if it is not the guidance, if it is not the Furqan?

When I returned from Khalwa at the hands of Shaykh al-Fayturi, radiyallahu 'anhu, one of his Fuqara asked me, "Now where will you go?" I replied, "After Makkah, where can I go – except Madinah?" From this came our work to elevate the School of Madinah, and later to restore the fallen Pillar of Zakat.

Now let us look again at Surat an-Najm (53:30-61), which contains all the secrets of this subject. Surat an-Najm begins, we could say, with the matter of the Mi'raj, and it ends, you could say, with defining the Fana'. Then, in Sufi language, it defines Baqa' from the thirtieth Ayat. This completes our study.

وَلِلَّهِ مَا فِي السَّمَاوَاتِ وَمَا فِي الْأَرْضِ
لِيَجْزِيَ الَّذِينَ أَسَاءُوا بِمَا عَمِلُوا وَيَجْزِيَ الَّذِينَ أَحْسَنُوا بِالْحُسْنَى ﴿٣١﴾
الَّذِينَ يَجْتَنِبُونَ كَبَائِرَ الْإِثْمِ وَالْفَوَاحِشَ إِلَّا اللَّمَمَ إِنَّ رَبَّكَ وَاسِعُ
الْمَغْفِرَةِ هُوَ أَعْلَمُ بِكُمْ إِذْ أَنْشَأَكُمْ مِنَ الْأَرْضِ وَإِذْ أَنْتُمْ أَجِنَّةٌ
فِي بُطُونِ أُمَّهَاتِكُمْ فَلَا تُزَكُّوا أَنْفُسَكُمْ هُوَ أَعْلَمُ بِمَنِ اتَّقَى ﴿٣٢﴾
أَفَرَأَيْتَ الَّذِي تَوَلَّى ﴿٣٣﴾ وَأَعْطَى قَلِيلًا وَأَكْدَى ﴿٣٤﴾ أَعِنْدَهُ عِلْمُ
الْغَيْبِ فَهُوَ يَرَى ﴿٣٥﴾ أَمْ لَمْ يُنَبَّأْ بِمَا فِي صُحُفِ مُوسَى ﴿٣٦﴾ وَإِبْرَاهِيمَ الَّذِي وَفَّى ﴿٣٧﴾
أَلَّا تَزِرُ وَازِرَةٌ وِزْرَ أُخْرَى ﴿٣٨﴾ وَأَنْ لَيْسَ لِلْإِنْسَانِ إِلَّا مَا سَعَى ﴿٣٩﴾
وَأَنَّ سَعْيَهُ سَوْفَ يُرَى ﴿٤٠﴾ ثُمَّ يُجْزَاهُ الْجَزَاءَ الْأَوْفَى ﴿٤١﴾ وَأَنَّ
إِلَى رَبِّكَ الْمُنْتَهَى ﴿٤٢﴾ وَأَنَّهُ هُوَ أَضْحَكَ وَأَبْكَى ﴿٤٣﴾ وَأَنَّهُ هُوَ أَمَاتَ وَأَحْيَا ﴿٤٤﴾
وَأَنَّهُ خَلَقَ الزَّوْجَيْنِ الذَّكَرَ وَالْأُنْثَى ﴿٤٥﴾ مِنْ نُطْفَةٍ إِذَا تُمْنَى ﴿٤٦﴾

وَأَنَّ عَلَيْهِ اِ۬لنَّشْأَةَ اَ۬لْأُخْرىٰ ﴿٤٧﴾ وَأَنَّهُۥ هُوَ أَغْنىٰ وَأَقْنىٰ ﴿٤٨﴾ وَأَنَّهُۥ هُوَ
رَبُّ اُ۬لشِّعْرىٰ ﴿٤٩﴾ وَأَنَّهُۥ أَهْلَكَ عَاداً اِ۬لُاولىٰ ﴿٥٠﴾ وَثَمُودَاْ فَمَآ أَبْقىٰ ﴿٥١﴾
وَقَوْمَ نُوحٖ مِّن قَبْلُ إِنَّهُمْ كَانُواْ هُمُۥ أَظْلَمَ وَأَطْغىٰ ﴿٥٢﴾ وَالْمُؤْتَفِكَةَ
أَهْوىٰ ﴿٥٣﴾ فَغَشّىٰهَا مَا غَشّىٰ ﴿٥٤﴾ فَبِأَيِّ ءَالَآءِ رَبِّكَ تَتَمَارىٰ ﴿٥٥﴾
هَٰذَا نَذِيرٞ مِّنَ اَ۬لنُّذُرِ اِ۬لُاولىٰ ﴿٥٦﴾ أَزِفَتِ اِ۬لْأٓزِفَةُ ﴿٥٧﴾ لَيْسَ لَهَا
مِن دُونِ اِ۬للَّهِ كَاشِفَةٌ ﴿٥٨﴾ أَفَمِنْ هَٰذَا اَ۬لْحَدِيثِ تَعْجَبُونَ ﴿٥٩﴾ وَتَضْحَكُونَ
وَلَا تَبْكُونَ ﴿٦٠﴾ وَأَنتُمْ سَٰمِدُونَ ﴿٦١﴾ فَاسْجُدُواْ لِلَّهِ وَاعْبُدُواْ ﴿٦٢﴾

Everything in the heavens and everything in the earth
belongs to Allah
so that He can repay those who do evil for what they did
and repay those who do good with the Very Best.

To whomever avoids the major wrong actions
and indecencies –
except for minor lapses –
truly your Lord is vast in forgiveness.
He has most knowledge of you
when He first produced you from the earth,
and when you were embryos in your mothers' wombs.
So do not claim purity for yourselves.
He knows best those who have Taqwa.

Have you seen him who turns away
and gives little, and that grudgingly?

Does he have knowledge of the Unseen,
enabling him to see?

Or has he not been informed what is in the texts of Musa
and of Ibrahim, who paid his dues in full:

that no burden-bearer can bear another's burden;
that man will have nothing but what he strives for;
that his striving will most certainly be seen;
that he will then receive repayment of the fullest kind;
that the ultimate end is with your Lord;
that it is He Who brings about both laughter and tears;
that it is He Who brings about both death and life;
that He created the two sexes – male and female –
out of a sperm-drop when it spurted forth;
that He is responsible for the second existence;
that it is He Who enriches and Who satisfies;
that it is He Who is the Lord of Sirius;
that He destroyed 'Ad, the earlier people,
and Thamud as well, sparing none of them,
and the people of Nuh before –
they were most unjust and exorbitant –
and the Overturned City which He turned upside down
so that what enveloped it enveloped it.

Which one of your Lord's blessings do you then dispute?

This is a warning like the warnings of old.
The Imminent is imminent!
No one besides Allah can unveil it.

Are you then amazed at this discourse
and laugh and do not cry,
treating life as a game?

Prostrate before Allah and worship Him!

At the last Ayat of this we have to make Sajda. Concentrate! Look at the Qur'an.

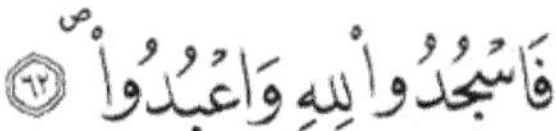

Prostrate before Allah and worship Him!

THE BOOK

OF

'AMAL

Eight Discourses
given between
October 27th 2007
and January 12th 2008
at the Nizamia Mosque,
Tokai, Cape Town

I

October 27th 2007

I want to introduce the subject of Mu'amala. Mu'amala is defined by the Rasul, sallallahu 'alayhi wa sallam: "Ad-Deen al-Mu'amala." The Deen is Mu'amala, the Deen is Behaviour. 'Behaviour' is not the best word, but it will do for the moment.

If the Deen is nothing but correct manners and correct behaviour, it is therefore the responsibility of every Muslim to know what that is and what is expected of him. For the Sufi it is more important because Imam al-Ghazali has warned in his 'Ihya al-'Ulum ad-Deen and other places that 'Ilm al-Mu'amala has to precede 'Ilm al-Mukashafa. In other words, the knowledges of behaviour have to precede the knowledge of the veiled matters, of the hidden things, of the Anwar – the lights, and the illuminations that come from Allah, subhanahu wa ta'ala. But prior to that is that you have the correct behaviour.

It would not be correct to negate Imam al-Ghazali, who is our great teacher, but without denying what he said, I would actually say that the opposite is true: 'Ilm al-Mukashafa precedes 'Ilm al-Mu'amala. Remembering that we have said that Mu'amala is the Deen itself, we therefore have to say what Mu'amala is. We are going to find the Qur'anic explanation of the source of Mu'amala in the Qur'an and we shall find it in Surat al-Baqara (2:144):

قَدْ نَرَىٰ تَقَلُّبَ وَجْهِكَ فِي ٱلسَّمَآءِ فَلَنُوَلِّيَنَّكَ
قِبْلَةً تَرْضَىٰهَا فَوَلِّ وَجْهَكَ شَطْرَ ٱلْمَسْجِدِ ٱلْحَرَامِ وَحَيْثُ مَا
كُنتُمْ فَوَلُّوا۟ وُجُوهَكُمْ شَطْرَهُۥ وَإِنَّ ٱلَّذِينَ أُوتُوا۟
ٱلْكِتَٰبَ لَيَعْلَمُونَ أَنَّهُ ٱلْحَقُّ مِن رَّبِّهِمْ
وَمَا ٱللَّهُ بِغَٰفِلٍ عَمَّا يَعْمَلُونَ ﴿١٤٤﴾

We have seen you looking up into heaven,
turning this way and that,
so We will turn you towards a direction
which will please you.
Turn your face, therefore, towards the Masjid al-Haram.
Wherever you all are, turn your faces towards it.
Those given the Book know it is the truth from their Lord.
Allah is not unaware of what they do.

Here we have the manifestation, the unveiling of Mu'amala, and it is Allah's bounty on the Muslims.

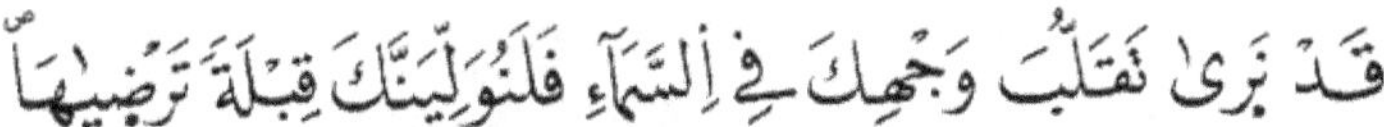

We have seen you looking up into heaven,
turning this way and that,
so We will turn you towards a direction
which will please you.

Allah, subhanahu wa ta'ala, is giving an order, giving us the Qibla, the direction in which the Muslims will worship. He says, "You have been looking for something and I am going to give it to you." This is the 'Amal of Allah, subhanahu wa ta'ala, on the Muslims. Remember that this is a Revealed Book, this is a Revelation that has come from Jibril and into the heart of Rasul, sallallahu 'alayhi wa sallam, and is then open to the people by the permission of Allah, subhanahu wa ta'ala. Remember that the Adab of Allah and everything in Qur'an flows to the Rasul, and from the Rasul to the people. "So We will turn you towards a direction which will please you." You could say this is to the Rasul, but it is also to all the Muslim people because Allah then says:

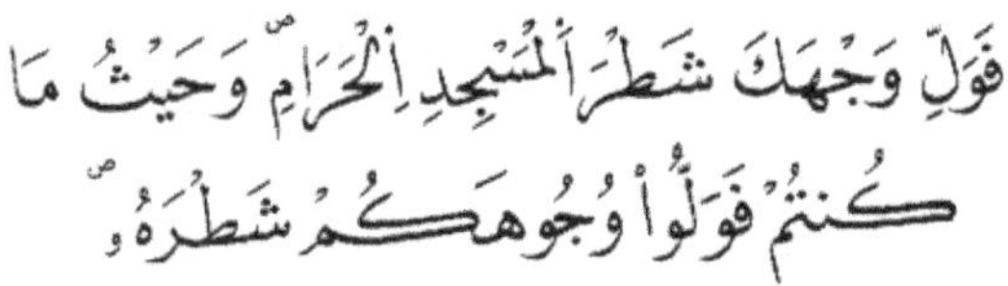

Turn your face, therefore, towards the Masjid al-Haram.
Wherever you all are, turn your faces towards it.

This is really the moment of the foundation of Islam. The granting of the Qibla happens while there is still the final putting-in-place of the Hajj. This is the initiatory creation of the new religion, and it is an act of Adab of Allah to his Messenger and to His people. Allah does not say, "I will turn you to a direction that is pleasing to Me." He says, "I will turn you to a direction which is pleasing to you." This is Adab. This is the Adab of Allah on His Messenger and on His people.

He then says, "Turn your face, therefore, towards the Masjid al-Haram." At that point He creates a new Deen with this act of courtesy. And He says, "Wherever you all are, turn your faces towards it." Now look at the next passage:

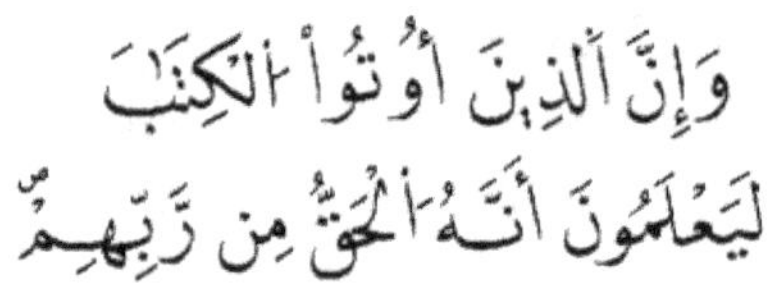

Those given the Book know
it is the truth from their Lord.

The Adab of the Muslims encompasses the situation of the people who have been given the Book. In other words, when this happens, everything they stood on is finished. But because they have been given the Book, they know it is the truth. At that moment, the old dispensation is finished, which is also why ANY talk of discourse or connection with, or collaboration with the jews and the christians is out of the question. They are finished! They are sacked from the practice of worship because they know from their Books that the Qibla is the foundation of the Deen – because they had another Qibla. They had one, and now it is over and finished, and now there is this new one, and this is for the people who love Allah, subhanahu wa ta'ala, and who follow the Rasul, sallallahu 'alayhi wa sallam. Surat an-Nisa (4:59):

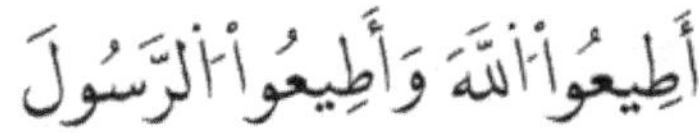

Obey Allah and obey the Messenger.

This is the command of Allah, subhanahu wa ta'ala. The final passage is:

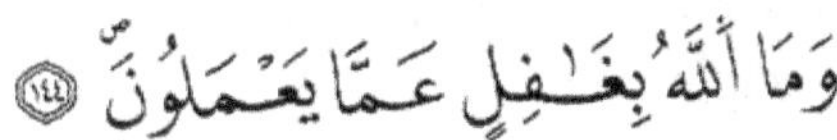

Allah is not unaware of what they do.

So Allah is not unaware of what they, the jews and the christians, do. The one who dispenses correct behaviour knows whether it is received well or whether it is not received well. If he is dispensing it then he has knowledge – the one of manners, of courtesy, is a man of knowledge. So if it is received, he knows if it is received, and if it is rejected, he knows if it is rejected. Sometimes hypocrites do it in a very special way. Cunning and diabolical people do it in a very clever way. But the one who has 'Amal, who has correct behaviour, he knows, because 'Amal itself is knowledge, it is Hikma.

We go back to what I said earlier: Ad-Deen al-Mu'amala. That is the foundation of the Deen. The indication of the Qibla is the beginning of the Deen, and facing the correct

Qibla is a Divine Illumination. By being given the Qibla of the Masjid al-Haram you have been given the point of reference. It is perfect manners, and it comes from Allah to Rasul, to the Muslim people.

The truth is that all real good manners come from the one of knowledge, and are dispensed to the ones either of ignorance or of innocence. It is the treating of these people in that way that has in it wisdom.

We said at the beginning of this that while Imam al-Ghazali's statement is that 'Ilm al-Mu'amala precedes 'Ilm al-Mukashafa, I say that the opposite is true, while not denying the principle upon which he says that. I give you an example: I was with my Shaykh, Shaykh Muhammad ibn al-Habib, rahimahullah, in the little room at the top of his tower in his Zawiya, and there was a very poor man from the desert who had some need to go to Marrakesh, which is on the other side of Morocco from Meknes, and with him were one or two of the Shaykh's Fuqara from Meknes. The Shaykh said, "You must go to Marrakesh," but then he saw that the man had no money, nothing. So he turned to one of his Fuqara and said, "Give him the money for his fare to Marrakesh," and the Faqir said, "Bismillah," and took out his purse and gave the money to the man. The poor man was overwhelmed and crying and he took the money and fell on his knees and started to kiss the man's knee and his foot, and the Faqir exclaimed, "No, no! Stop, stop!" Shaykh Muhammad ibn al-Habib became very angry and said, "Leave him be! Let him do it!" The Faqir was taken aback because he had done this good action, but here he was, being rebuked! The man again kissed his foot and said,

"Thank you, thank you!" and then left. Then Shaykh Muhammad ibn al-Habib turned on this poor fellow who had handed over the fare and said, "How dare you do that! You must not take away from him the right to cover his shame about his poverty." This made me see that the REAL Adab was not the giving of the money. The real Adab was knowing how to behave when you gave the money.

Also, the Rasul has said that the Sadaqa that is seen is less than the Sadaqa that is not seen, because then the Adab is strictly between Allah and the one who receives it. We are also told that if you have not thanked the giver, then you have not thanked Allah. Thus, I am saying that the whole matter of Adab is something that can only come by the one who is spiritually illuminated.

The first principle of all Adab is that you set the people who are lower than you above you, and you set the people who are higher than you, either below you or equal to you. That is why the ethos of politics is a matter of shaytan because there they do not recognise the person, they recognise the position. This is the opposite of behaviour, even when they appear to be correct. If you want a proof of this, look at any news-reel of a politician, and you will see him shaking hands one way, and his eyes going to where the next person is going to be that he is going to receive a greeting from – whereas the one of Adab would look at the person he is greeting because it is the man giving to you from himself.

So Adab is something which is unmasked in very small things, otherwise it never appears in the big things. The mark of the modern rich Muslims is that they treat their servants and the people below them abominably. Nowhere do you see people more badly treated than in Arabia and the Emirates – they treat people like dogs. But then that means that they are the dogs. This matter then of Adab is actually the end of all concepts of equality. Equality is a lie. It is a lie among the people who preach it, and it is a lie among the people who pretend to carry it out. People are not the same. People are not equal. Some are better than others – and I am not talking about their wealth but about their being. And some are less than others. The man of Allah is perpetually aware that things are not what they seem, so that one man may come to him and he may treat him with great Adab and courtesy because he sees he is a man of Allah, he sees that Allah loves this man, while another man he will treat with disdain. There are all different balances of this.

When Moulay al-'Arabi ad-Darqawi was sitting in his Zawiya in Fes with his Fuqara, a very rich Fasi merchant came in. He said to the Fuqara, "Get up and greet your master!" Why? Because this man fed them, and it was only fitting that they should greet him. Not because he was rich but because he fed the Fuqara. One of the great Sufis of Shaykh Muhammad ibn al-Habib, rahimahullah, Hajj Jilali, rahimahullah, he loved the Shaykh, and he said, "I want to go with you everywhere to be with you," and he said, "No. I will not allow you into my company unless you feed twenty-five people every day on your farm." Hajj Jilali said, "Bismillah." And every day he fed twenty-five people on his farm and he went everywhere with his Shaykh and he is buried next to him. This is Adab, and this Adab took him to the Next World.

II

NOVEMBER 3RD 2004

We will look at the first eleven Ayats of Surat Luqman:

بِسۡمِ ٱللَّهِ ٱلرَّحۡمَٰنِ ٱلرَّحِيمِ

الٓمٓ ١ تِلۡكَ ءَايَٰتُ ٱلۡكِتَٰبِ ٱلۡحَكِيمِ ٢ هُدٗى وَرَحۡمَةٗ لِّلۡمُحۡسِنِينَ ٣
ٱلَّذِينَ يُقِيمُونَ ٱلصَّلَوٰةَ وَيُؤۡتُونَ ٱلزَّكَوٰةَ وَهُم بِٱلۡأٓخِرَةِ هُمۡ
يُوقِنُونَ ٤ أُوْلَٰٓئِكَ عَلَىٰ هُدٗى مِّن رَّبِّهِمۡۖ وَأُوْلَٰٓئِكَ هُمُ ٱلۡمُفۡلِحُونَ ٥
وَمِنَ ٱلنَّاسِ مَن يَشۡتَرِي لَهۡوَ ٱلۡحَدِيثِ لِيُضِلَّ عَن سَبِيلِ ٱللَّهِ بِغَيۡرِ عِلۡمٖ
وَيَتَّخِذَهَا هُزُوًاۚ أُوْلَٰٓئِكَ لَهُمۡ عَذَابٞ مُّهِينٞ ٦ وَإِذَا تُتۡلَىٰ عَلَيۡهِ
ءَايَٰتُنَا وَلَّىٰ مُسۡتَكۡبِرٗا كَأَن لَّمۡ يَسۡمَعۡهَا كَأَنَّ فِيٓ أُذُنَيۡهِ وَقۡرٗاۖ فَبَشِّرۡهُ

بِعَذَابٍ أَلِيمٍ ﴿٧﴾ إِنَّ ٱلَّذِينَ ءَامَنُوا۟ وَعَمِلُوا۟ ٱلصَّٰلِحَٰتِ لَهُمْ جَنَّٰتُ
ٱلنَّعِيمِ ﴿٨﴾ خَٰلِدِينَ فِيهَا ۖ وَعْدَ ٱللَّهِ حَقًّا ۚ وَهُوَ ٱلْعَزِيزُ ٱلْحَكِيمُ ﴿٩﴾
خَلَقَ ٱلسَّمَٰوَٰتِ بِغَيْرِ عَمَدٍ تَرَوْنَهَا ۖ وَأَلْقَىٰ فِى ٱلْأَرْضِ رَوَٰسِىَ أَن
تَمِيدَ بِكُمْ وَبَثَّ فِيهَا مِن كُلِّ دَآبَّةٍ ۚ وَأَنزَلْنَا مِنَ ٱلسَّمَآءِ مَآءً
فَأَنۢبَتْنَا فِيهَا مِن كُلِّ زَوْجٍ كَرِيمٍ ﴿١٠﴾ هَٰذَا خَلْقُ ٱللَّهِ فَأَرُونِى مَاذَا
خَلَقَ ٱلَّذِينَ مِن دُونِهِۦ ۚ بَلِ ٱلظَّٰلِمُونَ فِى ضَلَٰلٍ مُّبِينٍ ﴿١١﴾

In the name of Allah, All-Merciful, Most Merciful

Alif Lam Mim
Those are the Signs of the Wise Book –
guidance and mercy for the good-doers:
those who establish Salat and pay Zakat
and are certain of the Akhira.

Such people are following guidance from their Lord.
They are the ones who are successful.

But there are some people who trade in distracting tales
to misguide people from Allah's Way
knowing nothing about it
and to make a mockery of it.
Such people will have a humiliating punishment.

When Our Signs are recited to such a person,
he turns away arrogantly as if he had not heard,
as if there was a great weight in his ears.

So give him news of a painful punishment.

For those who have Iman and do right actions
there are Gardens of Delight,
to remain in them timelessly, for ever.
Allah's promise is true.
He is the Almighty, the All-Wise.

It is Allah Who created the heavens
with no support – you can see them –
and cast firmly embedded mountains on the earth
so that it would not move under you,
and scattered about in it creatures of every kind.
And We send down water from the sky
and make every generous species grow in it.

This is Allah's creation.
Show me then what those besides Him have created!
The wrongdoers are clearly misguided.

This Surat is of great importance to us in relation to the theme you remember from our last gathering. We were looking at the understanding of 'Amal – Ad-Deen al-Mu'amala. We saw that 'Amal of itself is a Divine event and that 'Amal comes from Allah onto the people. So when we take up good action and good behaviour, we are actually embodying a quality that is borrowed from the Divine. For example, Rasul, sallallahu 'alayhi wa sallam, said that to come out of your house with a smiling face was part of the Deen. He referred to certain qualities as being "a portion of Nabawiyya". It is in this sense that all correct action, all courtesy and manners are themselves a showing-forth of a borrowed attribute that Allah, subhanahu wa ta‘ala, has placed on the Muminun.

We see here that Surat Luqman is, you could say, from one point of view because there are many things in it, the ‘Divine Manifesto’ of ‘Amal, of correct behaviour and courtesy. Before we come to the bit that immediately concerns us, we want to look at this prior aspect of this Surat, Surat Luqman, because it is from this that comes the overt statement about ‘Amal. What we find is that throughout the whole of Allah’s creation, He makes distinctions, and we cannot cover over these distinctions, because covering over these distinctions is failing to understand the wisdom, the Hikma, that is absolutely essential to correct understanding, and also for your correct behaviour in turn.

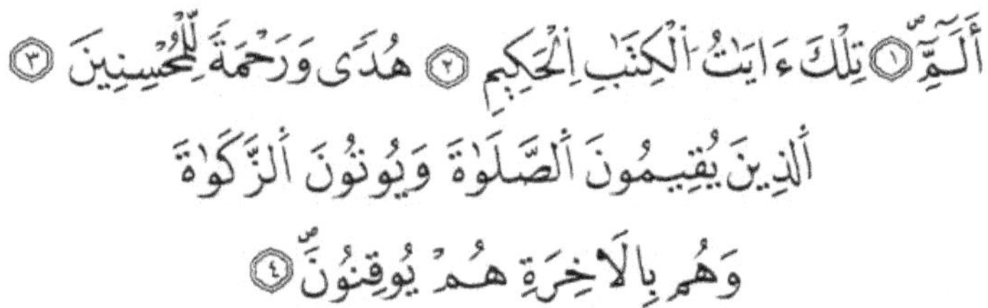

Alif Lam Mim
Those are the Signs of the Wise Book –
guidance and mercy for the good-doers:
those who establish Salat and pay Zakat
and are certain of the Akhira.

So already, the benefit, the guidance and the mercy is for the good-doers, the Muhsinin. The Muhsin is the one of Ihsan.

Ihsan is a Ruhani condition. If we go to the first Hadith in the collection of Imam Muslim, we find that the Angel Jibril questioned Rasul, sallallahu 'alayhi wa sallam, on the three aspects of the Deen: "What is Islam?" "What is Iman?" "What is Ihsan?" He replied: "Ihsan is to worship Allah as though you saw Him, and while you do not see Him, know that He sees you." This is what the Sufis call the reversal of knowledge and the reversal of the understanding that ignorant people have, because they see themselves as looking out on the world, and they make the judgments on the world, whereas the reality is that Allah sees His people and He makes the judgment:

الله معي الله ناظر إلي الله شاهد علي

Allah is with me, Allah sees me,
Allah is the Witness of my acts.

Alif Lam Mim
Those are the Signs of the Wise Book –
guidance and mercy for the good-doers.

Ihsan is a Ruhani knowledge. It is an understanding that is against the direct physical experience of existence – you worship as if you saw Him, but the reality is that Allah SEES YOU. Allah is looking on the people of His creation. Then the Muhsin, Allah defines as:

ٱلَّذِينَ يُقِيمُونَ ٱلصَّلَوٰةَ وَيُؤْتُونَ ٱلزَّكَوٰةَ
وَهُم بِٱلْءَاخِرَةِ هُمْ يُوقِنُونَ ٤

those who establish Salat and pay Zakat
and are certain of the Akhira.

So the ones who have this Ruhani quality are defined as the ones who establish Salat and pay Zakat and are certain of the Akhira. Look at the significance of this, and look at the crisis of the Muslims today and understand what it is. It is not a moral crisis, it is not a spiritual crisis, it is a crisis of 'Amal, of behaviour. Why? It is because throughout the Muslim world, Salat is established by the miracle of Allah. Among the people you see every time you go to Hajj, you see that there are millions of them imbued with the certainty of the Akhira. You can tell, you can see it in the Tawaf, you can see it at the Black Stone, you can see it at the Maqam al-Ibrahim – there are people who are certain of the Akhira. But what is missing is "pay Zakat", and this is 'Amal. The 'Amal of the Muhsin is Salat and Zakat, and this inner certainty of the Next World and the Unseen.

Zakat is not a given Sadaqa. I have to keep repeating it, because the so-called 'Ulama of the last century have thrown it out the window. They have turned Zakat into a Sadaqa so that it is a gift like any other gift, but it is not. Zakat is a TAKEN Sadaqa. There is one word in the Qur'an which categorically defines Zakat as "Take!" Surat at-Tawba (9:103):

II

Take Zakat from their wealth.

In other words, Zakat has to be taken. This is the practice of the Muslims, and has been the practice of the Muslims right up until the collapse of Khilafa in the great empires of Islam in the East – of the Mughals and the Osmanli.

When the Amr was removed, Zakat was destroyed. The argument we have with the people of Arabia is not the argument they want to have, which is criticising or worrying that we are somehow not correct in our Adab towards the dead Awliya. This is not the issue! The issue is: you made Bay'at to the Sultan and you broke that Bay'at when you took these rich, rich lands for yourselves, and at that minute you abolished Zakat. The rulers of Arabia said, "We do not want to be Khalif," when the English said, "Take it!" because already there was in them a belief which stems not from Madinah, which they have never respected, but from the Shi'a movement. The Shi'a movement, in its reality, is the denial of Amr. It is the denial of Amr. It exists on there not being a Ruler. They say that the Ruler has gone up the chimney and is hiding in the Unseen and is going to turn up when he is of no use to anybody, when the world is over, when he has nothing to rule! Because then the rule has passed to Allah, in the Judgment.

Thus, this abolition of Zakat took place in Arabia, and at that point the Muslims lost access to the Ruhani virtues that were available to them by this Guidance and Mercy. This is what you see today in the horrible, horrible tragedy of Pakistan – they establish Salat, but they do not pay Zakat, and the price they are paying for not paying Zakat is the most horrific price you can imagine.

This is important because Salat is 'Amal. Ad-Deen al-Mu'amala. Deen is 'Amal. Zakat is 'Amal. If you remove that, what do you do to the character of a man? A man who worships gains a quality, does he not? Now, the significant thing about paying Zakat is that in paying Zakat, you actually hand it over. You are assessed. Do you see the difference? They are all crying now in the North-West Provinces of Pakistan that they want to restore the Shari'at, but they do not know what the Shari'at is! It is not about putting women in black bags, it is about men paying up to their Amir from what they possess – handing it over – which makes them men. That is not at issue there because they have paper money, and the money of the country is worthless.

So you must understand that being assessed, and your paying of Zakat, changes your character. If you give, it can make you feel good, and make you feel that you are excellent. Having it taken from you makes you realise that it did not belong to you in the first place. It belonged to Allah and Allah is taking it back, it is His portion. Allah, subhanahu wa ta'ala, in a Hadith Qudsi said, "Fasting is Mine." But also, the property of Zakat is Allah's, and Zakat is for the poor.

This means a different kind of character. For example, in Cairo, at the point when it was a rich and flourishing Muslim city, the time came to collect Zakat, and there was a very rich merchant and his wife. He did not want to hand over his significant sum of money, so when the Zakat Collectors of the Amir came to the door, he said to the servant, "Let them wait." Meanwhile, he wrote out a document and signed over all his wealth to his wife. The Collectors then came in and he said to them, "Well, I have very little, I just have this." They said, "Alright, you owe so much." But they then said, "We would now like to see your wife." So the man said, "Just a moment," and the wife made out a document and signed over all her wealth back to him! She came out to the Collectors and told them, "I just have this." The Collectors were in this palace, wondering how these enormously rich people could have only these taxable goods!

So the Collectors reported the matter to the Mufti, and the Mufti in turn reported it to the Amir. The Amir said, "What are we to do?" and the Mufti replied, "Bring me the Imam Khatib." He brought him the Imam Khatib and instructed him what to do. The following Jumu'a, from the Mimbar – which remember is the politics of the Muslims, which is why in this country and in many places in Europe, the Mimbar has been taken away from the Muslims so that the Khutba does not come from the Mimbar which is power, but is reduced to a christian sermon from a christian lectern on the side – so the Imam stood on the Mimbar and said, "Our people have had the Zakat collected from them, and this Hajji so-and-so and his wife so-and-so did this. This is what they did to the Zakat Collectors! In the eyes of the Shari'at they are cleared. In the eyes of Allah, Allahu A'lam." And of course they were disgraced.

When these people say, "We want to bring back Shari'at!" you cannot bring back Shari'at unless it is underpinned by 'Amal, by behaviour, by people to whom these things matter. So when the Mimbar made that judgment, they were disgraced in their community. They were disgraced, but there was no punishment. The Shari'at in many things which are important does not have punishment because the event happens under the level of punishments with the 'Amal of how people view things, and how the Muslims approve or disapprove of something. Do you follow?

Here, Allah openly states:

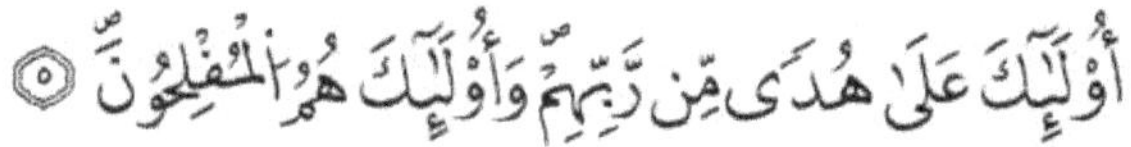

Such people are following guidance from their Lord.
They are the ones who are successful.

Allah is telling us that to have right action, which in Arabic one would call 'Birr' – to have an 'Amal that is pleasing means that you are going to be successful. It is a path of success. The path of correct behaviour is a path of success, it is not something which will bring on you punishment or which will make things hard for you and difficult for you. On the contrary, it unrolls for you a path of success because in doing it, you are in harmony with nature. You are in harmony with existence because the Deen is Fitra. The Deen is the natural state of things.

وَمِنَ ٱلنَّاسِ مَن يَشْتَرِى لَهْوَ ٱلْحَدِيثِ لِيُضِلَّ عَن سَبِيلِ ٱللَّهِ بِغَيْرِ عِلْمٍ
وَيَتَّخِذَهَا هُزُوًا ۚ أُو۟لَٰٓئِكَ لَهُمْ عَذَابٌ مُّهِينٌ ٦

But there are some people who trade in distracting tales
to misguide people from Allah's Way
knowing nothing about it and to make a mockery of it.
Such people will have a humiliating punishment.

Thus the categoric, functioning law of existence on this planet is that the people who provide the excuses to avoid the Way of Allah and who mock it and do not know what it is – they will have a humiliating punishment. This is a given of history itself. It is very important that you understand this. The people who trade in distracting tales to misguide people from Allah's Way are the ones who say, "You don't need this! We can work it all out for ourselves! We will use our reason and we will use our intellects, we will work it out and we won't need this thing. Everyone can make up his own mind, and everyone can have his own opinion and this is freedom. We can express this all freely and it'll all work out."

The 'working out' of it, as we have seen in the last two hundred years, is a litany of disasters of greater and greater proportions, until finally, at the beginning of a new century, we are informed that the whole earth is collapsing, the sea is poisoned, the air is toxic and the species are disappearing in front of us – the whole foundation of existence itself is disappearing under us! This is all because of the financial transaction which, again, is disobeying Allah and denying Zakat, and making and taking usury as the principle of finance, which is something that is abhorrent and forbidden, and against Fitra, against nature.

What we are told is that these people will have a humiliating punishment, and we see that a significant portion of the world is getting this humiliating punishment – just on an ecological level, just on a level of governance and justice and absence of justice. Even ancient justices that they had achieved over the centuries have been removed from the statute books in the new dictatorships of the modern State. Now we come to the next Ayat:

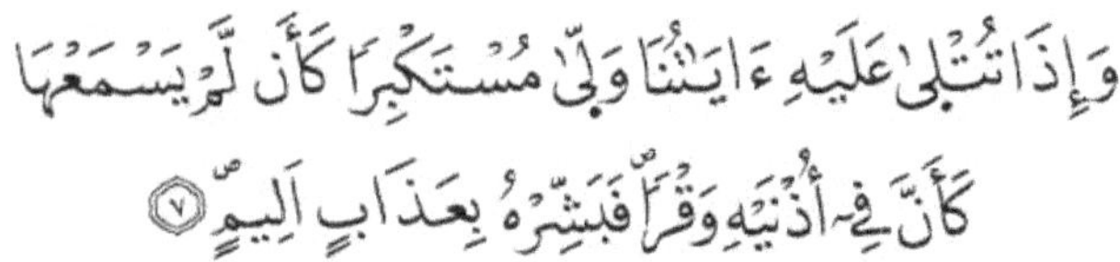

When Our Signs are recited to such a person,
he turns away arrogantly as if he had not heard,
as if there was a great weight in his ears.
So give him news of a painful punishment.

It is very important for you to take this understanding with you in your ordinary daily procedures of life. For example, when you turn on television – not the frivolous television but the enlightened television – it will tell you that they now have a programme on religion. They have now made this thing called 'Religion'. These people who trade in distracting tales say, "Pick the one you like! You are free to! It is a personal thing for you, but it must not spill out into the social discourse which is the market-place and finance." Part of this distraction these people make is to tell you that all religion is like this, it is something you have for yourself. "It is not a civic matter, and it absolutely must not come into the realm of governance – that, we will look after! You have your religion, but when it comes to government, we will do it. And modern government is that we make sure that you pay your taxes, and we absolutely guarantee that you will have no right to the access of the vastly wealthy who own the commodities of the earth – the gold, the platinum, the silver, the oil. You leave those alone! But you pay your taxes."

This is the reality we live in. What Allah, subhanahu wa ta'ala, is saying is: "Give them news of a painful punishment." We do not say to these people, "Well, we do not agree with you." No! We say to them, "You are in BIG trouble, in this world and the Next World."

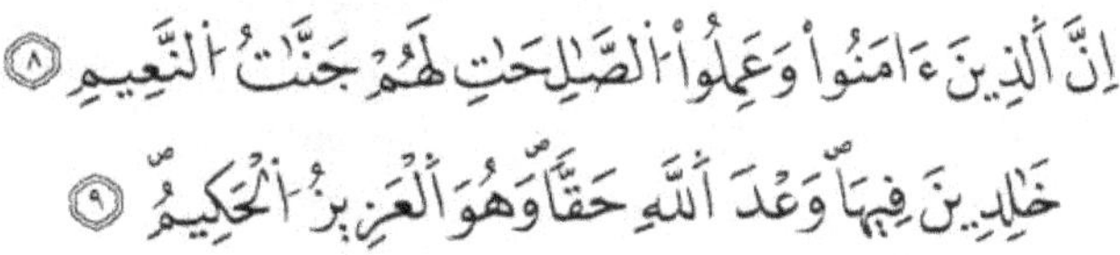

For those who have Iman and do right actions
there are Gardens of Delight,
to remain in them timelessly, for ever.
Allah's promise is true.
He is the Almighty, the All-Wise.

"For those who have Iman and do right actions" – Iman, and we are back to the Salihun, who are the people of Islah which means to fix, or to put things right. Those who have Iman are those who not only 'do right actions' but who put things right, who put things back on the Sirat al-Mustaqim, who put things back to how they should be, in harmony with what Allah has ordained. It is not enough that some noble person destroys Musharraf! The people have to be put back on the right path, and the right path is not being 'good' or 'nice', it is about what we have been looking at. They establish Salat and pay Zakat. The transaction is honest and straight-forward. People evaluate their brother with respect and also evaluate themselves with respect.

The language of the kuffar in our day and in the financial system which dominates all of us – we are all under its tyranny

– does not mention that at all. It only mentions how much it costs and how much it is worth. The people who have vast sums of money, undeservedly, then feel, "We must do something!" But giving money does not change the situation. It is not about flying to Africa and adopting 'a' child, when there are hundreds and thousands dying across Africa, it is putting things right. How do you put things right? You must ask, "Where is it against what Allah has ordained?" What has Allah ordained? He has ordained that there should be no usury, as Imam Malik said, "Not even to a blade of grass." That means the financial system has to be removed.

You ask, "How am I to remove the financial system?" First of all, it will be removed by our conviction that Allah is going to help us to move the thing so that when we put out our hand to it, before we have touched it, it has collapsed. It is like the Istikhara which tells you what you are to do, but even in making the Niyyat to do the Istikhara, Allah will tell you what to do before you say, "Allahu akbar," because the 'Amal is from the Niyyat.

If you change how you view it and you have trust in Allah, then the Rizq is coming before you put your hand out. That is why there is no person in greater darkness than the Muslim who ties dynamite to his belly, because he has given up believing in the Mercy of Allah, subhanahu wa ta'ala. Allah can fix it! But He will not fix it until we become the ones who want to put it right. For these people:

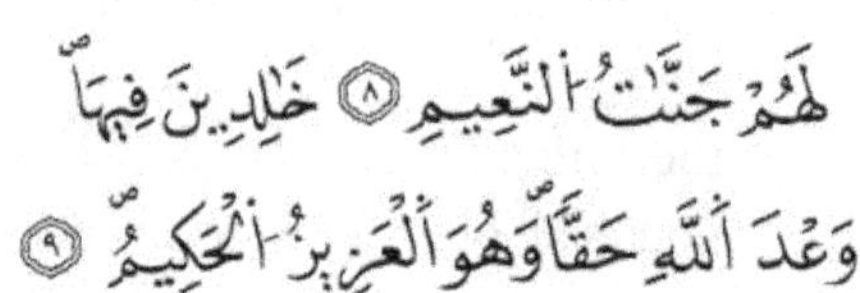

there are Gardens of Delight,
to remain in them timelessly, for ever.
Allah's promise is true.
He is the Almighty, the All-Wise.

Now let us look at the next Ayat:

خَلَقَ ٱلسَّمَٰوَٰتِ بِغَيۡرِ عَمَدٖ تَرَوۡنَهَاۖ وَأَلۡقَىٰ فِي ٱلۡأَرۡضِ رَوَٰسِيَ أَن
تَمِيدَ بِكُمۡ وَبَثَّ فِيهَا مِن كُلِّ دَآبَّةٖۚ وَأَنزَلۡنَا مِنَ ٱلسَّمَآءِ مَآءٗ
فَأَنۢبَتۡنَا فِيهَا مِن كُلِّ زَوۡجٖ كَرِيمٍ ١٠

It is Allah Who created the heavens
with no support – you can see them –
and cast firmly embedded mountains on the earth
so that it would not move under you,
and scattered about in it creatures of every kind.
And We send down water from the sky
and make every generous species grow in it.

In other words, Allah is telling us, "Look! We have given you a cosmic system that works. Under the principles by which Allah has created it, it is functioning." As Shaykh Ibn al-'Arabi said, "Allah rules the universe from inside the universe." He has put the laws in it which do it for Him, subhanahu wa ta'ala. It is not some primitive thing as the christian idea would have it, that has some kind of interventionist power. There is not a divinity that intervenes and goes 'Bang!' Allah has set it up so that the whole thing is moving by laws that He has put in it, and these laws never stop. They never stop. These laws go from everything to the glance, the glance of the eye. Is this not so? Allah knows the glance of the eye.

It is in this situation that we are being given this command to recognise the importance of our behaviour, of our 'Amal, of how we are in dealing with other people.

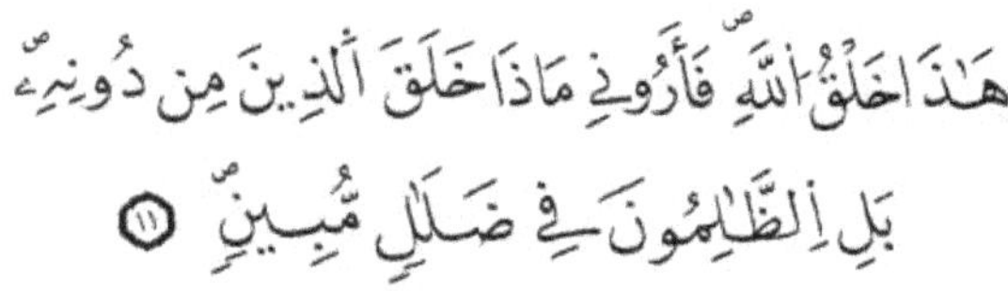

This is Allah's creation.
Show me then what those besides Him have created!
The wrongdoers are clearly misguided.

"This is Allah's creation." Khalq, in Arabic, actually means to create forms. Several meanings are contained in this one word. We are going around the outskirts of Divine Revelation!

هَٰذَا خَلْقُ ٱللَّهِ

"This is Allah's creation." Khalqullah. Let us make a whole sentence out of it: This is 'the form on which Allah has set everything up'. Allah has set up the whole thing so that it all absolutely works. The sky, the heavens, the earth, the sea – everything! All the elements have been set up by Divine Law. This Divine Law requires of us our free, spontaneous decision to be people of good action and correct, noble behaviour. We also find this word 'khalq' in Surat al-Qalam (68:4):

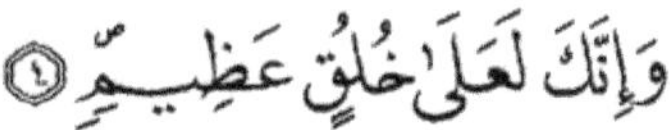

Indeed you are truly vast in character.

Or, staying with its root identity in the Qur'an, "Indeed you are created on a vast form." The best form is the one who is the Messenger of Allah, sallallahu 'alayhi wa sallam, who has the best action, the best behaviour. Sayyidatuna 'Aisha said, "He was the Qur'an walking," because he embodied all these wisdoms. The three dynamics of the life of Rasul, sallallahu 'alayhi wa sallam, his three qualities, were generosity, courage and worship. He was always generous because of his Islam, he was never afraid because of his Iman, and his worship was because of his Ihsan. He embodied them. This is YOUR responsibility through your life: to be raised up by performing in that way which is pleasing to Allah. You are on a Path of success and you will have success, and you will have an Iman that lasts until the last day of your life, inshallah.

III

NOVEMBER 10TH 2007

This is a continuation of what we were doing last week. We were looking at 'Amal as the foundation of the Deen. Ad-Deen al-Mu'amala. We were also looking at Surat Luqman, and just at the point where we came to the advice Luqman gave to his son, we stopped. We read up to the preliminary Ayats that led up to that, but so that we would neither belittle nor fail to grasp the importance of this counsel of Sayyiduna Luqman, 'alayhi salam, we had to make a stop.

Now we are going to look at another word. In Al-Bukhari and Ibn Hanbal we find the celebrated Hadith that Rasul, sallallahu 'alayhi wa sallam, said: "I was sent to ennoble good character."

'Mukarim' means to ennoble, or to make higher. Akhlaq is a word we so to speak stumbled over last time because we were not content with the terms which were being used. We did not like just the term 'character' because it is something much more sophisticated and complex than that. Khalq is really 'created form', is that not correct? Thus: "I was sent to ennoble the human form." 'Form', remember, is not a static thing. The human form, like that of the animal, is not like in a snapshot – to understand the form of the lion, for example, you have to understand how it lives with the other lions, how it breeds, how it hunts, its habitat – you have to know the whole life-cycle to know what the form of the lion is. The dead dog is not a dog, as the 'dogginess' has left it. The essentialness of the dog entails all its characteristics, of how it behaves – its loyalty, but also how it is treacherous, it is a hunter, it gobbles its food – all these things make up the form. This is very important because the Sufis have always insisted that this difference is where many of the Fuqaha have failed to understand the true nature of the Deen, because it cannot be fixed in principles, in principles of law. It always goes back to this Akhlaq, this living form of the character of the human creature.

So we take this Mukarim al-Akhlaq of the famous Hadith as in fact a process that from the time of Rasul, sallallahu 'alayhi wa sallam, is what is working, as it were, among the people of the Muslim Community. Their being affected by it is what raises up the Muslims to this capacity to create great civilisation and to create sciences, and all the many aspects Islam brings to enhance life on this planet.

Thus, we are going to look at another term. It is a term

which has almost vanished from the vocabulary of the people of Fiqh and 'Aqida, but significantly it has been taken up and turned into its opposite by the political Arabs. The term is 'Fata'. The plural in the masculine is Fityan, and in the feminine is Fatayat. The dictionary definition is 'a young man having attained the full vigour of his manhood'. There is another term which comes from it, and that is Fatya – Futya – which is the reply that shows enlightenment on a question. If a question is given and there is a reply which enlightens, that is Fatya – 'as if one had gained the power of that clarification'. So Fatya is a kind of illumination that allows one to see into a problem put in front of one.

We are going to look in our Qur'ans at Surat al-Anbiya' (21:51-67):

وَلَقَدْ ءَاتَيْنَآ إِبْرَٰهِيمَ رُشْدَهُۥ مِن قَبْلُ وَكُنَّا بِهِۦ
عَٰلِمِينَ ﴿٥١﴾ إِذْ قَالَ لِأَبِيهِ وَقَوْمِهِۦ مَا هَٰذِهِ ٱلتَّمَاثِيلُ ٱلَّتِىٓ
أَنتُمْ لَهَا عَٰكِفُونَ ﴿٥٢﴾ قَالُوا۟ وَجَدْنَآ ءَابَآءَنَا لَهَا عَٰبِدِينَ ﴿٥٣﴾ قَالَ
لَقَدْ كُنتُمْ أَنتُمْ وَءَابَآؤُكُمْ فِى ضَلَٰلٍ مُّبِينٍ ﴿٥٤﴾ قَالُوٓا۟ أَجِئْتَنَا
بِٱلْحَقِّ أَمْ أَنتَ مِنَ ٱللَّٰعِبِينَ ﴿٥٥﴾ قَالَ بَل رَّبُّكُمْ رَبُّ ٱلسَّمَٰوَٰتِ
وَٱلْأَرْضِ ٱلَّذِى فَطَرَهُنَّ وَأَنَا۠ عَلَىٰ ذَٰلِكُم مِّنَ ٱلشَّٰهِدِينَ ﴿٥٦﴾
وَتَٱللَّهِ لَأَكِيدَنَّ أَصْنَٰمَكُم بَعْدَ أَن تُوَلُّوا۟ مُدْبِرِينَ ﴿٥٧﴾
فَجَعَلَهُمْ جُذَٰذًا إِلَّا كَبِيرًا لَّهُمْ لَعَلَّهُمْ إِلَيْهِ يَرْجِعُونَ ﴿٥٨﴾
قَالُوا۟ مَن فَعَلَ هَٰذَا بِـَٔالِهَتِنَآ إِنَّهُۥ لَمِنَ ٱلظَّٰلِمِينَ ﴿٥٩﴾ قَالُوا۟

سَمِعْنَا فَتًى يَذْكُرُهُمْ يُقَالُ لَهُۥٓ إِبْرَٰهِيمُ ﴿٦٠﴾ قَالُوا۟ فَأْتُوا۟ بِهِۦ
عَلَىٰٓ أَعْيُنِ ٱلنَّاسِ لَعَلَّهُمْ يَشْهَدُونَ ﴿٦١﴾ قَالُوٓا۟ ءَأَنتَ فَعَلْتَ
هَٰذَا بِـَٔالِهَتِنَا يَٰٓإِبْرَٰهِيمُ ﴿٦٢﴾ قَالَ بَلْ فَعَلَهُۥ كَبِيرُهُمْ هَٰذَا
فَسْـَٔلُوهُمْ إِن كَانُوا۟ يَنطِقُونَ ﴿٦٣﴾ فَرَجَعُوٓا۟ إِلَىٰٓ أَنفُسِهِمْ
فَقَالُوٓا۟ إِنَّكُمْ أَنتُمُ ٱلظَّٰلِمُونَ ﴿٦٤﴾ ثُمَّ نُكِسُوا۟ عَلَىٰ رُءُوسِهِمْ
لَقَدْ عَلِمْتَ مَا هَٰٓؤُلَآءِ يَنطِقُونَ ﴿٦٥﴾ قَالَ أَفَتَعْبُدُونَ مِن
دُونِ ٱللَّهِ مَا لَا يَنفَعُكُمْ شَيْـًٔا وَلَا يَضُرُّكُمْ ﴿٦٦﴾ أُفٍّ
لَّكُمْ وَلِمَا تَعْبُدُونَ مِن دُونِ ٱللَّهِ أَفَلَا تَعْقِلُونَ ﴿٦٧﴾

We gave Ibrahim his right guidance early on,
and We had complete knowledge of him.
When he said to his father and his people,
"What are these statues you are clinging to?"
they said, "We found our fathers worshipping them."
He said, "You and your fathers are clearly misguided."
They said, "Have you brought us the truth
or are you playing games?"
He said, "Far from it! Your Lord
is the Lord of the heavens and the earth,
He who brought them into being.
I am one of those who bear witness to that.
By Allah, I will devise some scheme against your idols
when your backs are turned."

He broke them in pieces, except for the biggest one,

so that they would have it to consult!
They said, "Who has done this to our gods?
He is definitely one of the wrongdoers!"
They said, "We heard a young man mentioning them.
They call him Ibrahim."
They said, "Bring him before the people's eyes
so they can be witnesses."
They said, "Did you do this to our gods, Ibrahim?"
He said, "No, this one, the biggest of them, did it.
Ask them if they are able to speak!"

They consulted among themselves and said,
"It is you yourselves who are wrongdoers."
But then they relapsed back into their kufr:
"You know full well these idols cannot talk."

He said, "Do you then worship, instead of Allah,
what cannot help or harm you in any way?
Shame on you and what you worship besides Allah!
Will you not use your intellect?"

Now look at Ayat 60:

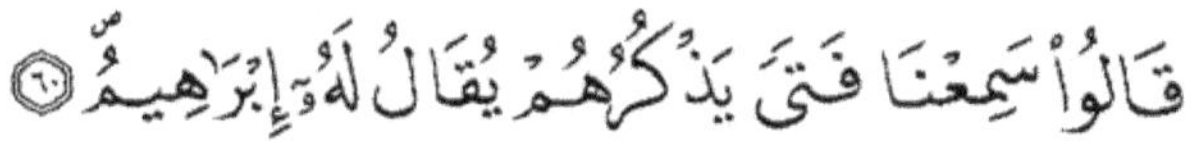

They said, "We heard a young man mentioning them.
They call him Ibrahim."

Here we meet the term 'Fata', and it is identifying Sayyid-una Ibrahim, 'alayhi salam, in this important event of early history. From this passage we derive three vital elements of Futuwwa. Firstly, Ibrahim is a youth. Secondly, Ibrahim teaches by an action, not words. He smashes the idols, and it is that action which turns the whole situation around. Another example I have seen of this in our own time is that Hajj 'Umar Pasha would argue with these people who thought they were so clever and knew everything about modern economy and the nature of the Gold Dinar, and nothing, nothing would penetrate their intellects at all. Then, when he produced the gold coin, and it went into their hands, another understanding went into their hearts because he made the action of giving them the gold coin. When our Hafidh's father presented the Gold Dinar to King Hasan II, at the moment he took it into his hand, everything changed. Because of that, the next day the King announced they would look into the collection of Zakat. Thus the second aspect of this is that, in this passage of the Qur'an, he teaches by an action and not words.

The third aspect is that, following that, he then calls on the intellect. The last Ayat reveals:

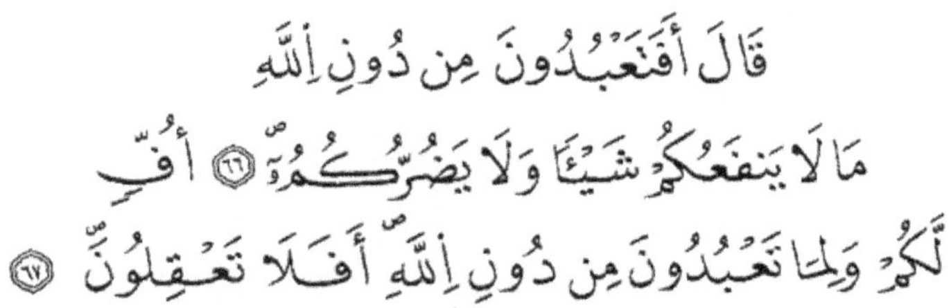

He said, "Do you then worship, instead of Allah,
what cannot help or harm you in any way?
Shame on you and what you worship besides Allah!
Will you not use your intellect?"

At that point, then, from the action, he brings in the intellect. So the intellect follows the action. We will see also that that in turn has, prior to it, something else.

We will now go to Surat al-Kahf (18:10 & 13):

إِذْ أَوَى ٱلْفِتْيَةُ إِلَى ٱلْكَهْفِ فَقَالُوا۟ رَبَّنَآ
ءَاتِنَا مِن لَّدُنكَ رَحْمَةً وَهَيِّئْ لَنَا مِنْ أَمْرِنَا رَشَدًا ١٠

When the young men took refuge in the cave and said,
"Our Lord, give us mercy directly from You
and open the way for us to right guidance
in our situation."

نَّحْنُ نَقُصُّ عَلَيْكَ نَبَأَهُم بِٱلْحَقِّ
إِنَّهُمْ فِتْيَةٌ ءَامَنُوا۟ بِرَبِّهِمْ وَزِدْنَٰهُمْ هُدًى ١٣

We will relate their story to you with truth.
They were young men who had Iman in their Lord
and We increased them in guidance.

Now we will look at Ayats 23 and 24 of the same Surat:

وَلَا تَقُولَنَّ لِشَا۟ىْءٍ إِنِّى فَاعِلٌ ذَٰلِكَ غَدًا ٢٣
إِلَّآ أَن يَشَآءَ ٱللَّهُ وَٱذْكُر رَّبَّكَ إِذَا نَسِيتَ
وَقُلْ عَسَىٰٓ أَن يَهْدِيَنِ رَبِّى لِأَقْرَبَ
مِنْ هَٰذَا رَشَدًا ٢٤

Never say about anything,
"I am doing that tomorrow,"
without adding "If Allah wills."
Remember your Lord when you forget,
and say, "Hopefully my Lord will guide me
to something closer to right guidance than this."

Why we put these together is because this counsel, as it were, comes after the event. The event is this 'initiation' by Allah, subhanahu wa ta'ala, of the youths in the cave. Again, they are defined as being Fata. It is the same term. In both the Qur'anic references we have seen, the ones concerning Sayyiduna Ibrahim, 'alayhi salam, and the ones concerning the youths in the cave, we notice that both events imply that they have been constrained to worship other-than-Allah. We confirm that they choose rather to have death than to worship something other than Allah. So in both cases there is a categoric rejection of worshipping idolatrously something that is other than the Divine. This is the event in which the youth fulfils his highest being – one case being one of the prophets of Allah, subhanahu wa ta'ala.

In Ayat 10, which we have just looked at, it indicates that they asked for direct knowledge from Allah – Rahma – here shown to be the foundation of knowledge.

ءَاتِنَا مِن لَّدُنكَ رَحْمَةً

So they asked for direct knowledge from Allah. That is something that was put into their hearts without anything between them and this illumination from Allah, subhanahu wa ta'ala. In this language of Tasawwuf that is called Tajalliyat – illumination into their hearts. This is the order of things. What we are seeing is direct knowledge from Allah. From the direct knowledge, the illumination from Allah, there comes right knowledge for their particular situation. Do you see? The discrimination comes after the illumination. Remember that last week I said I would respectfully contradict Imam Ghazali when he said 'Ilm al-Mukashafa had to come after 'Ilm al-Mu'amala. Although we understand why he said that, and it is a sensible thing to say, it is nevertheless not true because the reality is that the illumination comes from Allah, and it is that illumination which makes it possible for you to make the right action, to make the right judgment, because it comes from Allah.

So from the 'Ilm Laduni comes the right knowledge, Rahma itself, for their particular situation. Look at Ayat 13 again:

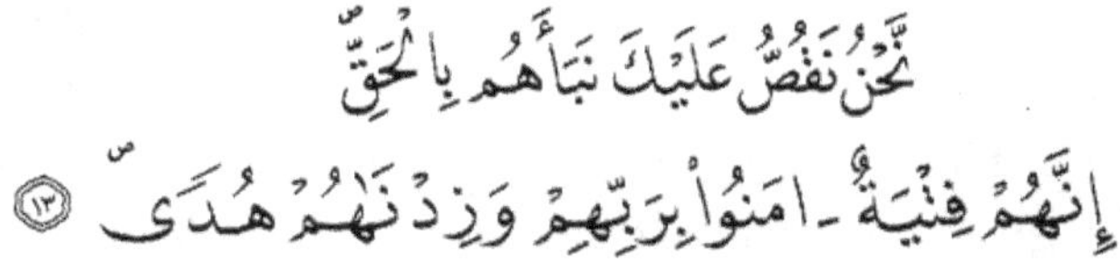

We will relate their story to you with truth.
They were young men who had Iman in their Lord
and We increased them in guidance.

So firstly, they had Iman. First, there was inwardness, and then they were given guidance, then they knew what to do. Iman preceded this specific knowledge of knowing what to do. The Furqan came after the illumination. Look at Surat al-Anbiya' (21:51). This is further confirmation of what we have been saying:

وَلَقَدْ ءَاتَيْنَآ إِبْرَٰهِيمَ رُشْدَهُۥ مِن قَبْلُ وَكُنَّا بِهِۦ عَٰلِمِينَ ﴿٥١﴾

We gave Ibrahim his right guidance early on,
and We had complete knowledge of him.

In his Tafsir, Tabari says: "This means that Allah gave him this when he was still a child." In other words, something was put into him in his childhood that was this Ruhani light which led him through his tremendous experiences he had as the Prophet of Allah, subhanahu wa ta'ala.

A very famous Sufi, Abu Hafs an-Nishaburi, who died around 265 A.H. was one of the great Fityan – one of the great people of Futuwwa, of Khorason, and he defined this science as: to teach by the action, not the word. Abu Hafs was a Murid of Abu Turab an-Nakhshabi, one of the oldest masters of Futuwwa. According to Hujwiri in his famous Kashf al-Mahjoub, he was also one of the teachers of Ibn Hanbal in Fiqh. It is very important in fact that you know that the great, great Sufis of the early days were absolutely laced in, locked in, connected with, and taught from and by the great Fuqaha and the great 'Ulama – even the ones who gave us our Madhhabs. It is very important you realise this because it is now covered over as if it were not the case. But here is this great Sufi who, according to Hujwiri, was one of the teachers of Ibn Hanbal in Fiqh.

In the mosque of Baghdad, Imam Junayd, who held Abu Hafs in the highest esteem, asked him before the assembled Shuyukh, "Abu Hafs, tell us, what is Futuwwa?" And Abu Hafs said, "You answer. For you have been granted a tongue of wisdom." Junayd replied, "For me, Futuwwa consists of abolishing the vision," meaning of the self, "and to break all the links," meaning with society. Abu Hafs replied, "What you say is very beautiful, but for me, Futuwwa consists above all in straight behaviour, and in not to ask anything from anybody." This is a devastating kind of opposite to the reply of the great Imam Junayd. "For me, Futuwwa consists above all in straight behaviour, and in not to ask anything from anybody." At this, Imam Junayd instructed everyone in the mosque of Baghdad to stand up out of respect for him, because he had given the unmatchable definition.

The arrival on earth of the Last Messenger, sallallahu 'alayhi wa sallam, heralded the renewal and laying down of the foundations of law and justice. It is a new and final Divine dispensation for mankind. 'Amal takes on a form: Nabawiyya. The Book and the Sunna reveal a new model for 'Amal. It is elevated. That is, the norm is raised up. 'Amal: 'Ayn–Mim–Lam: the Arabic word means 'to be active'. It is in its root the 'camel' itself. The camel, because it takes its meaning from its action, from its movement. The meaning of the camel is that it takes you from a place to a place.

The 'Amal in Islam is raised to higher degrees than mankind had known. 'Amal becomes transformed into Birr. Birr is a very complex word, a very important word in the Arabic language, and many 'Ulama have written books on the subject of Birr. Birr is 'just' action. More, it is just action in the light of Divine Guidance, which is what we have been talking about in relation to the youths in the cave and to the young Prophet Ibrahim, 'alayhi salam. Birr means therefore that the 'Amal is now transformed into something else which is not only action, but 'just action' in the light of Divine Guidance. Let us look at Surat ash-Shura (42:36-39):

فَمَآ أُوتِيتُم مِّن شَيْءٍ فَمَتَٰعُ ٱلْحَيَوٰةِ ٱلدُّنْيَا
وَمَا عِندَ ٱللَّهِ خَيْرٌ وَأَبْقَىٰ لِلَّذِينَ ءَامَنُوا۟ وَعَلَىٰ رَبِّهِمْ يَتَوَكَّلُونَ ﴿٣٦﴾
وَٱلَّذِينَ يَجْتَنِبُونَ كَبَٰٓئِرَ ٱلْإِثْمِ وَٱلْفَوَٰحِشَ وَإِذَا مَا غَضِبُوا۟ هُمْ
يَغْفِرُونَ ﴿٣٧﴾ وَٱلَّذِينَ ٱسْتَجَابُوا۟ لِرَبِّهِمْ وَأَقَامُوا۟ ٱلصَّلَوٰةَ وَأَمْرُهُمْ
شُورَىٰ بَيْنَهُمْ وَمِمَّا رَزَقْنَٰهُمْ يُنفِقُونَ ﴿٣٨﴾
وَٱلَّذِينَ إِذَآ أَصَابَهُمُ ٱلْبَغْىُ هُمْ يَنتَصِرُونَ ﴿٣٩﴾

Whatever you have been given is only
the enjoyment of the life of the dunya.
What is with Allah is better and longer lasting
for those who have Iman and trust in their Lord:
those who avoid major wrong actions and indecencies
and who, when they are angered, then forgive;
those who respond to their Lord and establish Salat,
and manage their affairs by mutual consultation
and give of what We have provided for them;
those who, when they are wronged, defend themselves.

This is the new dispensation that has been brought by the Rasul, sallallahu 'alayhi wa sallam, through the Revelation and through his own life and performance. This is a new dispensation – it has not been before. This is the Birr, and it is a dynamic. It is a rising in stations. This is the Mukarim al-Akhlaq of Rasul, sallallahu 'alayhi wa sallam. It is that the

Muslim becomes someone who, in the life process, improves himself all the time, all the time, all the time.

This is the motor power released by the Revelation and its Master. It is a striving, a reaching beyond, a self-transformation – it is Futuwwa. A Hanbali Faqih, Ibn Mi'mar, wrote a book of Fiqh called 'Kitab al-Futuwwa'. Islamic Futuwwa pre-dated and pre-designed the christian rules of chivalry which created the whole of European civilisation in the Middle Ages. Futuwwa is the adoption of an attitude and conduct, elevated, so that it is the image of the People of Jannah. According to Tabarani, one day Anas was ill. Some of the Companions came to visit him. Anas turned to his servant and said, "Give my friends something, even if it is only a piece of bread. I heard the Messenger say, sallallahu 'alayhi wa sallam, 'Excellence of behaviour is a quality of the People of the Garden.'"

Futuwwa is to maintain harmony among the brothers. Bayhaqi and Daraqutni record that Abu Sa'id, one of the Ahl as-Suffa, told that a man had prepared to entertain the Messenger and some Companions. When the food was laid out, one of the Companions did not eat, saying that he was fasting. The Messenger, sallallahu 'alayhi wa sallam, then said, "Your brother has invited us and gone to a lot of trouble!" Then he added: "Eat! Fast another day if you want."

Futuwwa is correctness in attitude and inner state. It has been reported from 'Urwah in Ibn Hanbal, Muslim and Tirmidhi, that Sufyan ibn 'Abdullah ath-Thaqafi said, "Oh Messenger! Give me a word in Islam thanks to which I will not need to question anyone after you." The Rasul, sallallahu 'alayhi wa sallam, replied, "Say: 'I believe in Allah,' and be straight."

Again, notice all this connectedness between the people of Fiqh – the 'Ulama – and the Sufis. Yusuf al-Husayn, the student of Ibn Hanbal, visited Abu Yazid al-Bistami, the great Sufi, and asked him, "Who do you counsel me to take as a friend?" Abu Yazid replied, "The one who will visit you when you are sick, and the one who will pardon you when you behave badly."

Futuwwa implies perfect harmony between the brothers. Al-Musayyib ibn Wahdi said, "Any brother to whom you say, 'Come!' and who replies, 'Where?' is not a true brother for you." Imam Junayd's Murid, Abu Bakr al-Kattani, said, "Futuwwa is to be aware of the lost time of ignorance and to take account of it wisely. I heard of a man who suddenly became aware that he was sixty years old. He counted his days for the first time and realised that they added up to twenty one thousand, five hundred days. The man became so full of fear, he passed out. When he was revived he said, How terrible! If I had done a wrong action every day, I would come before Allah covered in wrongs. But I have done wrong things tens of thousands of times a day!' and he passed out a second time. When they tried to revive him they saw that he was dead."

Fatiha.

IV

November 17th 2007

We will continue to deepen our knowledge of the science and practice of Futuwwa. This, in action, is the high Suluk of the Men of Allah. Abu'l Husayn al-Kalabadhi instructed his Murids thus: "Do not be concerned with your subsistence, it is guaranteed for you. But rather be concerned with the work that has been assigned to you." By that he meant what had been assigned to you in the Destiny of Allah, for you to perform in your life-time these good actions.

Dhul-Nun al-Misri instructed his Murids thus: "The one who looks into the imperfections of others is prevented from seeing his own imperfections. The one who keeps sight of his own faults no longer sees the faults of others." Futuwwa is to leave the path of accusations and head for the paths of forgiveness. A quarrel rose up between the 'Alim Ibn as-Sammak and some of his friends. During the argument, one of his friends said, "Let us meet tomorrow and continue this fight." Ibn as-Sammak replied, "No. Let us meet tomorrow in mutual pardon." The Murids of Ibn Junayd asked that he should not reply to the people who attended their sessions only to challenge Sufism and start polemics. Imam Junayd explained, "I see them differently from you. My hope is that they may grasp by chance a single word, that they may understand and that it might save them."

Imam Junayd told his followers, "I sat during ten years in the presence of masters who talked of the science of Tasawwuf without my understanding a word of their discourse. I knew they were speaking the truth, and that it was different from what I had always understood. Years later, they came to the door of my house and said to me, 'Junayd, such and such has happened, and we need you to give us your advice.'"

I once told the Imam of Shaykh Muhammad ibn al-Habib, rahimahullah, Imam Ibn 'Abdalwahhab, "The most I have learned, I learned sitting in the company of our Shaykh, although I understood only one out of ten things he was saying." The Imam was very pleased with me and said, "You are the one who succeeded. In due course it will come out from you."

Sari as-Saqati taught his Murids, "Leave five things: leave all that is perishing, men, passions, will to power, and seeking honours. Hold to five things: the blessings of the Jannah, that the world is worthless, sincerity which imposes fear of Allah, keeping company with the Awliya, and what is pleasing to Allah from which the ignorant turn away."

In the Musnad of Ibn Hanbal we find that the Messenger, sallallahu 'alayhi wa sallam, said, "One of the characteristics of the Muslim is that he does not busy himself with what does not concern him." Ma'ruf al-Karkhi, one of Imam Junayd's masters, said, "The fact that a Mumin uses his time in being occupied with what does not concern him, is a sign for him of Divine anger." Imam Junayd was asked, "What is the definition of the Sufi?" We take up our Qur'ans – and for Imam Junayd's reply we go to the first half of Ayat 23 in Surat al-Ahzab (33:23):

مِّنَ ٱلْمُؤْمِنِينَ رِجَالٌ صَدَقُوا۟ مَا عَـٰهَدُوا۟ ٱللَّهَ عَلَيْهِ

Among the Muminun there are men who have been true to the contract they made with Allah.

It has to be stressed that the greater mass of people today are less than whole human beings. Humanism, the worship of the species, has not produced humans, it has produced sub-humans. In exalting and looking up to 'man', they have placed themselves below man. Humanism has made both living men and the corpses of men identical. The masses of troops in World War I on both sides are identical. One mass of men charge out of the trenches, another mass of men mow them down. Half a million men in a day dead, and not an inch of territory gained. Germans in World War II rounding up and massacring millions of jews – but also, millions of jews submitting and letting themselves be slaughtered. In Russia, under the new regime of the Humanists – Communism – millions are herded into the Gulags and the Russian citizens obediently murder them. Not until Solzhenitsyn did one human voice speak up and expose the genocide.

The arrival of the Messenger, sallallahu 'alayhi wa sallam, meant a new dispensation for the whole of mankind. It offered a new code of conduct to the human creatures. On his part comes his dispensation to the Muminun in Surat at-Tawba (9:128-129):

لَقَدْ جَآءَكُمْ رَسُولٌ مِّنْ أَنفُسِكُمْ عَزِيزٌ
عَلَيْهِ مَا عَنِتُّمْ حَرِيصٌ عَلَيْكُم بِالْمُؤْمِنِينَ رَءُوفٌ
رَّحِيمٌ ﴿١٢٨﴾ فَإِن تَوَلَّوْا فَقُلْ حَسْبِيَ اللَّهُ لَآ إِلَٰهَ إِلَّا هُوَ
عَلَيْهِ تَوَكَّلْتُ وَهُوَ رَبُّ الْعَرْشِ الْعَظِيمِ ﴿١٢٩﴾

A Messenger has come to you from among yourselves.
Your suffering is distressing to him;
he is deeply concerned for you;
he is gentle and merciful to the muminun.
But if they turn away, say,
"Allah is enough for me.
There is no god but Him.
I have put my trust in Him.
He is the Lord of the Mighty Throne."

On our part, comes our contract with him. Look at Surat Al 'Imran (3:31-32). This is our contract that we have with him, but it is preceded by Allah ordering Rasul, sallallahu 'alayhi wa sallam:

قُلْ إِن كُنتُمْ تُحِبُّونَ ٱللَّهَ فَٱتَّبِعُونِى
يُحْبِبْكُمُ ٱللَّهُ وَيَغْفِرْ لَكُمْ ذُنُوبَكُمْ ۗ وَٱللَّهُ غَفُورٌ رَّحِيمٌ ﴿٣١﴾ قُلْ أَطِيعُوا۟
ٱللَّهَ وَٱلرَّسُولَ ۖ فَإِن تَوَلَّوْا۟ فَإِنَّ ٱللَّهَ لَا يُحِبُّ ٱلْكَٰفِرِينَ ﴿٣٢﴾

Say, "If you love Allah, then follow me
and Allah will love you and forgive you
for your wrong actions.
Allah is Ever-Forgiving, Most Merciful."

Say, "Obey Allah and the Messenger."
Then if they turn away,
Allah does not love the kafirun.

So, in the first Ayat, Allah commands the Rasul, sallallahu 'alayhi wa sallam. In his received command is embedded OUR received command.

قُلْ أَطِيعُوا۟ ٱللَّهَ وَٱلرَّسُولَ ۖ
فَإِن تَوَلَّوْا۟ فَإِنَّ ٱللَّهَ لَا يُحِبُّ ٱلْكَٰفِرِينَ ﴿٣٢﴾

Say, "Obey Allah and the Messenger."
Then if they turn away,
Allah does not love the kafirun.

So from this Divine and also Prophetic Contract, comes an open definition of the new dispensation.

It is reported from Anas ibn Malik and recorded in Imam Muslim that the Rasul, sallallahu 'alayhi wa sallam, said, "None of you is a Mumin until I am dearer to him than his children, his father and the whole of mankind." This is a completely new order, a completely new situation. Anas further told us that he also said, "None of you is a Mumin until one wants for one's brother what one wants for oneself." The Rasul, sallallahu 'alayhi wa sallam, is telling us what this new situation is. This second Hadith is the licence for Da'wa. If you have got the Deen of Islam, you want it for your brother. To this Abu Hurayra adds a further evidence. "Sallallahu 'alayhi wa sallam said, 'He who believes in Allah and the Last Day should treat his neighbour with kindness. He who believes in Allah and the Last Day should show hospitality to his guest.'" Now Rasul, sallallahu 'alayhi wa sallam, is laying down fundamental elements of the new order.

Here is the fourfold plan for a new social ethos, grounded in 'Ibada for Allah and love of the Messenger, sallallahu 'alayhi wa sallam. We have been given these four orders: You are not Mumin until you love Rasul, sallallahu 'alayhi wa sallam, more than your family and the whole of mankind. You are not Mumin until you want for your brothers what you want for yourself. If you believe in Allah and the Last Day you will treat your neighbour with kindness, and if you believe in Allah and the Last Day you will show hospitality to the guest.

I saw in our community in Spain that while they were inviting each other to their houses, the community was strong. The day they stopped inviting each other into their houses, conflict began among the houses. We go back to our Imam's definition of the Sufi from Surat al-Ahzab (33:23):

مِّنَ ٱلْمُؤْمِنِينَ رِجَالٌ صَدَقُوا۟ مَا عَٰهَدُوا۟ ٱللَّهَ عَلَيْهِ

Among the Muminun there are men who have been true
to the contract they made with Allah.

Now we know what the contract is. It is this foundation which marks out the elite of the human species – the Rijalallah, the Fuqara and the Faqirat. Allah openly explains about them in Surat an-Nur (24:36-38):

فِى بُيُوتٍ أَذِنَ ٱللَّهُ أَن تُرْفَعَ
وَيُذْكَرَ فِيهَا ٱسْمُهُۥ يُسَبِّحُ لَهُۥ فِيهَا بِٱلْغُدُوِّ وَٱلْـَٔاصَالِ ﴿٣٦﴾
رِجَالٌ لَّا تُلْهِيهِمْ تِجَٰرَةٌ وَلَا بَيْعٌ عَن ذِكْرِ ٱللَّهِ وَإِقَامِ ٱلصَّلَوٰةِ
وَإِيتَآءِ ٱلزَّكَوٰةِ ۙ يَخَافُونَ يَوْمًا تَتَقَلَّبُ فِيهِ ٱلْقُلُوبُ وَٱلْأَبْصَٰرُ ﴿٣٧﴾
لِيَجْزِيَهُمُ ٱللَّهُ أَحْسَنَ مَا عَمِلُوا۟ وَيَزِيدَهُم مِّن فَضْلِهِۦ ۗ
وَٱللَّهُ يَرْزُقُ مَن يَشَآءُ بِغَيْرِ حِسَابٍ ﴿٣٨﴾

In houses which Allah has permitted to be built
and in which His name is remembered,
there are men who proclaim His glory

morning and evening,
not distracted by trade or commerce
from the remembrance of Allah
and the establishment of Salat
and the payment of Zakat;
fearing a day when all hearts and eyes will be in turmoil –
so that Allah can reward them
for the best of what they did
and give them more from His unbounded favour.
Allah provides for anyone He wills without reckoning.

So the corollary of this is inevitable, given that this is the new dispensation given to mankind. From the human, live or a corpse, having been utterly worthless, utterly dispensable in the kafir world order, the human being has become an exalted creature with a Divine contract. We go to Surat al-Baqara (2:30):

وَإِذْ قَالَ رَبُّكَ لِلْمَلَٰٓئِكَةِ إِنِّي جَاعِلٌ فِي ٱلْأَرْضِ خَلِيفَةً قَالُوٓاْ
أَتَجْعَلُ فِيهَا مَن يُفْسِدُ فِيهَا وَيَسْفِكُ ٱلدِّمَآءَ وَنَحْنُ نُسَبِّحُ
بِحَمْدِكَ وَنُقَدِّسُ لَكَ قَالَ إِنِّيٓ أَعْلَمُ مَا لَا تَعْلَمُونَ ﴿٣٠﴾

When your Lord said to the angels,
"I am putting a Khalif on the earth,"
they said, "Why put on it
one who will cause corruption on it and shed blood
when we glorify You with praise
and proclaim Your purity?"
He said, "I know what you do not know."

This raising up of the human being to be Khalif-Representative of Allah, subhanahu wa ta'ala, means that the human being has meaning, has function. What is that function? We go to Surat adh-Dhariyat (51:56):

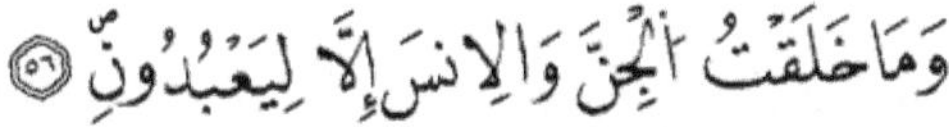

I only created jinn and man to worship Me.

Thus we can say that the human body is a kind of sacred vessel, filled with this Ruhani investiture. It means that the human is a protected creature. He cannot be destroyed except under the strictest rules – which we call 'Shari'at' – granting a right to kill in punishment and in Jihad fisabilillah. This especially sets suicide as the most terrible wrong action, as it is a betrayal of the Divine Contract. The Messenger of Allah, sallallahu 'alayhi wa sallam, told us, on the authority of Abu Hurayra in Imam Muslim's Collection:

> He who killed himself with a weapon will exist forever in the Fire of Jahannam. He will have that weapon and be thrusting it into his stomach forever. He who drank poison and killed himself will be taking it in the Fire of Jahannam where he is doomed to remain forever. He who killed himself by flinging himself from the top of a mountain will be perpetually plunging downwards in the Fire of Jahannam, forever.

In another recension, Thabit bin Dahaq reported his saying,

sallallahu 'alayhi wa sallam:

> He who killed himself with a thing will be tormented on the Day of Rising with that very thing.

The reference to these three sorts of suicide, in Arabic usage, also indicates that it is a general rule and therefore has no exception. It follows from this that a man who places such an instrument of suicide into a young man's hand is by that action guilty of two crimes: the murder of the one intending suicide, and also the deliberate incitement of a Muslim to send himself to Hell.

It must follow from this that the new awakening of mankind – which is the Message of Islam and the obedience and love of its Messenger, sallallahu 'alayhi wa sallam – is dependent on an end to the epoch of despair in the Mercy of Allah, currently functioning in the demented and ignorant Arab world.

The rebirth of Futuwwa in our time is incumbent on us. Firstly, challenging our ignorant brothers to set aside the false doctrines from the Age of Darkness of the Arab Nation. Thus our point of departure is in Surat al-A'raf (7:198-199):

وَإِن تَدْعُوهُمْ إِلَى ٱلْهُدَىٰ لَا يَسْمَعُوا۟ۖ
وَتَرَىٰهُمْ يَنظُرُونَ إِلَيْكَ وَهُمْ لَا يُبْصِرُونَ ﴿١٩٨﴾ خُذِ ٱلْعَفْوَ وَأْمُرْ
بِٱلْعُرْفِ وَأَعْرِضْ عَنِ ٱلْجَٰهِلِينَ ﴿١٩٩﴾

IV

If you call them to guidance, they do not hear.
You see them looking at you, yet they do not see.

Make allowances for people,
command what is right,
and turn away from the ignorant.

Futuwwa demands that we do not distance ourselves from our brothers because of their errors. They must be approached, welcomed, and brought back by good counsel. The Wahhabis are our brothers. Their Bida' is not Shirk. The Taliban are our brothers. Their errors are not Shirk. We must not let the kuffar divide us. Our concern for them comes from the obligation placed on us by our beloved Messenger, sallallahu 'alayhi wa sallam, to join with them in unity, made sincere by good counsel, for the Deen is nothing but good counsel.

V

December 1st 2007

The disaster of this last decade has been that through the ignorance and wrong actions of the Arab peoples, genuine teaching of Islam is not only denied to the kuffar but is distorted to the Muslim Nation. The Emirates television station 'Iqraa' pumps out an endless stream of pronouncements on the Deen in a sociological bubble, as if what was happening in Dubai simply did not exist.

This is a Deen whose scholars throughout our history always refused to be seen as a priesthood or a special caste, but who now can be observed wearing distinctive robes and underwriting every social process that the kafir world throws up, and licensing as permissible a whole raft of practices in commerce that stand as clearly forbidden in Qur'an and the Fiqh of the Salaf. The so-called extremists, even called insultingly the 'Islamists', declare that to put things right they want to establish the Shari'at as the means to an Islamic society.

They are mistaken, because these men have already crossed over from the Deen of Islam to the European system of law which is based on strict canonic principles which are to be used to encompass human behaviour. In other words, it is a system that in the first instance denies Divine decree, and in the second substitutes human reason and rulings on a people who already live without meaning or purpose.

Of course, we are not denying the Shari'at or setting it aside – what we must do is recognise the true nature of the Deen and the nature of the Muslim polity. The creation of a Muslim community is dependent on a set of processes – social and personal processes dynamically emerging and mutually sustaining each other.

If we examine the Muwatta' of Imam Malik, which is universally recognised as the greatest delineation of the Deen ever compiled, we find quite simply that its contents are divided into two major sections. Further, Imam Muslim's collection of Hadith, modelled structurally on the Muwatta', follows the same pattern.

The first half of the Muwatta' gives the detailed rules and practices that are required of us in 'Ibada. That is: belief in Tawhid, and confirmation of the ultimate Nabawiyyat of

V

the Rasul, sallallahu 'alayhi wa sallam, the detailed analysis and explication of every form of Salat, the parameters of Sawm and Zakat and the Fara'id and Sunnan of Hajj. The second half of the Muwatta' gives the detailed rules and practices that are required of us in Commerce, its instruments and its methods.

The Deen, therefore, is dependent on the Revelation itself, and the Messenger, sallallahu 'alayhi wa sallam, in his setting down and demonstrating the required Practice. Book – and Practice. So who is it for? Who is the Muslim? Let us look at the opening of the Book. We turn to Qur'an, and Surat al-Baqara (2:1-5):

بِسْمِ ٱللَّهِ ٱلرَّحْمَٰنِ ٱلرَّحِيمِ

الٓمٓ ﴿١﴾ ذَٰلِكَ ٱلْكِتَٰبُ لَا رَيْبَ فِيهِ هُدًى
لِّلْمُتَّقِينَ ﴿٢﴾ ٱلَّذِينَ يُؤْمِنُونَ بِٱلْغَيْبِ وَيُقِيمُونَ
ٱلصَّلَوٰةَ وَمِمَّا رَزَقْنَٰهُمْ يُنفِقُونَ ﴿٣﴾ وَٱلَّذِينَ
يُؤْمِنُونَ بِمَآ أُنزِلَ إِلَيْكَ وَمَآ أُنزِلَ مِن
قَبْلِكَ وَبِٱلْآخِرَةِ هُمْ يُوقِنُونَ ﴿٤﴾ أُوْلَٰٓئِكَ عَلَىٰ
هُدًى مِّن رَّبِّهِمْ وَأُوْلَٰٓئِكَ هُمُ ٱلْمُفْلِحُونَ ﴿٥﴾

In the name of Allah, All-Merciful, Most Merciful

Alif Lam Mim
That is the Book, without any doubt.

It contains guidance for those who have Taqwa:
those who have Iman in the Unseen and establish Salat
and spend from what We have provided for them;
those who have Iman in what has been sent down to you
and what was sent down before you,
and are certain about the Akhira.
They are the people guided by their Lord.
They are the ones who have success.

So what is it – what is Islam? Let us look at the famous first Hadith in Imam Muslim's Collection. Among the various important recensions, let us take that of Abu Hurayra, who told us that the Rasul, sallallahu 'alayhi wa sallam, said:

> "Ask me!" The Companions were overcome with awe and could not speak. Then a man came forward facing him, knees to knees, and said, "Rasulullah, what is Islam?" He replied: "You must not associate anything with Allah. Establish Salat and pay the Zakat. Keep the Fast of Ramadan. The man said, "You have told the truth. Now Rasulullah, what is Iman?" He said: "It is that you confirm that you believe in Allah, His Angels, His Books, His Messengers, the meeting with Him, the Day of Rising and the Divine Qadr in its entirety." He replied, "You have told the truth. Now, what is Ihsan?" The Rasul, sallallahu 'alayhi wa sallam, answered: "It is that you worship Allah as if you saw Him, and while you do not see Him, know that he sees you." The man said, "That is the truth. Now, when will be the Last Day?"

> The Rasul, sallallahu 'alayhi wa sallam, said, "The one who is asked knows no more than the one who asks. However, some of its signs are: when you see a slave-woman give birth to her master, when you see the barefoot, the naked, the deaf and dumb as masters of the earth, and when you see the herders of the black camels exalting in high buildings."

The Hadith continues:

> The man stood up and moved away. Rasulullah called out, "Bring him back to me!" They searched but could not find him. Sallallahu 'alayhi wa sallam said, "It was Jibril. He came to teach you when you did not ask yourselves."

Let us now look at the opening of Al-Muwatta' and the very first recension in the first chapter:

> He said, "Yahya ibn Yahya al-Laythi related to me from Malik ibn Anas from Ibn Shihab that one day 'Umar ibn 'Abdalaziz delayed the prayer. 'Urwa ibn az-Zubayr came and told him that al-Mughira ibn Shu'ba had delayed the prayer one day while he was in Kufa and Abu Mas'ud al-Ansari had come to him and said, 'What's this, Mughira? Don't you know that the Angel Jibril came down and prayed and the Messenger of Allah, sallallahu 'alayhi wa sallam, prayed. Then he prayed again, and the Messenger of Allah, sallallahu 'alayhi wa

> sallam, prayed. Then he prayed again, and the Messenger of Allah, sallallahu 'alayhi wa sallam, prayed. Then he prayed again, and the Messenger of Allah, sallallahu 'alayhi wa sallam, prayed. Then Jibril said, "This is what you have been ordered to do."' 'Umar ibn 'Abdalaziz said, "Be sure of what you relate, 'Urwa. Was it definitely Jibril who established the time of the prayer for the Messenger of Allah." 'Urwa said, "That is how it was related to Bashir ibn Abi Mas'ud al-Ansari by his father."

Here we have three distinct indications of what we are dealing with in taking on Islam, protecting it, and spreading it. It is a Divine transaction, dependent for its Revelation and emergence in the in-time reality, on an angelic transmission, and a delivery of the teaching and the Message, by the chosen final Messenger of mankind to – and at this point Islam emerges to the man or woman who will take on the Divine and revealed contract – the Muslim men and women. This means that the Divine Event – Qur'an and Messenger, and the angelic dimension in the Ghayb – all this was for me, for you, for the Muslim. This is why we are doomed to triumph, success and victory.

Only once this is understood can talk of Shari'at take place. Islam in its fullness is Jama'at – gathering. Even three travelling Muslims fall under the rule of Islam. One is an Amir. The Messenger, sallallahu 'alayhi wa sallam, warned us against travelling alone, saying that Shaytan is with the solitary. The Jama'at, not just one Muslim, is required for

Islam in its fullness to emerge. That in turn requires an appointment from among them of an Amir. Only then can the Jama'at proceed from Salat to Sawm and Zakat. Hajj is itself a journey, and so in turn it is dependent on an Amir.

This permits us to say that the emergence of the Amir, to whom Bay'at, that is allegiance, has been made, means at the same moment the Shari'at has emerged. The recognition of leadership, Amirate, is dependent on a prior recognition and knowledge of what a Muslim man is. In Sahih Muslim we find that Ibn 'Umar reported that Rasulullah, sallallahu 'alayhi wa sallam, declared: "You will find that people are like a hundred camels. You will only find one camel that is fit for riding."

The Sunna, the Practice of the Messenger, lays down the model of behaviour and social practice that defines in turn the Muslim peoples. Islam, therefore, is the social ennoblement of the raw material of the unformed human species, who up until then lie trapped in Jahiliyya, that is humanism, that is arrogance and that in turn is ignorance. In its place comes a new social nexus, that by its nature is both dynamic and elevating. It could be called a competition in qualities. This our Fuqaha called 'Birr'.

Birr is action – but action which is just. In its root it means 'solid land' as opposed to the sea which is ever-changing and unsure. From its root B-R-R also extends B-R-hamza, which is in its verb, 'to create', and from its noun, 'free', and also 'innocent'. Not just a naïve innocence but in its Qur'anic usage a very special freedom and innocence. Look at Surat an-An'am (6:75-79), noting particularly Ayat 78:

وَكَذَٰلِكَ نُرِيٓ إِبۡرَٰهِيمَ
مَلَكُوتَ ٱلسَّمَٰوَٰتِ وَٱلۡأَرۡضِ وَلِيَكُونَ مِنَ
ٱلۡمُوقِنِينَ ٧٥ فَلَمَّا جَنَّ عَلَيۡهِ ٱلَّيۡلُ رَءَا كَوۡكَبٗاۖ قَالَ هَٰذَا
رَبِّيۖ فَلَمَّآ أَفَلَ قَالَ لَآ أُحِبُّ ٱلۡأٓفِلِينَ ٧٦ فَلَمَّا رَءَا ٱلۡقَمَرَ
بَازِغٗا قَالَ هَٰذَا رَبِّيۖ فَلَمَّآ أَفَلَ قَالَ لَئِن لَّمۡ يَهۡدِنِي رَبِّي
لَأَكُونَنَّ مِنَ ٱلۡقَوۡمِ ٱلضَّآلِّينَ ٧٧ فَلَمَّا رَءَا ٱلشَّمۡسَ بَازِغَةٗ قَالَ
هَٰذَا رَبِّي هَٰذَآ أَكۡبَرُۖ فَلَمَّآ أَفَلَتۡ قَالَ يَٰقَوۡمِ إِنِّي بَرِيٓءٞ
مِّمَّا تُشۡرِكُونَ ٧٨ إِنِّي وَجَّهۡتُ وَجۡهِيَ لِلَّذِي فَطَرَ ٱلسَّمَٰوَٰتِ
وَٱلۡأَرۡضَ حَنِيفٗاۖ وَمَآ أَنَا۠ مِنَ ٱلۡمُشۡرِكِينَ ٧٩

Because of that We showed Ibrahim
the dominions of the heavens and the earth
so that he might be one of the people of certainty.

When night covered him he saw a star and said,
"This is my Lord!"
Then when it set he said,
"I do not love what sets."
Then when he saw the moon come up he said,
"This is my Lord!"
Then when it set he said,
"If my Lord does not guide me,
I will be one of the misguided people."
Then when he saw the sun come up he said,

"This is my Lord! This is greater!"
Then when it set he said,
"My people, I am free of what
you associate with Allah!
I have turned my face to Him
Who brought the heavens and earth into being,
a pure natural believer.
I am not one of the Mushrikun."

Let us look again at Ayat 78:

فَلَمَّا رَءَا ٱلشَّمْسَ بَازِغَةً قَالَ هَٰذَا رَبِّي هَٰذَآ أَكْبَرُ ۖ
فَلَمَّآ أَفَلَتْ قَالَ يَٰقَوْمِ إِنِّي بَرِيٓءٌ مِّمَّا تُشْرِكُونَ ﴿٧٨﴾

Then when he saw the sun come up he said,
"This is my Lord! This is greater!"
Then when it set he said,
"My people, I am free of what
you associate with Allah!

Now, read in the Arabic: "My people, I am free of what you associate with Allah!":

يَٰقَوْمِ إِنِّي بَرِيٓءٌ مِّمَّا تُشْرِكُونَ ﴿٧٨﴾

This 'Barri' is from Birr which we have been talking about. This allows us to say that the just action is of its nature and value and meaning that the actor acts in order to demonstrate that it confirms that the doer does not associate any power with Allah's Power. So Birr is the dynamic of living Islam. This is transmitted through Habib in Sahih Muslim:

> Yazid ibn Abu Habib reported that Na'im, the freed slave of Umm Salama reported to him that 'Abdallah ibn Amr said: "There came to the Messenger a young man who said, 'I pledge allegiance to your Hijra and Jihad, seeking only reward from Allah.' He was asked, 'Are one of your parents living?' He replied, 'Yes, of course, both are alive.' He was then asked, 'Do you want to seek a reward from Allah?' He said, 'Yes, I do,' at which the Rasulullah, sallallahu 'alayhi wa sallam, said, 'Go back to your parents and treat them kindly.'"

Now we go to Qur'an, and Surat al-Isra' (17:23-25):

وَقَضَىٰ رَبُّكَ أَلَّا تَعْبُدُوٓا۟ إِلَّآ إِيَّاهُ وَبِٱلْوَٰلِدَيْنِ إِحْسَٰنًا
إِمَّا يَبْلُغَنَّ عِندَكَ ٱلْكِبَرَ أَحَدُهُمَآ أَوْ كِلَاهُمَا فَلَا
تَقُل لَّهُمَآ أُفٍّ وَلَا تَنْهَرْهُمَا وَقُل لَّهُمَا قَوْلًا كَرِيمًا ﴿٢٣﴾ وَٱخْفِضْ
لَهُمَا جَنَاحَ ٱلذُّلِّ مِنَ ٱلرَّحْمَةِ وَقُل رَّبِّ ٱرْحَمْهُمَا كَمَا رَبَّيَانِى
صَغِيرًا ﴿٢٤﴾ رَّبُّكُمْ أَعْلَمُ بِمَا فِى نُفُوسِكُمْ إِن تَكُونُوا۟ صَٰلِحِينَ
فَإِنَّهُۥ كَانَ لِلْأَوَّٰبِينَ غَفُورًا ﴿٢٥﴾

Your Lord has decreed
that you should worship none but Him,
and that you should show kindness to your parents.
Whether one or both of them reach old age with you,
do not say "Ugh!" to them out of irritation
and do not be harsh with them
but speak to them with gentleness and generosity.
Take them under your wing,
out of mercy, with due humility
and say: "Lord, show mercy to them
as they did in looking after me when I was small."

Your Lord knows best what is in your selves.
If you are salihun,
He is Ever-Forgiving to the remorseful.

Thus this Hadith and this passage of Qur'an you can see are identical in their message, and so we have the first foundational order of Birr. The Muslim is also enjoined to keep amicable relations with his fellow Muslim. Abu Hurayra in our Sahih listed the acts of guidance from Rasul, sallallahu 'alayhi wa sallam, thus:

> Avoid suspicion, for it is the worst thing in talk. Do not be inquisitive about one another. Do not spy on one another. Do not envy anything of the other. Do not maintain a hostility against another. Do not bid against the other, in commerce, when he has made his bid. The Muslim is the brother of the Muslim. Do not oppress him. Do not humiliate him. Do not look down on him. All things of a Muslim are

> inviolable to other Muslims: his blood, his wealth, and his honour. "Allah does not look at your bodies, nor your faces, but he looks at your hearts" – and the Rasul pointed to his heart with his fingers.

Thawban, the freed slave of Rasulullah, sallallahu 'alayhi wa sallam, reported:

> The Messenger said: "He who visits the sick continues to remain in the Khurfat al-Jannah until he returns." He was asked, "What is the Khurfat al-Jannah?" He answered, "It is a place full of ripe fruit."

And lastly, from Abu Hurayra:

> Rasulullah told that a man set out to visit his brother Muslim in another town. Allah sent an Angel to wait for him on his way. He did so and stopped the man, asking, "Where are you going?" He said, "I intend to visit my brother Muslim in this town." "Has he done you some favour?" asked the Angel. "No," came the reply, "except that I love him for the sake of Allah, 'Azza wa Jalla." The Angel told him, "I have been sent to you from Allah to tell you that Allah loves you as you love him for Allah's sake."

These social norms indicate the existence of a genuine working Jama'at. Birr is the active evidence of the new Nomos on the earth. Islam.

V

Today we are witnessing the final enactment of the globalist kafir system. It has no ideology. It has no metaphysic. It has not even a leader. It is held together by a self-hating and mutually hating caucus of men from the dregs of human society. Devoid of background, upbringing or genetic quality. Racaille – the scum of the earth.

From where do they derive their illusion of power? Not from themselves. Not from their military strength – even they know it could only lead to mutual destruction. Not from their financial system which they already know is mathematically structured to come to an inevitable collapse. Their strength – their illusion of power, is uniquely based on a massively complex patterning of gas and petrol piping across the enormous land mass of western Asia and now spread across all Europe and the Middle East. Its epicentre is not the USA. It is Russia.

The once total hegemonic power of the USA based on the financial (paper and numbers) system has had to yield to the networked commodity wealth and control of Russia. The USA's last bid to control and halt this ascendance of commodity over finance was in the desperate bid to break the all-encompassing circuitry of gas-and-oil by an invasion of Iraq and Afghanistan. The failure of the first and the therefore inevitable collapse of the latter, insures a kafir unitary system covering the great land mass of the world. If you set up a map of present and planned pipelines you would see that the power of the money-regime of the USA is already spent, and the pipeline system has basically won. Allah explains our situation in Surat al-'Ankabut (29:41-45):

مَثَلُ ٱلَّذِينَ ٱتَّخَذُواْ مِن دُونِ ٱللَّهِ
أَوْلِيَآءَ كَمَثَلِ ٱلْعَنكَبُوتِ
ٱتَّخَذَتْ بَيْتًا وَإِنَّ أَوْهَنَ ٱلْبُيُوتِ لَبَيْتُ ٱلْعَنكَبُوتِ
لَوْ كَانُواْ يَعْلَمُونَ ﴿٤١﴾ إِنَّ ٱللَّهَ يَعْلَمُ مَا تَدْعُونَ مِن
دُونِهِۦ مِن شَيْءٍ وَهُوَ ٱلْعَزِيزُ ٱلْحَكِيمُ ﴿٤٢﴾ وَتِلْكَ
ٱلْأَمْثَٰلُ نَضْرِبُهَا لِلنَّاسِ وَمَا يَعْقِلُهَآ إِلَّا ٱلْعَٰلِمُونَ ﴿٤٣﴾
خَلَقَ ٱللَّهُ ٱلسَّمَٰوَٰتِ وَٱلْأَرْضَ بِٱلْحَقِّ إِنَّ فِي ذَٰلِكَ
لَأَيَةً لِّلْمُؤْمِنِينَ ﴿٤٤﴾ ٱتْلُ مَآ أُوحِيَ إِلَيْكَ مِنَ ٱلْكِتَٰبِ
وَأَقِمِ ٱلصَّلَوٰةَ إِنَّ ٱلصَّلَوٰةَ تَنْهَىٰ عَنِ ٱلْفَحْشَآءِ وَٱلْمُنكَرِ
وَلَذِكْرُ ٱللَّهِ أَكْبَرُ وَٱللَّهُ يَعْلَمُ مَا تَصْنَعُونَ ﴿٤٥﴾

The metaphor of those who take protectors besides Allah
is that of a spider which builds itself a house;
but no house is flimsier than a spider's house,
if they only knew.

Allah knows what you call upon besides Himself.
He is the Almighty, the All-Wise.

Such metaphors – We devise them for mankind;
but only those with knowledge understand them.

Allah created the heavens and the earth with truth.

V

There is certainly a Sign in that for the Muminun.

Recite what has been revealed to you of the Book
and establish Salat.
Salat precludes indecency and wrongdoing.
And remembrance of Allah is greater still.
Allah knows what you do.

It is in the illumination that we receive from these Ayats that we can see that the new Nomos, Islam, will sweep away the Spider's Web of Pipeline power. The people of Dhikr of Allah are already transcending the massive attempt to define Islam as nihilist and passéiste frenzy.

Birr will overwhelm the darkness. And from that will emerge the highest kind of men, the men who will rise from Birr to the Brotherhood of Futuwwa. Again the Awliya will walk, and are already walking, the earth.

VI

DECEMBER 8TH 2007

In recognising the law of Birr, the fundamental reality becomes clear. The realisation that just action – good action – is itself the confirmation of the Power of Allah, and the open declaration that Allah is One and nothing is associated with Him, defines the Deen as the transformative, indeed competitive process that elevates men and women above ignorance and arrogance, or Jahiliyya. Islam as 'Ibada IS Birr. Through and through. It is the elevation of mankind from the state of loss – Khusr, to the state of remembering.

Abu Hurayra narrated that the Rasulullah, sallallahu 'alayhi wa sallam, said: "Iman has around seventy branches. The best of it is saying that there is no god but Allah. The least of it is the removal of something injurious on the road."

This permits us to note the all-inclusive nature of the Deen. This in turn indicates that it is the duty, the taken-on duty of the Muslim to remove injustice and replace it with justice. To the false post-Islamic religion of the Shi'a the "covering of the earth with justice as it was before covered with injustice," is the affair of the Mahdi and the end of the world. To the Muslim it is the order of the day. The task of all the life-time. The task of Islam.

The evidence of this new order comes on the authority of Anas in the great Hadith narrated by Abdalwarith:

The Rasulullah, sallallahu 'alayhi wa sallam, said: "No person believes until I am dearer to him than the members of his household, his wealth, and the whole of mankind."

Anas ibn Malik related it also:

"None of you is a believer until I am dearer to him than his children, his father and the whole of mankind."

Look at the oath of Jarir Abu Amr: "I pledge allegiance to the Messenger of Allah, sallallahu 'alayhi wa sallam, on the establishment of Salat, the payment of Zakat, and Sidq and Nasiha for every Muslim." Nasiha is thus another stone in the wall of the Muslim's protection. It is more than counsel in the moral sense. It is counsel that brings with it the weight of the giver's affection and friendship. It has no disapproval, reproach or judgment in it. It is from the heart.

It heals because of the love the giver of Nasiha has for his fellow Muslim.

This permits us to say that those who speak of 'Islamic Principles' have failed to understand the Deen. We do not have principles based on reason and argument. We have concern and then counsel, and this is based on love. Abu Hurayra reported:

The Messenger of Allah, sallallahu 'alayhi wa sallam, said, "You will not enter the Jannah until you affirm your belief, and you will not believe until you love one another. Let me direct you to a thing which will foster love among you if you do it: spread the practice of saying, 'As-Salaamu 'alaykum.'"

This means that this greeting is said as a Du'a. It is not as a kafir salutation. It is not the, "Hey!" of the kafirun. It has to be said with the intention of asking the blessings of the Lord of Peace on the Muslim who is greeted. You must, especially Sufis, refrain from saying, "As-salaamu 'alaykum" in a frivolous, light and social manner. It is a Du'a. It is an act of worship of Allah. The Sahaba used to walk together, and if a group of them would go round a tree and one half went on one side and the other half went on the other, when they came to the other side of the tree they would say, "As-Salaamu 'alaykum." It was love, you see. Let us look at Surat an-Nisa' (4:86):

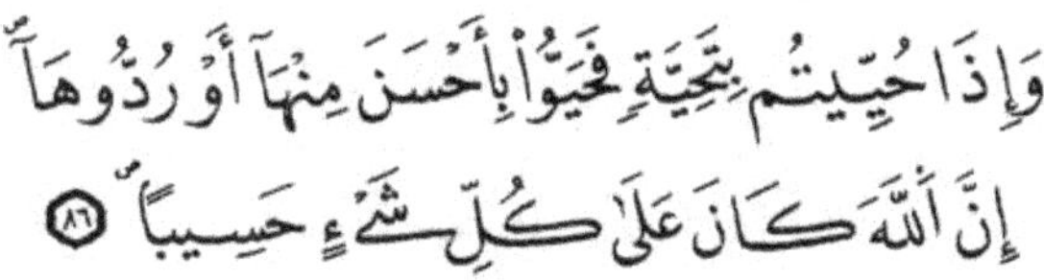

When you are greeted with a greeting,
return the greeting or improve on it.
Allah takes account of everything.

Thus the greeting itself is written for you and recorded for you, so it is a Du'a. What has emerged is that the life of the Muslim is enmeshed in a series of good actions which radiate out from love and respect for parents, out to the nearest neighbours, and on out to an all-encompassing active concern for the Muslims. Since this right action, which itself affirms Allah's dominion over the human situation, penetrates every sector of life, it places similar obligations and duties on the Muslims' dealings in wealth and commerce.

Just as Ramadan is the annual reminder and curb of appetites, both of food and sex, so too Zakat is the annual reminder and curb of both ownership and the deception that possession is permanent. The curb on ownership lies in the handing-over of the required amount. The curb on the illusion that we are the possessors lies in the necessity that our wealth be firstly assessed by the Zakat Collectors, and secondly that it should be TAKEN from us by the Collectors.

There is no Islam in the absence of Zakat and Salat. The two are almost in every case mentioned together in the Qur'an. Abu Hurayra reported:

> The Rasulullah, sallallahu 'alayhi wa sallam, sent 'Umar ibn al-Khattab to collect the Zakat. He was then informed that Ibn Jamil, Khalid bin Walid and Abbas, the uncle of the Rasul, sallallahu 'alayhi wa sallam, refused to hand it over.

> On hearing this the Rasulullah, sallallahu 'alayhi wa sallam, said, "Ibn Jamil is taking revenge, for he was destitute before Allah made him rich."

At that time Ibn Jamil was one of the munafiqun. This is in Surat at-Tawba (9:74-77):

يَحْلِفُونَ بِاللَّهِ مَا قَالُوا۟

وَلَقَدْ قَالُوا۟ كَلِمَةَ ٱلْكُفْرِ وَكَفَرُوا۟ بَعْدَ إِسْلَٰمِهِمْ
وَهَمُّوا۟ بِمَا لَمْ يَنَالُوا۟ وَمَا نَقَمُوٓا۟ إِلَّآ أَنْ أَغْنَىٰهُمُ ٱللَّهُ
وَرَسُولُهُۥ مِن فَضْلِهِۦ فَإِن يَتُوبُوا۟ يَكُ خَيْرًا لَّهُمْ وَإِن
يَتَوَلَّوْا۟ يُعَذِّبْهُمُ ٱللَّهُ عَذَابًا أَلِيمًا فِى ٱلدُّنْيَا وَٱلْءَاخِرَةِ
وَمَا لَهُمْ فِى ٱلْأَرْضِ مِن وَلِىٍّ وَلَا نَصِيرٍ ﴿٧٤﴾ وَمِنْهُم مَّنْ
عَٰهَدَ ٱللَّهَ لَئِنْ ءَاتَىٰنَا مِن فَضْلِهِۦ لَنَصَّدَّقَنَّ وَلَنَكُونَنَّ مِنَ
ٱلصَّٰلِحِينَ ﴿٧٥﴾ فَلَمَّآ ءَاتَىٰهُم مِّن فَضْلِهِۦ بَخِلُوا۟ بِهِۦ وَتَوَلَّوا۟ وَّهُم
مُّعْرِضُونَ ﴿٧٦﴾ فَأَعْقَبَهُمْ نِفَاقًا فِى قُلُوبِهِمْ إِلَىٰ يَوْمِ يَلْقَوْنَهُۥ
بِمَآ أَخْلَفُوا۟ ٱللَّهَ مَا وَعَدُوهُ وَبِمَا كَانُوا۟ يَكْذِبُونَ ﴿٧٧﴾

They swear by Allah that they said nothing,
but they definitely spoke the word of kufr
and returned to kufr after their Islam.
They planned something which they did not achieve
and they were vindictive for no other cause

than that Allah and His Messenger
had enriched them from His bounty.
If they were to make Tawba, it would be better for them.
But if they turn away, Allah will punish them
with a painful punishment in the dunya and the Akhira,
and they will not find any protector or helper on the earth.

Among them there were some
who made an agreement with Allah:
"If He gives us of His bounty
we will definitely give Sadaqa
and be among the Salihun."
But when He does give them of His bounty
they are tight-fisted with it and turn away,
so He has punished them
by putting hypocrisy in their hearts
until the day they meet Him
because they failed Allah in what they promised Him
and because they lied.

Later on, because of this matter, he asked forgiveness and returned to Islam. Thus refusal to be assessed and give Zakat is here openly indicated by Allah as a disaster for men. The Messenger then examined the other two. He said, sallallahu 'alayhi wa sallam:

> "As for Khalid, you are being unjust. He dedicated his armour and his weapons to the Way of Allah."

By this it meant that the Jihad excused him from needing to hand over the Zakat. He then said, sallallahu 'alayhi wa sallam:

> "As for Abbas, I shall be responsible for it, and an equal amount alongside that."

He added,

> "'Umar, bear in mind that the uncle of a man is like his father."

Thus, in the last case, only the making-up of his contribution by the Rasulullah himself, sallallahu 'alayhi wa sallam, exempted Abbas from the tax of Zakat.

Jarir ibn 'Abdullah reported:

> There came a group of Bedouins to the Rasulullah, sallallahu 'alayhi wa sallam, who said to him, "The Zakat Collectors came to us and they treated us unfairly." Whereupon the Rasulullah, sallallahu 'alayhi wa sallam, ordered them, "Please your Zakat Collectors." Jarir said, "Ever since I heard that from the Messenger of Allah, sallallahu 'alayhi wa sallam, no Zakat Collector ever left me but that he was pleased with me."

This is an evidence that being assessed and stripped of one's Zakat dues is a Ruhani affair, sweet and pleasing to the Muslim who by it feels the burdens of Dunya lifted from him and his heart at peace, as the Muslim also does on breaking his fast. As for those who reject or refrain from being taxed, the judgment is clear. We go back to Surat at-Tawba (9:34-35), starting at the second half of Ayat 34:

وَٱلَّذِينَ يَكْنِزُونَ ٱلذَّهَبَ وَٱلْفِضَّةَ
وَلَا يُنفِقُونَهَا فِى سَبِيلِ ٱللَّهِ فَبَشِّرْهُم بِعَذَابٍ أَلِيمٍ ﴿٣٤﴾
يَوْمَ يُحْمَىٰ عَلَيْهَا فِى نَارِ جَهَنَّمَ فَتُكْوَىٰ بِهَا جِبَاهُهُمْ
وَجُنُوبُهُمْ وَظُهُورُهُمْ هَٰذَا مَا كَنَزْتُمْ لِأَنفُسِكُمْ
فَذُوقُوا۟ مَا كُنتُمْ تَكْنِزُونَ ﴿٣٥﴾

As for those who hoard up gold and silver
and do not spend it in the Way of Allah,
give them the news of a painful punishment
on the Day it is heated up in the fire of Hell
and their foreheads, sides and backs are branded with it:
"This is what you hoarded for yourselves,
so taste what you were hoarding!"

In the light of the judgment we noted by the Rasulullah, sallallahu 'alayhi wa sallam, this situation refers both to the kuffar and to the munafiqun. Until the Zakat is collected after assessment, the guilty are clearly in Nifaq. In final Qur'anic confirmation of the Divinely discriminated difference between private Sadaqa and civic Zakat we turn to Surat al-Mujadala (58:13):

ءَأَشْفَقْتُمْ أَن تُقَدِّمُوا۟ بَيْنَ يَدَىْ نَجْوَىٰكُمْ صَدَقَٰتٍ فَإِذْ لَمْ تَفْعَلُوا۟
وَتَابَ ٱللَّهُ عَلَيْكُمْ فَأَقِيمُوا۟ ٱلصَّلَوٰةَ وَءَاتُوا۟ ٱلزَّكَوٰةَ
وَأَطِيعُوا۟ ٱللَّهَ وَرَسُولَهُۥ وَٱللَّهُ خَبِيرٌۢ بِمَا تَعْمَلُونَ ﴿١٣﴾

Are you afraid to give gifts of Sadaqa
before your private consultation?
If you do not and Allah turns to you,
at least establish Salat and pay Zakat,
and obey Allah and His Messenger.
Allah is aware of what you do.

So the giving of Sadaqa is distinguished from submission to the payment of Zakat. This permits us to say that we have understanding of the Deen. Until we have grasped this, we have not understood the Deen. And that the Deen is itself the functioning of the high 'Amal. It follows from this that there is another human community which rejects the Divine Contract. It is essential that we identify who they are since we have been commanded to love with the love of Allah and hate what He, glory be to Him, hates.

The enemy is denounced in Surat al-Fajr (89:17-20):

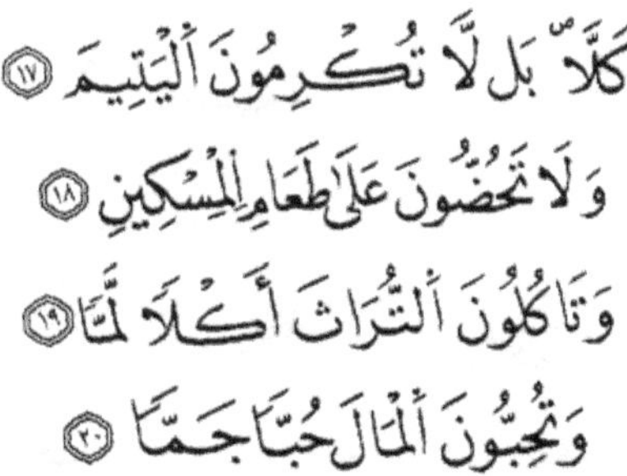

No indeed! You do not honour orphans
nor do you urge the feeding of the poor;
you devour inheritance with voracious appetites
and you have an insatiable love of wealth.

It follows from this that the community of safety and Allah's love is uniquely the community of Zakat and Salat. We now discover that this Divine Discrimination is not only an affair of this world but of the Next. It cannot any more be a matter of asking from us 'TOLÉRANCE' – but rather on our part WE must insist on justice for the poor. Let us look at Surat al-Haqqa (69:19-40):

فَأَمَّا مَنْ أُوتِيَ كِتَٰبَهُۥ بِيَمِينِهِۦ
فَيَقُولُ هَآؤُمُ ٱقْرَءُوا۟ كِتَٰبِيَهْ ﴿١٩﴾ إِنِّى ظَنَنتُ أَنِّى مُلَٰقٍ
حِسَابِيَهْ ﴿٢٠﴾ فَهُوَ فِى عِيشَةٍ رَّاضِيَةٍ ﴿٢١﴾ فِى جَنَّةٍ عَالِيَةٍ ﴿٢٢﴾ قُطُوفُهَا
دَانِيَةٌ ﴿٢٣﴾ كُلُوا۟ وَٱشْرَبُوا۟ هَنِيٓـًٔا بِمَآ أَسْلَفْتُمْ فِى ٱلْأَيَّامِ ٱلْخَالِيَةِ ﴿٢٤﴾
وَأَمَّا مَنْ أُوتِيَ كِتَٰبَهُۥ بِشِمَالِهِۦ فَيَقُولُ يَٰلَيْتَنِى لَمْ أُوتَ كِتَٰبِيَهْ ﴿٢٥﴾
وَلَمْ أَدْرِ مَا حِسَابِيَهْ ﴿٢٦﴾ يَٰلَيْتَهَا كَانَتِ ٱلْقَاضِيَةَ ﴿٢٧﴾ مَآ أَغْنَىٰ عَنِّى
مَالِيَهْ ﴿٢٨﴾ هَلَكَ عَنِّى سُلْطَٰنِيَهْ ﴿٢٩﴾ خُذُوهُ فَغُلُّوهُ ﴿٣٠﴾ ثُمَّ ٱلْجَحِيمَ
صَلُّوهُ ﴿٣١﴾ ثُمَّ فِى سِلْسِلَةٍ ذَرْعُهَا سَبْعُونَ ذِرَاعًا فَٱسْلُكُوهُ ﴿٣٢﴾
إِنَّهُۥ كَانَ لَا يُؤْمِنُ بِٱللَّهِ ٱلْعَظِيمِ ﴿٣٣﴾ وَلَا يَحُضُّ عَلَىٰ طَعَامِ ٱلْمِسْكِينِ ﴿٣٤﴾
فَلَيْسَ لَهُ ٱلْيَوْمَ هَٰهُنَا حَمِيمٌ ﴿٣٥﴾ وَلَا طَعَامٌ إِلَّا مِنْ غِسْلِينٍ ﴿٣٦﴾ لَّا يَأْكُلُهُۥٓ
إِلَّا ٱلْخَٰطِـُٔونَ ﴿٣٧﴾ فَلَآ أُقْسِمُ بِمَا تُبْصِرُونَ ﴿٣٨﴾ وَمَا لَا تُبْصِرُونَ ﴿٣٩﴾
إِنَّهُۥ لَقَوْلُ رَسُولٍ كَرِيمٍ ﴿٤٠﴾

VI

As for him who is given his Book in his right hand,
he will say, "Here, come and read my Book!
I counted on meeting my Reckoning."
He will have a very pleasant life
in an elevated Garden,
its ripe fruit hanging close to hand.

"Eat and drink with relish
for what you did before in days gone by!"

But as for him who is given his Book in his left hand,
he will say, "If only I had not been given my Book
and had not known about my Reckoning!
If only death had really been the end!
My wealth has been of no use to me.
My power has vanished."
"Seize him and truss him up.
Then roast him in the Blazing Fire.
Then bind him in a chain
which is seventy cubits long.
He used not to have Iman in Allah the Magnificent,
nor did he urge the feeding of the poor.
Therefore here today he has no friend
nor any food except exuding pus
which no one will eat except those
who were in error."

I swear both by what you see
and what you do not see,
that this is the word of a noble Messenger.

In our confrontation and obligatory conflict with the unjust, Allah indicates our Path to security and victory over them. The people of Allah are spiritually superior to the unjust. Look at Surat at-Tawba (9:20):

ٱلَّذِينَ ءَامَنُوا۟ وَهَاجَرُوا۟ وَجَٰهَدُوا۟ فِى سَبِيلِ ٱللَّهِ
بِأَمْوَٰلِهِمْ وَأَنفُسِهِمْ
أَعْظَمُ دَرَجَةً عِندَ ٱللَّهِ وَأُو۟لَٰٓئِكَ هُمُ ٱلْفَآئِزُونَ ٢٠

Those who have Iman and make Hijra
and do Jihad in the Way of Allah
with their wealth and themselves
have a higher rank with Allah.
They are the ones who are victorious.

This grants us a discovery of our own strength over Allah's enemies. Among us, there are those who are raised up to a higher condition. States and Station. In place of the material weaponry of Allah's enemies we find that Allah's Friends are armed with spiritual Ruhani power from Allah. Let us look at Surat al-Waqi'a (56:1-14):

بِسْمِ ٱللَّهِ ٱلرَّحْمَٰنِ ٱلرَّحِيمِ

إِذَا وَقَعَتِ ٱلْوَاقِعَةُ ١ لَيْسَ لِوَقْعَتِهَا كَاذِبَةٌ ٢ خَافِضَةٌ رَّافِعَةٌ ٣
إِذَا رُجَّتِ ٱلْأَرْضُ رَجًّا ٤ وَبُسَّتِ ٱلْجِبَالُ بَسًّا ٥ فَكَانَتْ هَبَآءً مُّنۢبَثًّا ٦
وَكُنتُمْ أَزْوَٰجًا ثَلَٰثَةً ٧ فَأَصْحَٰبُ ٱلْمَيْمَنَةِ مَآ أَصْحَٰبُ ٱلْمَيْمَنَةِ ٨

VI

وَأَصْحَٰبُ ٱلْمَشْـَٔمَةِ مَآ أَصْحَٰبُ ٱلْمَشْـَٔمَةِ ﴿٩﴾ وَٱلسَّٰبِقُونَ ٱلسَّٰبِقُونَ ﴿١٠﴾
أُو۟لَٰٓئِكَ ٱلْمُقَرَّبُونَ ﴿١١﴾ فِى جَنَّٰتِ ٱلنَّعِيمِ ﴿١٢﴾ ثُلَّةٌ مِّنَ ٱلْأَوَّلِينَ ﴿١٣﴾
وَقَلِيلٌ مِّنَ ٱلْـَٔاخِرِينَ ﴿١٤﴾

In the name of Allah, All-Merciful, Most Merciful

When the Great Event occurs,
none will deny its occurrence;
bringing low, raising high.

When the earth is convulsed
and the mountains are crushed
and become scattered dust in the air.

And you will be classed into three:
the Companions of the Right:
what of the Companions of the Right?
the Companions of the Left:
what of the Companions of the Left?
and the Forerunners,
the Forerunners.

Those are the Ones Brought Near
in Gardens of Delight.
A large group of the earlier people
but few of the later ones.

The Muqarrabun are, in the scientific language of the Sufis, the Awliya, the 'Arifin and the Salihun. Look how the kafir pig, Ataturk, was terrified of Mawlana Rumi, dead hundreds of years before, and did not dare set foot in Konya throughout his rule. How much more do the enemies of Allah fear and dread the living Awliya?

Now, in one of those particularly precious Suras, Allah lifts veils from His Power and how it functions in the world. We go to Surat al-Ma'arij (70:1-5):

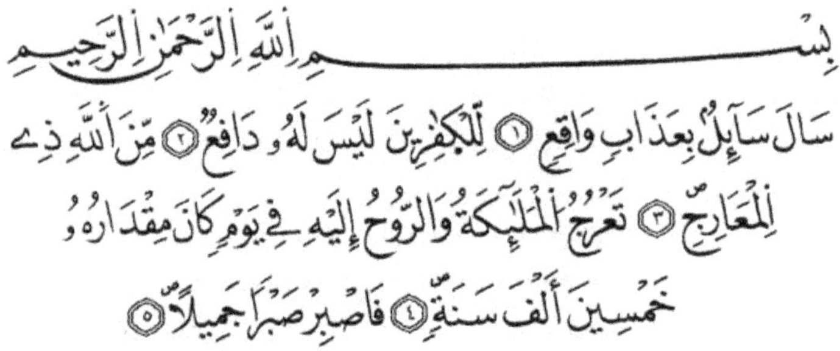

In the name of Allah, All-Merciful, Most Merciful

An inquirer asked about an impending punishment.

It is for the kafirun and cannot be averted
from Allah – the Lord of the Ascending Steps.
The Angels and the Spirit ascend to Him in a day
whose length is fifty thousand years.

Therefore be patient with a patience which is beautiful.

Here, we are given one of Allah's secret Names which encodes the structural nature of events in this and the Next World.

Shaykh Ibn 'Ajiba says: "These are the Ascending Steps that the Angels tread in carrying out their orders and their work. These are the degrees by which the Salihun ascend, and which the Muminun ascend on their Suluk."

Shaykh al-Akbar, Ibn 'Arabi, says: "These are the Stations through which creation rises from mineral to vegetal, then to the humans moving from one Station to another. These steps are the Stations and Manazil – Ranks, of the hearts, leading to the Station of Fana' in the Acts and the Attributes up to the Fana' in the Essence."

This brings us to the thunderbolt of the Suluk of Tasawwuf. Here is the unveiling in the Qur'an of the highest Stations. We go to Surat al-Balad (90:11-18), bearing in mind we have taken this Name of Allah, subhanahu wa ta'ala, which is Dhil-Ma'arij:

فَلَا ٱقۡتَحَمَ ٱلۡعَقَبَةَ ﴿١١﴾
وَمَآ أَدۡرَىٰكَ مَا ٱلۡعَقَبَةُ ﴿١٢﴾ فَكُّ رَقَبَةٍ ﴿١٣﴾ أَوۡ إِطۡعَٰمٞ فِي يَوۡمٖ ذِي
مَسۡغَبَةٖ ﴿١٤﴾ يَتِيمٗا ذَا مَقۡرَبَةٍ ﴿١٥﴾ أَوۡ مِسۡكِينٗا ذَا مَتۡرَبَةٖ ﴿١٦﴾ ثُمَّ كَانَ مِنَ ٱلَّذِينَ
ءَامَنُواْ وَتَوَاصَوۡاْ بِٱلصَّبۡرِ وَتَوَاصَوۡاْ بِٱلۡمَرۡحَمَةِ ﴿١٧﴾ أُوْلَٰٓئِكَ أَصۡحَٰبُ ٱلۡمَيۡمَنَةِ ﴿١٨﴾

But he has not braved the steep ascent.
What will convey to you what the steep ascent is?

It is freeing a slave
or feeding on a day of hunger
an orphaned relative

or a poor man in the dust;
then to be one of those who have Iman
and urge each other to steadfastness
and urge each other to compassion.
Those are the Companions of the Right.

The Qur'an lays out the task that has faced and today now faces the Muslim Ummah. We turn to Surat al-Mujadala (58:20-22):

إِنَّ ٱلَّذِينَ يُحَآدُّونَ ٱللَّهَ وَرَسُولَهُۥٓ أُوْلَٰٓئِكَ فِي ٱلۡأَذَلِّينَ ﴿٢٠﴾
كَتَبَ ٱللَّهُ لَأَغۡلِبَنَّ أَنَا۠ وَرُسُلِيٓۚ إِنَّ ٱللَّهَ قَوِيٌّ عَزِيزٞ ﴿٢١﴾
لَّا تَجِدُ قَوۡمٗا يُؤۡمِنُونَ بِٱللَّهِ وَٱلۡيَوۡمِ ٱلۡأٓخِرِ يُوَآدُّونَ مَنۡ حَآدَّ ٱللَّهَ وَرَسُولَهُۥ
وَلَوۡ كَانُوٓاْ ءَابَآءَهُمۡ أَوۡ أَبۡنَآءَهُمۡ أَوۡ إِخۡوَٰنَهُمۡ أَوۡ عَشِيرَتَهُمۡۚ أُوْلَٰٓئِكَ
كَتَبَ فِي قُلُوبِهِمُ ٱلۡإِيمَٰنَ وَأَيَّدَهُم بِرُوحٖ مِّنۡهُۖ وَيُدۡخِلُهُمۡ جَنَّٰتٖ
تَجۡرِي مِن تَحۡتِهَا ٱلۡأَنۡهَٰرُ خَٰلِدِينَ فِيهَاۚ رَضِيَ ٱللَّهُ عَنۡهُمۡ
وَرَضُواْ عَنۡهُۚ أُوْلَٰٓئِكَ حِزۡبُ ٱللَّهِۚ أَلَآ إِنَّ حِزۡبَ ٱللَّهِ هُمُ ٱلۡمُفۡلِحُونَ ﴿٢٢﴾

Those who oppose Allah and His Messenger,
such people will be among the most abased.
Allah has written, "I will be victorious,
I and My Messengers."
Allah is Most Strong, Almighty.

You will not find people
who have Iman in Allah and the Last Day

having love for anyone who opposes
Allah and His Messenger,
though they be their fathers, their sons,
their brothers or their clan.
Allah has inscribed Iman upon such people's hearts
and will reinforce them with a Ruh from Him
and admit them into Gardens
with rivers flowing under them,
remaining in them timelessly, for ever.
Allah is pleased with them and they are pleased with Him.
Such people are the party of Allah.
Truly it is the party of Allah who are successful.

We embark on our task with the promise of the Lord of the Worlds. We turn to Surat al-A'la (87:8):

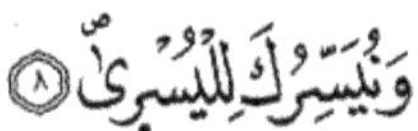

We will ease you to the Easy Way.

VII

December 15th 2007

We began our journey into the matter of 'Amal with a deliberate turning-upside-down of Imam al-Ghazali's famous definition: 'Ilm al-Mu'amala precedes 'Ilm al-Mukashafa.

The purpose of this reversal lay in the claim that the process and procedure of right action was itself dependent on a prior Ruhani illumination. Or, if you like, that a movement towards good action sprang from a Divinely designed capacity towards choosing what was pleasing to Allah, glory to be Him. To perceive the emergence from intention to right action implied an unveiling of the Destiny itself, and a glimpse of the secret of our lives which lies in our cognition that our act of will is from the Willer, the One Who Wills – Allah, glory be to Him.

Our first examination of this matter led us to an awareness that among the great Sufis the highest type of human creature is the man of Fata. Futuwwa was, as it were, the aimed-at science of Tasawwuf. Imam Junayd, Imam ibn Hanbal and Shaykh 'Abdalqadir al-Jilani competed in elevating it and in defining its contours.

What emerged from this exploration was that Futuwwa represented, as it were, the Himalayan aspects of nobility, but it was of the same earth, the same mineral as what lay in the slopes and valleys of human existence. It was not other, not cut off from, not an inaccessible zone, not of another element than what was the norm of Muslim behaviour.

The conclusion we have been forced to arrive at is that Futuwwa is the summit of what is the fundamental matter of the Deen. We discovered that this was the essential matter of Islam and it had been named by our 'Ulama as 'Birr'. From this came the knowledge that to the Muslim Ummah, right-action was in itself a Ruhani event which in itself represented an active and demonstrable declaration of Allah's Unity and that nothing can be compared to Him.

We then gained an insight from the Qur'an that Allah, 'Azza wa Jalla, had set up Ascending Steps of this Birr, that led to the highest Ma'rifa. We also found that Allah had linked the spiritual ascent of the Muslim to necessary acts of generosity, courage and rescue – in short, with the raising-up of lost humanity – mankind being a species in loss. Humanism thus being nothing more than the stoic and useless philosophy of loss. We go to the famous Surat al-'Asr (103:1-3):

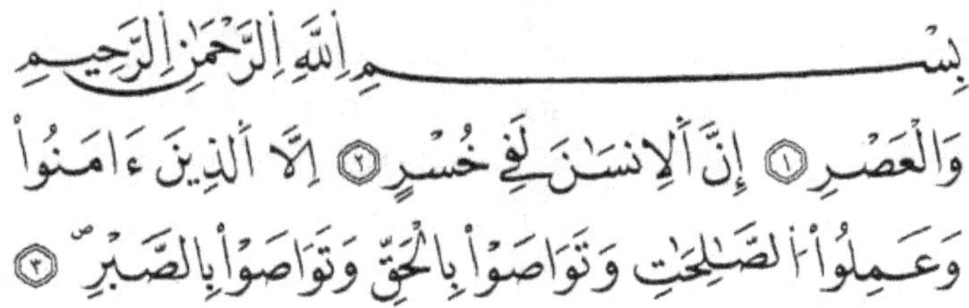

In the name of Allah, All-Merciful, Most Merciful

By the Late Afternoon,
truly man is in loss –
except for those who have Iman and do right actions
and urge each other to the truth
and urge each other to patience.

How is it that we, the Muslims, are able to see so clearly that men cannot arrive at knowledge and wisdom, let alone understanding, by thinking a way out of the human situation? Philosophy, a man-made construct, by its nature becomes more dark, more inaccessible, and more metaphoric. The philosopher, his life continuing, is forced to metaphors of hope: the light at the end of the tunnel, the bright clearing in the dark forest.

The answer is dual and lies in our dual Shahada. It declares the Oneness of Allah. It also links this to the Messengership of His Messenger, sallallahu 'alayhi wa sallam. The knowledge of Allah is linked, inexorably, to the event of the

Messenger. As Shaykh ibn al-Mashish explained: "If it were not for the means, the end would have escaped us."

Qadi 'Iyad said that the Messenger had plumbed "depths of knowledge which no mortal but him has reached." He confirmed that this can be verified "by anyone who studies the development of his states, the course of his life, the wisdom of his Hadith, his knowledge of what was in the Torah, the Injil, the Revealed Books, the wisdom of the sages and the history of past nations and their battles, making metaphors, managing people, establishing the laws of the Shari'at, laying the foundation of his incomparable Adab, and praiseworthy habits."

His greatest qualities of manhood were his 'Ibada, his generosity and his courage. These dynamic forces in his character are what have marked the whole World Muslim Community from his lifetime until today.

Ibn al-Munkadir heard Jabir ibn 'Abdullah say: "The Messenger of Allah, sallallahu 'alayhi wa sallam, was not asked for anything to which he said, 'No!'"

Anas said: "A man asked him for something and he gave him all the sheep between two mountains. The man returned to his people and said, 'Become Muslim. Muhammad gives the gift of a man who does not fear poverty.'"

He returned the captives of Hawazim who numbered six thousand. He gave Abbas so much gold that he could not carry it. Ninety thousand Dirham were brought to him and he placed them on a mat, and then he got up and distributed them. He did not turn away anyone who asked until he had given them all away.

Of his courage we find in Al-Bayhaqi:

> Ubayy ibn Khalaf caught sight of the Messenger during the Battle of Uhud, and Ubayy shouted out, "Where is Muhammad? May I not survive if he survives!" Now this Ubayy had previously been ransomed on the Day of Badr, and at that time he had declared, "I have a horse which I feed several measures of wheat every day. If I ride him I will kill you." The Messenger, sallallahu 'alayhi wa sallam, told him, "I will kill you, if Allah wills." So it was that on the Day of Uhud, when Ubayy saw the Messenger, sallallahu 'alayhi wa sallam, he drove his horse towards him. Some of the Muslims tried to block his way but the Rasul called out, "Leave him alone!" He then took a spear from Al-Harith ibn Simma and shook it in such a way that all the men fled from him, as flies scatter from the back of a camel when it shakes itself. Then the Rasul, sallallahu 'alayhi wa sallam, turned to face him and pierced him in the neck so that he swayed and fell from his horse. People said, "He has broken a rib," but he returned to the Quraysh and said, "Muhammad has killed me!" They said, "There's nothing wrong with you!" Ubayy replied, "Anyone would have been killed by what I have received. Did he not say, 'I will kill

you!’? By Allah, if he had spat on me, it would have killed me.” He died at Sarif on his way back to Makkah.

Allah tells us about him in Surat at-Tawba (9:128-129):

لَقَدْ جَآءَكُمْ رَسُولٌ مِّنْ أَنفُسِكُمْ عَزِيزٌ
عَلَيْهِ مَا عَنِتُّمْ حَرِيصٌ عَلَيْكُم بِالْمُؤْمِنِينَ رَءُوفٌ
رَّحِيمٌ ﴿١٢٨﴾ فَإِن تَوَلَّوْا فَقُلْ حَسْبِيَ اللَّهُ لَآ إِلَٰهَ إِلَّا هُوَ
عَلَيْهِ تَوَكَّلْتُ وَهُوَ رَبُّ الْعَرْشِ الْعَظِيمِ ﴿١٢٩﴾

A Messenger has come to you from among yourselves.
Your suffering is distressing to him;
he is deeply concerned for you;
he is gentle and merciful to the Muminun.
But if they turn away, say,
“Allah is enough for me.
There is no god but Him.
I have put my trust in Him.
He is the Lord of the Mighty Throne.”

Connected to that we look at Surat al-Anbiya’ (21:107). These are Allah’s statements of the Maqam of the Rasul, sallallahu ‘alayhi wa sallam:

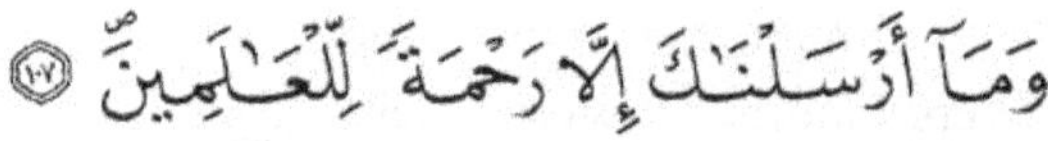

We have only sent you as a mercy to all the worlds.

And most importantly, we turn to Surat Saba' (34:28):

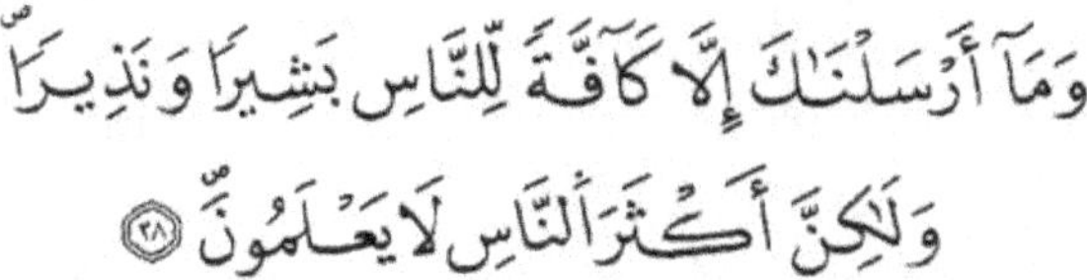

We only sent you for the whole of mankind,
bringing good news and giving warning.
But most of mankind do not know it.

The Divine Contract is that Allah educated His Messenger, and he in turn is sent to teach mankind. Look at the second part of the Ayat in Surat an-Nisa' (4:113):

وَأَنزَلَ ٱللَّهُ عَلَيۡكَ ٱلۡكِتَٰبَ وَٱلۡحِكۡمَةَ وَعَلَّمَكَ
مَا لَمۡ تَكُن تَعۡلَمُۚ وَكَانَ فَضۡلُ ٱللَّهِ عَلَيۡكَ عَظِيمٗا ١١٣

Allah has sent down the Book and Wisdom to you
and taught you what you did not know before.
Allah's favour to you is indeed immense.

The greatest of all honours in this world comes to him in Allah's exalting Islam above every other religion. We go to Surat at-Tawba (9:33):

هُوَ ٱلَّذِيٓ أَرۡسَلَ رَسُولَهُۥ بِٱلۡهُدَىٰ وَدِينِ ٱلۡحَقِّ
لِيُظۡهِرَهُۥ عَلَى ٱلدِّينِ كُلِّهِۦ وَلَوۡ كَرِهَ ٱلۡمُشۡرِكُونَ ٣٣

It is He who sent His Messenger
with guidance and the Deen of Truth
to exalt it over every other Deen,
even though the Mushrikun detest it.

So it follows that no Muslim may be invited to tolerance as if it somehow were morally superior and dominant over us. To those who preach and call you to 'tolerate' – tell them: "You are speaking another language. These words have no meaning for us. Learn a new language – one we have by Divine Revelation. Book and Sunna."

This brings us to the Miracle of the New Direction for Prayer, the physical setting of Islam over every prior religion. Turn to Surat al-Baqara (2:144-152):

قَدْ نَرَىٰ تَقَلُّبَ وَجْهِكَ فِي ٱلسَّمَآءِ فَلَنُوَلِّيَنَّكَ
قِبْلَةً تَرْضَىٰهَا فَوَلِّ وَجْهَكَ شَطْرَ ٱلْمَسْجِدِ ٱلْحَرَامِ وَحَيْثُ مَا
كُنتُمْ فَوَلُّوا۟ وُجُوهَكُمْ شَطْرَهُۥ وَإِنَّ ٱلَّذِينَ أُوتُوا۟
ٱلْكِتَٰبَ لَيَعْلَمُونَ أَنَّهُ ٱلْحَقُّ مِن رَّبِّهِمْ وَمَا ٱللَّهُ بِغَٰفِلٍ
عَمَّا يَعْمَلُونَ ﴿١٤٤﴾ وَلَئِنْ أَتَيْتَ ٱلَّذِينَ أُوتُوا۟ ٱلْكِتَٰبَ
بِكُلِّ ءَايَةٍ مَّا تَبِعُوا۟ قِبْلَتَكَ وَمَآ أَنتَ بِتَابِعٍ قِبْلَتَهُمْ
وَمَا بَعْضُهُم بِتَابِعٍ قِبْلَةَ بَعْضٍ وَلَئِنِ ٱتَّبَعْتَ أَهْوَآءَهُم
مِّنۢ بَعْدِ مَا جَآءَكَ مِنَ ٱلْعِلْمِ إِنَّكَ إِذًا لَّمِنَ ٱلظَّٰلِمِينَ ﴿١٤٥﴾
ٱلَّذِينَ ءَاتَيْنَٰهُمُ ٱلْكِتَٰبَ يَعْرِفُونَهُۥ كَمَا يَعْرِفُونَ أَبْنَآءَهُمْ

وَإِنَّ فَرِيقًا مِّنْهُمْ لَيَكْتُمُونَ ٱلْحَقَّ وَهُمْ يَعْلَمُونَ ﴿١٤٦﴾ ٱلْحَقُّ
مِن رَّبِّكَ فَلَا تَكُونَنَّ مِنَ ٱلْمُمْتَرِينَ ﴿١٤٧﴾ وَلِكُلٍّ وِجْهَةٌ
هُوَ مُوَلِّيهَا فَٱسْتَبِقُوا۟ ٱلْخَيْرَٰتِ أَيْنَ مَا تَكُونُوا۟ يَأْتِ بِكُمُ ٱللَّهُ
جَمِيعًا إِنَّ ٱللَّهَ عَلَىٰ كُلِّ شَىْءٍ قَدِيرٌ ﴿١٤٨﴾ وَمِنْ حَيْثُ خَرَجْتَ
فَوَلِّ وَجْهَكَ شَطْرَ ٱلْمَسْجِدِ ٱلْحَرَامِ وَإِنَّهُۥ لَلْحَقُّ مِن رَّبِّكَ وَمَا ٱللَّهُ
بِغَٰفِلٍ عَمَّا تَعْمَلُونَ ﴿١٤٩﴾ وَمِنْ حَيْثُ خَرَجْتَ فَوَلِّ وَجْهَكَ شَطْرَ
ٱلْمَسْجِدِ ٱلْحَرَامِ وَحَيْثُ مَا كُنتُمْ فَوَلُّوا۟ وُجُوهَكُمْ شَطْرَهُۥ لِئَلَّا
يَكُونَ لِلنَّاسِ عَلَيْكُمْ حُجَّةٌ إِلَّا ٱلَّذِينَ ظَلَمُوا۟ مِنْهُمْ
فَلَا تَخْشَوْهُمْ وَٱخْشَوْنِى وَلِأُتِمَّ نِعْمَتِى عَلَيْكُمْ
وَلَعَلَّكُمْ تَهْتَدُونَ ﴿١٥٠﴾ كَمَآ أَرْسَلْنَا فِيكُمْ رَسُولًا مِّنكُمْ
يَتْلُوا۟ عَلَيْكُمْ ءَايَٰتِنَا وَيُزَكِّيكُمْ وَيُعَلِّمُكُمُ ٱلْكِتَٰبَ
وَٱلْحِكْمَةَ وَيُعَلِّمُكُم مَّا لَمْ تَكُونُوا۟ تَعْلَمُونَ ﴿١٥١﴾ فَٱذْكُرُونِىٓ أَذْكُرْكُمْ
وَٱشْكُرُوا۟ لِى وَلَا تَكْفُرُونِ ﴿١٥٢﴾

We have seen you looking up into heaven,
turning this way and that,
so We will turn you towards a direction
which will please you.
Turn your face, therefore, towards the Masjid al-Haram.
Wherever you all are, turn your faces towards it.

Those given the Book know it is the truth from their Lord.
Allah is not unaware of what they do.

If you were to bring every Sign to those given the Book,
they still would not follow your direction.
You do not follow their direction.
They do not follow each other's direction.
If you followed their whims and desires,
after the knowledge that has come to you,
you would then be one of the wrongdoers.

Those We have given the Book recognise it
as they recognise their own sons.
Yet a group of them knowingly conceal the truth.

The truth is from your Lord,
so on no account be among the doubters.

Each person faces a particular direction
so race each other to the good.
Wherever you are, Allah will bring you all together.
Truly Allah has power over all things.

Wherever you come from,
turn your face to the Masjid al-Haram.
This is certainly the truth from your Lord.
Allah is not unaware of what you do.

Wherever you come from,
turn your face to the Masjid al-Haram.
Wherever you are, turn your faces towards it
so that people will have no argument against you –
except for those among them who do wrong

and then you should not fear them but rather fear Me –
and so that I can complete My blessing to you
so that hopefully you will be guided.

For this We sent a Messenger to you from among you
to recite Our Signs to you and purify you
and teach you the Book and Wisdom
and teach you things you did not know before.

Remember Me – I will remember you.
Give thanks to Me and do not be ungrateful.

This tremendous passage takes us from the Divine Command to establish the new world religion, itself turned to the most ancient House of Allah, the Masjid al-Haram. It then reveals to us that those of earlier dispensations have fallen into conflict and ignorance. It then makes plain that the deciding element of the new religion is defined in the Book and the Example of the Messenger as a guide and model for mankind. This in turn promises, as Ruhani reward, Divine Knowledge – Ma'rifa. Allah says: "Remember Me – I will remember you."

What we discern from these revealed Qur'anic secrets is a dynamic interaction from Allah to His Messenger and from him, sallallahu 'alayhi wa sallam, to his Ummah. Surat Al 'Imran (3:31-32):

قُلْ إِن كُنتُمْ تُحِبُّونَ ٱللَّهَ فَٱتَّبِعُونِى
يُحْبِبْكُمُ ٱللَّهُ وَيَغْفِرْ لَكُمْ ذُنُوبَكُمْ ۗ وَٱللَّهُ غَفُورٌ رَّحِيمٌ ٣١ قُلْ أَطِيعُوا۟
ٱللَّهَ وَٱلرَّسُولَ ۖ فَإِن تَوَلَّوْا۟ فَإِنَّ ٱللَّهَ لَا يُحِبُّ ٱلْكَٰفِرِينَ ٣٢

Say, "If you love Allah, then follow me
and Allah will love you and forgive you
for your wrong actions.
Allah is Ever-Forgiving, Most Merciful."

Say, "Obey Allah and the Messenger."
Then if they turn away,
Allah does not love the kafirun.

There remains always the warning to the kafirun and the only rescue for them: Obey Allah and the Messenger.

To us, the Muslims, remains the Path of Islam.
We love Allah – so
We follow the Messenger – so
Allah loves us and forgives us.
This is the Deen, and this is its 'Amal.

Fatihah

VIII

JANUARY 12TH 2008

We have been examining the affair of 'Amal, and have recognised that it is the primal matter of the Deen. To understand it more deeply we began with the Surat Luqman since it contains the exalted counsel of Luqman to his son. Our first discovery was of such importance that we did not get to the actual advice itself, for what preceded it in this Surat was crucial teaching on Tawhid and Allah's Power.

Now that we are ready to examine the counsel, we must prepare ourselves for a further opening of knowledge. Just as Luqman's counsel is preceded by the warnings and good news from Allah, we will discover that the personal guidance given by Luqman is in turn followed up by grave pronouncements addressed by Allah, subhanahu wa ta'ala, to the human race itself – mankind.

This is going to force us to a very uncompromising position, one that gives linkage to these two counsels. We go to Surat Luqman (31:13-15):

وَإِذْ قَالَ لُقْمَٰنُ لِٱبْنِهِۦ وَهُوَ يَعِظُهُۥ
يَٰبُنَيَّ لَا تُشْرِكْ بِٱللَّهِ إِنَّ ٱلشِّرْكَ لَظُلْمٌ عَظِيمٌ ﴿١٣﴾
وَوَصَّيْنَا ٱلْإِنسَٰنَ بِوَٰلِدَيْهِ حَمَلَتْهُ
أُمُّهُۥ وَهْنًا عَلَىٰ وَهْنٍ وَفِصَٰلُهُۥ فِى عَامَيْنِ أَنِ ٱشْكُرْ لِى
وَلِوَٰلِدَيْكَ إِلَىَّ ٱلْمَصِيرُ ﴿١٤﴾ وَإِن جَٰهَدَاكَ عَلَىٰٓ أَن تُشْرِكَ بِى
مَا لَيْسَ لَكَ بِهِۦ عِلْمٌ فَلَا تُطِعْهُمَا وَصَاحِبْهُمَا فِى ٱلدُّنْيَا مَعْرُوفًا
وَٱتَّبِعْ سَبِيلَ مَنْ أَنَابَ إِلَىَّ ثُمَّ إِلَىَّ مَرْجِعُكُمْ
فَأُنَبِّئُكُم بِمَا كُنتُمْ تَعْمَلُونَ ﴿١٥﴾

When Luqman said to his son, counselling him,
"My son, do not associate anything with Allah.
Associating others with Him is a terrible wrong."

We have instructed man concerning his parents.
Bearing him caused his mother great debility
and the period of his weaning was two years:
"Give thanks to Me and to your parents.
I am your final destination.

But if they try to make you associate something with Me
about which you have no knowledge,
do not obey them.
Keep company with them
correctly and courteously in this world
but follow the Way of him who turns to Me.
Then you will return to Me and I will inform you
about the things you did."

There are two vital elements to be taken from these Ayats. The first is that Adab due to parents is linked in character to the activity of worship by the slave of Allah:

أَنِ ٱشْكُرْ لِى وَلِوَٰلِدَيْكَ

Give thanks to Me and to your parents.

The tenure of behaviour expected of the Mumin to his parents is characterised as 'correct' and 'courteous'.

The second element is the limit set on the contract of obedience and care:

وَٱتَّبِعْ سَبِيلَ مَنْ أَنَابَ إِلَىَّ

But follow the Way of him who turns to Me.

Now, to us, that directly refers to the Rasul, sallallahu 'alayhi wa sallam, as that is his perfect description. It can however be extended to the guidance from within the Muslim

Community that calls to right action and could find itself denied or opposed by parents.

The next Ayats continue the counsel. We turn to Surat Luqman (31:16-19):

يَٰبُنَيَّ إِنَّهَآ إِن تَكُ مِثْقَالَ حَبَّةٖ مِّنْ خَرْدَلٖ فَتَكُن
فِي صَخْرَةٍ أَوْ فِي ٱلسَّمَٰوَٰتِ أَوْ فِي ٱلْأَرْضِ يَأْتِ بِهَا ٱللَّهُۚ إِنَّ ٱللَّهَ
لَطِيفٌ خَبِيرٞ ﴿١٦﴾ يَٰبُنَيَّ أَقِمِ ٱلصَّلَوٰةَ وَأْمُرْ بِٱلْمَعْرُوفِ وَٱنْهَ عَنِ
ٱلْمُنكَرِ وَٱصْبِرْ عَلَىٰ مَآ أَصَابَكَۖ إِنَّ ذَٰلِكَ مِنْ عَزْمِ ٱلْأُمُورِ ﴿١٧﴾
وَلَا تُصَعِّرْ خَدَّكَ لِلنَّاسِ وَلَا تَمْشِ فِي ٱلْأَرْضِ مَرَحًاۖ إِنَّ
ٱللَّهَ لَا يُحِبُّ كُلَّ مُخْتَالٖ فَخُورٖ ﴿١٨﴾ وَٱقْصِدْ فِي مَشْيِكَ
وَٱغْضُضْ مِن صَوْتِكَۚ إِنَّ أَنكَرَ ٱلْأَصْوَٰتِ لَصَوْتُ ٱلْحَمِيرِ ﴿١٩﴾

“My son, even if something weighs as little
as a mustard-seed
and is inside a rock
or anywhere else in the heavens or earth,
Allah will bring it out.
Allah is All-Pervading, All-Aware.
My son, establish Salat
and command what is right and forbid what is wrong
and be steadfast in the face of all that happens to you.
That is certainly the most resolute course to follow.
Do not avert your face from people out of haughtiness
and do not strut about arrogantly on the earth.

Allah does not love anyone who is vain or boastful.
Be moderate in your tread and lower your voice.
The most hateful of voices is the donkey's bray."

The first of these Ayats reassures the Mumin that Allah governs the universe from within the universe, so that all creation is obedient and also active in fulfilling the destinies of men. The second Ayat is clear and radiant. The two subsequent Ayats confirm that the Muslims are expected to try to attain to that perfect behaviour which is shown to us by our beloved Messenger, sallallahu 'alayhi wa sallam.

It is following this noble counsel that Allah reveals the setting against which this good behaviour may expect to find itself enacted. Here we come to this other matter that I said would appear after the counsel to the son. Thus we go to Surat Luqman (31:33):

يَٰٓأَيُّهَا ٱلنَّاسُ ٱتَّقُوا۟ رَبَّكُمْ
وَٱخْشَوْا۟ يَوْمًا لَّا يَجْزِى وَالِدٌ عَن وَلَدِهِۦ وَلَا مَوْلُودٌ هُوَ
جَازٍ عَن وَالِدِهِۦ شَيْـًٔا ۚ إِنَّ وَعْدَ ٱللَّهِ حَقٌّ ۖ فَلَا تَغُرَّنَّكُمُ
ٱلْحَيَوٰةُ ٱلدُّنْيَا وَلَا يَغُرَّنَّكُم بِٱللَّهِ ٱلْغَرُورُ ﴿٣٣﴾

Mankind! Have Taqwa of your Lord and fear a day
when no father will be able to atone for his son,
or son for his father, in any way.
Allah's promise is true.
So do not let the life of the dunya delude you
and do not let the Deluder delude you concerning Allah.

So the Mumin is called to this highest behaviour, this noble action, against the world situation of disintegrating and degrading behaviour from mankind at large. Let us look at Surat Fatir (35:3–7):

يَٰٓأَيُّهَا ٱلنَّاسُ ٱذْكُرُوا۟ نِعْمَتَ ٱللَّهِ عَلَيْكُمْ ۚ هَلْ مِنْ خَٰلِقٍ غَيْرُ ٱللَّهِ
يَرْزُقُكُم مِّنَ ٱلسَّمَآءِ وَٱلْأَرْضِ ۚ لَآ إِلَٰهَ إِلَّا هُوَ ۖ فَأَنَّىٰ تُؤْفَكُونَ ﴿٣﴾
وَإِن يُكَذِّبُوكَ فَقَدْ كُذِّبَتْ رُسُلٌ مِّن قَبْلِكَ ۚ وَإِلَى ٱللَّهِ تُرْجَعُ
ٱلْأُمُورُ ﴿٤﴾ يَٰٓأَيُّهَا ٱلنَّاسُ إِنَّ وَعْدَ ٱللَّهِ حَقٌّ ۖ فَلَا تَغُرَّنَّكُمُ ٱلْحَيَوٰةُ
ٱلدُّنْيَا ۖ وَلَا يَغُرَّنَّكُم بِٱللَّهِ ٱلْغَرُورُ ﴿٥﴾ إِنَّ ٱلشَّيْطَٰنَ لَكُمْ عَدُوٌّ
فَٱتَّخِذُوهُ عَدُوًّا ۚ إِنَّمَا يَدْعُوا۟ حِزْبَهُۥ لِيَكُونُوا۟ مِنْ أَصْحَٰبِ ٱلسَّعِيرِ ﴿٦﴾
ٱلَّذِينَ كَفَرُوا۟ لَهُمْ عَذَابٌ شَدِيدٌ ۖ وَٱلَّذِينَ ءَامَنُوا۟ وَعَمِلُوا۟ ٱلصَّٰلِحَٰتِ
لَهُم مَّغْفِرَةٌ وَأَجْرٌ كَبِيرٌ ﴿٧﴾

Mankind! remember Allah's blessing to you.
Is there any creator other than Allah
providing for you from heaven and earth?
There is no god but Him.
So how have you been perverted?

If they deny you, Messengers before you were also denied.
All matters return to Allah.

Mankind! Allah's promise is true.
Do not let the life of the dunya delude you
and do not let the Deluder delude you about Allah.

Shaytan is your enemy
so treat him as an enemy.
He summons his party so they will be
among the people of the Searing Blaze.
Those who are kafir will suffer a harsh punishment.
But those who have Iman and do right actions
will receive forgiveness and an immense reward.

It is clear from this that in every age, the Muslims are set down on a ferocious conflict where mankind struggles to triumph in possessing power and wealth and dominion over others. It is in this way that the modern Muslim has to see that the Divine project offered in Islam sets itself against the project of mankind on the whole, who have turned their heads from this. So we now look again at Surat Fatir (35:15-21). It is very important you follow the meanings of this very carefully:

يَـٰٓأَيُّهَا ٱلنَّاسُ أَنتُمُ ٱلْفُقَرَآءُ إِلَى ٱللَّهِ
وَٱللَّهُ هُوَ ٱلْغَنِيُّ ٱلْحَمِيدُ ﴿١٥﴾ إِن يَشَأْ
يُذْهِبْكُمْ وَيَأْتِ بِخَلْقٍ جَدِيدٍ ﴿١٦﴾ وَمَا ذَٰلِكَ عَلَى ٱللَّهِ بِعَزِيزٍ ﴿١٧﴾
وَلَا تَزِرُ وَازِرَةٌ وِزْرَ أُخْرَىٰ ۚ وَإِن تَدْعُ مُثْقَلَةٌ إِلَىٰ حِمْلِهَا
لَا يُحْمَلْ مِنْهُ شَيْءٌ وَلَوْ كَانَ ذَا قُرْبَىٰٓ ۗ إِنَّمَا تُنذِرُ ٱلَّذِينَ
يَخْشَوْنَ رَبَّهُم بِٱلْغَيْبِ وَأَقَامُوا۟ ٱلصَّلَوٰةَ ۚ وَمَن تَزَكَّىٰ فَإِنَّمَا
يَتَزَكَّىٰ لِنَفْسِهِۦ ۚ وَإِلَى ٱللَّهِ ٱلْمَصِيرُ ﴿١٨﴾ وَمَا يَسْتَوِى ٱلْأَعْمَىٰ
وَٱلْبَصِيرُ ﴿١٩﴾ وَلَا ٱلظُّلُمَـٰتُ وَلَا ٱلنُّورُ ﴿٢٠﴾ وَلَا ٱلظِّلُّ وَلَا ٱلْحَرُورُ ﴿٢١﴾

Mankind! You are the poor in need of Allah
whereas Allah is the Rich Beyond Need, the Praiseworthy.
If He wills He can dispense with you
and bring about a new creation.
That is not difficult for Allah.

No burden-bearer can bear another's burden.
If someone weighed down
calls for help to bear his load,
none of it will be borne for him,
even by his next of kin.
You can only warn those
who fear their Lord in the Unseen
and establish Salat.
Whoever is purified, is purified for himself alone.
Allah is your final destination.

The blind and seeing are not the same
nor are darkness and light
nor are cool shade and fierce heat.

The situation that we are in is one that has been continuous and unchanging from the end of the Khalifate of Sultan 'Abdulhamid II of Istanbul, rahimahullah. From that point on the Muslims turned their backs on the Deen and accepted, with significant exceptions, this way of mankind which felt that it could, by its own strength, create a new society and make everybody rich and make everybody prosperous. We then entered into that hellish century called the Twentieth Century. From its very beginning, here in South Africa, the Boer War led to the First World War and on to the so-called Second World War – both of which were one continuous war. Only after all that, there was to emerge the macabre spectacle of one country slowly taking control of the whole of the world system, almost totally, and the Muslims, in all of that, have had a most shameful record.

This is because the Muslim became an individual and said, "I will accept everything they do, and I will just go on and will try to make some money out of it and store some under the bed for a rainy day, and I will send my son to their colleges to learn how he then can be one of them. And the best that can be is that my son turns out to be a successful version of the kuffar." That has been the situation of the Muslims throughout the whole world.

The 'Ulama, especially in the Subcontinent, when the kuffar took over the Mughal Empire, fled from Delhi, the capital of power and Amr on which Islam was based, and some went to Deoband and some went to Barelwi, and they said, "We have lost the Amr, so now you must follow us," and in that instant they became Shi'a. They said, "The rulers are unjust and cruel but we will give you the proper teaching, and we will wait, because when the Mahdi comes everything will be cleaned up at the end of the world." This is the situation that has befallen all of us.

In all of this, there remains one community that, in itself, has been corrupted so that one part of it withdrew simply to a kind of worship of the Awliya and 'Arifin of the past, and so there was a kind of dead Sufism. Because that was a polarity, it then caused another sect that was trying somehow to rescue the Muslims by purification of the Deen to say, "The enemy is this other extremity – the ones who worship the tombs." But BOTH of these had rejected the element on which Islam is based and founded which is the Amr, which is Command, without which, as we have seen earlier in this series of studies, it is impossible for there to be Salat, it is impossible for there to be Zakat, it is impossible for there to be Ramadan itself in its beginnings and ends, and it is impossible for there to be Hajj.

Thus, the responsibility of the Muslims is set against this warning to mankind of what they must take on, because we are Bani Adam. We have to take on the warning of Allah to the human race because the warning of Luqman to his son is not in itself enough. That is why Allah, subhanahu wa ta'ala, makes after it these devastating Ayats where He calls on mankind and warns mankind that the path they are on is not going to succeed and cannot succeed. Allah, subhanahu wa ta'ala, says in Surat az-Zukhruf (43:33-35):

وَلَوْلَآ أَن يَكُونَ ٱلنَّاسُ أُمَّةً وَٰحِدَةً
لَّجَعَلْنَا لِمَن يَكْفُرُ بِٱلرَّحْمَٰنِ
لِبُيُوتِهِمْ سُقُفًا مِّن فِضَّةٍ وَمَعَارِجَ عَلَيْهَا يَظْهَرُونَ ﴿٣٣﴾
وَلِبُيُوتِهِمْ أَبْوَٰبًا وَسُرُرًا عَلَيْهَا يَتَّكِـُٔونَ ﴿٣٤﴾
وَزُخْرُفًا ۚ وَإِن كُلُّ ذَٰلِكَ لَمَّا مَتَٰعُ ٱلْحَيَوٰةِ ٱلدُّنْيَا ۚ
وَٱلْءَاخِرَةُ عِندَ رَبِّكَ لِلْمُتَّقِينَ ﴿٣٥﴾

Were it not that mankind
might all become one community,

We would have given those who reject the All-Merciful
silver roofs to their houses
and silver stairways to ascend
and silver doors to their houses
and silver couches on which to recline,
and gold ornaments.
All that is merely the trappings of the life of the dunya.
But the Akhira with your Lord
is for those who have Taqwa.

So the awakening of the Muslims and the revival of the Deen of Islam will come when a generation of Muslims step forward and disassociate themselves from this madness on which the main body of mankind have embarked. That will manifest itself in their disconnection from the false wealth on which the whole system is based, for wealth belongs to Allah. Allah says in Surat Fatir very clearly (35:15):

يَٰٓأَيُّهَا ٱلنَّاسُ أَنتُمُ ٱلْفُقَرَآءُ إِلَى ٱللَّهِ ۖ وَٱللَّهُ هُوَ ٱلْغَنِىُّ ٱلْحَمِيدُ ﴿١٥﴾

Mankind! You are the poor in need of Allah
whereas Allah is the Rich Beyond Need, the Praiseworthy.

This is the terrible responsibility that has fallen on the Muslims of today. In that sense, it is not the kuffar who are to be blamed for the disaster that has fallen on a whole zone of the world, from Iraq to the gates of China, because right next to that terrible devastation is the macabre, extravagant, apparent wealth of the richness of the Arab world. Right next to this devastation and poverty and suffering and mass-murder are these Arabs who have taken on this pseudo-wealth and have built themselves these skyscrapers in the desert.

In all of this the whole body of Muslims have let this happen, have remained silent, and those who think that ANY form of violent murder of innocents – which the kuffar call 'Terrorism' – can accomplish anything, must realise that that is precisely the escape vent, the relief vent, which guarantees that nothing will happen, and nothing will be changed because the only thing that will change things is when the Muslims disconnect from the wealth they have acquired in this false-wealth system and realise that: "Mankind! You are the poor in need of Allah, whereas Allah is the Rich Beyond Need, the Praiseworthy." And that wealth belongs to Allah, and this is not real wealth that they have, it is a fantasy.

The horrible thing is that you find in Johannesburg, and you find also in London and France and North Africa, that the so-called wealthy Muslims still think they can put the money under the bed, and hand some to their sons who already are taking drugs and crashing their cars and dying. This is the reality in which we live. So the awakening of the Muslims is not to awaken to a petty violence called Terrorism but to confront the massive violence of the slaughter of innocent people in Iraq and the Subcontinent and north of it – this is the responsibility of the Muslims, and it is the responsibility of the people who have studied the Deen and who have learned the Qur'an and know what its meanings are. This is what has to be grasped. The message of the Qur'an is absolutely exact today as it was at the time it was revealed to Rasul, sallallahu 'alayhi wa sallam.

Therefore, the counsel of Luqman cannot in itself satisfy the demand that Allah makes, because Allah makes a demand on the human creature to fulfil the Divine Contract. Allah, subhanahu wa ta'ala, says in Surat al-Ahzab (33:72-73):

إِنَّا عَرَضْنَا ٱلْأَمَانَةَ عَلَى ٱلسَّمَٰوَٰتِ
وَٱلْأَرْضِ وَٱلْجِبَالِ فَأَبَيْنَ أَن يَحْمِلْنَهَا وَأَشْفَقْنَ مِنْهَا وَحَمَلَهَا
ٱلْإِنسَٰنُ إِنَّهُۥ كَانَ ظَلُومًا جَهُولًا ﴿٧٢﴾ لِّيُعَذِّبَ ٱللَّهُ ٱلْمُنَٰفِقِينَ
وَٱلْمُنَٰفِقَٰتِ وَٱلْمُشْرِكِينَ وَٱلْمُشْرِكَٰتِ وَيَتُوبَ ٱللَّهُ
عَلَى ٱلْمُؤْمِنِينَ وَٱلْمُؤْمِنَٰتِ وَكَانَ ٱللَّهُ غَفُورًا رَّحِيمًا ﴿٧٣﴾

We offered the Trust to the heavens,
the earth and the mountains
but they refused to take it on and shrank from it.
But man took it on.
He is indeed wrongdoing and ignorant.

This was so that Allah might punish
the men and women of the Munafiqun,
and the men and women of the Mushrikun,
and turn towards the men and women of the Muminun.
Allah is Ever-Forgiving, Most Merciful.

* * * * *

In these Ayats we have looked at in Surat Fatir, the final guidance to the Muminin is that they must continue on the Sabil of Allah, despite the world condition in which they find themselves. Allah gives strength and power from Him, for here He tells us that mankind are but a lesser part of a cosmic creation, and one that is entirely Allah's creation. So for this we turn to Surat Ghafir (40:57-58):

لَخَلْقُ ٱلسَّمَٰوَٰتِ وَٱلْأَرْضِ أَكْبَرُ
مِنْ خَلْقِ ٱلنَّاسِ وَلَٰكِنَّ أَكْثَرَ ٱلنَّاسِ لَا يَعْلَمُونَ ﴿٥٧﴾
وَمَا يَسْتَوِى ٱلْأَعْمَىٰ وَٱلْبَصِيرُ وَٱلَّذِينَ ءَامَنُوا۟ وَعَمِلُوا۟
ٱلصَّٰلِحَٰتِ وَلَا ٱلْمُسِىٓءُ قَلِيلًا مَّا يَتَذَكَّرُونَ ﴿٥٨﴾

The creation of the heavens and earth
is far greater than the creation of mankind.
But most of mankind do not know it.

The blind and the seeing are not the same.

Nor are those who have Iman and do right actions
the same as evildoers.
What little heed they pay!

The doctrine of the kuffar is what they call 'Humanism'. But the human, in worshipping the human, is below-human – they have become sub-human in order to worship the human as an ideal. But what Allah is telling us is that even to worship mankind is an idolatry because that is but a small part of the creation. The idea that the power could be invested in the humans in absurd when Allah is saying, "LOOK! The Power is with the Creator of all the universe of which the humans are one tiny, tiny part."

So we worship Allah Who has created them and the whole universe, whereas they are still worshipping this one little bit, and that is the idolatry, the kufr, of modern times. "The creation of the heavens and earth is far greater than the creation of mankind. But most of mankind do not know it." Again, Allah, subhanahu wa ta'ala, repeats this message that "The blind and the seeing are not the same."

لَخَلْقُ السَّمَٰوَٰتِ وَالْأَرْضِ أَكْبَرُ
مِنْ خَلْقِ النَّاسِ وَلَٰكِنَّ أَكْثَرَ النَّاسِ لَا يَعْلَمُونَ ﴿٥٧﴾
وَمَا يَسْتَوِي الْأَعْمَىٰ وَالْبَصِيرُ وَالَّذِينَ ءَامَنُوا وَعَمِلُوا
الصَّٰلِحَٰتِ وَلَا الْمُسِيٓءُ قَلِيلًا مَّا يَتَذَكَّرُونَ ﴿٥٨﴾

The creation of the heavens and earth
is far greater than the creation of mankind.
But most of mankind do not know it.

The blind and the seeing are not the same.

Nor are those who have Iman and do right actions
the same as evildoers.
What little heed they pay!

I go back to this image of the modern Muslim as a businessman. It is to me much more offensive than the most terrible aspect of the kufr of the kafirun, because they have embarked on a Shari'at that is not the Shari'at of Islam and they are content with it. Not only are they content with it but they even think that from it they can dispense help and support to the Muslims and to the cause of Islam.

You have to understand that to participate in the procedures of what is called the Capitalist System of finance in any way, is absolutely to prevent the emergence of a worshipping community among the human beings. It is to prevent it! They ask, "Do you want me to be poor then?" I have met in my life-time individual Muslims who have given up being business-men, and they are the ones who have had success. The ones who have held on to it have had calamity upon calamity. I saw an excellent man who bought a skyscraper in the Lebanon saying, "I am a good Muslim and I'm giving this to my mother because this will be a Waqf for her and give her income for the rest of her life." I said to him, "Sell it immediately! Get rid of it because it will be destroyed!" He said, "No, no, no, you don't understand. I have to fulfil my task as a Muslim."

Within the year the thing had been burned out of existence. It was destroyed. You cannot build a life on the financial transactions of something that already has been condemned by Allah, subhanahu wa ta'ala. But some strange psychosis has entered into modern men, and into modern Muslims, whereby they think that they can do this. It cannot continue. If you turn on the television and look in the news-papers – it is crashing. This bank is collapsing, that bank is going to the wall. The matter is at its end-game anyway. How many sons have crashed their Mercedes? How many sons have taken drugs and been destroyed?

But this still continues, and nowhere is it more prevalent than in South Africa. Alongside the well-being of a wealthy

Muslim community, they have not lifted one finger to do Da'wa to the people of the country. You have to understand the extremity with which this takes place. And yet the moment the kuffar are drowned in a tsunami, they pour their money out to help those people – and all the money they gave went to those who ran the brothels along the coast of Thailand, for they were the important victims of the tsunami.

This is the world we live in. But this cannot be the world that YOU live in. It is your generation. It is your responsibility. If you want purification, then the purification has to begin where there is one enormous gap in the Deen of Islam, which is Zakat, and it cannot be restored until there is Amr to order the collecting of the Zakat, and until the money is real money of gold and silver. This is our responsibility, but this cannot be done if you send your sons to university to learn Business Management – to be good kuffar. Better that you leave the whole thing and you become happy drunks until you fall down, choked in your own vomit. At least that is consistent. This is the dilemma facing the Muslims of today.

That is why the whole project of Terrorism is so infuriating and upsetting. Not because of the innocent people who are killed by it, but because in fact it prolongs the process of kufr. It is the licence for the whole thing to continue, because if that is the message of Islam then they say: "Business as usual." But the message of the Muslims is: "Put down the paper money, and the whole affair collapses." This will take a kind of intoxication that will not come by the people of ratiocination, because the 'reasonable' people have revealed themselves as hypocrites. They may be reasonable, but they are reasonable hypocrites.

Surat an-Nisa (4:59):

أَطِيعُواْ اللَّهَ وَأَطِيعُواْ الرَّسُولَ

Obey Allah and obey the Messenger.

If you take that seriously, you will open a path to Islam and you will see it happen in your life-time. Allah gives the news of that certainty on which all true 'Amal is based. We go to Surat Ghafir (40:64-65):

اللَّهُ الَّذِى جَعَلَ لَكُمُ الْأَرْضَ قَرَارًا وَالسَّمَآءَ بِنَآءً
وَصَوَّرَكُمْ فَأَحْسَنَ صُوَرَكُمْ وَرَزَقَكُم مِّنَ الطَّيِّبَٰتِ
ذَٰلِكُمُ اللَّهُ رَبُّكُمْ فَتَبَارَكَ اللَّهُ رَبُّ الْعَٰلَمِينَ ﴿٦٤﴾
هُوَ الْحَىُّ لَآ إِلَٰهَ إِلَّا هُوَ فَادْعُوهُ مُخْلِصِينَ لَهُ الدِّينَ
الْحَمْدُ لِلَّهِ رَبِّ الْعَٰلَمِينَ ﴿٦٥﴾

It is Allah who made the earth a stable home for you
and the sky a dome,
and formed you, giving you the best of forms,
and provided you with good and wholesome things.
That is Allah, your Lord.
Blessed be Allah, the Lord of all the worlds.

He is the Living –

there is no god but Him –
so call on Him, making your deen sincerely His.
Praise be to Allah, the Lord of all the worlds.

Let us look at that again:

ٱللَّهُ ٱلَّذِى جَعَلَ لَكُمُ ٱلْأَرْضَ قَرَارًا وَٱلسَّمَآءَ بِنَآءً
وَصَوَّرَكُمْ فَأَحْسَنَ صُوَرَكُمْ وَرَزَقَكُم مِّنَ ٱلطَّيِّبَٰتِ
ذَٰلِكُمُ ٱللَّهُ رَبُّكُمْ فَتَبَارَكَ ٱللَّهُ رَبُّ ٱلْعَٰلَمِينَ ﴿٦٤﴾
هُوَ ٱلْحَىُّ لَآ إِلَٰهَ إِلَّا هُوَ فَٱدْعُوهُ مُخْلِصِينَ لَهُ ٱلدِّينَ
ٱلْحَمْدُ لِلَّهِ رَبِّ ٱلْعَٰلَمِينَ ﴿٦٥﴾

It is Allah who made the earth a stable home for you
and the sky a dome,
and formed you, giving you the best of forms,
and provided you with good and wholesome things.
That is Allah, your Lord.
Blessed be Allah, the Lord of all the worlds.

He is the Living –
there is no god but Him –
so call on Him, making your deen sincerely His.
Praise be to Allah, the Lord of all the worlds.

Al-Hamdulillahi Rabbil-'alamin.

Fatihah.

THE BOOK

OF

SAFAR

Six Discourses
given between
July 5th 2008
and October 17th 2008
at the Jumu'a Mosque of Cape Town

I

JULY 5TH 2008

Allah the Exalted says in Surat al-Qadr (97:1-5):

بِسْمِ ٱللَّهِ ٱلرَّحْمَٰنِ ٱلرَّحِيمِ

إِنَّآ أَنزَلْنَٰهُ فِى لَيْلَةِ ٱلْقَدْرِ ١ وَمَآ أَدْرَىٰكَ مَا لَيْلَةُ ٱلْقَدْرِ ٢

لَيْلَةُ ٱلْقَدْرِ خَيْرٌ مِّنْ أَلْفِ شَهْرٍ ٣ تَنَزَّلُ ٱلْمَلَٰٓئِكَةُ وَٱلرُّوحُ

فِيهَا بِإِذْنِ رَبِّهِم مِّن كُلِّ أَمْرٍ ٤ سَلَٰمٌ هِىَ حَتَّىٰ مَطْلَعِ ٱلْفَجْرِ ٥

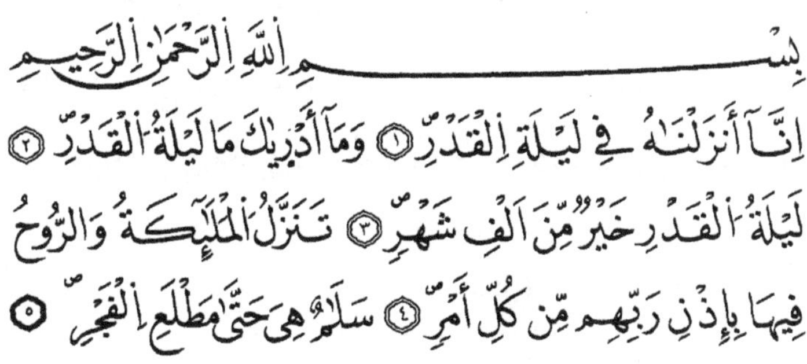

In the name of Allah, All-Merciful, Most Merciful

Truly We sent it down on the Night of Power.
And what will convey to you what the Night of Power is?

The Night of Power is better than a thousand months.
In it the angels and the Ruh descend
by their Lord's authority
with every ordinance.

It is Peace –
until the coming of the dawn.

The Night of Power, in it the Angels and the Ruh descend by their Lord's authority. So we find that the Qur'an itself is hurtling from beyond the beyond-time-and-space from the 'Arsh, down into the heart of the Rasul, sallallahu 'alayhi wa sallam – awaiting the Divine impulse that Sayyiduna Jibril would open to Rasul, sallallahu 'alayhi wa sallam, at the significant moment of event that merited the opening of these lights into the world of time and space. We now turn to Surat al-Quraysh (106):

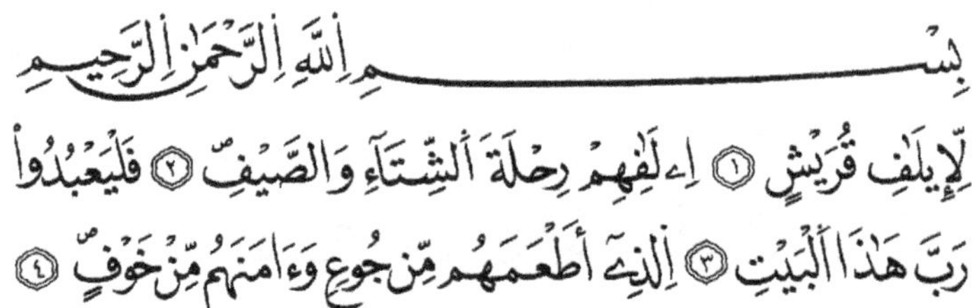

In the name of Allah, All-Merciful, Most Merciful
In acknowledgment of
the established tradition of Quraysh,
their tradition of the winter and summer caravans:
so let them worship the Lord of this House
who has preserved them from hunger
and secured them from fear.

We find in this Surat that Allah honours the Quraysh for their caravans of the summer and the winter. Allah indicates by this that the winter and the summer caravan have to be linked to the worship of the Lord of the House. Then this has to be connected to a knowledge that Allah has preserved them from hunger and secured them from fear. Therefore, by the process of the caravan, they have knowledge of Allah's power and compassion towards them. The significance and importance of the journey is that it is the means by which the people get to know of this tremendous mercy and compassion of Allah, subhanahu wa ta'ala.

Now we go to Surat at-Tariq (86:11-14):

By Heaven with its cyclical systems
and the earth with its splitting seeds,
it is truly a Decisive Word.
It is no joke.

Allah, subhanahu wa ta'ala, tells us that the heavens are designed on a movement, on a journey, that is circular – the heavens are moving in this circular motion as the foundational reality of existence. "And the earth with its splitting seeds." So you go from the stars and the cosmos to the seeds which are also moving, they are moving and breaking open to give life to the earth. The whole cosmic system is journeying, is on Safar. And Allah, subhanahu wa ta'ala, says that this is no joke. It is not something poetic and pretty, but the foundational reality on which He has set up His creation. Now we go to Surat at-Takwir (81:1-21):

بِسۡمِ ٱللَّهِ ٱلرَّحۡمَٰنِ ٱلرَّحِيمِ
إِذَا ٱلشَّمۡسُ كُوِّرَتۡ ﴿١﴾ وَإِذَا ٱلنُّجُومُ ٱنكَدَرَتۡ ﴿٢﴾ وَإِذَا ٱلۡجِبَالُ
سُيِّرَتۡ ﴿٣﴾ وَإِذَا ٱلۡعِشَارُ عُطِّلَتۡ ﴿٤﴾ وَإِذَا ٱلۡوُحُوشُ حُشِرَتۡ ﴿٥﴾
وَإِذَا ٱلۡبِحَارُ سُجِّرَتۡ ﴿٦﴾ وَإِذَا ٱلنُّفُوسُ زُوِّجَتۡ ﴿٧﴾ وَإِذَا ٱلۡمَوۡءُۥدَةُ
سُئِلَتۡ ﴿٨﴾ بِأَيِّ ذَنۢبٖ قُتِلَتۡ ﴿٩﴾ وَإِذَا ٱلصُّحُفُ نُشِرَتۡ ﴿١٠﴾ وَإِذَا ٱلسَّمَآءُ
كُشِطَتۡ ﴿١١﴾ وَإِذَا ٱلۡجَحِيمُ سُعِّرَتۡ ﴿١٢﴾ وَإِذَا ٱلۡجَنَّةُ أُزۡلِفَتۡ ﴿١٣﴾ عَلِمَتۡ
نَفۡسٞ مَّآ أَحۡضَرَتۡ ﴿١٤﴾ فَلَآ أُقۡسِمُ بِٱلۡخُنَّسِ ﴿١٥﴾ ٱلۡجَوَارِ ٱلۡكُنَّسِ ﴿١٦﴾
وَٱلَّيۡلِ إِذَا عَسۡعَسَ ﴿١٧﴾ وَٱلصُّبۡحِ إِذَا تَنَفَّسَ ﴿١٨﴾ إِنَّهُۥ لَقَوۡلُ رَسُولٖ
كَرِيمٖ ﴿١٩﴾ ذِي قُوَّةٍ عِندَ ذِي ٱلۡعَرۡشِ مَكِينٖ ﴿٢٠﴾ مُّطَاعٖ ثَمَّ أَمِينٖ ﴿٢١﴾

In the name of Allah, All-Merciful, Most Merciful
When the sun is compacted in blackness,
when the stars fall in rapid succession,
when the mountains are set in motion,
when the camels in foal are neglected,
when the wild beasts are all herded together,
when the oceans surge into each other,
when the selves are arranged into classes,
when the baby girl buried alive is asked
for what crime she was killed,
when the Pages are opened up,

when the Heaven is peeled away,
when the Fire is set ablaze,
when the Garden is brought up close:
then each self will know what it has done.

No! I swear by the planets with their retrograde motion,
swiftly moving, self-concealing,
and by the night when it draws in,
and by the dawn when it exhales,
truly it is the speech of a noble Messenger,
possessing great strength,
securely placed with the Lord of the Throne,
obeyed there, trustworthy.

You see the situation where Allah is revealing that everything in creation is in this dynamic activity of moving. Every-thing is moving. Everything is in action – every single aspect of life, as we saw in these Ayats. This is the actual condition in which the human finds himself. We shall see that it also involves the human creature. So let us look now at Surat al-Baqara (2:35-39):

وَقُلْنَا يَٰٓـَٔادَمُ اُ۟سْكُنَ اَنتَ
وَزَوْجُكَ اَ۬لْجَنَّةَ وَكُلَا مِنْهَا رَغَدًا حَيْثُ شِئْتُمَا وَلَا تَقْرَبَا
هَٰذِهِ اِ۬لشَّجَرَةَ فَتَكُونَا مِنَ اَ۬لظَّٰلِمِينَ ٣٥ فَأَزَلَّهُمَا اَ۬لشَّيْطَٰنُ
عَنْهَا فَأَخْرَجَهُمَا مِمَّا كَانَا فِيهِ وَقُلْنَا اَ۪هْبِطُواْ بَعْضُكُمْ لِبَعْضٍ
عَدُوٌّ وَلَكُمْ فِے اِ۬لْأَرْضِ مُسْتَقَرٌّ وَمَتَٰعٌ اِلَىٰ حِينٍ ٣٦ فَتَلَقَّىٰ
ءَادَمُ مِن رَّبِّهِۦ كَلِمَٰتٍ فَتَابَ عَلَيْهِ إِنَّهُۥ هُوَ اَ۬لتَّوَّابُ اُ۬لرَّحِيمُ ٣٧

قُلْنَا اهْبِطُوا مِنْهَا جَمِيعًا فَإِمَّا يَأْتِيَنَّكُم مِّنِّي هُدًى فَمَن تَبِعَ هُدَايَ
فَلَا خَوْفٌ عَلَيْهِمْ وَلَا هُمْ يَحْزَنُونَ ﴿٣٨﴾ وَالَّذِينَ كَفَرُوا وَكَذَّبُوا
بِآيَاتِنَا أُولَٰئِكَ أَصْحَابُ النَّارِ هُمْ فِيهَا خَالِدُونَ ﴿٣٩﴾

We said, "Adam, live in the Garden, you and your wife,
and eat freely from it wherever you will.
But do not approach this tree and so become wrongdoers."

But Shaytan made them slip up by means of it,
expelling them from where they were.
We said, "Go down from here as enemies to each other!
You will have residence on the earth
and enjoyment for a time."

Then Adam received some words from his Lord
and He turned towards him.
He is the Ever-Returning, the Most Merciful.

We said, "Go down from it, every one of you!
Then when guidance comes to you from Me,
those who follow My guidance
will feel no fear and will know no sorrow."

But those who are kafir and deny Our Signs
are the Companions of the Fire,
remaining in it timelessly, for ever.

Here we find three elements. Allah sends the family of Adam out from the Garden, they are expelled, and sent on this journey to the earth. That is the first aspect of it. Then, "Adam received some words from his Lord," in other words, it is because of this event that you have the creation, the arrival on the planet Earth, of the reality of Nabawiyya. So Adam, 'alayhi salam, is invested with a message from his Lord for mankind. So the beginning of this relationship Allah has towards the human creature, subhanahu wa ta'ala, if we can use such a word as relationship, is Nabawiyya, which is the link or the opening by which Allah opens this knowledge to the sons of Adam. Allah, subhanahu wa ta'ala, says: "Those who follow My guidance will feel no fear and will know no sorrow. But those who are kafir and deny Our Signs are the Companions of the Fire." In other words, without that journey, Nabawiyya would not take place and would not even be necessary. So the beginning of the reality of knowledge for human beings comes from this journey. If they had not taken this journey they would not have been open to this knowledge in the wisdom of Allah, subhanahu wa ta'ala.

Now we go to Surat al-Muminun (23:23-29):

وَلَقَدْ أَرْسَلْنَا نُوحًا إِلَىٰ قَوْمِهِۦ فَقَالَ يَٰقَوْمِ ٱعْبُدُوا۟
ٱللَّهَ مَا لَكُم مِّنْ إِلَٰهٍ غَيْرُهُۥٓ أَفَلَا تَتَّقُونَ ﴿٢٣﴾ فَقَالَ ٱلْمَلَؤُا۟ ٱلَّذِينَ
كَفَرُوا۟ مِن قَوْمِهِۦ مَا هَٰذَآ إِلَّا بَشَرٌ مِّثْلُكُمْ يُرِيدُ أَن يَتَفَضَّلَ
عَلَيْكُمْ وَلَوْ شَآءَ ٱللَّهُ لَأَنزَلَ مَلَٰٓئِكَةً مَّا سَمِعْنَا بِهَٰذَا فِىٓ
ءَابَآئِنَا ٱلْأَوَّلِينَ ﴿٢٤﴾ إِنْ هُوَ إِلَّا رَجُلٌۢ بِهِۦ جِنَّةٌ فَتَرَبَّصُوا۟ بِهِۦ
حَتَّىٰ حِينٍ ﴿٢٥﴾ قَالَ رَبِّ ٱنصُرْنِى بِمَا كَذَّبُونِ ﴿٢٦﴾ فَأَوْحَيْنَآ إِلَيْهِ

أَنِ ٱصْنَعِ ٱلْفُلْكَ بِأَعْيُنِنَا وَوَحْيِنَا فَإِذَا جَآءَ أَمْرُنَا وَفَارَ ٱلتَّنُّورُ
فَٱسْلُكْ فِيهَا مِن كُلٍّ زَوْجَيْنِ ٱثْنَيْنِ وَأَهْلَكَ إِلَّا مَن سَبَقَ عَلَيْهِ
ٱلْقَوْلُ مِنْهُمْ وَلَا تُخَٰطِبْنِى فِى ٱلَّذِينَ ظَلَمُوٓا۟ إِنَّهُم مُّغْرَقُونَ ﴿٢٧﴾
فَإِذَا ٱسْتَوَيْتَ أَنتَ وَمَن مَّعَكَ عَلَى ٱلْفُلْكِ فَقُلِ ٱلْحَمْدُ لِلَّهِ
ٱلَّذِى نَجَّىٰنَا مِنَ ٱلْقَوْمِ ٱلظَّٰلِمِينَ ﴿٢٨﴾ وَقُل رَّبِّ أَنزِلْنِى مُنزَلًا مُّبَارَكًا
وَأَنتَ خَيْرُ ٱلْمُنزِلِينَ ﴿٢٩﴾

We sent Nuh to his people and he said,
"My people, worship Allah.
You have no god other than Him.
So will you not have Taqwa?"
The ruling circle of those of his people
who were kafir said,
"This is nothing but a human being like yourselves
who simply wants to gain ascendancy over you.
If Allah had wanted He would have sent Angels down.
We never heard of anything like this
among our ancestors, the earlier peoples.
He is nothing but a man possessed
so wait a while and see what happens to him."
He said, "My Lord, help me
because of their calling me a liar!"

We revealed to him: "Build the Ship
under Our supervision and as We reveal.
When Our command comes
and water bubbles up from the earth,

load into it a pair of every species,
and your family – except for those among them
against whom the word has already gone ahead.
And do not address Me concerning those who do wrong.
They shall be drowned.
When you and those with you
are settled in the Ship,
then say: 'Praise be to Allah who has rescued us
from the people of the wrongdoers!'
And say: 'My Lord, land me in a blessed landing-place.
You are the best Bringer to Land.'"

Here we have the famous narration of Sayyiduna Nuh, 'alayhi salam. What is interesting to grasp is this same situation in which Allah sends the family of Nuh on a journey which was, as it were, against all the odds. It is a terrifying journey – sending them out on the flood waters and guaranteeing him against all the people whom he has been negated by and has had to fight against. Then he is ordered to make this Du'a: "My Lord, land me in a blessed landing place. You are the best Bringer to Land."

Let us all recite it:

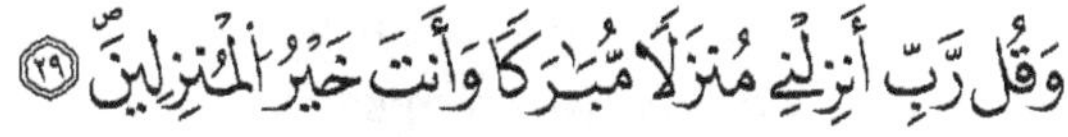

"My Lord, land me in a blessed landing place.
You are the best Bringer to Land."

Now let us look at Surat al-Anbiya' (21:71-75):

وَنَجَّيْنَٰهُ وَلُوطًا إِلَى ٱلْأَرْضِ
ٱلَّتِى بَٰرَكْنَا فِيهَا لِلْعَٰلَمِينَ ﴿٧١﴾ وَوَهَبْنَا لَهُۥٓ
إِسْحَٰقَ وَيَعْقُوبَ نَافِلَةً وَكُلًّا جَعَلْنَا صَٰلِحِينَ ﴿٧٢﴾
وَجَعَلْنَٰهُمْ أَئِمَّةً يَهْدُونَ بِأَمْرِنَا وَأَوْحَيْنَآ إِلَيْهِمْ فِعْلَ
ٱلْخَيْرَٰتِ وَإِقَامَ ٱلصَّلَوٰةِ وَإِيتَآءَ ٱلزَّكَوٰةِ وَكَانُوا۟ لَنَا
عَٰبِدِينَ ﴿٧٣﴾ وَلُوطًا ءَاتَيْنَٰهُ حُكْمًا وَعِلْمًا وَنَجَّيْنَٰهُ مِنَ
ٱلْقَرْيَةِ ٱلَّتِى كَانَت تَّعْمَلُ ٱلْخَبَٰٓئِثَ إِنَّهُمْ كَانُوا۟ قَوْمَ سَوْءٍ
فَٰسِقِينَ ﴿٧٤﴾ وَأَدْخَلْنَٰهُ فِى رَحْمَتِنَآ إِنَّهُۥ مِنَ ٱلصَّٰلِحِينَ ﴿٧٥﴾

We delivered both him and Lut
to the land which We had blessed for all beings.
And in addition to that We gave him Ishaq and Ya'qub
and made both of them Salihun.
We made them leaders, guiding by Our command,
and revealed to them how to do good actions
and establish Salat and pay Zakat,
and they worshipped Us.
We gave right judgement and knowledge to Lut
and rescued him from the city
which committed disgusting acts.
They were evil people who were deviators.
We admitted him into Our mercy.
He was one of the Salihun.

When Allah, subhanahu wa ta'ala, says, "We delivered both him and Lut," He is referring to Sayyiduna Ibrahim and Sayyiduna Lut, 'alayhum salam. So of these great Prophets, Allah says:

وَنَجَّيْنَٰهُ وَلُوطًا إِلَى ٱلْأَرْضِ
ٱلَّتِى بَٰرَكْنَا فِيهَا لِلْعَٰلَمِينَ ﴿٧١﴾

We delivered both him and Lut
to the land which We had blessed for all beings.

So the journey is what precedes Allah's introducing them to a land which is blessed. In other words, this is exactly the same as the Ayats we have just seen previously – Allah's bringing people to a blessed place because they have made this journey, fisabilillah, against all the odds of safety. Now we go to Surat Yusuf (12:109):

وَمَآ أَرْسَلْنَا مِن قَبْلِكَ إِلَّا رِجَالًا
يُوحَىٰٓ إِلَيْهِم مِّنْ أَهْلِ ٱلْقُرَىٰٓ ۗ أَفَلَمْ يَسِيرُوا۟ فِى ٱلْأَرْضِ
فَيَنظُرُوا۟ كَيْفَ كَانَ عَٰقِبَةُ ٱلَّذِينَ مِن قَبْلِهِمْ ۗ وَلَدَارُ
ٱلْءَاخِرَةِ خَيْرٌ لِّلَّذِينَ ٱتَّقَوْا۟ ۗ أَفَلَا تَعْقِلُونَ ﴿١٠٩﴾

The significance of what we are about to look it, is that it is the end of the long narration in a unique Surat in Qur'an which simply tells the story of Sayyiduna Yusuf, 'alayhi salam. It is a series of journeys over years, bringing great suffering to the father of Yusuf, and great trouble, distress and conflict to his brothers, and a long, long travail for Yusuf which, again, ends with this tremendous apotheosis of Rahma and the reunification of Yusuf with his father in the wonderful phrase in Qur'an where his father says: "I can smell Yusuf's scent!" It is beautiful. With the culmination of this life-long journey, in this Ayat, Allah explains the pattern of existence:

We sent none before you but men inspired with revelation
from among the people of the cities.
Have they not travelled in the land
and seen the final fate of those before them?
The abode of the Akhira is better
for those who have Taqwa.
So will you not use your intellect?

Allah says: "Will you not use your intellect?" So the function of the intellect is to recognise that the journey is to Allah. The destiny is to Allah. In the Qur'an, Allah openly gives away secrets of existence. It only requires you to look into it with reflection and the things open up for you. "We sent none before you but men inspired with revelation from among the people of the cities. Have they not travelled in the land and seen the final fate of those before them?" So the function of travelling in the land is to see the fate of the ones who were before you. You cannot fail to see, wherever you go, what happened to people. And what happened to people was that in turning from Allah and disobeying Allah, disaster crashed down on them. But there are those people who, with this knowledge, are lifted out, they are rescued from the flood. They are rescued from the Fire. And He says:

وَلَدَارُ ٱلْآخِرَةِ خَيْرٌ لِّلَّذِينَ ٱتَّقَوْا۟ ۗ أَفَلَا تَعْقِلُونَ ﴿١٠٩﴾

The abode of the Akhira is better
for those who have Taqwa.
So will you not use your intellect?

Now we come to Sayyiduna Musa, 'alayhi salam, in Surat al-Qasas. Again, this story is actually called 'The Story'. The story of Yusuf is a story and this is the other story. We go to Ayats 5-20:

وَنُرِيدُ أَن نَّمُنَّ عَلَى ٱلَّذِينَ
ٱسْتُضْعِفُوا۟ فِى ٱلْأَرْضِ وَنَجْعَلَهُمْ أَئِمَّةً وَنَجْعَلَهُمُ ٱلْوَٰرِثِينَ ﴿٥﴾
وَنُمَكِّنَ لَهُمْ فِى ٱلْأَرْضِ وَنُرِىَ فِرْعَوْنَ وَهَٰمَٰنَ وَجُنُودَهُمَا
مِنْهُم مَّا كَانُوا۟ يَحْذَرُونَ ﴿٦﴾

We desired to show kindness to those
who were oppressed in the land
and to make them leaders
and make them inheritors
and establish them firmly in the land,
and to show Pharaoh and Haman and their troops
the very thing that they were fearing from them.

Look at what Allah is telling us. Allah, subhanahu wa ta'ala, has decreed that something should happen, and this is HOW He makes it happen. It is something that is not there, but the outcome will be this.

وَنُرِيدُ أَن نَّمُنَّ عَلَى ٱلَّذِينَ
ٱسۡتُضۡعِفُواْ فِي ٱلۡأَرۡضِ وَنَجۡعَلَهُمۡ أَئِمَّةٗ وَنَجۡعَلَهُمُ ٱلۡوَٰرِثِينَ ٥
وَنُمَكِّنَ لَهُمۡ فِي ٱلۡأَرۡضِ وَنُرِيَ فِرۡعَوۡنَ وَهَٰمَٰنَ وَجُنُودَهُمَا
مِنۡهُم مَّا كَانُواْ يَحۡذَرُونَ ٦ وَأَوۡحَيۡنَآ إِلَىٰٓ أُمِّ مُوسَىٰٓ أَنۡ أَرۡضِعِيهِۖ
فَإِذَا خِفۡتِ عَلَيۡهِ فَأَلۡقِيهِ فِي ٱلۡيَمِّ وَلَا تَخَافِي وَلَا تَحۡزَنِيٓۖ
إِنَّا رَآدُّوهُ إِلَيۡكِ وَجَاعِلُوهُ مِنَ ٱلۡمُرۡسَلِينَ ٧ فَٱلۡتَقَطَهُۥٓ
ءَالُ فِرۡعَوۡنَ لِيَكُونَ لَهُمۡ عَدُوّٗا وَحَزَنًاۗ إِنَّ فِرۡعَوۡنَ
وَهَٰمَٰنَ وَجُنُودَهُمَا كَانُواْ خَٰطِـِٔينَ ٨ وَقَالَتِ ٱمۡرَأَتُ
فِرۡعَوۡنَ قُرَّتُ عَيۡنٖ لِّي وَلَكَۖ لَا تَقۡتُلُوهُ عَسَىٰٓ أَن يَنفَعَنَآ
أَوۡ نَتَّخِذَهُۥ وَلَدٗا وَهُمۡ لَا يَشۡعُرُونَ ٩ وَأَصۡبَحَ فُؤَادُ
أُمِّ مُوسَىٰ فَٰرِغًاۖ إِن كَادَتۡ لَتُبۡدِي بِهِۦ لَوۡلَآ أَن
رَّبَطۡنَا عَلَىٰ قَلۡبِهَا لِتَكُونَ مِنَ ٱلۡمُؤۡمِنِينَ ١٠ وَقَالَتۡ
لِأُخۡتِهِۦ قُصِّيهِۖ فَبَصُرَتۡ بِهِۦ عَن جُنُبٖ وَهُمۡ لَا يَشۡعُرُونَ ١١
وَحَرَّمۡنَا عَلَيۡهِ ٱلۡمَرَاضِعَ مِن قَبۡلُ فَقَالَتۡ هَلۡ أَدُلُّكُمۡ
عَلَىٰٓ أَهۡلِ بَيۡتٖ يَكۡفُلُونَهُۥ لَكُمۡ وَهُمۡ لَهُۥ نَٰصِحُونَ ١٢
فَرَدَدۡنَٰهُ إِلَىٰٓ أُمِّهِۦ كَيۡ تَقَرَّ عَيۡنُهَا وَلَا تَحۡزَنَ وَلِتَعۡلَمَ
أَنَّ وَعۡدَ ٱللَّهِ حَقّٞ وَلَٰكِنَّ أَكۡثَرَهُمۡ لَا يَعۡلَمُونَ ١٣

I

وَلَمَّا بَلَغَ أَشُدَّهُۥ وَاسْتَوَىٰٓ ءَاتَيْنَٰهُ حُكْمًا وَعِلْمًا ۚ وَكَذَٰلِكَ
نَجْزِى الْمُحْسِنِينَ ﴿١٤﴾ وَدَخَلَ الْمَدِينَةَ عَلَىٰ حِينِ غَفْلَةٍ مِّنْ
أَهْلِهَا فَوَجَدَ فِيهَا رَجُلَيْنِ يَقْتَتِلَانِ هَٰذَا مِن شِيعَتِهِۦ وَهَٰذَا مِنْ
عَدُوِّهِۦ ۖ فَاسْتَغَٰثَهُ الَّذِى مِن شِيعَتِهِۦ عَلَى الَّذِى مِنْ عَدُوِّهِۦ فَوَكَزَهُۥ
مُوسَىٰ فَقَضَىٰ عَلَيْهِ ۖ قَالَ هَٰذَا مِنْ عَمَلِ الشَّيْطَٰنِ ۖ إِنَّهُۥ عَدُوٌّ مُّضِلٌّ
مُّبِينٌ ﴿١٥﴾ قَالَ رَبِّ إِنِّى ظَلَمْتُ نَفْسِى فَاغْفِرْ لِى فَغَفَرَ لَهُۥٓ ۚ إِنَّهُۥ هُوَ
الْغَفُورُ الرَّحِيمُ ﴿١٦﴾ قَالَ رَبِّ بِمَآ أَنْعَمْتَ عَلَىَّ فَلَنْ أَكُونَ ظَهِيرًا
لِّلْمُجْرِمِينَ ﴿١٧﴾ فَأَصْبَحَ فِى الْمَدِينَةِ خَآئِفًا يَتَرَقَّبُ فَإِذَا الَّذِى
اسْتَنصَرَهُۥ بِالْأَمْسِ يَسْتَصْرِخُهُۥ ۚ قَالَ لَهُۥ مُوسَىٰٓ إِنَّكَ لَغَوِىٌّ
مُّبِينٌ ﴿١٨﴾ فَلَمَّآ أَنْ أَرَادَ أَن يَبْطِشَ بِالَّذِى هُوَ عَدُوٌّ لَّهُمَا قَالَ يَٰمُوسَىٰٓ
أَتُرِيدُ أَن تَقْتُلَنِى كَمَا قَتَلْتَ نَفْسًۢا بِالْأَمْسِ ۖ إِن تُرِيدُ إِلَّآ أَن
تَكُونَ جَبَّارًا فِى الْأَرْضِ وَمَا تُرِيدُ أَن تَكُونَ مِنَ الْمُصْلِحِينَ ﴿١٩﴾
وَجَآءَ رَجُلٌ مِّنْ أَقْصَا الْمَدِينَةِ يَسْعَىٰ قَالَ يَٰمُوسَىٰٓ إِنَّ الْمَلَأَ
يَأْتَمِرُونَ بِكَ لِيَقْتُلُوكَ فَاخْرُجْ إِنِّى لَكَ مِنَ النَّٰصِحِينَ ﴿٢٠﴾

We desired to show kindness to those
who were oppressed in the land
and to make them leaders
and make them inheritors

and establish them firmly in the land,
and to show Pharaoh and Haman and their troops
the very thing that they were fearing from them.

We revealed to Musa's mother, "Suckle him and then
when you fear for him, cast him into the sea.
Do not fear or grieve – We will return him to you
and make him one of the Messengers."

The family of Pharaoh picked him up
so that he might be an enemy
and a source of grief to them.
Certainly Pharaoh and Haman
and their troops were in the wrong.

The wife of Pharaoh said,
"A source of delight for me and for you –
do not kill him.
It may well be that he will be of use to us
or perhaps we could adopt him as a son."
They were not aware.

Musa's mother felt a great emptiness in her heart
and she almost gave him away –
only We fortified her heart so that
she would be one of the Muminun.

She said to his sister, "Go after him."
And she kept an eye on him from afar
and they were not aware.

We first made him refuse all wet-nurses,

so she said, "Shall I show you to a household
who will feed him for you and be good to him?"

That is how We returned him to his mother
so that she might delight her eyes and feel no grief
and so that she would know that Allah's promise is true.
But most of them do not know this.

And when he reached his full strength and maturity,
We gave him judgement and knowledge.
That is how We recompense good-doers.

He entered the city at a time
when its inhabitants were unaware
and found two men fighting there –
one from his party and the other from his enemy.
The one from his party asked for his support
against the other from his enemy.
So Musa hit him, dealing him a fatal blow.
He said, "This is part of Shaytan's handiwork.
He truly is an outright and misleading enemy."

He said, "My Lord, I have wronged myself. Forgive me."
So He forgave him.
He is the Ever-Forgiving, the Most Merciful.

He said, "My Lord, because of Your blessing to me,
I will never be a supporter of evildoers."

Morning found him in the city, fearful and on his guard.
Then suddenly the man
who had sought his help the day before,

shouted for help from him again.
Musa said to him, "You are clearly a misguided man."

But when he was about to grab the man
who was their common enemy,
he said, "Musa! Do you want to kill me
just as you killed a person yesterday?
You only want to be a tyrant in the land,
you do not want to be a reformer."

A man came running from the furthest part of the city,
saying, "Musa, the Council
are conspiring to kill you, so leave!
I am someone who brings you good advice."

In this last Ayat we find, "A man came running from the furthest part of the city," and we find this also in Surat Ya Sin (36:19):

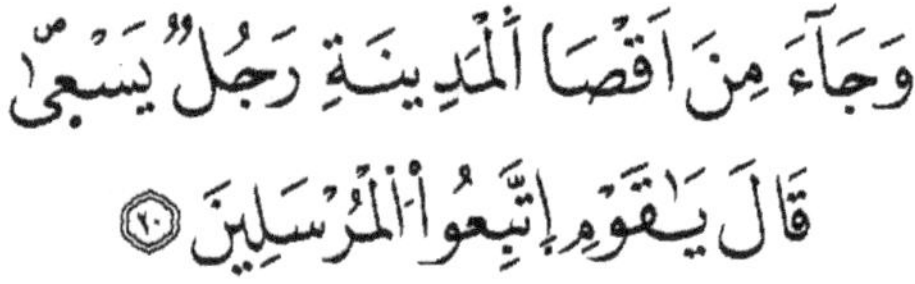

A man came running from the far side of the city, saying,
'My people! follow the Messengers!'

It is this echo whereby, in these crises of life, there is someone who comes and says, "Follow the Messengers!" It is not the Messenger himself but someone who says, "Follow the Messengers!" Here, it is someone who comes running and says, "I come to give you good advice," but what is good advice is from Allah, subhanahu wa ta'ala. Thus an essential part of wisdom is that Allah sends people with the right words, and you hear it, and you act by the good, and then you get the good, you get the benefit.

We will look now at Ayats 29 and 30 of the same Surat:

فَلَمَّا قَضَىٰ مُوسَى أَلَاجَلَ وَسَارَ بِأَهْلِهِۦٓ ءَانَسَ مِن جَانِبِ
اِ۬لطُّورِ نَارًا قَالَ لِأَهْلِهِ اِ۪مْكُثُوٓاْ إِنِّيَ ءَانَسْتُ نَارًا
لَّعَلِّيَ ءَاتِيكُم مِّنْهَا بِخَبَرٍ اَوْ جِذْوَةٍ مِّنَ اَلنَّارِ لَعَلَّكُمْ تَصْطَلُونَ ﴿٢٩﴾
فَلَمَّآ أَتَيٰهَا نُودِيَ مِن شَٰطِيِٕ اِ۬لْوَادِ اِ۬لَايْمَنِ فِي اِ۬لْبُقْعَةِ
اِ۬لْمُبَٰرَكَةِ مِنَ اَلشَّجَرَةِ أَنْ يَّٰمُوسَيٰٓ إِنِّيَ أَنَا اَ۬للَّهُ رَبُّ اُ۬لْعَٰلَمِينَ ﴿٣٠﴾

When Musa had fulfilled the appointed term
and had set off with his family,
he noticed a fire from one side of the Mount.
He said to his family, "Stay here, I can see a fire.
Hopefully I will bring you back some news from it
or a burning branch from the fire
so that you will be able to warm yourselves."

But when he reached it a voice called out to him
from the right hand side of the valley
in the part which was full of blessing,
from out of the bush:
"Musa, I am Allah, the Lord of all the worlds."

The last part of this, is Ayat 43 in Surat al-Qasas:

وَلَقَدْ ءَاتَيْنَا مُوسَى ٱلْكِتَـٰبَ
مِنۢ بَعْدِ مَآ أَهْلَكْنَا ٱلْقُرُونَ ٱلْأُولَىٰ
بَصَآئِرَ لِلنَّاسِ وَهُدًى وَرَحْمَةً لَّعَلَّهُمْ يَتَذَكَّرُونَ ﴿٤٣﴾

We gave Musa the Book
after destroying the earlier nations,
to awaken people's hearts and as a guidance and a mercy
so that hopefully they would pay heed.

So look at this journey of Sayyiduna Musa, which begins with him as a helpless baby in a basket in the river, and it takes him through all these adventures where he kills someone. Look at the vicissitude, look at the trials he has! And the journey continues, and its final outcome is that he is appointed Messenger, and he then has a direct meeting with Allah, subhanahu wa ta'ala, in the coming upon the fire on the mountain. So this is the journey. Without the journey of Sayyiduna Musa, the event cannot happen – without this tremendous journey on the river and through this great wealthy kingdom where he has to struggle to stay alive – and it ends with the meeting with his Lord.

Now we go to Surat as-Saffat (37:139-148):

وَإِنَّ يُونُسَ لَمِنَ ٱلْمُرْسَلِينَ ﴿١٣٩﴾
إِذْ أَبَقَ إِلَى ٱلْفُلْكِ ٱلْمَشْحُونِ ﴿١٤٠﴾ فَسَاهَمَ
فَكَانَ مِنَ ٱلْمُدْحَضِينَ ﴿١٤١﴾ فَٱلْتَقَمَهُ ٱلْحُوتُ وَهُوَ مُلِيمٌ ﴿١٤٢﴾

فَلَوْلَآ أَنَّهُۥ كَانَ مِنَ ٱلْمُسَبِّحِينَ ﴿١٤٣﴾ لَلَبِثَ فِى بَطْنِهِۦٓ إِلَىٰ
يَوْمِ يُبْعَثُونَ ﴿١٤٤﴾ فَنَبَذْنَٰهُ بِٱلْعَرَآءِ وَهُوَ سَقِيمٌ ﴿١٤٥﴾ وَأَنۢبَتْنَا
عَلَيْهِ شَجَرَةً مِّن يَقْطِينٍ ﴿١٤٦﴾ وَأَرْسَلْنَٰهُ إِلَىٰ مِاْئَةِ أَلْفٍ أَوْ
يَزِيدُونَ ﴿١٤٧﴾ فَـَٔامَنُوا۟ فَمَتَّعْنَٰهُمْ إِلَىٰ حِينٍ ﴿١٤٨﴾

Yunus too was one of the Messengers.
When he ran away to the fully laden ship
and cast lots and lost.
Then the fish devoured him and he was to blame.
Had it not been that he was a man who glorified Allah,
he would have remained inside its belly
until the Day they are raised again.
So We cast him up onto the beach and he was sick,
and We caused a gourd tree to grow over him.
We sent him to a hundred thousand or even more.
They had Iman
and so We gave them enjoyment for a time.

Thus the journey of Yunus is into the depths of a triple darkness. He was in the darkness of the night, in the belly of the whale and in the darkness of the depths of the ocean. So out of this journey into triple darkness, Allah takes him and gives him followers, raises him up and makes him one of the Messengers. Now the last of these narrations we come to is in Surat al-Isra‘ (17:1):

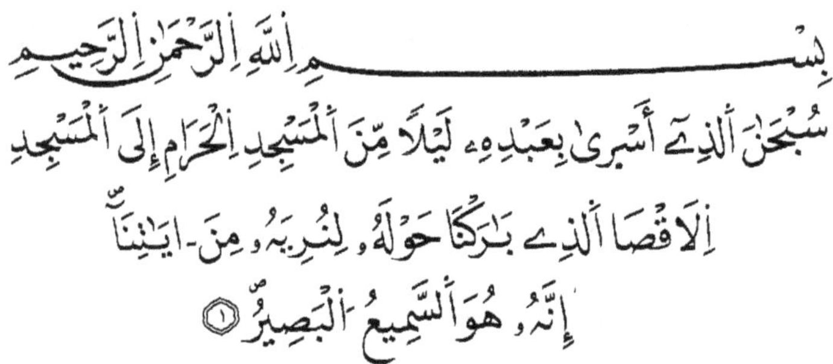

In the name of Allah, All-Merciful, Most Merciful
Glory be to Him who took His slave on a journey by night
from the Masjid al-Haram to the Masjid al-Aqsa,
whose surroundings We have blessed,
in order to show him some of Our Signs.
He is the All-Hearing, the All-Seeing.

Here the Rasul, sallallahu 'alayhi wa sallam, also has this same experience as these other Prophets, but Allah, subhanahu wa ta'ala, took him through the air, from the haram of Makkah to al-Aqsa of Jerusalem. He took him to that meeting which is described as being within two bows-lengths of the Lord of the Universe. In other words, to within the proximity that is the closest conceivable, which, in the language of the Arabs, is the nearest that a person is allowed to approach a king. In other words, it was an intimacy of the most extreme limit of what is permitted.

What we have seen is that all the elements of creation are on a journey, and whichever one of the elements you are encountering can take you to the meeting with your Lord, which, in the language of Tasawwuf, is Fana' fillah. Sayyiduna Yunus had his Fana' in the Essence, in water. Sayyiduna

Ibrahim in fire, Sayyiduna Musa in earth, in seeing the bush, and Rasul, sallallahu 'alayhi wa sallam, in being taken through the air from one part of this world to the other.

So the point of this is that this is how existence is. It is itself a journey – but everything is on a journey, even the actual atoms. Everything is moving, everything is alive – everything! Remember how Rasul, sallallahu 'alayhi wa sallam, spoke to the stones. He spoke to the dead in the well at Badr. You must remember that this is the true nature of existence. This is why, for the Sufis, Safar is OBLIGATORY. You HAVE to get up and get out! This is an age where men have become enslaved. They want salaries, they want to be safe, they want to be secure, they have a debt and they want to pay their debt! No, no, no! You were born to have knowledge of Allah, subhanahu wa ta'ala, and for this you must make the journey. You have to travel. Travel in the land. You have to SEE.

This is your obligation. You must wake up from this sleep-walking of the age we live in and realise and see what Allah has done with the world – what the creation is – see its beauty and see the terrible majesty that happens to those who have turned away from Allah, and you must understand what is happening wherever you go. Also you must seek those people of knowledge from whom you can take benefit so that on the highway you will encounter the man who comes running from the furthest part of the city and says: "Follow the Messengers!" and opens a door for you.

This is the destiny for the elite of the Elite. This is the Tariqa of Shaykh as-Shadhili and Shaykh Muhammad ibn al-Habib and Shaykh al-Fayturi.

II

JULY 26TH 2008

We are continuing our theme from our last meeting, the theme of Safar, on the journey, on travel. Now we are looking at a very deep matter of one of the great unveilings that are in the Qur'an, for people who look into these matters and take the Qur'an seriously. We are looking at the Safar of Allah's Times, and the Safar of men.

Firstly we shall look at Surat al-A'raf (7:143):

وَلَمَّا جَآءَ مُوسَىٰ لِمِيقَٰتِنَا وَكَلَّمَهُۥ
رَبُّهُۥ قَالَ رَبِّ أَرِنِىٓ أَنظُرْ إِلَيْكَ قَالَ لَن تَرَىٰنِى وَلَٰكِنِ
ٱنظُرْ إِلَى ٱلْجَبَلِ فَإِنِ ٱسْتَقَرَّ مَكَانَهُۥ فَسَوْفَ تَرَىٰنِى فَلَمَّا
تَجَلَّىٰ رَبُّهُۥ لِلْجَبَلِ جَعَلَهُۥ دَكًّا وَخَرَّ مُوسَىٰ صَعِقًا فَلَمَّآ
أَفَاقَ قَالَ سُبْحَٰنَكَ تُبْتُ إِلَيْكَ وَأَنَا۠ أَوَّلُ ٱلْمُؤْمِنِينَ ﴿١٤٣﴾

When Musa came to Our appointed time
and his Lord spoke to him,
he said, "My Lord, show me Yourself
so that I may look at You!"
He said, "You will not see Me,
but look at the mountain.
If it remains firm in its place,
then you will see Me."
But when His Lord manifested Himself to the mountain,
He crushed it flat
and Musa fell unconscious to the ground.
When he regained consciousness he said,
"Glory be to You! I make Tawba to You
and I am the first of the Muminun!"

Here we come on something which you must reflect on very deeply – and it does not mean in any way that we are going to lose the understanding of Tawhid that we, as Sufis, already have. Nothing can be associated with Allah. Is this not the foundational statement of Tawhid? "La sharikalak." – "Nothing connected to You." But we find that Allah, subhanahu wa ta'ala, uses the Qur'an in very important moments, He refers to "Our appointed time". So:

وَلَمَّا جَآءَ مُوسَىٰ لِمِيقَٰتِنَا

"When Musa came to Our appointed time."

Also, we find in the Qur'an that Allah, subhanahu wa ta'ala, sometimes says, "We," as opposed to, "I," and this is because He is referring to the Essence of His Being, of His Self.

So He says, "We," – "When Musa came to OUR appointed time," so Musa is in the world, in the realm of the world's time, and now he comes to a meeting which is "Our appointed time." Allah's time is not measured time. The time of Allah is one of the secrets of Allah. Here, we have a meeting of two measurements of time. There is the time of the universe and there is the time that Allah specifies to Himself – the time that He has chosen. You must understand that when the slave is truly the slave, then he lives under this knowledge. Look at Surat Ta Ha (20:6-8):

لَهُۥ مَا فِى ٱلسَّمَٰوَٰتِ وَمَا فِى ٱلْأَرْضِ وَمَا بَيْنَهُمَا
وَمَا تَحْتَ ٱلثَّرَىٰ ﴿٦﴾ وَإِن تَجْهَرْ بِٱلْقَوْلِ
فَإِنَّهُۥ يَعْلَمُ ٱلسِّرَّ وَأَخْفَى ﴿٧﴾ ٱللَّهُ لَآ إِلَٰهَ إِلَّا هُوَ
لَهُ ٱلْأَسْمَآءُ ٱلْحُسْنَىٰ ﴿٨﴾

Everything in the heavens
and everything on the earth
and everything in between them
and everything under the ground
belongs to Him.

Though you speak out loud,
He knows your secrets
and what is even more concealed.

Allah, there is no god but Him.
The Most Beautiful Names are His.

What we are seeing is that the human creature is tuned to this Divine Reality which is so utterly, uncompromisingly absolute and sublime and magnificent, and here is the human creature tuned to One, of Whom you could say, "Everything in the heavens and everything on the earth and everything in between them and everything under the ground belongs to Him." The human creature is faced with this Divine Reality which is totally overwhelming.

While the slave is obedient in awaiting Allah's time, his ardour and desire are already there. As the fire smoulders under the stones, awaiting the breath of wind to awaken it, Allah restrains his beloved slave to be ready for His time. In other words, the human creature is trying to tune his time in the world – his world-time – to be ready for that point at which Allah's time breaks into this world of existence. We look again at Surat Ta Ha (20:81-82):

وَمَآ أَعْجَلَكَ عَن قَوْمِكَ يَـٰمُوسَىٰ ﴿٨٣﴾
قَالَ هُمْ أُوْلَآءِ عَلَىٰٓ أَثَرِى وَعَجِلْتُ إِلَيْكَ رَبِّ لِتَرْضَىٰ ﴿٨٤﴾

"Why have you hurried on ahead of your people, Musa?"
He said, "They are following in my tracks.
I have hurried on ahead to You, My Lord,
to gain Your good pleasure."

Allah asks: "Why have you hurried on ahead of your people, Musa?" – Why are you anticipating what I have already set up? Musa is out of tune with what Allah has already decreed. Allah is asking, "Why are you rushing to it?" This is the nature of man – not the bad man or the ignorant man, but this is the man of knowledge – but he wants, and what he wants He tells us: "They are following in my tracks. I have hurried on ahead to You, My Lord," so Sayyiduna Musa is hurrying to this moment and Allah, subhanahu wa ta'ala, is cautioning him and keeping him the slave, keeping him obedient, and therefore He is actually slowing him down! In the in-time world of events he was not ready.

وَمَآ أَعۡجَلَكَ عَن قَوۡمِكَ يَٰمُوسَىٰ ﴿٨٣﴾

قَالَ هُمۡ أُوْلَآءِ عَلَىٰٓ أَثَرِي وَعَجِلۡتُ إِلَيۡكَ رَبِّ لِتَرۡضَىٰ ﴿٨٤﴾

"Why have you hurried on ahead of your people, Musa?"
He said, "They are following in my tracks.
I have hurried on ahead to You, My Lord,
to gain Your good pleasure."

Allah's power, which He reveals to us in the Qur'an, is held between two times. There are the times He has fixed by His Rububiyyat, the movements of the creation: its weather, its locations, the DNA of the human creature. This is the time of existence, of the creation. There is another set of times which are His, fixed by Him, and they are hidden between the Qadr and the Qadaa. They are hidden because they are the moment of the destiny: when the point comes of Allah's, not interfering, but manifesting Tajaliyyat of light, when He has decreed it. So he finds His prophet, which He set up for this highest of knowledges, running ahead of himself to get to it! And He, subhanahu wa ta'ala, says, "No! You have to be there 'in time' for this meeting. You cannot anticipate this meeting because you are the helpless slave and you have to know that in order to experience what I have ready for you."

Now, again in Surat Ta Ha, we go to Ayat 114:

فَتَعَٰلَى ٱللَّهُ ٱلْمَلِكُ ٱلْحَقُّ ۗ وَلَا تَعْجَلْ بِٱلْقُرْءَانِ مِن قَبْلِ
أَن يُقْضَىٰٓ إِلَيْكَ وَحْيُهُۥ ۖ وَقُل رَّبِّ زِدْنِى عِلْمًا ﴿١١٤﴾

High exalted be Allah, the King, the Real!
Do not rush ahead with the Qur'an
before its revelation to you is complete,
and say: "My Lord, increase me in knowledge."

Here we see in the Qur'an Allah, subhanahu wa ta'ala, having this same way of dealing with another of his Prophets – the greatest and the last of His Prophets, telling Rasul, sallallahu 'alayhi wa sallam: "Do not rush ahead with the Qur'an." Do you see what we are seeing? What we found with Sayyiduna Musa, we now find with Sayyiduna Muhammad, sallallahu 'alayhi wa sallam – Allah is saying, "Steady! Wait! Do not rush until it is the right time."

فَتَعَٰلَى ٱللَّهُ ٱلْمَلِكُ ٱلْحَقُّ ۗ وَلَا تَعْجَلْ بِٱلْقُرْءَانِ مِن قَبْلِ
أَن يُقْضَىٰٓ إِلَيْكَ وَحْيُهُۥ ۖ وَقُل رَّبِّ زِدْنِى عِلْمًا ﴿١١٤﴾

High exalted be Allah, the King, the Real!
Do not rush ahead with the Qur'an

before its revelation to you is complete,
and say: "My Lord, increase me in knowledge."

Here, Allah reveals to mankind how He, Allah, subhanahu wa ta'ala grooms His chosen ones so that they learn this Adab of the highest elite – to connect the natural time to the time of destiny. Our 'Ulama say: "Allah educated Rasul, sallallahu 'alayhi wa sallam," and people object to that as if to say, "It is not good manners to say that about Rasul," sallallahu 'alayhi wa sallam. They do not understand that it is on this level. Allah's teaching Rasul, sallallahu 'alayhi wa sallam, is a matter of refining his actions so that he has the highest Ma'rifa of Allah, subhanahu wa ta'ala.

Now we look at Surat Al-An'am (6:3-4):

هُوَ ٱلَّذِي خَلَقَكُم مِّن طِينٖ ثُمَّ قَضَىٰٓ أَجَلٗاۖ
وَأَجَلٞ مُّسَمًّى عِندَهُۥۖ ثُمَّ أَنتُمۡ تَمۡتَرُونَ ٢ وَهُوَ ٱللَّهُ
فِي ٱلسَّمَٰوَٰتِ وَفِي ٱلۡأَرۡضِ يَعۡلَمُ سِرَّكُمۡ وَجَهۡرَكُمۡ وَيَعۡلَمُ مَا تَكۡسِبُونَ ٣

It is He who created you from clay
and then decreed a fixed term,
and another fixed term is specified with Him.
Yet you still have doubts!

He is Allah in the heavens and in the earth.
He knows what you keep secret
and what you make public
and He knows what you earn.

ثُمَّ قَضَىٰٓ أَجَلًا ۖ

"And then decreed a fixed term." This is the first 'time'. What we might call the 'in-time' time. The time of the universe, the time of everything under the 'Arsh.

وَأَجَلٌ مُّسَمًّى عِندَهُۥ ۖ

"And another fixed term is specified with Him." So there are two times. Allah is saying it openly here in the Qur'an. There are two times. "And another fixed term is specified with Him."

هُوَ ٱلَّذِى خَلَقَكُم مِّن طِينٍ ثُمَّ قَضَىٰٓ أَجَلًا ۖ
وَأَجَلٌ مُّسَمًّى عِندَهُۥ ۖ ثُمَّ أَنتُمْ تَمْتَرُونَ ﴿٢﴾ وَهُوَ ٱللَّهُ
فِى ٱلسَّمَٰوَٰتِ وَفِى ٱلْأَرْضِ ۖ يَعْلَمُ سِرَّكُمْ وَجَهْرَكُمْ وَيَعْلَمُ مَا تَكْسِبُونَ ﴿٣﴾

It is He who created you from clay
and then decreed a fixed term,
and another fixed term is specified with Him.
Yet you still have doubts!

He is Allah in the heavens and in the earth.
He knows what you keep secret
and what you make public
and He knows what you earn.

"He is Allah in the heavens and in the earth." So He is Allah in the visible world of measured time, and in the heavens He is also Allah in the Ghayb, destining and decreeing from beyond space and time. "He knows what you keep secret and what you make public and He knows what you earn." Look how Allah puts the most ordinary mundane thing of existence and puts it under this Command of Allah, subhanahu wa ta'ala. Thus this high, high knowledge is totally linked to knowing what you earn. In other words, your whole existence is locked into the knowledge of Allah, subhanahu wa ta'ala.

This secret time is again revealed to us in the story of Sayyiduna Musa, in Surat al-A'raf (7:142-143):

وَوَٰعَدْنَا مُوسَىٰ ثَلَٰثِينَ لَيْلَةً
وَأَتْمَمْنَٰهَا بِعَشْرٍ فَتَمَّ مِيقَٰتُ رَبِّهِۦٓ أَرْبَعِينَ لَيْلَةً ۚ وَقَالَ
مُوسَىٰ لِأَخِيهِ هَٰرُونَ ٱخْلُفْنِى فِى قَوْمِى وَأَصْلِحْ وَلَا تَتَّبِعْ
سَبِيلَ ٱلْمُفْسِدِينَ ﴿١٤٢﴾ وَلَمَّا جَآءَ مُوسَىٰ لِمِيقَٰتِنَا وَكَلَّمَهُۥ
رَبُّهُۥ قَالَ رَبِّ أَرِنِىٓ أَنظُرْ إِلَيْكَ ۚ قَالَ لَن تَرَىٰنِى وَلَٰكِنِ
ٱنظُرْ إِلَى ٱلْجَبَلِ فَإِنِ ٱسْتَقَرَّ مَكَانَهُۥ فَسَوْفَ تَرَىٰنِى ۚ فَلَمَّا
تَجَلَّىٰ رَبُّهُۥ لِلْجَبَلِ جَعَلَهُۥ دَكًّا وَخَرَّ مُوسَىٰ صَعِقًا ۚ فَلَمَّآ
أَفَاقَ قَالَ سُبْحَٰنَكَ تُبْتُ إِلَيْكَ وَأَنَا۠ أَوَّلُ ٱلْمُؤْمِنِينَ ﴿١٤٣﴾

We set aside thirty nights for Musa
and then completed them with ten,
so the appointed time of his Lord
was forty nights in all.
Musa said to his brother Harun,
"Be my Khalif among my people.
Keep order and do not follow the way of the corrupters."

When Musa came to Our appointed time
and his Lord spoke to him,
he said, "My Lord, show me Yourself
so that I may look at You!"
He said, "You will not see Me,
but look at the mountain.
If it remains firm in its place,
then you will see Me."
But when His Lord manifested Himself to the mountain,
He crushed it flat
and Musa fell unconscious to the ground.
When he regained consciousness he said,
"Glory be to You! I make Tawba to You
and I am the first of the Muminun!"

That last phrase, "I am the first of the Muminun," is Sayyiduna Musa's taking on the empowerment of Allah, subhanahu wa ta'ala, as the Prophet of his time: "I am the first of the Muminun – I am the Messenger of Allah." Musa accepts this destiny.

وَوَٰعَدْنَا مُوسَىٰ ثَلَٰثِينَ لَيْلَةً
وَأَتْمَمْنَٰهَا بِعَشْرٍ فَتَمَّ مِيقَٰتُ رَبِّهِۦٓ أَرْبَعِينَ لَيْلَةً

We set aside thirty nights for Musa
and then completed them with ten,
so the appointed time of his Lord
was forty nights in all.

Again, see how Allah has divided this into two. It is His time, but He has divided it into two. He has distinguished the last ten nights from the earlier thirty nights. In that sense we see that the last ten represent the hidden time of Ma'rifa. It is all a time with his Lord, but you could say it is the meeting with the Act and the Sifat – the Attributes, and the final ten nights represent the encounter with the Dhat, the Essence, the Tajaliyyat adh-Dhat and the Fana' of existence which comes in the amazing explanation of Allah's showing Himself to the mountain.

Thus, firstly Musa hears his Lord speak to him, then his desire awakens in him a hastening of his, Musa's time, and he asks for the vision of his Lord. In that sense also, he goes ahead in a way which is still not the correct Adab. His yearning and love are still not the correct Adab. Then the record of what happened is in Allah's time, outside of, or, more correctly, beyond the space-time of the universe.

وَلَمَّا جَآءَ مُوسَىٰ لِمِيقَٰتِنَا وَكَلَّمَهُۥ
رَبُّهُۥ قَالَ رَبِّ أَرِنِىٓ أَنظُرْ إِلَيْكَ قَالَ لَن تَرَىٰنِى وَلَٰكِنِ
ٱنظُرْ إِلَى ٱلْجَبَلِ فَإِنِ ٱسْتَقَرَّ مَكَانَهُۥ فَسَوْفَ تَرَىٰنِى فَلَمَّا
تَجَلَّىٰ رَبُّهُۥ لِلْجَبَلِ جَعَلَهُۥ دَكًّا وَخَرَّ مُوسَىٰ صَعِقًا فَلَمَّآ
أَفَاقَ قَالَ سُبْحَٰنَكَ تُبْتُ إِلَيْكَ وَأَنَا۠ أَوَّلُ ٱلْمُؤْمِنِينَ ﴿١٤٣﴾

When Musa came to Our appointed time
and his Lord spoke to him,
he said, "My Lord, show me Yourself
so that I may look at You!"
He said, "You will not see Me,
but look at the mountain.
If it remains firm in its place,
then you will see Me."
But when His Lord manifested Himself to the mountain,
He crushed it flat
and Musa fell unconscious to the ground.
When he regained consciousness he said,
"Glory be to You! I make Tawba to You
and I am the first of the Muminun!"

We find in Ibn Hanbal, in his Kitab al-Zuhud, this Hadith:

> The Rasulullah, sallallahu 'alayhi wa sallam, said: "The one who worships Allah sincerely for forty Subh prayers, there appears from his Lord wisdom from his heart to his tongue."

So from his Nabawiyyat, Rasulullah, under his dispensation, tells the people that he who reaches this level of adoration of Him, there will appear from their Lord wisdom that will come from his heart to his tongue. This is a very big secret revealed by Rasulullah, sallallahu 'alayhi wa sallam.

Before the Tajalli of Allah on the mountain, the mountain travels by Allah until its form disintegrates and disappears. The mountain is gone, but the dust remains.

Now we look at Surat al-Hashr (59:21):

لَوْ أَنزَلْنَا هَٰذَا ٱلْقُرْءَانَ عَلَىٰ
جَبَلٍ لَّرَأَيْتَهُۥ خَٰشِعًا مُّتَصَدِّعًا مِّنْ خَشْيَةِ ٱللَّهِ ۚ وَتِلْكَ
ٱلْأَمْثَٰلُ نَضْرِبُهَا لِلنَّاسِ لَعَلَّهُمْ يَتَفَكَّرُونَ ﴿٢١﴾

If We Had sent down this Qur'an onto a mountain,
you would have seen it humbled,
crushed to pieces out of fear of Allah.
We make such examples for people
so that hopefully they will reflect.

So you see what we are arriving at here. It is overwhelming when you connect it to the prior Ayat about Sayyiduna Musa.

So the secret of Ikhlas is that in the Mukhlis the first determined time, the universal time of Allah is, we could say, not synchronised – because the other is not measurable – but that that time becomes identical with Allah's time. And, as you know, nothing can be associated with it, it is Allah's way of expressing it so that we can understand. So the two journeys become one event.

This term, Safar, is used because it comes from unveiling. We have been talking all this time about Safar as 'journey', but Safar is an unveiling. "Usfiru" is "He unveils." One says of the woman, "She unveils herself" – "Safarat an-Wajiha" – she unveils her face. What we are saying is that this Safar, this movement is itself the unveiling of the Majesty and

Power of Allah, subhanahu wa ta'ala. Let us look at Surat al-Muddaththir (74:32-37):

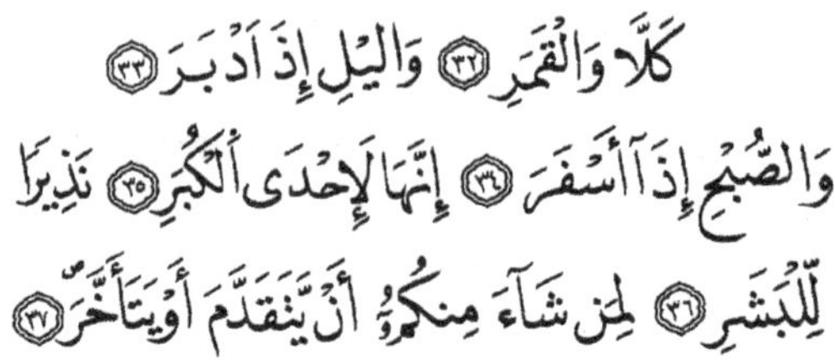

No indeed! By the moon
and the night when it withdraws
and the dawn when it grows bright,
it truly is one of the greatest of all things,
a warning to human beings:
for any of you who want to go forward
or hang back.

"By the moon and the night when it withdraws." So, when the created forms of the existent world withdraw and:

وَالصُّبْحِ إِذَآ أَسْفَرَ ٣٤

You see it is the term, Safar. It is really, "And the dawn when it unveils itself." What we are seeing is the meeting of these two times. The creational time which is darkness and solid covers over, then the Subh unveils itself – the Tajalliyat of light from Allah, subhanahu wa ta'ala. It is the cross-over of these two things which are only divided by the Barzakh which sets everything between Allah, subhanahu wa ta'ala, and His creation.

We can conclude from this that for this unveiling of Allah, subhanahu wa ta'ala, the Mumin has to be prepared. His preparation is to recognise that that moment comes into the in-time when he has submitted to the realities of the in-time. He is not rushing forward any more than he is pulling back. This allows us to deduce from this that if man ignores his Hal – if a man is ignorant of the states he is passing through – he ignores his Waqt, he ignores the time that he is living in, in that instant. If he does not know his state, he does not know the moment that he is living in.

If man ignores his Waqt, he ignores his Nafs. He ignores himself. If man ignores his Nafs, then man ignores his Rabb. While it is not a Hadith, the great Sufis say it and the great 'Alim, ar-Razi, who was almost a rationalist, quoted it often – the famous saying:

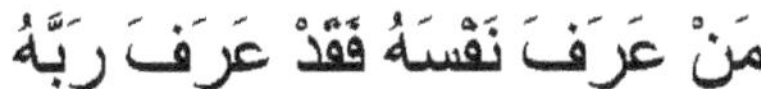

He who knows his self, knows his Lord.

III

August 2nd 2008

We are taking the theme of Safar, and our first examination was looking at the journeys the great Prophets took in the past, in their fulfilling their task allotted to them by Allah, subhanahu wa ta'ala, as Messengers and Prophets. Then we looked at the Safar of time itself, and how we found in the Qur'an that there are two times referred to: the time inside the universe – the time that we understand, the time that is over events – and then there is the time of Allah which is, of course, in the Unseen, and is not measurable because Allah is, and nothing is associated with him. Nevertheless, He has indicated that He has times and these are moments of unveiling when the Unseen makes appear in the manifest great events like the investing of a man with the position of being a Messenger of Allah, subhanahu wa ta'ala.

Now we are going to look at the Safar of the Qur'an. For this we shall turn to Surat al-Qadr (97):

إِنَّا أَنزَلْنَٰهُ فِى لَيْلَةِ ٱلْقَدْرِ ۝ وَمَآ أَدْرَىٰكَ مَا لَيْلَةُ ٱلْقَدْرِ ۝ لَيْلَةُ ٱلْقَدْرِ خَيْرٌ مِّنْ أَلْفِ شَهْرٍ ۝ تَنَزَّلُ ٱلْمَلَٰٓئِكَةُ وَٱلرُّوحُ فِيهَا بِإِذْنِ رَبِّهِم مِّن كُلِّ أَمْرٍ ۝ سَلَٰمٌ هِىَ حَتَّىٰ مَطْلَعِ ٱلْفَجْرِ ۝

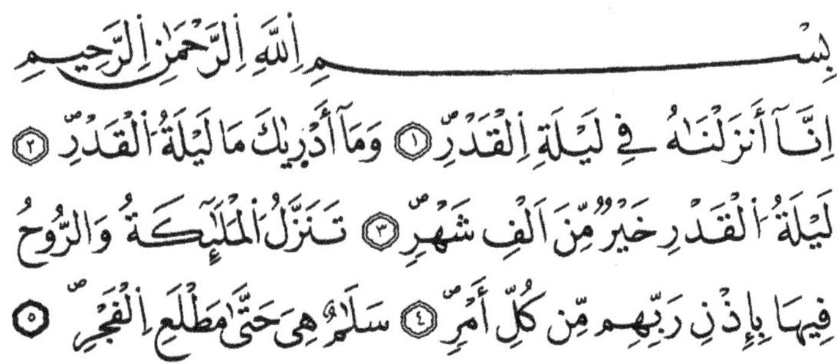

In the name of Allah, All-Merciful, Most Merciful
Truly We sent it down on the Night of Power.
And what will convey to you what the Night of Power is?
The Night of Power is better than a thousand months.

In it the Angels and the Ruh descend
by their Lord's authority
with every ordinance.

It is Peace – until the coming of the dawn.

Ibn Abbas and others have said that it is a Madinan Surat. We will now see what Ibn 'Atiyya says in his famous commentary:

The pronoun 'hu' in "Anzalnahu" refers to the Qur'an, and the meaning is not explicit.

Ibn Abbas and others have said:

> Allah sent it down entirely on the Night of Power to the lowest heaven.

The lowest heaven is what is called As-Sama' ad-Dunya – the worldly heaven. Then Ibn Abbas said:

> He gathered it with Muhammad, sallallahu 'alayhi wa sallam, over twenty years.

The Hadith of Rasul, sallallahu 'alayhi wa sallam, says:

> Seek for it in the last ten nights of Ramadhan.

Sayyidatuna 'Aisha, radiyallahu 'anha, said,

> I fear within myself the sending down of the Qur'an and the Night of Power.

You must appreciate what this means. "I fear within myself the sending down of the Qur'an". When you reflect that in the Qur'an there is the defence of Sayyidatuna 'Aisha, so there was sent down the Qur'an which contains in it that defence of Sayyidatuna 'Aisha before the unfolding of the event which led to her being accused and exonerated by Allah, subhanahu wa ta'ala. Therefore she understood, from a Ruhani point of view, the immensity of this Revelation, because she was the proof of it.

It is a night that Allah has distinguished and made better than a thousand nights. Ibn Abbas and others have said:

> It has been called the Night of Power because on that

> night Allah determines deaths, provision, and all occurences in the world, and He informs the Angels of it.

Az-Zuhri said:

> The Night of Power is immense and the honour of it is immense.

Abu Bakr al-Waraq said:

> It was called the Night of Power because it is unique. There has not been anything like it. It has a great place with Allah. The Night of Power is in the odd nights of the last ten nights of Ramadhan.

Malik said:

> It means the last nine nights, starting with the twenty-first.

Ibn Abbas and a group of the Sahaba said:

> It is the twenty-seventh night.

Ibn Abbas also said:

> The Rizq is determined on the twenty-seventh. On that night the provision of your life is determined.

Ibn 'Attiya said that the Rasulullah, sallallahu 'alayhi wa sallam, said:

One who observes the Night of Power with Iman and accountability, Allah will forgive his wrong actions.

إِنَّآ أَنزَلۡنَٰهُ فِي لَيۡلَةِ ٱلۡقَدۡرِ ١ وَمَآ أَدۡرَىٰكَ مَا لَيۡلَةُ ٱلۡقَدۡرِ ٢
لَيۡلَةُ ٱلۡقَدۡرِ خَيۡرٞ مِّنۡ أَلۡفِ شَهۡرٖ ٣ تَنَزَّلُ ٱلۡمَلَٰٓئِكَةُ وَٱلرُّوحُ
فِيهَا بِإِذۡنِ رَبِّهِم مِّن كُلِّ أَمۡرٖ ٤

Truly We sent it down on the Night of Power.
And what will convey to you what the Night of Power is?
The Night of Power is better than a thousand months.

In it the Angels and the Ruh descend
by their Lord's authority
with every ordinance.

Ibn 'Attiya says that the Ruh referred to is Jibril.

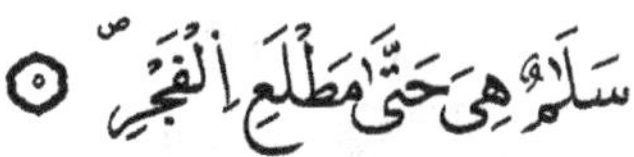

It is Peace – until the coming of the dawn.

Ash-Shabi al-Mansur says that "Peace" here means greetings from the Angels to the Muminun. So it is a Divine event where the Unseen world appears and manifests itself to the Muminun. Peace refers to the night of the twenty-seventh. It is very interesting because Ibn Abbas, who is full with these enormous secrets and insights as you know, because of his closeness to Rasul, sallallahu 'alayhi wa sallam, said:

> This word 'Peace', is the twenty-seventh word in the Surat and this is the evidence that that is the night on which the Qur'an was sent down.

Of course, "Until the coming of the dawn" means that at that point the matter ends.

This descent, this journey, according to Hadith, was to the nearest heaven and from there into the heart of the Messenger. Now let us look at Surat al-Waqi'a (56:75):

And I swear by the falling of the stars

This word 'Nujum' is the word that is used to describe this descent of the Qur'an into the heart of the Rasul, sallallahu 'alayhi wa sallam. This indicates the intermittent flashing of the lights of the descent from the heavens into the heart of Sallallahu 'alayhi wa sallam. So this journey never ceases as long as tongues recite the Qur'an silently and aloud.

Now look at Surat ad-Dukhan (44:1-6):

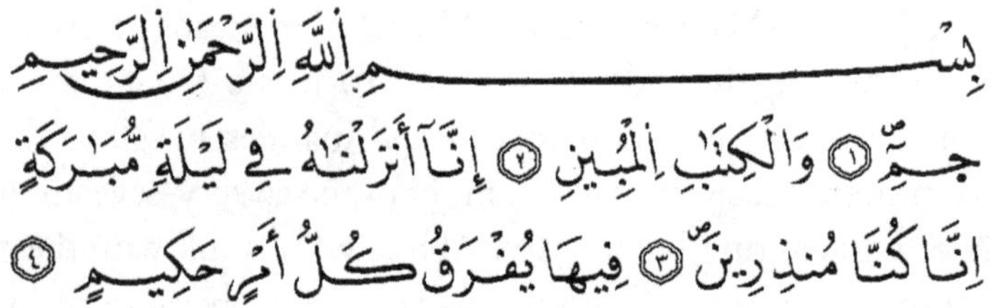

أَمْرًا مِّنْ عِندِنَآ ۚ إِنَّا كُنَّا مُرْسِلِينَ ﴿٥﴾ رَحْمَةً مِّن رَّبِّكَ
إِنَّهُۥ هُوَ ٱلسَّمِيعُ ٱلْعَلِيمُ ﴿٦﴾

In the name of Allah, All-Merciful, Most Merciful

Ha Mim
By the Book which makes things clear.

We sent it down on a blessed night –
We are constantly giving warning.
During it every wise decree is specified
by a command from Our presence.
We are constantly sending out
as a mercy from your Lord.
He is the All-Hearing, the All-Knowing.

Do you see the importance of the word 'Kuna'? Allah is saying: "We sent it down," and then He says that "We are continually sending it down." Do you follow? This is the whole point! "We are continually sending it down." "We sent it down of the Night of Power and We are continually sending it down."

Now go back to Surat al-Qadr and look at the fourth Ayat:

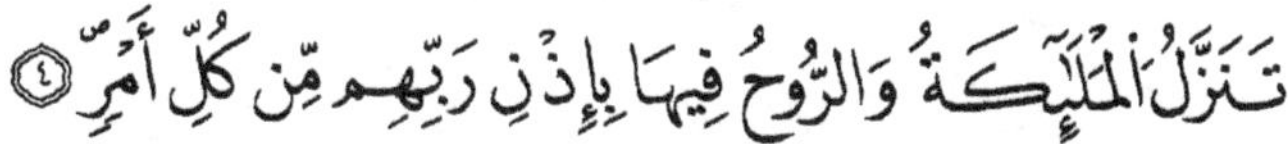

In it the Angels and the Ruh descend
by their Lord's authority
with every ordinance.

What you are required to understand of this is that the Qur'an was sent down on the Night of Power, but that Allah is continually sending it down, "With every ordinance," with every command. This descent has two elements: the Divine Command, and the pure servant. The Command, to be received, requires a pure heart, thus the entering of the descent, the Revelation, is the arrival at a pure heart. On the Night of Power it descends into the heart of Rasul, sallallahu 'alayhi wa sallam, is that not true? Also, every time someone recites the Qur'an – this event that has come into the world – aloud or silently, there is a descent into that person's heart of the Qur'an. Do you see the immensity of this situation?

The descent is unified as Qur'an and it is distinguished as Furqan. So it is a Ruhani event of the gatheredness of the Qur'an and at the same time it is a Furqan, as it gives distinguishing, particular illuminations to the one whose heart receives it and whose tongue then speaks it. Now look again at Surat ad-Dukhan (44:1-8):

بِسْمِ اللَّهِ الرَّحْمَٰنِ الرَّحِيمِ

حمٓ ﴿١﴾ وَالْكِتَابِ الْمُبِينِ ﴿٢﴾ إِنَّا أَنزَلْنَاهُ فِي لَيْلَةٍ مُّبَارَكَةٍ
إِنَّا كُنَّا مُنذِرِينَ ﴿٣﴾ فِيهَا يُفْرَقُ كُلُّ أَمْرٍ حَكِيمٍ ﴿٤﴾
أَمْرًا مِّنْ عِندِنَا إِنَّا كُنَّا مُرْسِلِينَ ﴿٥﴾ رَحْمَةً مِّن رَّبِّكَ إِنَّهُ هُوَ
السَّمِيعُ الْعَلِيمُ ﴿٦﴾ رَبِّ السَّمَاوَاتِ وَالْأَرْضِ وَمَا بَيْنَهُمَا
إِن كُنتُم مُّوقِنِينَ ﴿٧﴾ لَا إِلَٰهَ إِلَّا هُوَ يُحْيِي وَيُمِيتُ
رَبُّكُمْ وَرَبُّ آبَائِكُمُ الْأَوَّلِينَ ﴿٨﴾

In the name of Allah, All-Merciful, Most Merciful

Ha Mim
By the Book which makes things clear.
We sent it down on a blessed night –
We are constantly giving warning.
During it every wise decree is specified
by a command from Our presence.
We are constantly sending out
as a mercy from your Lord.
He is the All-Hearing, the All-Knowing:
the Lord of the heavens and the earth
and everything in between them,
if you are people with certainty.
There is no god but Him –
He gives life and causes to die –
your Lord and the Lord of your forefathers,
the previous peoples.

The third Ayat of this is:

During it every wise decree is specified.

Thus it is a Qur'an and it is a Furqan. It is both a gathered, Ruhani event, and it contains in it discrimination – particular references and guidances in matters of this world. It is known among the Awliya and the Salihun that certain of the Elite have spoken Ayats, never having learned the

Qur'an. It is said that Abu Yazid of Bistami, before his death, knew all the Qur'an by heart, no-one having taught him by the normal methods. The Qur'an journeys in its descent continually and ceaselessly, as we have seen from the words of the Qur'an.

The memorisation of the Qur'an by Abbas does not pass that memorisation to Zayid. The memorisation into one heart does not pass it on to another heart. It only enters that heart which is prepared for it. When the master gives the student an Ayat, it descends into the heart of the student from the heart of the master, and the student retains it. If the heart of the student is distracted, the Qur'an, again, has to descend on the teacher that it may again descend on the student who then is ready to receive it. The Qur'an is alive. The Qur'an is in perpetual descent, following the Messenger having received it in its first primal descent. If someone says, "Allah has sent down the Qur'an on me," he is not lying, for the Qur'an travels ceaselessly to descend on the one who retains it.

This is what we are dealing with in this matter of Qur'an. This is why the kuffar do not understand why we have this intensity and passion for the Book of Allah, subhanahu wa ta'ala.

In the Divine Revelation, as it was sent down on the Messenger, sallallahu 'alayhi wa sallam, Jibril was instructed to teach him the Adab of the slave in transmitting the Message of the Rabb. In other words, the Messenger himself had to be disciplined into this matter of letting it out, not to anticipate the moment of letting it out. Look at Ta Ha (20:114):

III

فَتَعَٰلَى ٱللَّهُ ٱلْمَلِكُ ٱلْحَقُّ ۗ وَلَا تَعْجَلْ بِٱلْقُرْءَانِ مِن قَبْلِ
أَن يُقْضَىٰٓ إِلَيْكَ وَحْيُهُۥ ۖ وَقُل رَّبِّ زِدْنِى عِلْمًا ﴿١١٤﴾

High exalted be Allah, the King, the Real!
Do not rush ahead with the Qur'an
before its revelation to you is complete,
and say: "My Lord, increase me in knowledge."

"High exalted be Allah, the King, the Real!" This first statement is an exaltation of Allah, the Supreme Power. The second is: "Do not rush ahead with the Qur'an before its revelation to you is complete." So you see these two coming together.

This event involves the man – being Rasul, sallallahu 'alayhi wa sallam – and receiving the Message. It is man and his reality that IS the incomparable Qur'an. From his own presence, to the Divine Presence, its hiddenness is the Laylat al-Qadr, the Night of Power. Each descent of the Message on the Rasul is therefore the Haqq of that moment. That moment's reality is Allah Himself. When one of the Sahaba told the Messenger, sallallahu 'alayhi wa sallam, that he found himself that morning truly a Mumin, Sallallahu 'alayhi wa sallam replied:

لكلّ حقّ حقيقة

"From every truth, the Reality."

If you found that in your experience, then it is a Divine event. It is Haqiqat.

We go to Surat al-Qalam (68:4):

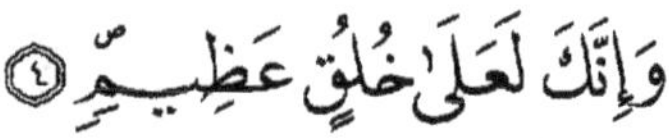

Indeed you are truly vast in character.

Of course, the word 'Khalq' in Arabic is much more rich in meaning than 'character'. Khalq is, in itself, a term of the created form of something. So Allah, subhanahu wa ta'ala, is saying: "You are truly on a tremendous form." Now, Sayyidatuna 'Aisha was asked, "What was he like?" and she replied:

كَانَ خُلُقُهُ الْقُرْآنَ

"His Khalq was the Qur'an."

So the form of Rasul, sallallahu 'alayhi wa sallam, was the Qur'an itself. So the form of the Qur'an was the man, and the man was Rasul, sallallahu 'alayhi wa sallam.

IV

AUGUST 9TH 2008

Please be very still, and look at your Qur'ans, and concentrate.

The last time, we were discussing the Safar of the Qur'an. This time we are going to look at the Safar to the Ayats – to the Signs of Allah, subhanahu wa ta'ala. Let us now look at the result of this event of the Qur'an's descent onto the heart of the Rasul, sallallahu 'alayhi wa sallam, and thus its presence permanently in the heaven of the Dunya. We will look at Surat al-Isra' (17:1):

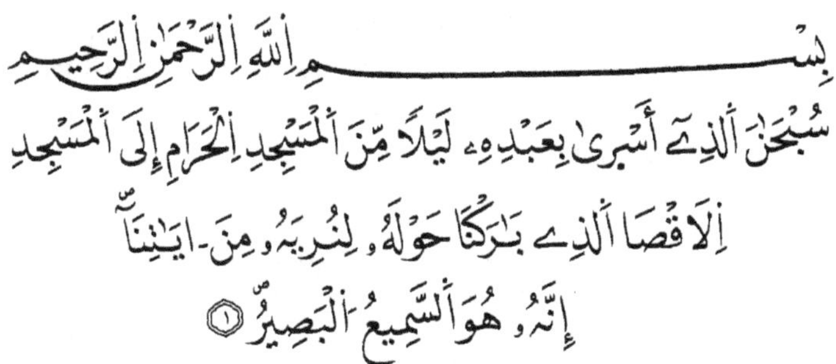

In the name of Allah, All-Merciful, Most Merciful
Glory be to Him who took His slave
on a journey by night
from the Masjid al-Haram to the Masjid al-Aqsa,
whose surroundings We have blessed,
in order to show him some of Our Signs.
He is the All-Hearing, the All-Seeing.

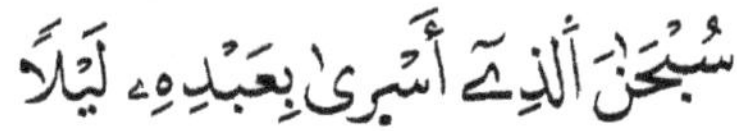

Glory be to Him who took His slave
on a journey by night.

This reference to His slave confirms that his journey was bodily. Now, look at the beginning of the phrase.

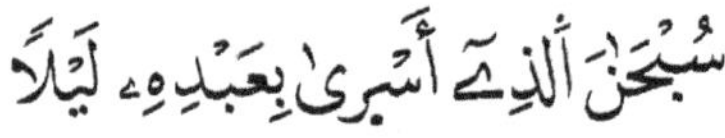

Glory be to Him who took His slave
on a journey by night.

"Glory be to Him" is indicating Allah. In Arabic it is called Dami al-Ghayb – the pronoun of absence. It is referring to Allah by a pronoun of absence. The one who is not present is a grammatical term. In other words it is not a physical presence. It is referring to Allah in a very high manner. "Glory be to Him" is the pronoun of absence.

سُبۡحَٰنَ ٱلَّذِيٓ أَسۡرَىٰ بِعَبۡدِهِۦ لَيۡلٗا

Glory be to Him who took His slave
on a journey by night.

The "His" is also a pronoun in the third person, the pronoun of absence. The grammar of this gives us, in speaking of Allah, an absence in an absence – there are two references to absence. This is Ghayb al-Ghayb. This indicates to us the highest, exalted nature of what is happening.

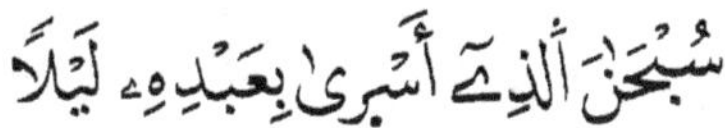

Glory be to Him who took His slave
on a journey by night

The Messenger here is specifically mentioned in his station of 'slave', of 'Abd. He is then taken to the two places of Sujud:

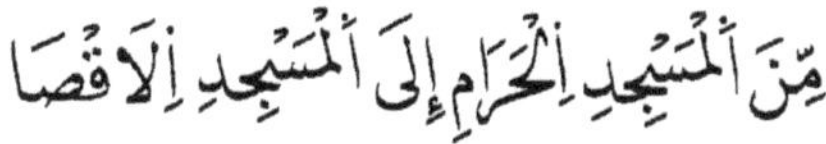

From the Masjid al-Haram to the Masjid al-Aqsa.

So he is taken to the two places of Sujud, the Masjid being the place of prostration. Sujud is slavery. But the two Mosques, however, indicate the highest. The two Mosques indicate the place of sacredness, of purity – Haram, and distance – al-Aqsa.

Here we see that Allah, subhanahu wa ta'ala, has placed Rasul, sallallahu 'alayhi wa sallam, in his lowest condition of his humanness, of being slave, and the slaveness is Sujud, and He has taken him, nevertheless, to the highest and most exalted places – the Haram and the Aqsa. One is set aside as sacred, and the other is far, distant.

Now, of the Signs, Allah tells us in Surat al-Fussilat (41:53):

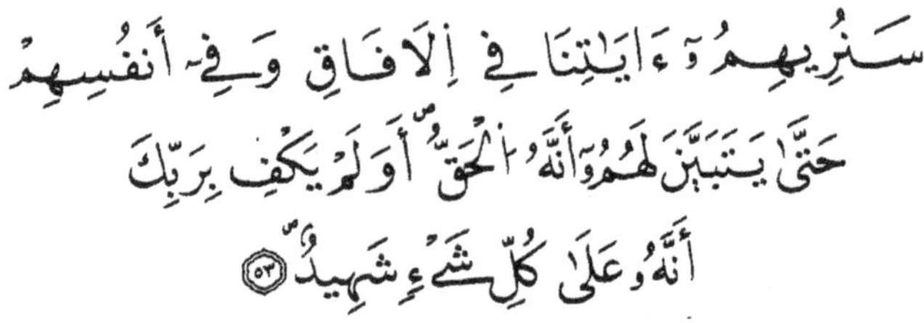

We will show them Our Signs on the horizon
and within themselves
until it is clear to them that it is the Truth.
Is it not enough for your Lord
that He is a witness of everything?

Here we see the first aspect of these Signs, because we are coming to look at what was this event that took place on the Night Journey.

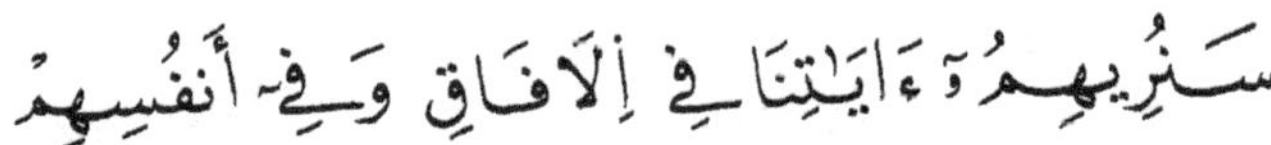

We will show them Our Signs on the horizon
and within themselves.

Hold on to that, and we will go to Surat adh-Dhariyat (51:20-21):

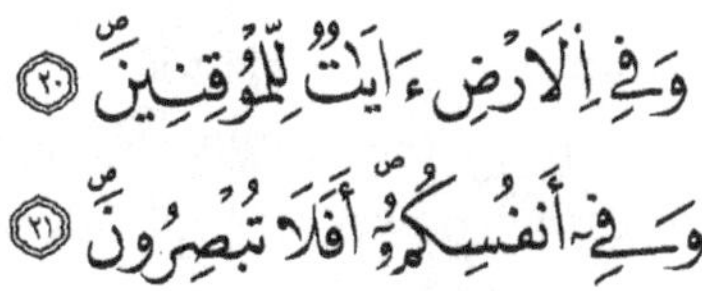

There are certainly Signs in the earth
for people with certainty –
and in yourselves as well. Do you not then see?

What we are seeing, is that Allah, subhanahu wa ta'ala, is bringing Rasul, sallallahu 'alayhi wa sallam, into a condition of consciousness, of knowledge – of Ma'rifa of himself from two aspects. One which is Signs on the horizon, and then Signs which are in himself. So let us go to Surat an-Najm (53:1-9):

بِسْمِ ٱللَّهِ ٱلرَّحْمَٰنِ ٱلرَّحِيمِ
وَٱلنَّجْمِ إِذَا هَوَىٰ ﴿١﴾ مَا ضَلَّ صَاحِبُكُمْ وَمَا غَوَىٰ ﴿٢﴾ وَمَا يَنطِقُ عَنِ
ٱلْهَوَىٰٓ ﴿٣﴾ إِنْ هُوَ إِلَّا وَحْىٌ يُوحَىٰ ﴿٤﴾ عَلَّمَهُۥ شَدِيدُ ٱلْقُوَىٰ ﴿٥﴾
ذُو مِرَّةٍ فَٱسْتَوَىٰ ﴿٦﴾ وَهُوَ بِٱلْأُفُقِ ٱلْأَعْلَىٰ ﴿٧﴾ ثُمَّ دَنَا فَتَدَلَّىٰ ﴿٨﴾
فَكَانَ قَابَ قَوْسَيْنِ أَوْ أَدْنَىٰ ﴿٩﴾

In the name of Allah, All-Merciful, Most Merciful
By the star when it descends,

your companion is not misguided or misled –
nor does he speak from whim.

It is nothing but Revelation revealed,
taught him by one immensely strong,
possessing power and splendour.
He stood there stationary –
there on the highest horizon.
Then he drew near and hung suspended.
He was two bow-lengths away
or even closer.

So the two bow-lengths is one of the Signs of the horizon, of the created world, of Allah's creation. "Or even closer" is the station of election and love. In the next Ayat we find:

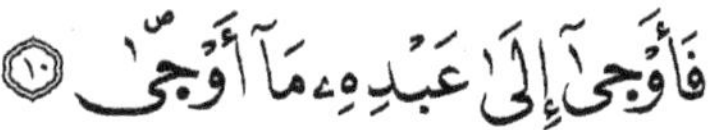

Then He revealed to His slave what He revealed.

This represents the night meeting of the self of his self – of the self of the self of Rasulullah, sallallahu 'alayhi wa sallam, with the absence of His absence. Do you see? "He revealed to His slave what He revealed" represents the night meeting of the self of the self of Rasul, sallallahu 'alayhi wa sallam, with the absence of His, Allah's, absence – with the innermost reality that we can speak of, of Allah, subhanahu wa ta'ala.

This is confirmed by the next two Ayats:

His heart did not lie about what he saw.
What! Do you dispute with him about what he saw?

The heart does not lie, for it is a Ma'rifa that has been given to Rasul, sallallahu 'alayhi wa sallam, and known thus only to the Rasul, sallallahu 'alayhi wa sallam. Allah tells him that the heart does not lie. The next Ayat is: "What! Do you dispute with him about what he saw?" Now, it is a Ma'rifa known only to the Rasul, sallallahu 'alayhi wa sallam, in his inwardness, so it cannot be denied, or confirmed. There cannot be any proof brought against it or for it. We find that this is confirmed by the Ayat:

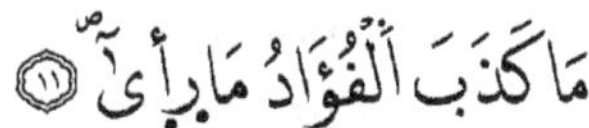

His heart did not lie about what he saw.

Here we come upon something very interesting. Allah says in the Qur'an – and this is translated by all the translators as "His heart did not lie," but this is not actually the correct, precise meaning of the Arabic, because the Arabic word here is not Qalb, but Fuadh. This is another matter. Fuadh is not the same as Qalb. Fuadh, in the Ruhalmani Tafsir, is the breast. He says: "Or we could say it is the 'inner heart' or the 'heart of the heart' because the root of Fuadh, Fa-A-Dh, is 'he struck his heart'. The other meaning of the root is 'to shoot a gazelle'. The gazelle, in the language of the Arabs and of many peoples, is the treasure, it is the most precious matter of the hunt. So:

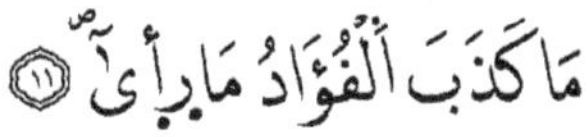

His heart did not lie about what he saw.

The next Ayat says:

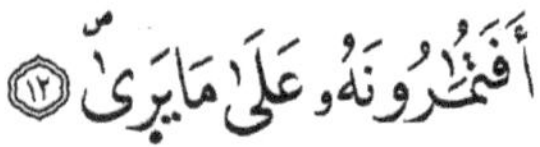

What! Do you dispute with him about what he saw?

That Ayat puts it above any idea that it could be questioned, because it is a Ma'rifa known only to the Rasul, sallallahu 'alayhi wa sallam, and is not accessible to denial or confirmation. This is the indication that this event was something which gave the highest knowledge to Rasul, sallallahu 'alayhi wa sallam, what our 'Ulama of Tasawwuf call Ma'rifatullah. It is a recognition, but we see that what it indicates here is the core of his being in the state of annihilation from the cosmos, but going from a knowledge of the horizon to this other knowledge which is in the heart. Then we find that even to speak of the heart is not enough. Allah, subhanahu wa ta'ala, says in Surat al-Hajj (22:46):

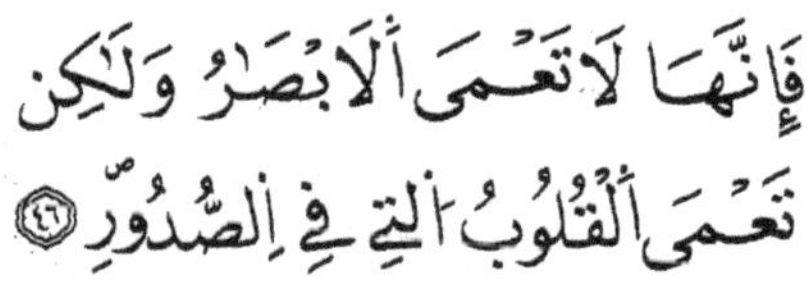

It is not their eyes which are blind
but the hearts in their breasts which are blind.

Just as there is the heart which is blind, there is also the heart that sees, there is the heart of Ma'rifa. Of course, that is not a seeing with a sensory seeing, but a knowledge of a much more exalted and incomparable kind. So, this matter of the Night journey, the Isra' of Rasul, sallallahu 'alayhi wa sallam, indicates his high and highest station among men, based on his slavehood – utterly determined by his slavehood – as we have seen from these Ayats.

We ask Allah, subhanahu wa ta'ala, to give us a knowledge of the Qur'an and benefit from it.

V

October 10th 2008

First of all I want to welcome all the Fuqara from every part of the world, as we now have Fuqara here coming from all over the world, and most importantly, we welcome our brothers from Russia because they bring with them a whole body of Russian Muslims from the capital – a body of men stretching from Moscow to Vladivostok. The Tariqa is established in Russia, and with it, the disciplines of The School of the 'Amal of the Ahl al-Madinah. This is a big, big historical event which presages very well for the future of Islam in the world. It is why I want to take one phrase which recurs in the Qur'an in that way that the Qur'an has an almost musical structure which repeats itself, as in a symphony the theme is repeated, but when it is repeated it is changed slightly in meaning so that depth and emotion are added to it. So this phrase which recurs in several Ayats, you shall see how it deepens its meanings as it progresses.

The subject of what I want to say is because you are here, because you are Fuqara and you have travelled, and you have travelled for the sake of Allah. This, apart from the obligatory right of Hajj, the travel of the people who love Allah, who travel for the sake of Allah, to meet other living Muslims – this is the life-blood, this is the venous system on which the Deen of Islam lives and survives. If this travel did not take place, the Hajj could not take place, because it is this turbulence and awakening in the heart that makes men and women yearn to visit the House of Allah. The visiting of the houses of the Fuqara also has a great secret in it because embedded in it is that same secret that is fulfilled in the Tawaf of a house that is the House of all mankind, as Allah designates it. It is His House, but it is a House for all mankind.

We are now living in a very strange time. In our lifetime, and in your lifetimes, we have seen the collapse of a whole formal structure that was understood and accepted in almost all the world, as a basic pattern of law which was based on a certain respect for people which had been trumpeted by the atheist and the kuffar – the Humanists, in trumpeting the 'Rights of Man'. In our lifetime, we have seen the most horrible abandoning of a kind of discipline that men put on their violence in times of war and aggression – and we saw this collapse completely. And the country that presented itself as the leaders of society, the ones who were taking the world to a new level of justice and this famous 'humanity', we saw them smash all the structures of International Law and smash all the principles and rights due to men in war in the terrible, inescapable shame of Guantanamo and Abu Ghraib prison.

There is no going back from that. There is no repairing it. There is no punishing the guilty. There is no saying they are sorry. There is no apologising. There is no way back. We have witnessed the collapse of the moral order – what was left of it – which was based on the remnants of the christian religion.

Now we are in a situation where there is basically no law. The Nation States have collapsed, and we now have war-lords who are answerable in fact to no individual nation – I am referring to NATO – and here we all are in the middle of it all, and every time you get into an airport and you have come this way to travel you see the humiliation and the degradation visited on the Muslims worldwide by a society which in itself is collapsing, bankrupt, and with the macabre discovery that their money is disappearing and they do not know how it happened. They cannot explain it.

Now, Allah, subhanahu wa ta'ala, warns people. I want you to understand that you must not travel naively, you must travel with understanding and see what Allah has prepared you for in travelling because from one point of view, it is not nice, it is not pleasant, it is not tourism, but it is a deep, deep, deep opportunity to understand how existence works, how human beings behave, and what the message of it is. Look at Surat Fatir (35:44):

أَوَلَمْ يَسِيرُوا۟ فِى ٱلْأَرْضِ فَيَنظُرُوا۟ كَيْفَ كَانَ عَٰقِبَةُ ٱلَّذِينَ مِن
قَبْلِهِمْ وَكَانُوٓا۟ أَشَدَّ مِنْهُمْ قُوَّةً ۚ وَمَا كَانَ ٱللَّهُ لِيُعْجِزَهُۥ مِن
شَىْءٍ فِى ٱلسَّمَٰوَٰتِ وَلَا فِى ٱلْأَرْضِ ۚ إِنَّهُۥ كَانَ عَلِيمًا قَدِيرًا ﴿٤٤﴾

We find in the Bewley version this:

Have they not travelled in the land
and seen the final fate of those before them?
They were far greater than them in strength.
Allah cannot be withstood in any way,
either in the heavens or on earth.
He is All-Knowing, All-Powerful.

So you see that this travel you have made to come to one of the furthest points of the earth is in fact to liberate you, to free you from the bonds that have held back the Muslims because we have been held back from the time that the Khilafa was destroyed, and the time that the Dinar and the Dirham were doctrinally abolished by the kuffar. When they took away the golden rupee and gave India the paper rupee, overnight the richest country became a country of beggars. What you have to understand is that by this journey, you cannot ever be the same again. You cannot go back to believing that reality is what you get on the television news. You have to have this Qur'anic perspective which frees you to be ready for the next stage which is the coming together of the people who love Allah and who are able to raise up the whole world with them, the way these people have cast the whole world down – not just into

V

prisons and torture but into bankruptcy. Look now at Surat ar-Rum (30:9):

أَوَلَمْ يَسِيرُوا۟ فِى ٱلْأَرْضِ
فَيَنظُرُوا۟ كَيْفَ كَانَ عَـٰقِبَةُ ٱلَّذِينَ مِن قَبْلِهِمْ
كَانُوٓا۟ أَشَدَّ مِنْهُمْ قُوَّةً وَأَثَارُوا۟ ٱلْأَرْضَ وَعَمَرُوهَآ أَكْثَرَ
مِمَّا عَمَرُوهَا وَجَآءَتْهُمْ رُسُلُهُم بِٱلْبَيِّنَـٰتِ فَمَا كَانَ ٱللَّهُ
لِيَظْلِمَهُمْ وَلَـٰكِن كَانُوٓا۟ أَنفُسَهُمْ يَظْلِمُونَ ﴿٩﴾

Have they not travelled in the earth
and seen the final fate of those before them?
They had greater strength than them
and cultivated the land
and inhabited it in far greater numbers than they do.
Their Messengers also came to them with the Clear Signs.
Allah would never have wronged them –
but they wronged themselves.

Let us listen to the last phrase again:

فَمَا كَانَ ٱللَّهُ لِيَظْلِمَهُمْ
وَلَـٰكِن كَانُوٓا۟ أَنفُسَهُمْ يَظْلِمُونَ ﴿٩﴾

Allah would never have wronged them –
but they wronged themselves.

So obedience to Allah is to be right by yourself, to act rightly with yourself, and that is to write for yourself a good life. You must write for yourselves a good life. A good life is when you start living first of all for your brothers and for your sisters, for the close ones, the Fuqara, the people of the Jama'at, and then you can extend it out beyond that circle who know each other and who love each other. You can raise up the world because they have what they need. You have what they do not have. If you go to any major country in the world today, its government is betraying its people. Its government has lied to its people and nowhere is that more clearly so than in South Africa, where the Freedom Charter had removed from it the very physical means which would have raised up the people from the townships and from the scandalous poverty of these isolated zones which after ten years, are not only exactly where they were, but they are ten years further in decay and disgrace.

It is this outer community which we have to reach out to and unify. This is the task you can only grasp and take on by being freed through travel and by seeing that Allah has punished these people, but also that they have not served themselves. The Fuqara are the ones who serve themselves by serving others. The Khidma of the Faqir is what makes him noble above everybody else. The Fuqara give, and the governments and the State take.

When the great first conqueror entered India, when he arrived at Peshawar he rode with his army and he distributed thousands of gold Dinars to the people. Now when the heads of these kafir enslaving States go into these cities, it costs that city hundreds and thousands of Dinar of gold to pay for their security because everybody wants to kill them! That is the difference. The Muslims go in and they give to the people, and the people love them. It is this generosity of which our Imam was speaking today. Now look at Surat

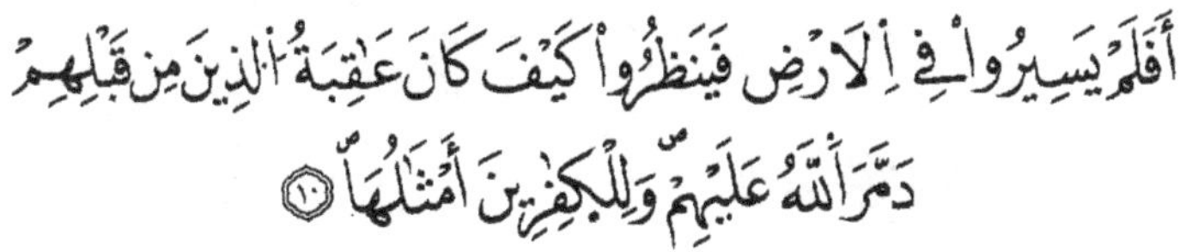

Muhammad (47:10), sallallahu 'alayhi wa sallam:

Have they not travelled about the earth
and seen the final fate of those before them?
Allah destroyed them utterly.
And those who are kafir will suffer the same fate.

And those who are kafir will suffer the same fate. This is the world you are living in. This is what you are seeing when you travel about. Go here in Cape Town, from the Waterfront and from Constantia, and then go to the great Muslim community of the Cape Flats and see what has been done to people by this enslaving government. They are themselves slaves of people whom nobody has elected because these people have the wealth and the real money. The gold which is dug out of the earth does not go into the hands of the poor, it goes into a plane and straight over to the United States.

So this is the message: The kafir will suffer the same fate. For this we travel the earth to understand what is going on. But this also makes you free, and it makes you free to realise that in living your life you need the Fuqara, you ARE the

Fuqara, and it is your love for each other which will be the model for everyone to take because it is mutual help and mutual support, it is mutual feeding and concern – the very aspects that are totally missing in the whole political spectrum of what is current living in the industrial societies.

فَسِيرُواْ فِي الْأَرْضِ
فَانظُرُواْ كَيْفَ كَانَ عَاقِبَةُ الْمُكَذِّبِينَ ﴿٣٦﴾

Now look at Surat an-Nahl (16:36):

Travel about the earth and see the final fate of the deniers.

This is the first part of the message of this gathering here in Cape Town. "Travel about the earth and see the final fate of the deniers." You see it all around you. But then, recognise what Abu Madyan said, the Ghawth of the Sufis:

The pleasure of life is only in the company of the Fuqara.
They are the Sultans, the masters, the princes.

They are the Sultans, the masters, the princes, because they are the people of Khidma. They are people of Khidma with their hands, but they are people of Khidma with their Hikma. They serve the people with right guidance and a good word, and a healing word, that they are those who make the whole situation of the world continue to exist. If the Awliya of the Sufic Tariqa, known and unknown, inside Tariqas and outside Tariqas, these people who love Allah and love the people of Allah, if these people ceased to exist, the world could not exist. If the queen insect of the termitiary is destroyed, then the termitiary is destroyed. It is these people's love that keeps the whole thing going. It is not the whale or the forests or the Amazon that we have to be worried about. It is these people who love Allah and who speak the name of Allah, if these people were to disappear, then we would have reached the end of the matter.

It is our business to keep it alive, and to keep it dynamic because there is more to be done and there is greater glory to be achieved for Allah, subhanahu wa ta'ala, and you are the people to do this. You have been blessed by Allah, you have been picked by Allah, and you have been brought

وَإِن يُرِيدُوٓا۟ أَن يَخْدَعُوكَ فَإِنَّ حَسْبَكَ ٱللَّهُ هُوَ ٱلَّذِىٓ أَيَّدَكَ
بِنَصْرِهِۦ وَبِٱلْمُؤْمِنِينَ ﴿٦٢﴾ وَأَلَّفَ بَيْنَ قُلُوبِهِمْ لَوْ أَنفَقْتَ مَا فِى
ٱلْأَرْضِ جَمِيعًا مَّآ أَلَّفْتَ بَيْنَ قُلُوبِهِمْ وَلَٰكِنَّ ٱللَّهَ أَلَّفَ
بَيْنَهُمْ إِنَّهُۥ عَزِيزٌ حَكِيمٌ ﴿٦٣﴾ يَٰٓأَيُّهَا ٱلنَّبِىُّ حَسْبُكَ ٱللَّهُ
وَمَنِ ٱتَّبَعَكَ مِنَ ٱلْمُؤْمِنِينَ ﴿٦٤﴾

together by Allah. Allah says in Surat al-Anfal (8:62-64):

If they intend to deceive you,
Allah is enough for you.
It is He who supported you with His help
and with the muminun,
and unified their hearts.
Even if you had spent everything on the earth,
you could not have unified their hearts.

But Allah has unified them.
He is Almighty, All-Wise.

O Prophet! Allah is enough for you,
and for the muminun who follow you.

That is the truth. And that is the truth which has brought us together. The arrival of our friends from Russia is an evidence of the success of this. It is also a signal that you must visit them in Russia and you must visit the Fuqara in Pakistan and in India. Pass over the Middle East because it is a lost desert. Apart from the Holy places there is no reason to have anything to do with it, it is doomed. But visit the brothers and sisters in India and in Pakistan and Indonesia, and then Uzbekistan when that shaytan has gone. Go into Tajikistan. Go into Kyrgyzstan. This is your future. The future is there. This place of Cape Town for the people of Cape Town is a place you must jump off from because there is no indication of any justice or any social elevation or education from the political class who are tearing each other to bits with their greed to get at the wealth of which they are only given a little bit by its masters, who have got it all hidden away in Switzerland.

This is the world we live in. You must travel in the land and you must see. If you travel that way, you only stop for the House of Allah and to visit Rasul, sallallahu 'alayhi wa sallam, and then on to the renewal of Islam which will certainly come with the people of the Subcontinent and from these great Stans which have been sleeping and sleeping, and which are now waking up.

V

Also, the Russian people, who have nowhere to turn but to Allah, subhanahu wa ta'ala, and Rasul, sallallahu 'alayhi wa sallam. We make Fatiha for the blessings of the future and all the Fuqara, and for success for all the Fuqara, and mercy to all the Muslims of Cape Town. We ask Allah, subhanahu wa ta'ala, to bless all the family of Sufi Sahib whose mosque we are in – a great Wali. He came to this country and he put down nine mosques all over the country and without them there would not have been a trace left. He did that because of his love for Allah and because he was from a Tariqa of intoxication, a Tariqa of adoration, of love of Rasul, sallallahu 'alayhi wa sallam, of love of Allah, the Chistiyya Tariqa. It is because of that, that we are here tonight. We are his guests, and the guests of his family. It is such a tremendous thing, you cannot imagine how important it is. If you go to Ladysmith you see one of the most beautiful mosques in the world. It is in the middle of nowhere, and he put it there! But when you see it, everything changes. The land becomes blessed. Everything changes. We are very blessed to belong to a Tariqa that has links to the Chistiyya and its great past, and its family are still alive in the Tariqa and alive in service to Allah, subhanahu wa ta'ala. We ask Allah to bless the family of the Habibia and we ask Allah to keep us in close friendship and alliance with them. We ask Allah, subhanahu wa ta'ala, to restore the Jama'at as a living thing in which the people serve each other.

VI

October 17th 2008

Safar on the 'Bismillah'

Our journey ends tonight with the opening of the Opening:

Let us start at the beginning of the Beginning. Qur'an opens with the exalted "Bismillahir-Rahmanir-Rahim." That great opening phrase opens with the Bismillah. So let us look at this in detail.

Bismillah – Bismi – Bi.

'Bi' is in English what we call a preposition. In Arabic it is defined as Harf – letter, but precisely it is 'Harf Jarr', meaning a modifying letter, literally 'a pulling letter'. The preposition – Harf Jarr, PULLS the noun into having a Kasra. The Ajrumiyya defines it thus: "Prepositions do not have the characteristics or indications of the noun or verb." Therefore it modifies but does not connect.

'Ism' is from S-M-A and means 'to be high above'. From its plural we get Samawati – the Heavens. From the same root is S-M-Y which means 'to name'. This permits us to say that its name – naming – is a heavenly affair. The position of the People of the Sunna is:

> If it is true that ISM is derived from Height, Allah was described by it before creation existed, after it existed, and will be when it is annihilated, and creatures have no effect on the Names or Attributes.
>
> It is the Mu'tazili who derive Ism from SIMA, which means 'a sign'. They say: "Before time, Allah was without name or attribute. When He created creatures, THEY gave Him Names and Attributes. When He annihilates them He will again have no name or attribute. This is against the position of the Community. This is worse than their claim that His Word is created. Allah is exalted above this.

So, right at the beginning – at the first phrase of the Book, we encounter the pure indication of Tawhid, which lets us make our key preposition: The Name is the thing named. This was defined by Qadi Abu Bakr al-Baqillani:

> If someone says "Allah is Knowing", his words indicate the Essence, which is described as being knowing. So the Name is Knowing and it is what is Named. It is the same when someone says "Allah is the Creator." The Creator is the Lord, and it is the Name itself. In this, our view, the Name is the Named itself with no distinction.

Ibn Hassar said:

> The People of Bida' deny the Attributes when they claim that namings have no meaning except the Essence. That is why they say that the Name is not the Named. Whoever affirms the Attributes, affirms that the Names have meanings which are the qualities of the Essence. In this correct view they are not expressions, but they are Names.

Now, for the Name to be understood, recognised, and then literally verbalised, the faculty of capacity to name has to precede the naming. Naming demands the namer. Let us look at the Divine investiture by Allah of the human creature as namer. Surat al-Baqara (2:30):

وَإِذْ قَالَ رَبُّكَ لِلْمَلَٰٓئِكَةِ إِنِّي جَاعِلٌ فِي ٱلْأَرْضِ خَلِيفَةً ۖ قَالُوٓاْ
أَتَجْعَلُ فِيهَا مَن يُفْسِدُ فِيهَا وَيَسْفِكُ ٱلدِّمَآءَ وَنَحْنُ نُسَبِّحُ
بِحَمْدِكَ وَنُقَدِّسُ لَكَ ۖ قَالَ إِنِّيٓ أَعْلَمُ مَا لَا تَعْلَمُونَ ﴿٣٠﴾

> When your Lord said to the Angels,
> "I am putting a Khalif on the earth,"
> they said, "Why put on it one who will
> cause corruption on it and shed blood
> when we glorify You with praise
> and proclaim Your purity?"
> He said, "I know what you do not know."

At-Tabari has said that 'putting' means 'creating'. The Prophet, sallallahu 'alayhi wa sallam, said, "The earth was smoothed out from Makkah." Hence its name as the Mother of Cities. Khalifa in the form of an active particle means 'the one who replaced the Angels before Him on the earth.' It may be in the passive mode giving the meaning of 'one who is sent as a representative.' Al-Qurtubi, in his renowned Ahkam al-Qur'an, makes this important judgment:

> This Ayat is sound evidence for having a leader and a Khalif who is obeyed so that he will be a focus for the cohesion of society, and the rulings of the Khalifate will be carried out. None of the Imams of the Community disagree about the obligatory nature of having such a leader, except for what is related from al-Asamim (literally, the Deaf), who lived up to the meaning of his name and was indeed deaf to the Shari'at, and those who take his position who say that the Khalifate is permitted rather than mandatory if the Community undertake all the obligations on their own without the need for a ruler to enforce them.

> The Companions agreed to make Abu Bakr Khalif after the disagreement which took place between the Muhajirun and the Ansar. If it had been a definite obligation that the ruler had to be from Quraysh, there would have been no point in the argument and debate which took place. When Abu Bakr died, he delegated the task of being Khalif to 'Umar, and no one said that it was not mandatory. Its obligatory nature indicated that it is one of the pillars of the Deen which supports the Muslims. Praise be to Allah, the Lord of the Worlds."

The next Ayat informs us about the investiture of Adam as namer of all things. Surat al-Baqara (2:31):

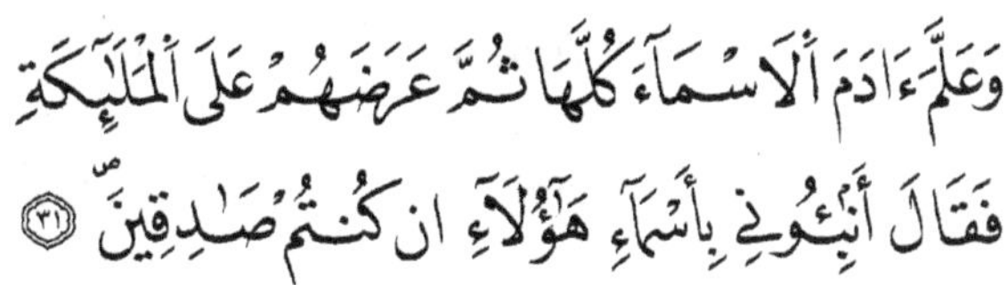

He taught Adam the names of all things.
Then He arrayed them before the Angels and said,
"Tell me the names of these if you are telling the truth."

A respected Sufi of our Habibiyya-Darqawiyya once asked me in the Tafilalet desert of Morocco, "Did Adam have a Book?" I said that I did not know. He replied, "Yes. He did. It was Alif, Ba, Ta, Tha…" In other words, what he was explaining was that the teaching of the names was language itself. This in turn means that Allah had created man – Adam's kunya is Abu'l-Bashir, which means 'Father of

Humanity' – both with an intellect to grasp language and a physique to express it: tongue, palate, lips and the vocal chords.

This allows us to say that the beginning of mankind is the beginning of language. We find, corroborating this, that ancient languages first manifest with a complex grammar and large vocabulary, and that language then 'dies' of simplification and decrease of terms.

At the core of language is its return to He Who created it. So the naming of Allah is the speaking of the Name of the Giver of Names. Here, inevitably, scholarship stutters as it strives to give roots to the root. It has driven Sufis in misguided but intoxicated search for the Greatest Great Name. The truth is, and I mean the Qur'an, that the Supreme Name is ALLAH itself. Imam ash-Shafi', Al-Khattabi and Al-Ghazali, and confirmed by al-Khalil, said that the Name itself is Allah. Surat al-Waqi'a (56:99) ends:

So glorify the Name of your Lord, the Magnificent!

This takes us to the Bismillah in that it is completed by the connection of the two Supreme Attributes: Ar-Rahman and Ar-Rahim. There is general agreement that these two Names indicate in the first, general compassion, and in the second, specific acts of mercy on the Mumin. Allah makes the importance and primacy of these Names clear in the Qur'an. Look at Surat al-Isra' (17:110):

قُلِ ٱدْعُواْ ٱللَّهَ أَوِ ٱدْعُواْ ٱلرَّحْمَٰنَ
أَيًّا مَّا تَدْعُواْ فَلَهُ ٱلْأَسْمَآءُ ٱلْحُسْنَىٰ

Say: "Call on Allah or call on the All-Merciful,
whichever you call upon,
the Most Beautiful Names are His."

Here is the clear Tawhid that indicates Allah by His Names and Attributes. Let us look at Surat an-Naml (27:29-31):

قَالَتْ يَٰٓأَيُّهَا ٱلْمَلَؤُاْ إِنِّىٓ أُلْقِىَ إِلَىَّ كِتَٰبٌ كَرِيمٌ ﴿٢٩﴾
إِنَّهُۥ مِن سُلَيْمَٰنَ وَإِنَّهُۥ بِسْمِ ٱللَّهِ ٱلرَّحْمَٰنِ ٱلرَّحِيمِ ﴿٣٠﴾
أَلَّا تَعْلُواْ عَلَىَّ وَأْتُونِى مُسْلِمِينَ ﴿٣١﴾

She said, "Council! a noble letter has been delivered to me.
It is from Sulayman and says:
'In the name of Allah, All-Merciful, Most Merciful.
Do not rise up against me,
but come to me in submission.'"

Here, the invocation of the full Bismillah demands submission to Allah's Prophet, Sulayman, 'alayhi salam.

We find in Surat al-Hud (11:41):

وَقَالَ ٱرْكَبُواْ فِيهَا بِسْمِ ٱللَّهِ مَجْر۪ىٰهَا وَمُرْسَىٰهَآ
إِنَّ رَبِّى لَغَفُورٌ رَّحِيمٌ ﴿٤١﴾

He said, "Embark in it.
In the name of Allah be its voyage and its landing!
Truly my Lord is Ever-Forgiving, Most Merciful."

Then in Surat al-An'am (6:118), we find:

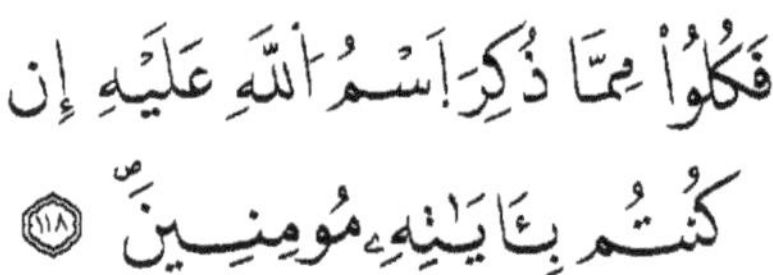

Eat that over which the name of Allah has been mentioned,
if you have Iman in His Signs.

From this we find that the Bismillah is the door to the actions of the Muminun. From the act of Dhikr to the written word, on to the opening of the meal and eating and drinking – Bismillahir-Rahmanir-Rahim.

To sum up: the Bismillah in itself, by its indications, and being an indication, defines the fundamental truths of Tawhid. Thus, Bi, as we have established, in grammar, as Harf Jarr, is that which pulls the noun, or we could say it is that which activates it. The Bi is therefore an action. It is the Act.

Ism, the noun itself, represents the Name. The Name cannot be named but by its own empowerment. The recognition of 'Name' is the Divinely decreed and necessary attribute which entails in itself, by implication, having capacity: Seer, Hearer, Doer, Knower, Living – in effect the Mother-Attributes, from which all the other attributes emerge.

VI

Allah is, of course, the Named, the One, Unique, without association, Essence, and yet while of Himself exalted in this way, is by Divine Revelation, inextricably bonded to two of the key-Names: the Merciful and the Compassionate. So, the Bismillah is by Divine Revelation, the Bismillahir-Rahmanir-Rahim. Act-Attribute-Essence.

Here is the great declaration which opens the Qur'an, and the Surat is the open declaration of Tawhid which sets Islam as the crown and triumph over all previous stages of religion.

———o———

This book is set in BEMBO, which was cut
by the punch-cutter Francesco Griffo
for the Venetian printer-publisher
Aldus Manutius in early 1495
and first used in a pamphlet
by a young scholar
named Pietro
Bembo.